Sovereignty, Nationalism, and the Quest for Homogeneity in Interwar Europe

Sovereignty, Nationalism, and the Quest for Homogeneity in Interwar Europe

Edited by
Emmanuel Dalle Mulle,
Davide Rodogno, and Mona Bieling

BLOOMSBURY ACADEMIC
LONDON • NEW YORK • OXFORD • NEW DELHI • SYDNEY

BLOOMSBURY ACADEMIC
Bloomsbury Publishing Plc
50 Bedford Square, London, WC1B 3DP, UK
1385 Broadway, New York, NY 10018, USA
29 Earlsfort Terrace, Dublin 2, Ireland

BLOOMSBURY, BLOOMSBURY ACADEMIC and the Diana logo are
trademarks of Bloomsbury Publishing Plc

The open access publication of this book has been published with the support
of the Swiss National Science Foundation.

First published in Great Britain 2023
Paperback edition published 2024

Copyright © Emmanuel Dalle Mulle, Davide Rodogno and Mona Bieling, 2023

Emmanuel Dalle Mulle, Davide Rodogno and Mona Bieling have asserted their right under
the Copyright, Designs and Patents Act, 1988, to be identified as Editor of this work.

Cover image: Composition with Grid #1, abstract painting by Piet Mondriaan,
1918 © incamerastock / Alamy

This work is published open access subject to a Creative Commons
Attribution-NonCommercial-NoDerivatives 4.0 International licence (CC BY-NC-ND 4.0,
https://creativecommons.org/licenses/by-nc-nd/4.0/). You may re-use, distribute,
and reproduce this work in any medium for non-commercial purposes, provided
you give attribution to the copyright holder and the publisher and provide a link to the
Creative Commons licence.

Bloomsbury Publishing Plc does not have any control over, or responsibility for, any
third-party websites referred to or in this book. All internet addresses given in
this book were correct at the time of going to press. The author and publisher regret
any inconvenience caused if addresses have changed or sites have ceased to exist,
but can accept no responsibility for any such changes.

A catalogue record for this book is available from the British Library.

A catalog record for this book is available from the Library of Congress.

ISBN: HB: 978-1-3502-6338-3
PB: 978-1-3502-6337-6
ePDF: 978-1-3502-6339-0
eBook: 978-1-3502-6340-6

Typeset by Integra Software Services Pvt. Ltd.

To find out more about our authors and books visit www.bloomsbury.com
and sign up for our newsletters.

To Eric Weitz

Contents

List of Tables	ix
Notes on Contributors	x
Acknowledgments	xiv
List of Abbreviations	xv

1 Introduction: Sovereignty, Nationalism, and the Quest for Homogeneity in Interwar Europe *Emmanuel Dalle Mulle, Davide Rodogno, and Mona Bieling*   1

Part 1   Minorities and the Transition from Empires to Nation-states

2 Making Minorities and Majorities: National Indifference and National Self-determination in Habsburg Central Europe *Pieter M. Judson*   21

3 "Prison of the Nations?" Union and Nationality in the United Kingdom, 1870–1925 *Alvin Jackson*   39

4 Nationalism, Religion, and Minorities from the Ottoman Empire to the Republic of Turkey *Erol Ülker*   61

Part 2   The Minority Question across Europe: Comparing Policies, Regimes, and Resistance

5 Assessing the "Paris System": Self-determination and Ethnic Violence in Alsace-Lorraine and Asia Minor, 1919–23 *Volker Prott*   85

6 Sovereignty and Homogeneity: A History of Majority-Minority Relations in Interwar Western Europe *Emmanuel Dalle Mulle and Mona Bieling*   105

7 Exercising Minority Rights in New Democracies: Germans and Jews in Interwar Poland, Romania, and Latvia, 1919–33 *Marina Germane*   125

8 A Double-edged Sword: The Political Use of National Heterogeneity in the Soviet Union during the Interwar Period *Sabine Dullin*   147

Part 3 Majorities and Minorities as Social Constructs: Negotiating Identity Ascription

9 Nationalism and Vernacular Cosmologies: Revisiting the Concept of National Indifference and the Limits of Nationalization in the Second Polish Republic *Olga Linkiewicz* 171

10 Survival and Assimilation: Loyalism in the Interwar Irish Free State *Brian Hughes* 191

11 Navigations of National Belonging: Legal Reintegration after the Return of Alsace to France, 1918–39 *Alison Carrol* 211

Part 4 Minority Mobilization beyond the Nation-state

12 Internationalist Patriots? Minority Nationalists, Ethnic Minorities, and the Global Interwar Stage, 1918–39 *Xosé M. Núñez Seixas and David J. Smith* 233

13 Transnational Collaborations among Women's Organizations and Questions of Minorities and Macedonia, 1925–30 *Jane K. Cowan* 257

Coda

14 The Difference Nationalism Makes: Jews and Others in the Twentieth Century *Omer Bartov* 283

Index 296

Tables

1 Comparison of Asia Minor and Alsace-Lorraine   97

Notes on Contributors

Omer Bartov is Samuel Pisar Professor of Holocaust and Genocide Studies at Brown University and the author of nine books. His recent publications include *Erased: Vanishing Traces of Jewish Galicia in Present-Day Ukraine* (Princeton University Press, 2007), *Anatomy of a Genocide: The Life and Death of a Town Called Buczacz* (Simon & Schuster, 2018), winner of the National Jewish Book Award, and *Tales from the Borderlands: Making and Unmaking the Galician Past* (Yale University Press, 2022). His edited volumes include *Shatterzone of Empires: Coexistence and Violence in the German, Habsburg, Russian, and Ottoman Borderlands* (Indiana University Press, 2013), *Voices on War and Genocide: Three Accounts of the World Wars in a Galician Town* (Berghahn, 2020), and *Israel-Palestine: Lands and Peoples* (Berghahn, 2021). Bartov's novel, *The Butterfly and the Axe*, will be published in 2023.

Mona Bieling is a doctoral student at the Department of International History and Politics at the Geneva Graduate Institute, and a Landhaus Fellow at the Rachel Carson Center for Environment and Society in Munich. Her PhD dissertation is entitled "Landscape and Power in Mandate Palestine, 1917–1948." Previously, she worked as Teaching Assistant at the Graduate Institute and as Research Assistant for the SNSF-funded project "The Myth of Homogeneity. Minority Protection and Assimilation in Western Europe, 1919–1939."

Alison Carrol is Reader in European History at Brunel University London, where she teaches on different aspects of French, European, and borderland histories in the nineteenth and twentieth centuries. She is the author of *The Return of Alsace to France, 1918–1939*, which was published by Oxford University Press in 2018, as well as numerous articles and chapters on the experiences of the Alsatian population following their return to French rule at the end of the First World War.

Jane K. Cowan is Emeritus Professor of Anthropology at the University of Sussex. While her early work investigated gender, power, identity, and the body, in recent years she has been exploring the nexus of rights claiming and international governance at the League of Nations' Minorities Section and, with Julie Billaud, the Universal Periodic Review, a UN human rights mechanism. Her publications include *Dance and the Body Politic in Northern Greece* (Princeton University Press, 1990, Winner of 1991 Chicago Folklore Prize), *Macedonia: The Politics of Identity and Difference* (Pluto Press, 2000), *Culture and Rights: Anthropological Perspectives* (with M. Dembour and R. Wilson, Cambridge University Press, 2001), and "Between Learning and Schooling: The Politics of Human Rights Monitoring at the Universal Periodic Review" (with J. Billaud, *Third World Quarterly*, 2015).

Emmanuel Dalle Mulle is a postdoctoral researcher at the Complutense University of Madrid and a research fellow of the Albert Hirschman Centre on Democracy. His current project, entitled "The Myth of Homogeneity," examines comparatively majority-minority relations in Belgium, Italy, and Spain during the interwar years. Specialized in the history and politics of nationalism, his research interests include self-determination movements, majority-minority relations, the history of the welfare state, and the history of human rights.

Sabine Dullin is Professor of History at SciencesPo Paris. Specialized in modern Russia and the USSR, her work has ranged from the political history of the Soviet State to the international and transnational dimensions of communism and border studies. She is one of the founding editors of the French journal in global and transnational history *Monde(s). Histoire, espaces, relations*. Among her books are *L'Ironie du destin. Une histoire des Russes et de leur Empire, 1853–1991* (Payot, 2021) and *La frontière épaisse. Aux origines des politiques soviétiques 1920–1940* (EHESS Editions, 2014), which was recently published in Russian.

Marina Germane is a postdoctoral research fellow at the ERC-funded project "Non-Territorial Autonomy as Minority Protection in Europe. An Intellectual and Political History of a Travelling Idea" based at the Institute for East European History of the University of Vienna. She is currently working on a monograph about the internationalisation of minority rights and transnational minority activism during the twentieth century.

Brian Hughes lectures in the Department of History at Mary Immaculate College, University of Limerick, Ireland, and is Director of the Irish Association of Professional Historians. Among other publications on the Irish Revolution (c.1912–23) and its aftermath, he is the author of *Defying the IRA? Intimidation, Coercion, and Communities during the Irish Revolution* (Liverpool University Press, 2016) and, with Conor Morrissey, editor of *Southern Irish Loyalism, 1912–1949* (Liverpool University Press, 2020).

Alvin Jackson is Sir Richard Lodge Professor of History at the University of Edinburgh. His books include *The Two Unions: Ireland, Scotland and the Survival of the United Kingdom, 1707–2007* (Oxford University Press, 2012/13) and his edited *Oxford Handbook of Modern Irish History* (Oxford University Press, 2014/17). He is currently working on a comparative study of multinational union states in a project funded by the Leverhulme Trust. He is a Fellow of the Royal Society of Edinburgh, an honorary Member of the Royal Irish Academy, and a Member of the Academia Europaea.

Pieter M. Judson currently holds the Chair in Nineteenth and Twentieth Century History at the European University Institute in Florence. He is the author of works on empire, nationalism, national indifference, liberalism, and gender in Habsburg Central Europe. His most recent book, *The Habsburg Empire. A New History* (Harvard University Press, 2016) is being translated into twelve languages.

Olga Linkiewicz is Assistant Professor at the Tadeusz Manteuffel Institute of History, Polish Academy of Sciences. She specializes in the history of modern Eastern Europe, the history of social sciences, and memory studies, which include fieldwork experience in Ukraine, Belarus, and Poland. Her book *Localness and Nationalism: Rural Communities in Interwar Eastern Galicia* (Universitas, 2018, in Polish) was awarded the "Polityka" magazine History Award for the best debut and the Kazimierz Moczarski Prize for the best history book in 2019. Her current research activity includes the completion of a book about the interchange of knowledge between Polish social scientists and American internationalists from the interwar period up to the early Cold War.

Xosé M. Núñez Seixas is Full Professor of Modern History at the University of Santiago de Compostela. He previously taught at the Ludwig Maximilian University of Munich and has published widely on the comparative history of nationalist movements and national and regional identities. His last books include *Die bewegte Nation: Der spanische Nationalgedanke, 1808–2019* (Hamburger Edition, 2019), the edited volume *The First World War and the Nationality Question in Europe* (Brill, 2020), and *The Spanish Blue Division on the Eastern Front, 1941–1945. War, Occupation, Memory* (University of Toronto Press, 2022).

Volker Prott is Senior Lecturer in Modern History at Aston University in Birmingham, UK. His fields of interest include the history of nationalism and borders, ethnic violence, and humanitarian politics in the twentieth century. His first monograph, *The Politics of Self-Determination: Remaking Territories and National Identities in Europe, 1917–1923*, was published with Oxford University Press in 2016. He is currently working on foreign interventions in the Cold War, focusing on the Congo Crisis in the 1960s and the Indo-Pakistani conflict (1947–50 and 1971). The project explores the conflicted rise of transnational politics before the "boom" of foreign interventions since the 1990s.

Davide Rodogno is Professor of International History and Politics at the Geneva Graduate Institute. Among his publications are *Fascism's European Empire* (Cambridge University Press, 2006), *Against Massacre: Humanitarian Interventions in the Ottoman Empire (1815–1914)* (Princeton University Press, 2011), and *Night on Earth – A History of International Humanitarianism in the Near East 1918–1930* (Cambridge University Press, 2021).

David J. Smith holds the Alec Nove Chair in Russian and East European Studies at the University of Glasgow. He has written extensively on issues of ethno-politics, minority activism, and conflict regulation in Central and Eastern Europe, in both historical and contemporary perspectives. His book *Ethnic Diversity and the Nation State* (with John Hiden, Routledge, 2012) examined the relationship between the European Nationalities Congress and the League of Nations. More recently, he co-authored (with Marina Germane and Martyn Housden) the article "'Forgotten Europeans': Transnational Minority Activism in the Age of European Integration" (*Nations and Nationalism*, 2018). In 2022 Smith was elected UK Representative to the Council of Europe Advisory Committee on the Framework Convention for the Protection of National Minorities.

Erol Ülker is a faculty member at Işık University, Department of International Relations. Ülker obtained his BA in International Relations from Istanbul University (1999). He holds two MA degrees from the Political Science and International Relations Department of Boğaziçi University (2003) and the Nationalism Studies Program of the Central European University (2004). He received his PhD in History from the University of Chicago in 2013, with a dissertation entitled "Sultanists, Republicans, Communists: The Turkish National Movement in Istanbul, 1918–1923." His research interests include nationalism, migration, socialist and communist movements, and labor politics in Ottoman and Turkish history.

Acknowledgments

This volume is a collective work that would not have been possible without the support of several persons and institutions. We would like to acknowledge their help and thank them very much for their support. The research behind this project received funding from the Swiss National Science Foundation (project no. 169568) and the European Union's Horizon 2020 research and innovation programme (Marie Skłodowska-Curie grant agreement no. 847635). The Pierre Du Bois Foundation for the Study of Current History also supported the publication process. The Department of International History and Politics of the Graduate Institute of International and Development Studies, Geneva, and the Department of Political History, Theory and Geography of the Complutense University of Madrid have both hosted projects related to this publication. Some of the contributing authors presented their chapters at the workshop *Sovereignty, Nationalism and Homogeneity in Europe between the Two World Wars*, which took place at the Geneva Graduate Institute on February 27–28, 2020, and that we co-organized with the Albert Hirschman Centre on Democracy. It was the last event held before the first lockdown caused by the Covid-19 pandemic. The participants in the workshop benefited from the comments of some dedicated discussants, notably Bojan Aleksov, Sandrine Kott, Andre Liebich, and Eric Storm. Additionally, Dr. Emily Jenkins edited some of the chapters of the volume, while Alessandro Ambrosino has contributed to the research behind this project.

The volume was initially planned to conclude with a contribution by Eric Weitz. His chapter was supposed to be based on the memorable keynote that he gave during our February 2020 workshop. Eric left us prematurely in July 2021. We thank him for everything he has done for us. We will not forget his passion for history, and for the history of minorities and of human rights in particular. We will not forget his contagious smile, his subtle sense of humor, and the beautiful art of not taking oneself too seriously.

List of Abbreviations

ADBR   *Archives Departémentales du Bas-Rhin* (Departmental Archives of the Lower Rhine, France)

AMM   *Archives Municipales de Mulhouse* (Municipal Archives of Mulhouse, France)

AMVCUS *Archives Municipales de la Ville et Communauté Urbaine de Strasbourg* (Municipal Archives of the City and the Urban Community of Strasbourg, France)

AN   *Archives Nationales* (National Archives, France)

ASSR   Autonomous Soviet Socialist Republic

AST   *Archivio di Stato di Trieste* (Trieste State Archives, Italy)

BCA   *Devlet Arşivleri Başkanlığı Cumhuriyet Arşivi* (Directorate of State Archives / The Republic Archive, Turkey)

BWU   Bulgarian Women's Union

CEN   Congress of European Nationalities

CUP   Committee of Union and Progress

DP   Displaced Persons

DV   *Deutscher Verband* (German Association)

FO   Foreign Office (UK)

GUS   Central Statistical Office (Poland)

IGC	Irish Grants Committee
ILA	International Law Association
IPU	Inter-Parliamentary Union
IRA	Irish Republican Army
IWSA	International Woman Suffrage Alliance
LA	*Letterenhuis* Antwerp (Belgium)
LoN	League of Nations
LONA	League of Nations Archives (Geneva)
LSE	London School of Economics
MOPR	International Red Aid
MP	Member of Parliament
MWU	Macedonian Women's Union
NARA	National Archives and Records Administration (US)
NKVD	Ministry of Internal Affairs (Soviet Union)
NLI	National Library of Ireland
NTA	Non-Territorial Autonomy
OGPU	Joint State Political Directorate (Soviet Union)
PRONI	Public Record Office of Northern Ireland
PTSD	Post-Traumatic Stress Disorder

RIC	Royal Irish Constabulary
RSFSR	Russian Soviet Federative Socialist Republic
SE	*Staatsarchiv Eupen* (Eupen State Archives, Belgium)
SILRA	Southern Irish Loyalists Relief Association
SSR	Soviet Socialist Republics
TD	Teachta Dála (member of parliament)
TBMM	*Türkiye Büyük Millet Meclisi Zabıt Ceridesi* (Minutes of the Grand National Assembly of Turkey)
TNA	The National Archives (UK)
TSDiAL	*Tsentralnyi derzhavnyi istorychnyi arkhiv Ukrainy* (Central Historical Archive, Ukraine)
UIA	*Union Internationale des Associations pour la Société des Nations* (International Federation of League of Nations' Societies)
USSR	Union of Soviet Socialist Republics
UUC	Ulster Unionist Council
VDM	*Verband der Deutschen Minderheiten in Europa* (Association of German Minorities in Europe)
WILPF	Women's International League for Peace and Freedom

1

Introduction: Sovereignty, Nationalism, and the Quest for Homogeneity in Interwar Europe

Emmanuel Dalle Mulle, Davide Rodogno, and Mona Bieling

The aftermath of the Great War significantly changed the history of nationalism, putting into motion processes that still influence European politics today. Although nationalism arose in the late eighteenth century,[1] it became one of the pillars, both domestically and internationally, of sovereignty and political legitimation by the end of the Great War. At the 1919 Paris Peace Conference, the victorious powers agreed upon a new international system "focused on populations and an ideal of state sovereignty rooted in national homogeneity."[2] The principle of self-determination became a rallying cry for political leaders claiming to represent "oppressed peoples" across the globe.[3] Self-determination promised a future of freedom from foreign domination. It also foreshadowed vicious conflicts about membership of and loyalty to legitimate sovereign communities. In European states that were already independent before 1919, nationalism served to enhance processes of inclusion and exclusion. It solidified allegiances and crystallized geographies, borders and, broadly speaking, societies. In newly independent states, nationalism became the political framework around which the nation and the nation-state were built. In most cases, nationalism postulated national and cultural homogeneity, but this rarely resembled lived realities in those countries. Consequently, between the two World Wars, minority questions sparked struggles and violent conflict throughout Europe, from East and West to North and South.[4]

Minority questions did not disappear after 1945. They are still a daily topic of discussion in contemporary politics. The massive population transfers that coincided with the end of the Second World War constituted a radical attempt to reduce the potential for ethnic strife in Central and Eastern Europe.[5] This objective was achieved only in part, as multinational states persisted in the continent, notably in Yugoslavia and the Soviet Union. Ideological rather than national forms of identification became dominant after 1945. However, the declining legitimacy of communism in the 1980s created a fertile ground for the mobilization of national, ethnic, and linguistic cleavages, which in the meantime had been reinforced, rather than repressed by state authorities in these two countries. The early 1990s brought a spike in nationalist conflicts, most visibly in former Yugoslavia, and with this brought a renewed academic and political interest in minority rights.[6] These conflicts did not remain confined to the western Balkans and the former Soviet Union. In the last quarter of the twentieth century and the first decades of the twenty-first, self-determination movements have grown stronger in several Western European regions and have even threatened the stability and territorial integrity of well-established states. The 2014 Scottish independence referendum and the row between the Spanish and Catalan governments over the organization of a similar consultation on self-determination are only the most visible recent instances of a broader European phenomenon.[7] Furthermore, throughout the continent, parties of the populist radical right have resurfaced after several decades of exclusion from politics. With these parties gaining strength, demands for bolder forms of national assertion and greater intolerance of cultural difference have gained currency too.[8]

As in the interwar period, nationalist contestation is to be found throughout Europe. Although the institutional architecture of the European continent has changed dramatically since the end of the Second World War, most notably with the establishment of the European Union, nationalism remains a key principle of political legitimacy.[9] Examining how nationalism promoted a generalized quest for homogeneity in a Europe at the peak of its transition from dynastic to popular sovereignty promises to offer relevant insights for contemporary affairs.

In 1919, European intellectual and political elites began to neatly compartmentalize state populations into minorities and majorities. While the term "minority" existed before the Paris Peace Conference, it is only in the immediate postwar period that it began to be widely used in the contemporary meaning of a non-dominant group deemed to be different from a putative "majority" on the basis of cultural, linguistic, religious, and/or ethnic criteria.[10] Seeking the establishment of "perpetual" peace, the victorious powers set up a system of international protection of minority rights and, in an unprecedented step, entrusted its enforcement to an inter-governmental organization, the League of Nations. The minority treaties, modeled after the agreement between the Allied and Associated Powers and Poland, bestowed upon "persons belonging to racial, religious or linguistic minorities" negative rights of non-discrimination, equality before the law, and religious freedom. The treaties also granted minorities positive rights to set up social, charitable, educational, and religious institutions and an equitable share of public funds to support them.[11] The strange formulation whereby individuals, not minorities, were the holders of rights was a cunning solution expedient to protect minority groups while avoiding to grant them the status of international law subjects. Most European statesmen were afraid of creating a "state within the state."[12] The treaties "required a group subject and obliterated it at the same time."[13]

The procedure established in the years immediately after the end of the Peace Conference allowed private individuals, as well as organizations claiming to represent minorities, to send petitions to the League's Minorities Section. These petitions did not have legal standing, and international bureaucrats in Geneva often dismissed them as non-receivable on the basis of restrictive criteria designed to reduce the flow of petitions examined by the League's Council to a minimum. That notwithstanding, the system allowed specific groups in selected countries to appeal to an international institution to denounce rights violations committed by the state where they lived. The former League's bureaucrat Lucy Mair did not hesitate to call the treaties "the greatest abdication of sovereignty that has been made by an independent state."[14]

Yet such abdication was not universal. The Great Powers limited the application of this system to the newly independent states that arose from the fall of the Eastern European empires, as well as to some older states in the area such as Bulgaria, Greece, and Romania.[15] Resorting to older civilizational arguments and considering the question of national minorities as one of the causes of the war, the Great Powers deemed it necessary to place the new states under international supervision.[16] This decision constituted a humiliation that was profoundly resented by the so-called "minority states." Along with the League of Nation's Mandates in extra-European territories, the minority treaties de facto established a three-tiered hierarchical system with fully sovereign (Western) states at the top, people "not yet able to stand by themselves"[17] at the bottom, and "semi-civilized" Eastern European countries under the League's supervision in the middle.[18] The decision to limit minority protection to some countries also offered ground for Great Power intervention into the domestic affairs of the states forced to sign minority treaties, a practice that some scholars have directly linked to the privileges offered to Western citizens and Christian minorities by the capitulations system in the Ottoman Empire.[19]

The unequal application of the treaties reflected both new and old understandings of sovereignty shared among European political elites. Nineteenth-century conceptions of sovereignty had emphasized the absolute power of the state. The First World War had clearly exposed the perils of unfettered state authority. The League of Nations was a novel attempt, if not to bind sovereignty, at least to coordinate it. Yet ideas of international legal constraints were mapped onto civilizational stereotypes. As the South African statesman Jan Smuts emphasized at the Paris Peace Conference, "the peoples left behind by the decomposition of Russia, Austria, and Turkey are mostly untrained politically; many of them are either incapable of or deficient in power of self-government; they are mostly destitute and will require much nursing toward economic and political independence."[20] The asymmetry of the minority treaties, and the creation of the League's Mandates, signaled a transition from an absolute to a "graded" conception of sovereignty, with the "gradation" being based on the degree of approximation to the ideal typical of the (Western) European homogenous nation-state. It was both an attempt to universalize this model of political organization and to mark the unbridgeable difference between non-Western populations and Western modernity.[21]

However, civilizational stereotypes do not completely explain the asymmetry of the minority treaties. Widespread assumptions about the irrelevance of minority questions in Western Europe contributed to that too. Several Western European actors denied the existence of minorities in Western Europe, even if in fact national and cultural homogeneity in their states was more a myth than a reality.[22] Already in 1915, the British historian Arnold Toynbee, who would later be one of the masterminds behind British plans for peace in Paris, self-confidently asserted that when looking for something similar to the Western European homogeneous nation-state in Eastern Europe, one could simply not find it.[23] In the appendix to his *Nationality and War*, addressing cases that might have contradicted his assertion, he described the populations of the

Basque Country and Catalonia simply as Basque- and Catalan-speaking Spaniards. He also predicted the inevitable merger of Flemings and Walloons into the Belgian nation. Seven years later, in a work that became a standard reference on the subject of minorities, the French ambassador Jacques Fouques Duparc located the origins of the "minority problem" in differences of language, race, and religion that—he stressed— were immense in Eastern Europe. Western Europe, on the other hand, "more stable in its political organization, had lost even the memory" of such "barriers" between groups.[24] Such self-confident statements found an echo in political circles as well. In 1925, reacting to a Lithuanian proposal for a general convention on the protection of minorities, the French delegate at the League of Nations, Henry de Jouvenel, replied that "if France has not signed such [minority] treaties, it is because she has no minorities. To find minorities in France, one would have to invent them." During that same meeting, his British counterpart, Lord Robert Cecil, dismissed the Lithuanian plans affirming that he did not fear "the cantankerous Welsh because none existed."[25]

This myth of Western European homogeneity has influenced the international historiography on European interwar minorities. In spite of repeated calls for "de-pathologizing" Eastern Europe[26] and awareness of the existence of minority questions in European countries not subjected to the minority treaties, most studies have focused, geographically speaking, on the so-called "minority belt" extending from the Baltic states to Turkey.[27] This is especially the case with works looking at extreme forms of exclusion and homogenization that have accompanied the rise of the nation-state in the first half of the twentieth century. Although these contributions have suggested a universal connection between modernity, nation-states, and forms of cultural homogenization, their emphasis on extremely violent policies, including genocide, ethnic cleansing, and population transfer, has made them privilege few selected cases in the East. Overlooking "softer" nation-building programs, these investigations have tended to leave Western Europe out of the picture.[28]

Recently, some authors have begun challenging this East-West divide showing how the history of majority-minority relations in interwar Europe defies simple categorizations pitting a heterogeneous, repressive East against a homogeneous, tolerant West. Tara Zahra has questioned the commonplace idea of France as a homogeneous nation-state, as well as blind interpretations of French nationalism as a civic script. At the end of the Second World War, both France and the newborn Czechoslovakia were confronted with the challenge of integrating sizable German-speaking minorities of unsure national identification into the fabric of the state. Zahra shows that, contrary to stereotypical understandings of East and West, between the autumn of 1918 and the spring of 1919 French officials dealt with their own minority challenge in Alsace-Lorraine through ethnic "identity cards, purges, expropriation and expulsion."[29]

Zahra correctly emphasizes that the point of her comparison is not to suggest that majority-minority issues were the same in the two halves of the continent. Her aim rather lies in examining the diversity within each aggregate and the specific historical factors that explain convergence or divergence. A similar concern is evident in the comparative work of Timothy Wilson and Volker Prott. Wilson dissects inter-ethnic violence from below in Ulster and Upper Silesia in 1918–22. Prott inquires into how international, national, and local factors contributed to promoting or restraining ethnic violence in the contested regions of Alsace-Lorraine and Asia Minor between 1917 and 1923. Both confirm that nationalist and ethnic violence was not a uniquely Eastern European story, but rather informed postwar events in Western European locales as well. At the same time, their accounts do not hide away from the conclusion that violence was indeed greater in Upper Silesia and Asia Minor than in Ulster and Alsace-Lorraine, respectively. Both historians reach this conclusion after rigorous historical examination, and both of them explain this outcome with reference to specific historical and, sometimes, contingent factors.[30] Their *modus procedendi* is key to understanding how all contributors to this book approach the study of majority-minority relations.

We intend to take the challenge to the East-West divide one step further. Anchoring specific case studies to the wider European context, we question the twin myths of Western European homogeneity and Eastern European heterogeneity, of Western European civic tolerance and Eastern European ethnic rejection of cultural and national difference. Our purpose is not to suggest that majority-minority relations evolved in the same way across Europe, but to offer a granular comparison between different European experiences.[31] By including Western European states in this discussion, we offer new historical insights into the relation between sovereignty, nationalism, and the quest for cultural and national homogeneity that allow us to identify factors favoring or restraining processes of assimilation and exclusion in different European places.

The contributions to this volume aim at bridging not only East and West, but also top-down, bottom-up, comparative case study, and transnational approaches. We consider minority questions as issues that need to be looked at from different angles and bring together different methodological perspectives to provide the most comprehensive view possible of majority-minority relations between the two World Wars. The following three premises inform our analysis.

Firstly, building on Rogers Brubaker's work on nationalism in Eastern Europe, we emphasize the multi-layered nature of nationalist conflicts. Brubaker's framework focuses on how nationalist conflicts result from the interplay of multiple actors operating at different scales (national minorities, nationalizing states, and external national homelands).[32] Similarly, our contributors examine majority-minority relations as resulting from the dynamic interaction of state authorities, their policies toward minorities, and the reaction of minority representatives/organizations; the attitude of ordinary people toward the frequently rival claims of state authorities and minority representatives; diplomats, minority representatives, and international and nongovernmental organizations negotiating majority-minority relations internationally.

Secondly, we question the assumption that interwar Western Europe was a paradigmatic model of accomplished national integration.[33] We consider Western European states as "nationalizing states" that pursued policies of cultural homogenization because their dominant elites perceived them as "incomplete" or "unrealized" nation-states.[34]

Thirdly, the contributors to this book do not assume that nationalism was a decisive factor at all levels of people's existence. While recognizing the pervasive nature of nationalism in modern societies, our authors see "nationhood" as "a variable property of groups" that becomes salient at certain moments, but not at others, as something that "happens" in specific situations.[35] Throughout the 2000s, scholars working on the history of the Habsburg Empire have embraced this methodological approach and, focusing on everyday experiences, have introduced the concept of national indifference. With it, these authors identified different behaviors adopted by ordinary people to counter the nationalizing attempts of state authorities or minority nationalist activists that primarily converged around the three following types: giving priority to non-national forms of identification (religious, class, local, professional, etc.); switching opportunistically from one national self-understanding to another; and sticking to previously existing dual identities accompanied by bilingualism and intermarriage across different national communities.[36]

National indifference has been criticized on many grounds. As ordinary people left few records of their thoughts, feelings, and actions, national indifference is mostly deduced from nationalist activists who complained about the lack of commitment to the national cause of their "co-nationals." The expression "national indifference" itself comes from the discourses of such militants. The indirect nature of this evidence clearly limits the conclusions that can be drawn from it.[37] Furthermore, the term "indifference" risks being too broad to serve as a meaningful analytical tool and would probably gain accuracy if broken down into more precise components pointing to specific behaviors, such as national "agnosticism," instrumentalism, or the prevalence of local geographical forms of identification over national ones. Finally, most of the literature on national indifference focuses on the period prior to the Paris Peace Conference, when nationalism was institutionalized as a major principle of legitimacy in domestic and international politics. The relevance of national indifference in the interwar years is still largely untested.[38] As Tara Zahra has suggested with regard to the Central and Eastern European context, "the collapse of the Habsburg empire into self-declared nation-states in 1918 rendered the outright refusal of nationality nearly impossible"—a conclusion that is echoed in some of the contributions to this volume.[39] These limitations notwithstanding, the national indifference framework poses valid questions for any analysis of majority-minority relations: does nationalism work? If yes, under which circumstances? What does nationhood mean to ordinary people and how does it influence their everyday life?

Building on Brubaker's model and the considerations on national indifference made above, we engage with three dimensions of interwar majority-minority relations asking specific questions and providing new insights. First, several contributors examine majority-minority relations from a *comparative top-down perspective*. International historians have emphasized how in Eastern Europe the "Paris system"—according to the felicitous term coined by Eric Weitz[40]—and the League of Nations, as its guarantor, promoted a world order "that treated clearly separable homogenous nation-states as the accepted norm" and cast diversity as "a potential problem."[41] The authors who focus on this comparative dimension go one step further by examining the impact of this new world order not only in Eastern European cases, but also in supposedly homogeneous Western European countries. They examine state policies seeking patterns of majority-minority relations as well as investigate whether there is a nexus between policies and political regimes. Additionally, some contributions inquire into how minority actors, notably political elites in minority regions, reacted to state policies and whether homogenization occurred, or was attempted, within minority groups rather than at the state level. These contributions find that the Paris system unleashed repressive policies of exclusion or assimilation in France (Volker Prott) and Italy (Emmanuel

Dalle Mulle and Mona Bieling) as well as in Poland (Marina Germane) and in the USSR (Sabine Dullin), while democratic institutions put in place mechanisms for the acceptance and protection of national and cultural difference in Estonia (until 1934) as much as in Belgium (Dalle Mulle and Bieling). Our comparative cases suggest that factors such as the nature of the political regime (liberal-democratic, authoritarian, or hybrid), the power of the state to enforce its own decision, and the commitment of international actors to specific territorial decisions influenced outcomes on the ground in unpredictable ways that do not follow a superficial East-West dichotomy.[42]

The chapters addressing the previous dimension largely consider majorities and minorities as uncontested entities. This is an approximation that we accept in order to pursue specific research objectives. We also recognize the need to complement this top-down comparative view with a *bottom-up approach*, which is the second dimension that this volume covers. The chapters that focus on this dimension challenge the assumption that minorities are coherent communities and interrogate the triangular relationship between state institutions, minority nationalist elites, and ordinary people deemed as belonging to minorities. They dissect how the populations of minority regions negotiated their identities between the often rival claims of state institutions and minority organizations. They further investigate whether national indifference is an adequate label to describe such interactions. These contributions simultaneously build on and move away from the concept of national indifference. On the one hand, the authors who adopt this bottom-up perspective recognize the validity of the national indifference paradigm in challenging old interpretive schemes about mass nationalization at the beginning of the interwar period. On the other hand, they all point to the fact that in the new international order ushered in by the Paris Peace Conference the space for indifference, although still existing, shrank considerably and especially so in border regions inhabited by minority groups. In the coda, Omer Bartov offers an insightful explanation of the reasons why nationalization progressively extended its reach further into the general population in Europe and beyond. Several contributors also make an effort to narrow down the capacious concept of national indifference to more precise and distinguishable behaviors. They identify "navigations of national belonging" in Alsace-Lorraine (Alison Carrol), describe strategies of "hedging" and "fence-sitting" in Ireland (Brian Hughes), and examine "vernacular cosmologies" that provided meaning to interwar individuals in Eastern Poland (Olga Linkiewicz).

Despite striving to avoid methodological nationalism through comparative analysis and a focus on the interaction of actors operating at different scales, notably local realities and central state institutions, the chapters addressing the previous two dimensions mostly consider majority-minority relations within state borders. However, some authors do look at majority-minority relations from a *transnational perspective*, which is the third dimension that this book covers. They expand Brubaker's model by considering not only the influence of "external national homelands," but also that of international organizations such as the League of Nations and transnational actors advocating minority rights. Their chapters inquire into how international and nongovernmental organizations approached minority protection throughout the interwar years, which strategies minority actors pursued within the international arena, and whether minority representatives cooperated or competed for international recognition of their claims. Two sets of actors are the key characters in the chapters that adopt this perspective: activists advocating for minority rights in the international sphere, notably around the Congress for European Nationalities and the Women's International League for Peace and Freedom (WILPF), and the civil servants of the League of Nations' Minorities Section. On the one hand, these contributions point out how minority activists came from all over Europe—not only from states subjected to the minority treaties—and propose a re-assessment of the Congress, as an organization that until the early 1930s pursued a moderate, liberal policy of minority rights promotion and was careful to avoid political radicalization on the ground (Xosé Manoel Núñez-Seixas and David Smith). On the other hand, they show how transnational networks were complex webs of interaction in which certain organizations, such as WILPF, could act as mediators between local minority activists and bureaucrats at the League of Nations in Geneva, thus further problematizing Brubaker's model. These chapters also remind us that, although nationhood is a critical prism through which to understand these transnational interactions during the interwar period, other dynamics tied to gender, class, race, and civilizational hierarchies contributed to shaping them too (Jane Cowan).

Engaging with these questions, the volume brings together East and West, as well as top-down and bottom-up approaches. Examining both nation-states' ingrained tendencies to promote national homogenization and factors that restrained such tendencies, we aim at advancing and nuancing the current understanding of minority questions in interwar Europe. We are aware that national identities, promoted either by the state or by minority actors, were not hegemonic in the interwar period. Europeans held a number of different simultaneous forms of identification. Among territorial ones, local, urban, regional, and pan-ethnic self-understandings all became more prominent and generated allegiances that stood along national belonging in a complex set of relations of competition, collaboration, contradiction, indifference, or symbiosis.[43] However, nationhood was a key category in interwar Europe. In a number of contexts and everyday situations, being deemed to hold the "wrong" national tag could have far-reaching consequences for a great many individuals. We invite the readers of this volume not to forget that multiple, concomitant, and, at times, concurrent forms of identification coexisted in interwar Europe. We deliberately chose to focus on nationalizing states, national minorities, and external national homelands, since their interplay bore heavily on European politics and daily life.

Outline

Part One addresses the theme of "Minorities and the Transition from Empires to Nation-states." This part sets the context for the rest of the book by looking at the different ways in which empires and nation-states have dealt with issues of cultural heterogeneity before, during, and shortly after the First World War. Proposing an unusual juxtaposition that might intrigue historians investigating empires, this part examines three empires (Austria-Hungary, the United Kingdom, and the Ottoman Empire) that, although on different scales, experienced crisis and partition at the end of the Great War.

Within the context of the First World War and the early interwar years, Pieter Judson revisits some of his earlier theses on national indifference, the compatibility of the Habsburg Empire with self-determination claims, and the record of imperial institutions in dealing with cultural difference. Judson inquires into what national belonging meant for ordinary people living in the Empire and shows how, in many ways, imperial forms of governance in the Austrian part of the Dual Monarchy gave more space to people to speak the language they preferred and to embrace a wider array of self-understandings than the nation-states which followed the fall of the Habsburg Empire. Then, Alvin Jackson's chapter brings the United Kingdom and its different "unions" into a wider European comparative framework. His starting point is the surprising acknowledgment that, despite the widespread awareness among specialists of the composite nature of the United Kingdom, in comparative studies, this has often been examined as a nation-state rather than a union state. Jackson, by contrast, considers the United Kingdom as a composite monarchy sharing many of the characteristics of similar continental kingdoms that were later replaced by nation-states. He dissects the centrifugal and centripetal forces that led to the partial break-up of the Union, with the secession of Ireland in 1921, but also Britain's continued survival (and the survival of the British Empire) in the immediate postwar period. Erol Ülker closes this first part by approaching the transition from the Ottoman Empire to the Republic of Turkey from the perspective of the relationship between the Turkish population and ethnoreligious minorities. Covering the years from the Young Turks Revolution (1908) to the Treaty of Lausanne (1923), Ülker dissects the rise of Turkish nationalism and the implementation of ever-more extreme homogenizing policies, from the purge of non-Muslims from the labor force to forced migration and resettlement. The chapter concludes that although there was a clear transition toward increasing homogenization, Turkish nationalists pursued a range of measures toward non-Turkish minorities that are considerably more complex and varied than recognized by traditional accounts. This first part thus introduces some of the main themes of the wider volume: the bridging of East and West, national indifference as a conceptual tool, and evidence that the Paris system did favor the unleashing of homogenizing tendencies throughout Europe.

Part Two, entitled "The Minority Question across Europe: Comparing Policies, Regimes and Resistance," looks at majority-minority relations in interwar Europe mostly from a top-down comparative vantage point. More specifically, it comparatively scrutinizes the measures adopted by different states toward populations considered to be minorities and the strategies followed by the groups in question in several Eastern and Western European countries. The main goal is to bridge the East-West divide in the relevant historiography, showing that minority questions existed throughout the continent and that countries not submitted to the League's minority system did not necessarily deal with cultural difference in more tolerant ways that the states of the minority belt.

Volker Prott opens this part by testing the Paris system, the new international order established at Versailles that tied state sovereignty to a vaguely defined national legitimacy of the state. Comparing self-determination and ethnic violence in Alsace-Lorraine and Asia Minor, Prott highlights how a temptation to use force to implement the Paris system was inherent in the postwar international regime. At the same time, through an exhaustive analytical framework, he singles out the factors that contributed to restraining the excesses of homogenization, as well as those that favored the degeneration of majority-minority contact into processes of large-scale violence. In the following chapter, Emmanuel Dalle Mulle and Mona Bieling consider Belgium, Italy, and Spain as cases of Western European countries that, in different ways, experienced both attempts at state-led national homogenization and relevant sub-state nationalist mobilization. They argue that some of these Western European states behaved as nationalizing states, pursuing highly coercive forms of assimilation toward some minority groups, as exemplified by certain interwar regimes in Italy and Spain. Moreover, they show how homogenization can occur at the regional rather than the state level and be called for by the leaders of specific minorities, as illustrated by interwar Belgium. Dalle Mulle and Bieling provide further evidence of the built-in tendencies toward homogenization promoted by the Paris system.

Marina Germane shifts the focus of this part of the volume to Central and Eastern Europe by comparing minority policy and the strategies adopted by minority representatives in Latvia, Poland, and Romania. Germane follows German and Jewish minority representatives while simultaneously examining policies of accommodation and assimilation adopted by state authorities in these three countries. Zooming in on debates around electoral reform in Poland, educational policy in Romania, and cultural autonomy in Latvia, Germane assesses the preconditions for successful minority cooperation between the members of these two minorities. She investigates the limits of successful domestic mobilization showing how, by the mid-1920s, disillusion with the postwar promises of minority protection pushed activists to expand their lobbying efforts to the transnational sphere. Sabine Dullin closes this part with an innovative contribution on the Soviet Union's ambiguous nationality policy. Dullin emphasizes how the USSR was the only post-imperial state that combined federal construction of the state and ethnic personal identification. Furthermore, the Bolsheviks' understanding of national sovereignty and state power was not linked to cultural and linguistic homogeneity, but rather promoted the development of national cultures. At the same time, Soviet leaders were obsessed with border control, capitalist infiltrations, and war scare. When collectivization turned the countryside upside down and pushed peasants to rebel, the diasporic nations and ethnic minorities living in the borderlands came to be perceived as dangerous potential fifth columns, becoming the targets of collective punishment, forced displacement, and terror.

Part Three, entitled "Majorities and Minorities as Social Constructs: Negotiating Identity Ascription," nuances and deconstructs some of the assumptions adopted in Part Two. The contributions gathered here inquire into processes of identity ascription and examine how ordinary people negotiated their identities between the often opposing injunctions of state authorities and minority representatives. They explore instrumental conceptions of rival forms of identification and instances of national indifference among non-elites. They capture a more focused image of "majority-minority" relations in interwar Europe—one that complements the conclusions reached in the previous part. More generally, this part dissects the situational and negotiated nature of identity in different European contexts, while, at the same time, pointing to the limits of national indifference in an increasingly nationalizing interwar Europe.

Using the Second Polish Republic as a case study, Olga Linkiewicz examines the nature of local conflicts in rural areas of interwar Eastern Europe. Linkiewicz focuses on popular reactions to the language plebiscite carried out by Polish authorities in 1924 and shows that, in their everyday interactions, rural peasants behaved in accordance with the principles of a vernacular cosmology that defies simple classification within the opposing extremes of national indifference and full Polish nationalization. The chapter provides a nuanced interpretation of ordinary responses to state-led nation-building and contributes to clarifying the national indifference paradigm. Similarly, Brian Hughes explores strategies of "everyday" resistance pursued by Irish loyalists during and after the Irish Revolution (1916–23). By looking at the experiences of ordinary people, he further dissects the meaning of loyalism, suggesting how this ranged from attachment to the monarchy and the Empire, with obvious links to similar lingering allegiances in continental Europe, to a political identity descending from a Protestant faith shared across the Irish Sea, although Hughes' chapter also includes Catholic loyalists (a minority within the minority). Extending his analysis well into the 1920s and early 1930s, Hughes follows dynamics of integration and assimilation within an Irish Republic that openly promoted a Catholic and Gaelic identity. Dynamics of integration and assimilation are also central to the last contribution within this part. Alison Carrol revisits Germany's return of Alsace to France exploring how different groups within Alsatian society navigated, and resisted, state plans for the region's integration. French politicians initially thought that the incorporation of the area would be straightforward, but they had to confront a reality in which locals had much more complex and varied opinions about their feelings of belonging. Carrol shows that concern for unrest pushed the state to adopt more flexible policies of integration than those initially pursued, creating spaces in which alternative (regional) understandings of identity could flourish. At the same time, many of these flexible solutions were the result of temporary compromises that slowly turned into permanent arrangements more out of contingency and necessity than by design.

The final set of chapters, gathered under the title "Minority Mobilization beyond the Nation-State," follows minority representatives across borders and gauges their efforts to lobby foreign governments and international organizations in favor of the defense of minority rights. Part Four also examines the reception of petitions at the League of Nations and focuses on some women's organizations concerned with questions of minorities.

Activists are the protagonists of Xosé M. Núñez Seixas and David Smith's contribution. Beginning with a broad assessment of transnational networks of minority representatives and their strategies of advocacy across the continent, both East and West, the authors zero in on the Congress of European Nationalities (CEN), the most important nongovernmental organization concerned with the defense of minority rights in interwar Europe. Núñez Seixas and Smith examine the emergence of a transnational nationality theory that aimed to overcome the limitations of the Paris system. Despite its failure, these efforts bore witness to the existence of a broad spectrum of actors looking for alternatives to the dominant model of the homogeneous nation-state in the interwar years. Subsequently, Jane Cowan explores in depth the triangular, asymmetric, and not fully reciprocal relations between the Women's

International League for Peace and Freedom (WILPF), Bulgarian and Macedonian female activists concerned with the fate of the Macedonian minority in Greece and Serbia, and the male-dominated Minorities Section of the League of Nations. Cowan uses the minority question in Macedonia as a prism to study the League's minority petition procedure as a site of mobilization and contestation, as well as to examine the engagement of and collaboration between women belonging to different geographical and political contexts. The chapter further investigates how, in their interactions, these actors navigated hierarchies of gender, class, race, and civilization. Including women as another marginalized group, Cowan's chapter poses important questions of how better to incorporate gender dimensions into all of our work.

Omer Bartov closes this volume with a broad-ranging coda on what he defines as "the conundrum of national indifference." Bartov argues that national indifference correctly reminds us to avoid taking nationalist arguments at face value and to be skeptical when faced with easy claims of mass nationalization. Yet even a cursory look at the history of the twentieth century prompts the equally valid conclusion that historians downplay the power of nationalism at their own peril—as the recent Russian invasion of Ukraine has reminded us. Building on a wide variety of cases, from Eastern Poland to France, Germany, and Israel, Bartov suggests that the emancipation of the peasantry in several European countries unleashed widespread and profound top-down processes of cultural and linguistic homogenization. Zealous "nationalizers" patrolled up and down state territories and border regions to spread national consciousness among fellow citizens. While often frustrated in their efforts, the polarizing effect of the First World War and the postwar institutionalization of nationalism described earlier in this introduction gave them a decisive boost. As Bartov's and many other contributions suggest, although nationhood did not become the only, nor consistently the most important, form of identification for a sizable share of the European population, as a result of this quest for homogeneity, the space for national indifference shrank considerably between the two World Wars, in Poland and Romania, but also in Italy, France, and Ireland.

Notes

1   By nationalism we mean an ideology holding that "the political and the national unit should be congruent." See Ernest Gellner, *Nations and Nationalism* (Ithaca: Cornell University Press, 1983), 1. Although there is no consensus on the precise origins of nationalism in the historiography, most authors consider the late eighteenth century and the French Revolution as a decisive moment for its development and spread. For different approaches see John Breuilly, *Nationalism and the State* (Manchester: Manchester University Press, 1982); Benedict Anderson, *Imagined Communities: Reflections on the Origin and Spread of Nationalism* (London: Verso, 1983); Eric Hobsbawm, *Nations and Nationalism since 1780: Programme, Myth, Reality* (Cambridge: Cambridge University Press, 1990); Liah Greenfeld, *Nationalism: Five Roads to Modernity* (Cambridge: Harvard University Press, 1992); Anthony Smith, *Myths and Memories of the Nation* (Oxford: Oxford University Press, 1999).

2   Eric Weitz, "From the Vienna to the Paris System: International Politics and the Entangled Histories of Human Rights, Forced Deportations, and Civilizing Missions," *The American Historical Review* 113, no. 5 (2008): 1314.
3   Erez Manela, *The Wilsonian Moment: Self-determination and the International Origins of Anticolonial Nationalism* (Oxford: Oxford University Press, 2007).
4   Jennifer Jackson Preece, *National Minorities and the European Nation-states System* (Oxford: Clarendon Press, 1998), 11.
5   On population transfers during and after the Second World War, see Matthew Frank, *Making Minorities History: Population Transfer in Twentieth-Century Europe* (Oxford: Oxford University Press, 2017).
6   On the role of nationalism in the dissolution of former Yugoslavia, see Aleksandar Pavković, "Anticipating the Disintegration: Nationalisms in Former Yugoslavia, 1980–1990," *Nationalities Papers* 25, no. 3 (1997): 427–40. On renewed interest in minority rights in the 1990s see Patrick Thornberry, *International Law and the Rights of Minorities* (Oxford: Clarendon Press, 1991); Andre Liebich and André Reszler, eds., *L'Europe centrale et ses minorités: vers une solution européenne?* (Geneva: Graduate Institute Publications, 1993); Will Kymlicka, *Multicultural Citizenship: A Liberal Theory of Minority Rights* (Oxford: Oxford University Press, 1995); Jennifer Jackson Preece, "National Minority Rights vs. State Sovereignty in Europe: Changing Norms in International Relations?," *Nations and Nationalism* 3, no. 3 (1997): 345–64.
7   On the growth of self-determination movements in Western Europe, see Michael Keating, *Nations against the State: The New Politics of Nationalism in Quebec, Catalonia and Scotland* (London: Macmillan, 1995); Montserrat Guibernau, *Nations without States: Political Communities in a Global Age* (Oxford: Polity Press, 1999); Emmanuel Dalle Mulle, *The Nationalism of the Rich: Discourses and Strategies of Separatist Parties in Catalonia, Flanders, Northern Italy and Scotland* (London: Routledge, 2017).
8   On the populist radical right, see Herbert Kitschelt, *The Radical Right in Western Europe: A Comparative Analysis* (Ann Arbor: University of Michigan Press, 1995); Cas Mudde, *Populist Radical Right Parties in Europe* (Cambridge: Cambridge University Press, 2007).
9   Especially in the case of banal nationalism. See Michael Billig, *Banal Nationalism* (London: Sage, 1995).
10 On the history of the terms minority and majority, see Till van Rahden, *Minority and Majority as Asymmetrical Concepts: The Perils of Democratic Equality and Fantasies of National Purity* (Workshop Sovereignty, Nationalism and Homogeneity in Europe between the two World Wars, Graduate Institute, Geneva, 2020). Although one could say that the terms minority and majority were invented in 1919, they also inherited features of the concept of nationality, which was widely used in imperial contexts and continued to circulate after the end of the First World War. On the differences and continuities between the concepts of minority and nationality, see Natasha Wheatley, "Making Nations into Legal Persons between Imperial and International Law: Scenes from a Central European History of Group Rights," *Duke Journal of Comparative and International Law* 28, no. 3 (2018): 481–94; Anna Adorjáni and László Bence Bari, "National Minority: The Emergence of the Concept in the Habsburg and International Legal Thought," *Acta Universitatis Sapientiae, European and Regional Studies* 16, no. 1 (2019): 7–37; Börries Kuzmany,

"Non-Territorial National Autonomy in Interwar European Minority Protection and Its Habsburg Legacies," in *Remaking Central Europe: The League of Nations and the Former Habsburg Lands*, ed. Peter Becker and Natasha Wheatley (Oxford: Oxford University Press, 2020), 316.

11 *Treaty between the Principal Allied and Associated Powers and Poland*, June 28, 1919, http://ungarisches-institut.de/dokumente/pdf/19190628-3.pdf (accessed June 27, 2022).

12 Fouques Duparc, Jacques, *La protection des minorités, de race, de langue et de religion, étude de droit des gens* (Paris: Dalloz, 1922), 42.

13 Natasha Wheatley, "Spectral Legal Personality in Interwar International Law: On New Ways of Not Being a State," *Law and History Review* 35, no. 3 (2017): 777. For a discussion on whether the rights enshrined in the minority treaties were individual or collective rights, see Emmanuel Dalle Mulle and Mona Bieling, "The Ambivalent Legacy of Minority Protection for Human Rights," *Schweizerische Zeitschrift Für Geschichte—Revue Suisse d'histoire* 71, no. 2 (2021): 272.

14 Quoted in Jane K. Cowan, "Who's Afraid of Violent Language? Honour, Sovereignty and Claims-making in the League of Nations," *Anthropological Theory* 3, no. 3 (2003): 273.

15 The treaties applied to Albania, Austria, Bulgaria, Czechoslovakia, Estonia, Finland, Greece, Hungary, Iraq, Latvia, Lithuania, Poland, Romania, Turkey, Yugoslavia, the territory of Memel, and Upper Silesia. See Pablo de Azcárate, *League of Nations and National Minorities an Experiment* (Washington and New York: Carnegie endowment for international peace, 1945), 94–5.

16 Mark Mazower, "Minorities and the League of Nations in Interwar Europe," *Daedalus* 126, no. 2 (1997): 53.

17 *The Covenant of the League of Nations*, article 22, https://avalon.law.yale.edu/20th_century/leagcov.asp (accessed June 27, 2022).

18 Lerna Ekmekcioglu, "Republic of Paradox: The League of Nations Minority Protection Regime and the New Turkey's Step-Citizens," *International Journal of Middle East Studies* 46, no. 4 (2014): 666–7.

19 Laura Robson, "Capitulations Redux: The Imperial Genealogy of the Post-World War I 'Minority' Regimes," *The American Historical Review* 126, no. 3 (2021): 978–1000. Andre Liebich interprets minority rights as an attempt to "compensate" defeated parties in post-conflict negotiations. See Andre Liebich, "Minority as Inferiority: Minority Rights in Historical Perspective," *Review of International Studies* 34, no. 2 (2008): 243–63.

20 Jan Smuts, "The League of Nations: A Practical Suggestion," in *The Drafting of the Covenant*, ed. David Hunter Miller, vol. 2 (New York: Putnam, 1928), 26.

21 Antony Anghie, *Imperialism, Sovereignty and the Making of International Law* (Cambridge: Cambridge University Press, 2012). On sovereignty see also Stephen D. Krasner, *Sovereignty: Organized Hypocrisy* (Princeton: Princeton University Press, 1999).

22 Mazower, "Minorities and the League," 53.

23 Arnold Toynbee, *Nationality & the War* (London: Dent & Sons, 1915), 476–504.

24 Fouques Duparc, *La protection des minorités*, 17. See also Carlile Aylmer Macartney, "Minorities: A Problem of Eastern Europe," *Foreign Affairs* 9, no. 4 (1931): 677.

25 League of Nations, *Sixième Assemblée, 1925. Procès-verbal de la quatrième séance de la sixième commission*, September 16, 9–11, Centre d'Archives diplomatiques de la Courneuve, 242QO-87.

26 Tara Zahra, "The 'Minority Problem' and National Classification in the French and Czechoslovak Borderlands," *Contemporary European History* 17, no. 2 (2008): 143; Pieter Judson, *The Habsburg Empire: A New History* (Cambridge: Harvard University Press, 2016), 39; Maarten Van Ginderachter and Jon E. Fox, *National Indifference and the History of Nationalism in Modern Europe* (London: Routledge, 2018), 248; Timothy Snyder, "Introduction," in *The Balkans as Europe, 1821–1914*, ed. Timothy Snyder and Katherine Younger (Rochester: Rochester University Press, 2018), 1–10. See also recent works that have emphasized the contribution of Central and Eastern Europe to the creation of the post-First World War global order through the creation of international, rather than national, institutions. Peter Becker and Natasha Wheatley, eds., *Remaking Central Europe: The League of Nations and the Former Habsburg Lands* (Oxford: Oxford University Press, 2020); Natasha Wheatley, "Central Europe as Ground Zero of the New International Order," *Slavic Review* 78, no. 4 (2019): 900–11.

27 Raymond Pearson, *National Minorities in Eastern Europe: 1848–1945* (New York: St. Martin's Pr., 1983); Stephan Horak, *Eastern European National Minorities, 1919–1980: A Handbook* (Littleton: Libraries unlimited, 1985); Paul Smith, *Ethnic Groups in International Relations* (Aldershot: Dartmouth, 1991); Christian Raitz von Frentz, *A Lesson Forgotten: Minority Protection under the League of Nations: The Case of the German Minority in Poland, 1920–1934* (Münster: Lit-Verlag, 1999); Martin Scheuermann, *Minderheitenschutz contra Konfliktverhütung?: Die Minderheitenpolitik des Völkerbundes in den zwanziger Jahren* (Marburg: Verlag Herder-Instut, 2000); Carole Fink, *Defending the Rights of Others* (Cambridge: Cambridge University Press, 2006); Umut Özsu, *Formalizing Displacement: International Law and Population Transfers* (Oxford: Oxford University Press, 2014); Sarah Shields, "Forced Migration as Nation-Building: The League of Nations, Minority Protection, and the Greek-Turkish Population Exchange," *Journal of the History of International Law* 18, no. 1 (2016): 120–45; Carolin Liebisch-Gümüş, "Embedded Turkification: Nation Building and Violence within the Framework of the League of Nations 1919–1937," *International Journal of Middle East Studies* 52, no. 2 (2020): 229–44.

28 Norman Naimark, *Fires of Hatred: Ethnic Cleansing in Twentieth-century Europe* (Cambridge: Cambridge University Press, 2002); Michael Mann, *The Dark Side of Democracy: Explaining Ethnic Cleansing* (Cambridge: Cambridge University Press, 2009); Donald Bloxham, "The Great Unweaving: Forced Population Movement in Europe, 1875–1949," in *Removing Peoples: Forced Removal in the Modern World*, ed. Richard Bessel and Claudia Haake (Oxford: Oxford University Press, 2009), 167–208; Omer Bartov and Eric Weitz, eds., *Shatterzone of Empires: Coexistence and Violence in the German, Habsburg, Russian, and Ottoman Borderlands* (Bloomington and Indianapolis: Indiana University Press, 2013); Mark Levene, *Devastation: Volume I: The European Rimlands 1912–1938* (Oxford: Oxford University Press, 2013); Philipp Ther, *The Dark Side of Nation-states: Ethnic Cleansing in Modern Europe* (Oxford: Berghahn Books, 2016); Frank, *Making Minorities History*.

29 Tara Zahra, "The 'Minority Problem,'" 148.

30 Timothy Wilson, *Frontiers of Violence: Conflict and Identity in Ulster and Upper Silesia 1918–1922* (Oxford: Oxford University Press, 2010); Volker Prott, *The Politics of Self-Determination: Remaking Territories and National Identities in Europe, 1917–1923* (Oxford: Oxford University Press, 2016). For other, more limited, attempts to expand comparative analyses to Western European countries, see Frank, *Making Minorities History*, 99–118; Marcus Payk and Roberta Pergher, eds., *Beyond*

Versailles: Sovereignty, Legitimacy, and the Formation of New Polities after the Great War (Bloomington: Indiana University Press, 2019), 143–64.

31 Although including the League's Mandates in our comparative analysis would certainly provide an additional insightful perspective on the topic of this edited volume, it would also risk stretching our efforts too widely. On minorities in the Mandates see Benjamin White, *The Emergence of Minorities in the Middle East: The Politics of Community in French Mandate Syria* (Edinburgh: Edinburgh University Press, 2011); Laura Robson, *States of Separation Transfer, Partition, and the Making of the Modern Middle East* (Oakland: University of California Press, 2017).

32 Rogers Brubaker, *Nationalism Reframed: Nationhood and the National Question in the New Europe* (Cambridge: Cambridge University Press, 1996), 55–78.

33 This is what most of the literature on nation-building has generally done. For a summary and an early critique, see Anthony Birch, *Nationalism and National Integration* (London: Unwin Hyman, 1989). The point has been repeated by Brubaker, *Nationalism Reframed*, 81–2. For a recent innovative work on the subject that in part questions earlier views of nation-building in Western Europe, see Andreas Wimmer, *Nation Building* (Princeton: Princeton University Press, 2018).

34 For a definition of "nationalizing states" see Brubaker, *Nationalism Reframed*, 9.

35 Ibid., 19. See also Rogers Brubaker, Mara Loveman, and Peter Stamatov, "Ethnicity as Cognition," *Theory and Society* 33, no. 1 (2004): 31–64.

36 See Pieter Judson, *Guardians of the Nation: Activists on the Language Frontiers of Imperial Austria* (Cambridge: Harvard University Press, 2006); Zahra, "Imagined Noncommunities"; Maarten Van Ginderachter and Jon Fox, "Introduction," in Van Ginderachter and Fox, *National Indifference*, 1–14.

37 See John Breuilly, "What Does It Mean to Say That Nationalism Is 'Popular'," in *Nationhood from Below. Europe in the Long Nineteenth Century*, ed. Maarten Van Ginderachter and Marnix Beyen (London: Palgrave, 2012), 23–46; Laurence Cole, "Differentiation or Indifference? Changing Perspectives on National Identification in the Austrian Half of the Habsburg Monarchy," in Van Ginderachter and Beyen, *Nationhood from Below*, 96–119.

38 For exceptions, see Tara Zahra, *Kidnapped Souls: National Indifference and the Battle for Children in the Bohemian Lands, 1900–1948* (Ithaca: Cornell University Press, 2008); Ginderachter and Fox, *National Indifference*.

39 Zahra, "Imagined Non-Communities," 101.

40 Weitz, "From the Vienna to the Paris System," 1314.

41 Liebisch-Gümüş, "Embedded Turkification," 11. See also Shields, "*Forced Migration*"; Özsu, *Formalizing Displacement*, 1–20.

42 On the factors that explain variations, see especially Volker Prott's and Emmanuel Dalle Mulle and Mona Bieling's chapters in this volume.

43 On these various territorial identities and their relationship with nationhood and the nation-state, see Celia Applegate, *A Nation of Provincials: The German Idea of Heimat* (Berkeley: University of California Press, 1990); Joost Augusteijn and Eric Storm, *Region and State in Nineteenth-Century Europe Nation-Building, Regional Identities and Separatism* (Houndmills, Basingstoke, Hampshire; New York: Palgrave Macmillan, 2013); Alon Confino, *The Nation as a Local Metaphor: Württemberg, Imperial Germany, and National Memory, 1871–1918* (Chapel Hill: The University of North Carolina Press, 1997); Alexander Geppert, *Fleeting Cities: Imperial Expositions in "Fin-de-Siècle" Europe* (Basingstoke: Palgrave Macmillan, 2010); Stéphane Gerson, *The Pride of Place: Local Memories and Political Culture in Nineteenth-Century France*

(Ithaca: Cornell University Press, 2003); Xosé-Manoel Núñez and Maiken Umbach, "Hijacked Heimats: National Appropriations of Local and Regional Identities in Germany and Spain, 1930–1945," *European Review of History: Revue Européenne d'histoire* 15, no. 3 (2008): 295–316; Xosé Manoel Nuñez Seixas and Eric Storm, *Regionalism and Modern Europe: Identity Construction and Movements from 1890 to the Present* (London: Bloomsbury Academic, 2019); Maiken Umbach, "A Tale of Second Cities: Autonomy, Culture, and the Law in Hamburg and Barcelona in the Late Nineteenth Century," *The American Historical Review* 110, no. 3 (2005): 659–92.

Part One

Minorities and the Transition from Empires to Nation-states

2

Making Minorities and Majorities: National Indifference and National Self-determination in Habsburg Central Europe

Pieter M. Judson

In December of 1918, Tomáš Garrigue Masaryk, first president of the Czechoslovak Republic and former deputy to the Austrian imperial parliament, published an essay titled "The Problem of Small Nations and States." The essay sought to explain the world-historical import of the very recent collapse of Austria-Hungary[1] and its territorial division among several self-styled nation-states. In so doing, the essay also cited recent history both to justify and to legitimize an emerging new territorial order from which the new Czechoslovak state had greatly benefited. Masaryk's historical argument placed Czechoslovakia at the forefront of an inexorable historical process. "On the whole," he wrote (perhaps somewhat over-optimistically), "multinational empires are an institution of the past, of a time when material force was held high and the principle of nationality had not yet been recognized." He then proceeded to make a key argument that explained both why the principle of nationality had not been recognized in the past, and why the present age represented a critical break with the past. "Because," Masaryk explained, "democracy had not been recognized."[2]

In writing about the continuities and breaks encapsulated in Habsburg Central Europe's post-imperial transitions, I regularly quote Masaryk's essay. His words beautifully capture the enduring presumptions that have framed and often continue to influence the way many historians, journalists, and politicians depict the events of 1918–20.[3] In particular, these words express most historians' conception of the relationship of "empire" to "nation." In this view, empires preceded so-called nation-states chronologically. But empires had also allegedly repressed developing nations, while nations had only gained the opportunity to replace empire once democracy had become a global force for change. These presumptions have also given meaning to our twentieth-century understandings of concepts like "minority" or "majority," as they apply to the self-styled nation-states that replaced the empires of the Habsburgs, Ottomans, Hohenzollerns, and Romanovs. In Habsburg Central Europe, so the story goes, nations were exceptionally interspersed among each other. It was therefore impossible to draw clear territorial borders between nations without leaving some members of one nation in a neighboring nation-state.

This chapter questions the fundamental presumptions about empire and nation (and thus implicitly about majority and minority) that underlie the logic of the Masaryk quotation, especially the self-evident link between democracy and nation-statehood. I start by explaining the ways in which imperial structures and nationalist movements shaped each other in the nineteenth century, also showing that the two were hardly at odds with each other. Placing the twin phenomena of what I and others have referred to as "national indifference" next to Rogers Brubaker's "situational nationalism" at the center of the analysis, I pose an alternative understanding of the relationships between empire and nation that I believe lasted well into the post-1918 era in Central and Eastern Europe. Finally, I point out that the efforts of the successor states themselves to ascribe nationality using the full powers of the law and administration made them more "prisons of the peoples" than the empire of the Habsburgs had been.

In the empire of the Habsburgs, unlike in the Ottoman Empire for example, linguistic practice rather than religious practice originally defined nationhood as the Austrian Constitutional Laws (1867) and the Hungarian Law of Nationalities (1868) established it.[4] Here we also need to emphasize that no linguistically defined group (or what would come to be called nationality) in fact comprised a majority of the population, either in the Empire as a whole or in the two states that together constituted the Dual Monarchy after 1867. In the Austrian half of Austria-Hungary, all such language groups might constitute a majority or a minority of the population in the different regions where they were located. Nevertheless, and despite the claims of later nationalist propaganda, this imperial Austrian state had no official state nationality or language. The German language did serve as a common language for internal communication within the imperial bureaucracy and German was the official language of command for the common Austro-Hungarian military. Still, while German nationalists might use the term *Staatsvolk* to describe their nationality, this particular and nationalist relationship to the state was never more than a claim, and certainly not something recognized by the state. On the other hand, Hungarian did become the official language of administration and education in the Hungarian state after 1867, although informal local administrative practice in some regions often featured other languages simply for lack of local Hungarian speakers.[5]

After the breakup of the Dual Monarchy, and following the Hungarian example, the successor states called themselves nation-states and each claimed to embody a linguistically—or culturally—defined nation. Those inhabitants of the new state who did not belong to the defining nation—and these often represented a substantial portion of the population—were often legally categorized as belonging to specific "minorities."[6] At the same time, however, each post-1918 ruling nationality (or "majority") had developed a mythology under the Habsburg Monarchy that claimed many of its members had in fact been "de-nationalized" by a hostile neighboring nation or by the imperial government. After 1918 some states even attempted to "re-nationalize" those whose families were perceived to have "gone astray" and to have joined the "wrong national community" under the Empire.[7]

But let us return for a moment to Masaryk's bold claim for the post-imperial successor states in Central, Southern, and Eastern Europe, and about how they differed from the Habsburg Monarchy. Masaryk asserted that multinational empires had depended on force to hold subject nationalities in thrall, implying that it would have been impossible to hold these nations together in an imperial structure in any other way than by means of coercion. The contemporary recognition of democracy as the necessary principle for state organization in the twentieth century, however, had allegedly ended this forced imposition of imperial rule from above. It was democracy that facilitated the creation of linguistically based nation-states from below. When the people had the opportunity to speak for themselves, according to this view, they had chosen nation-statehood. On one level Masaryk meant this as an argument to legitimate the creation of new states like Poland, Yugoslavia, and his own Czechoslovakia. It also legitimated the territorial aggrandizement of the Italian and Romanian empires that proclaimed themselves nation-states as well. And such arguments were necessary in 1918. After all, the victorious allies—especially the United States—had not easily been convinced about the wisdom of partitioning Austria-Hungary until the very last months of the War.[8] Their basis in democracy, or in a form of self-determination, protected these states from accusations of imperial and territorial aggrandizement against their neighbors.

A territorial disposition that to us today appears as natural and normal, however, was nevertheless problematic and potentially highly unstable in 1919. Why, for example, should the peace conferences have risked de-stabilizing the region further by condoning the partition of Austria-Hungary and legitimizing untested new states, especially when the Bolshevik revolution threatened so many parts of Europe? Could one really trust the optimistic assertions of some nationalist politicians who—when circumstances required it—could also claim to be fully inexperienced in the arts of politics precisely because of their people's alleged vassalage inside Austria-Hungary?[9] And how could the allies, themselves openly imperialist, justify the dismemberment of a fellow imperial regime without questioning their own legitimacy, a legitimacy that was indeed debated throughout the world in 1919?[10]

These immediate concerns may well explain Masaryk's particular assertions about the qualitative differences between empires and nation-states. They do not, however, oblige us to accept these assertions at face value, as I fear too many historians have done in the century since 1920. The rest of this chapter examines critically the aspects of empire, nationhood, and democracy raised in Masaryk's statement to better understand how the legacies of the Habsburg Empire shaped the ways in which issues of minority and majority populations were conceived in the interwar period and remain influential even today. In particular, these legacies help us to understand why, for example, matters of minorities and so-called "ethnic mosaics" have traditionally been cast as topics particular to Central and Eastern Europe and not to Europe in general. Finally, the chapter also seeks to remind us that many Europeans around 1900 may have felt little or no significant and enduring tie to a national community.

My examples are drawn from the institutional, administrative, and political practices of the Habsburg Monarchy, and from popular attitudes within Habsburg society. First, I trace the ways in which systems of national identification developed as byproducts of imperial structures and practices around language use (one could even say as products of unintended imperial encouragement). Second, I investigate the question of the subject (or agent) of that democracy that was allegedly finally recognized in 1918.

Who in fact was given the choice to determine her or his political fate after the War? Third, using the concept of national indifference, I assess the nationalist character and significance of the revolutions that ended Habsburg rule in Central Europe, and their implications for subsequent systems of managing so-called national majorities and minorities.

Empire and Nationhood

Masaryk's quotation placed multinational empires and nation-states at opposite ends of an imagined spectrum of forms of political organization. Force is the dominant consolidating principle at one end of this spectrum and democracy is the dominant principle at the other end. Only force, Masaryk asserts, could have held so many different nations within empires. Yet the most rudimentary examination of the history of the Habsburg Monarchy in the nineteenth century reveals a far different and more complex picture of the relationship between concepts of empire and nation. As political concepts whose fundamental meanings changed radically during the nineteenth century, nation and empire in fact developed in close relationship to each other and were often mutually constitutive of each other. Each gave the other meaning, and the programs pursued by each did not necessarily exclude those of the other. Far from being understood as polar opposites, empire and nation could be seen as close allies. To put it simply, most nationalists in the Habsburg Monarchy had good reason to be imperial patriots, and most imperial propagandists used concepts of nationhood to strengthen their justifications of empire.

Twentieth-century nationalists often claimed in retrospect that after centuries during which the Empire had successfully suppressed the national principle, in the early nineteenth century so-called nationalist "awakeners" had made "sleeping" peoples conscious again that they belonged to national communities. These national communities were usually understood to be rooted in distinctive language use going back centuries, sometimes over a thousand years to the time of the ancient Romans or earlier. This version of history increasingly asserted that despite their spatial proximity to each other, people who used different languages in the nineteenth century descended from different national communities distinguished not only by language use but also by recognizably different cultures. The so-called "awakeners," following Herder's imagery for the "sleeping Slavs," were claimed to have been early activists, nationalists who sought to revive the use of national languages that had fallen into disuse under the Empire. In cases where a language had little written history, their object was to codify the language, to give it a modern grammar and vocabulary. Some of these "awakeners" were folklorists who sought to rescue local folk cultures from oblivion, in a century where standardized written communication rapidly replaced more traditional oral forms. Some were interested in preserving oral languages through codification, defining certain languages as dialects of larger languages. Many argued over which dialect constituted the purest form of a spoken language that could then serve as the basis for a written language. In the early nineteenth century, for example, there was no agreed-upon "Slovene language," nor in fact was there a recognized written Serb or Slovak language. Instead, activists and linguists debated the significance of regional differences and similarities, giving some spoken languages distinctive grammars. The individuals who later were called "awakeners" often had not shared particularly nationalist goals. But later activists recast their work in specifically nationalist terms.[11]

The work of the early "awakeners" allegedly produced popular movements that soon demanded cultural and political rights for their nations and eventually brought down empires to achieve those rights. In fact, however, it was largely the Habsburg state itself that unintentionally created the conditions that promoted this linguistic concept of cultural and political nationhood in the nineteenth century. The Habsburgs' holdings had constituted—like many other states in Europe—a composite state that included territories governed under quite different legal traditions and customs and that employed different vernacular and bureaucratic languages. The Habsburgs did not begin to develop a common and integrated imperial state structure until the eighteenth century, and this process was neither simple nor easy to impose on their varied regional holdings. In fact, up until 1804, when Emperor Franz II of the Holy Roman Empire proclaimed himself Emperor Franz I of Austria, there had been no Austrian empire. In 1815, imperial Austria was one of Europe's youngest states.

The Habsburg Empire and National Difference

Although the Habsburgs held the title of Holy Roman Emperor (of the German Nation) since the late fifteenth century, they did not associate themselves with a single national language in their own realms. They saw themselves—at least in theory—as rulers of a universal empire, in the same way that they proclaimed themselves protectors of a universal Catholic Church. What did this mean in practice? The developing Habsburg state ruled over territories that historically used a range of different languages for official and local functions. The Habsburgs had not opposed the use of local languages for official and semi-official purposes, or for local primary education. Even the failed efforts of Joseph II in the 1780s, or of Francis Joseph in the 1850s, to enforce the German language as a kind of official bureaucratic language, never sought to end fully the use of other languages at the local or regional level.[12] Proclamations were made locally in more than one language, and until 1847, the Hungarian Diet, for example, conveniently used Latin in its deliberations, a policy that meant that no one had the advantage of speaking her or his own language in the Diet's proceedings. This institutional recognition of linguistic diversity was a result of pragmatism in a traditionally composite state.[13]

During this period, even the term "nation" did not at first carry the same ethno-linguistic connotations that it would by the end of the nineteenth century. In 1800 "nation" more often referred to the privileged members of a regional diet. It was they who constituted the nation, not the ordinary people who might or might not share a similar language. Nation could also refer to a single region that might well encompass inhabitants who spoke a diverse range of languages, such as the "Moravian nation" or the "Hungarian nation." But unlike cases in other parts of the world or in earlier periods where the term "nation" had held such different meanings, nationhood in Habsburg Austria in the nineteenth century became defined overwhelmingly by the question of language use, reinforced in some cases by religious practice.

Both in imperial Austria and in the emergent Hungarian state, the 1848–9 revolutions saw a critical transformation in understandings and treatment of language differences. Although nationhood remained a slippery concept, used by many actors to advance very different agendas, the focus on linguistic practice as the basis for national difference became decisive. In imperial Austria, for example, the new parliament faced the question of what language in which to conduct its business. The deputies debated in German, as a common language of the university educated, but they made concessions, for example, when Galician peasant deputies arrived in Vienna who required translations to understand the proceedings. When it came time to draft a constitution for Austria, a parliamentary committee debated how best to organize the imperial administration to enable the citizens to use their own languages in primary education or in communication with the bureaucracy. Paragraph 4 of the Kremsier Parliament's draft bill of rights gave every nation of the Empire equal rights to use its language and develop its nationality.[14]

When again in 1867 liberals wrote constitutions and laws for each half of the new Dual Monarchy, they again transformed this pragmatic policy into a question of rights. In Austria, the constitutional issue of language use was debated in a way that sought to guarantee both the distinctive historic rights of the individual provinces that used specific languages, and the imperial citizen's common right to use one's own distinctive language in daily life situations. In the context of this discussion, deputies consciously referred to "minorities." Bohemian German liberal Eduard Herbst (1820–92), soon to be Minister of Justice, asked his colleagues in the parliament: "Since this large empire, thanks to a unique fate, unites in itself such a diversity of nations, don't we have to find the providential unity of the empire, in the protection it gives to the individuals and minorities that are dispersed everywhere?"[15] Legal historian Joachim Pirker notes, however, that in general the deputies in 1867 preferred to speak of the rights of individuals and of nations rather than of majorities and minorities.[16]

In Hungary the rights of different nationalities were embodied in a particular law rather than in a constitution. Drafted by Baron Josef Eötvös (1813–71), the original law proposed a liberal framework to guarantee a range of rights to non-Hungarian speakers, but as individuals not as members of nations. Unlike Austrian constitutional law, the Hungarian law did not concede collective rights to language groups or nations, but rather to individuals. The details of the law's application were left to future legislation and starting in the 1870s that legislation generally worked to restrict the rights of non-Hungarian speakers to use their languages in public life.[17]

Although after 1867 both the Austrian and Hungarian states guaranteed certain kinds of rights to users of officially recognized languages, they did so in very different ways and with different effects. In both contexts, however, speakers of different languages became understood as members of diverse nations when taken as a whole, although no one in either state was legally assigned to a nation, and no one needed legally to belong to one. These policies produced two important developments. First, the two states—for very different reasons—started to collect statistics about the numbers of speakers of different languages. In the Austrian case this practice was meant to help determine language use in schools, the courts, and in the local and provincial administration. By comparison, in Hungary the census sought to measure the successes and failures of the so-called "Magyarization" policies intended to make all Hungary's citizens into speakers of the Hungarian language, at least as a second language if not as a "mother tongue." Secondly, the constitutional articulation of language rights led to a steady buildup of case law and administrative practice around language use both in the Austrian state and in the shared imperial institutions such as the military.[18] These legal decisions articulated principles that often survived in the legal codes of successor states in the interwar period later and that regulated specific policies around what came to be known as "minority rights."[19] The application of Austrian principles of language use for the common military also produced considerable friction between Hungary's rulers and the imperial government. The Hungarian political classes opposed the application of the more liberal Austrian language laws to the military. In fact, they sought to create their own military force altogether, something the emperor-king, keenly aware of his military prerogative, refused to countenance.

It was generally court cases in Austria in the 1870s and 1880s that shaped administrative practices around language use, answering such questions as "how many speakers of a second language in a district required the hiring of teachers or bureaucrats who could speak that language?" Such considerations led to legally defined minority languages coming into being at the level of local districts and crownlands (provinces) in Austria. For a language to be recognized officially in a crownland, for example, it had to be reported in the census by at least 20 percent of the residents. For a language group to demand a state-funded minority language school in a district (Austria had an eight-year educational requirement for all boys and girls after 1868), the courts ruled that a minimum of forty school-age children within a two-hour walking distance of the school had to speak that language.[20] In a military regiment, if 20 percent of the recruits spoke a particular language, then the officers (up to the level of captain) were obligated to use that language, not in military commands, but in normal communication.[21]

I mention these administrative details for four reasons. First to remind us that at the level of the state in Austria there were no linguistic or national majorities or minorities. The term "minority" was used contextually starting in 1867, but it did not have the same significance it would have after 1918. This was partly because the state as a whole had no official nation, nor did it ascribe an immutable linguistic or national identity to its citizens. Secondly, I raise these details to emphasize that the law enabled nationalist activists to assert increasingly that language use was legally the premier sign of national belonging, whether or not an individual actually felt a sense of belonging to a nation. Nationalist activists of all kinds in Austria regularly—and misleadingly—treated the census as a moment that measured their demographic strengths and weaknesses.[22] Thirdly, as mentioned above, after 1918 a state like Czechoslovakia adopted many of these familiar regional administrative practices such as the 20 percent rule to determine whether a language group qualified for what were now called "minority rights" in a particular district. Fourthly, and as mentioned above, in the self-styled nation-states after 1918, membership in a language group was no longer a question of a person's un-reflected behavior or personal choice, as it had been in Austria-Hungary. Under the successor states it was now up to government agencies, police detectives, and the testimonies of meddling neighbors to determine authentic national belonging, by carrying out intrusive investigations of an individual's or family's history, sociability, and home life.[23]

How Empire and Nation Could Fit Together

Another reason to explore the details of the imperial system is that its structures and rules about language use produced a vibrant political system organized largely around linguistic demands expressed in nationalist political terms. It was not merely the courts and bureaucrats that determined how constitutional rights were implemented, but the political parties as well. Masaryk may have argued that the Empire was held together by force but in fact, it was held together largely by the efforts of regional—usually nationalist—political parties that sought to gain as many tangible benefits for themselves and their voters as possible. These benefits ranged from appointments to influential bureaucratic posts to extra funding for new schools. Before the First World War, nationalist political parties had every incentive to maintain this system. Several nationalist parties even gained significant forms of local political autonomy for their linguistic nations. Some, like the Czech, Hungarian, Italian, and Polish nationalists, even built empires of patronage within the larger Empire, and were quite committed to maintaining the system. Even when their most radical deputies performed outrageous acts of nationalist hostility toward each other in public, they often depended on the state to maintain their positions of power.[24]

Politics in the Habsburg Monarchy—especially the Austrian half—revolved around ongoing efforts by nationalist politicians to win ever-more ambitious forms of linguistic and political rights and autonomy for their alleged national communities. To do so, they argued increasingly that extreme cultural differences separated their nation from other nations to the point where national differences could become racialized. In imperial Austria, all of this took place within the context of a relatively liberal—and at some levels even proto-democratizing—political system that was comparable to many of the systems one encountered in other contemporary European states.[25] We have trouble seeing this point in part because the nationalists themselves never openly declared themselves satisfied with one victory or another. By definition, of course, nationalists can never express full satisfaction about anything. Their political influence depends on maintaining a sense of heroic struggle and unfair victimization.

At the same time, during the nineteenth century the Empire and its propagandists developed new definitions and visions for empire that relied on nation as much as nations used the structures of empire to develop their politics. After the unifications of Italy and Germany removed Habsburg influence from these former sites of power and prestige, the Empire could no longer portray itself in the universal European terms of the Holy Roman Empire/German Nation of the past. Instead, propagandists and scientists increasingly portrayed the Empire as a kind of protective shield that encompassed many nations while fostering their cultural and civilizational advancement. This vision of empire too required a cataloging of the various nations and their cultural accomplishments or deficiencies. The most famous of these imperial efforts was the so-called *Kronprinzenwerk, Österreich-Ungarn in Wort und Bild* (*Austria-Hungary in Word and Image*). This series of volumes, each devoted to a crownland or region of the Empire, was inspired by Crown Prince Rudolf in 1883 who also wrote an introduction to the series before his suicide in 1889. The series was published in both German and Hungarian editions, and included essays commissioned by two editorial staffs from 423 experts on the flora, fauna, geology, and ethnographic diversity of each region. The series documented the diversity of the Empire and its peoples, and implicitly argued for the role of the state in the work of bringing higher levels of culture and civilization to the different regions.[26]

Given the agitation by nationalist politicians, on the one hand, and the efforts of imperial propagandists, on the other, it would be easy to assume that by 1900 most citizens of the Dual Monarchy had a strong sense of attachment to one national community or another. While historians have assumed for a long time that populations in Habsburg Central Europe had become fully nationalized by 1900, lingering doubts remained among the nationalists themselves about the effectiveness of their mobilizing efforts. Historical research and theorizing in the past two decades have also disputed the all-too-easy presumption about firm popular national loyalties and their significance. After all, it was nationalists themselves who originated the term "national indifference," both with condescension and anxiety, applying it to those problematic people who apparently did not demonstrate adequate loyalty to the nation in their daily lives. They also applied other terms such as national "amphibians" or "hermaphrodites" to people who appeared to waver between languages and nations, or they labeled them backward and ill-informed.[27] For historians in the past fifteen years, the term "national indifference" (or "indifference to nation") characterizes a broad range of attitudes that shaped an individual's perception of a given situation along with her or his loyalties. Those of us who developed the concept wanted to move away from the question "who was a nationalist in what nation?" or "who was not-national?" Rather, we have tried to examine situations that produced group identities and to ask in what situations people may have seen the world through the lens of nationhood, to use Rogers Brubaker's terminology, or in what situations that lens of nation lost its relevance. This approach to the question of behavior or attitude moves us away from ideas of fixed, authentic, or even fluid identities. Instead, it invites us to evaluate *why* the idea of nation might be important in one situation and not in another.[28]

Nationalists at the time understood "indifference" as behaviors that contradicted a person's own authentic national interest. If there were two different language schools in a town, to which one did a family send its children? When the decennial Austrian census was taken, which language did family members report as their "language of daily use?" In an election, which national party did a voter support? To which local social clubs did a person belong? When it came to consumption or church attendance, which shops did an individual patronize, which church services did she attend? The answers to these questions, it was presumed, demonstrated where an individual's national loyalties lay. The problem with this presumption was that in real life, people often made a variety of choices that contradicted or confirmed one or the other or both national interests. In regions or crownlands where more than one language was spoken, husband and wife might even report different languages of daily use on the census or change their answers over time. Farming families sent their children on exchanges with a family that used a different language, in order to acquaint the child with both provincial languages. Knowledge of both languages sometimes made good economic sense and might help a child's social mobility. In multilingual regions of Bohemia some families attempted to send their children to different schools in different years for the same purpose. This was often the case because increasingly after 1867, schools rarely taught both provincial languages.[29]

By the end of the nineteenth century, in crownlands where nationalist political conflict was strongest, both sets of nationalists might compete for the national loyalties of a single family. This competition was especially harsh when children registered for the coming school year, or when the decennial census was taken. The dynamic of competition often radicalized nationalists on all sides as they competed for the same people and they also developed cultural or psychological explanations to rationalize why someone might be indifferent and "betray" the national community.[30]

For many people, however, it seems that nationhood was important in some particular situations, and quite unimportant or irrelevant to many other situations. Moreover, nationhood was only one of several kinds of loyalties, such as religious, local, regional, or imperial patriotic that defined people's outlooks. Most of these identifications tended to define and reinforce each other, rather than to contradict each other. This was the case, for example, for the military veterans analyzed by Laurence Cole whose organizations proudly proclaimed their regional identifications, their use of their national language, and their patriotic loyalty to Emperor/King and fatherland.[31] These elements were not particular and could not easily be separated out from each other, precisely because they both defined and reinforced each other's meanings. In this way, nationalist and imperial identifications often reinforced each other.

The outbreak of war in 1914 did little at first to undermine this general reality. However, from the very start of the war several influential elite military and bureaucrats (along with certain nationalists) expressed deep mistrust toward other nationalist political parties or language groups that—without any evidence—they presumed to be disloyal to the Empire. In August and September of 1914, this mistrust often manifested itself in brutal persecutions against Ruthenes/Ukrainian-speaking civilians unfairly suspected of Russian sympathies, or Slovene or Serb speakers suspected of pro-Serbia feelings. Early on government officials even encouraged or "tolerated" local popular initiatives taken against perceived traitors that could take the form of informing on one's neighbors in a kind of mass hysteria.[32] All of this became possible thanks to the authority granted a military high command that distrusted all popular politics and used its emergency powers to impose a harsh military dictatorship that abandoned the rule of law for three years.

Stories of the wartime treachery of some national groups were most often used either to impugn a rival nationalist group, or to hide the fundamental incompetence of Austria-Hungary's military leaders and their strategies. It is true that some Austro-Hungarian POWs in Russia or Italy were freed in exchange for their agreement to fight with the Allies against Austria-Hungary, but we should not generalize these behaviors to entire populations, for which there is no evidence. Finally, we should keep in mind that the only wartime armed nationalist revolt against an imperial power occurred not in Habsburg Austria-Hungary, but rather in Ireland in 1916.[33]

National Revolution, Democracy, Nationhood

How then should we evaluate the events celebrated as national revolutions that brought down the Habsburg Monarchy in 1918, keeping in mind the conceptual tool of national indifference? On the one hand, the death of Emperor-King Francis Joseph and the accession of his young grandnephew, Charles I, reversed many elements of the brutal military dictatorship that alienated so many citizens since 1914. Charles amnestied political prisoners, pressured the Hungarian government to expand the suffrage, and reopened the Austrian Parliament (the Hungarian parliament had continued to function during the war). His government also created and generously funded a new ministry of social welfare. But these reversals hardly revived confidence in the Empire. Instead, greater freedom simply unleashed more open political opposition to and criticism of a regime that had demanded unyielding sacrifice from its people but could not provide them with the necessities to survive. For this reason, the revolutionary events that produced the fall of the Habsburg Monarchy were primarily about human survival.

By 1918, since the imperial state was no longer able to ensure its people's physical survival, the administrative links to the various regions began to crumble. State officials could no longer control strikes or popular violence or pogroms, and they could no longer guarantee even minimal food or fuel supplies. Local administrators who found themselves hard pressed to find solutions to impossible problems could expect no help from the imperial state. When they took independent action, it was for regionalist reasons and in regional contexts, rather than for nationalist reasons. The crownland territorial divisions within which local bureaucrats worked to prevent a complete breakdown of order, to provide populations with sustenance for survival, or in which they adjudicated conflicting property claims, also did not coincide with the territorial boundaries later claimed by nationalist politicians for their nation-states. When some regional actors took control in Styria (later claimed by Austria and Yugoslavia) or in Transylvania (later claimed by Hungary and Romania), their seizures of power received a retrospective nationalist interpretation.

For other reasons, the regional conditions also favored later nationalist interpretations of revolutionary events. As local people and institutions sought solutions to food, fuel, medical, and housing crises, they abandoned the imperial center to manage survival on their own. And when, for example, the new Imperial Ministry of Welfare doled out millions of crowns to local experts to distribute to people, those local experts were generally activist members of nationalist organizations in the crownlands. It was their nationalist organizations and not the Empire that reaped the credit for having helped local populations.[34] By the time the war was clearly lost in September 1918, there was no longer a functioning central state. For all these reasons, we cannot date the Empire's fall to a specific or even to a symbolic date. In a manner typical of the layered forms of sovereignty of empire, the Monarchy simply retrospectively granted increasing degrees of political autonomy to break-away regions and the self-styled "national councils" that constituted themselves as regional authorities.

People also turned increasingly away from the imperial center and to local and regional officials for their survival. Moreover, unless they were in a major city, they may not have even known much about the proclamations of various new states that occurred in October and November of 1918. Several of the new states that arose in the wake of imperial collapse only lasted for a few weeks or months. Most of these rose and fell on military strength or weakness. Some were products of local efforts to manage the food crisis and maintain social stability. How many of us recall the Western Ukrainian Republic or German Bohemia (with its two capitals at Teplitz/Teplice and Reichenberg/Liberec), the Hutsul Republic, German Southern Moravia, or the short-lived Miners' Republic in Istria? These entities have mostly been forgotten because eventually they fell to the superior power of Polish, Czechoslovak, or Italian nationalist armed forces. But their primary purpose—and the reason they held some legitimacy in the last months of 1918—was their commitment to provide stability, continuity, and above all survival within their borders. For the short time they existed, people treated these "statelets" as the legitimate successors to the failed Empire, as the hundreds of petitions and denunciations from ordinary people to the officials of the state of *Deutschböhmen*, for example, attest.

As we know from subsequent history, and from the Masaryk quotation at the outset, a great deal of effort has been expended retrospectively to give these changes a more pointedly nationalist significance. This was most obvious in the diverse ways that today's successor states commemorated the centennial of the events of 1918 that had brought them into being or enlarged their territories. None of them incorporate their imperial histories into their national histories. All of them maintain a largely nationalist explanation for the foundation or expansion of their states after 1918. But as recent research has demonstrated, these local revolutionary administrations often involved a forced collaboration of nationalists from different sides, simply to manage survival. To call these revolutions national revolutions would be a stretch.[35]

Let me return one final time to Masaryk's view of the issue of imperial force as opposed to national democracy to reconsider these national revolutions specifically in the context of claims about democracy. Masaryk inferred that nation-statehood was the necessary outcome of the implementation of a democratic system. The "national self-determination" of the time implied that it was individuals who had risen up collectively to choose a new state form. Not surprisingly, after years of starvation, misery, and a harshly unjust dictatorship, Austro-Hungarians had indeed lost faith in the legitimacy of their state, just as many Germans, Russians, French, Italians, and Irish had lost faith in theirs. But the presumption that democracy would necessarily produce a nation-state form begs the question of the democratic subject at the very heart of this issue.

If we ask, "who is the subject, the actor, the beneficiary, of this democracy?" we can see the problem more clearly. In 1919 it was the idea of the nation itself, the collectivity (or more accurately its nationalist spokespeople), whose democratic rights were at the center of most discourse and politics. It was not, however, the individual. The link between the idea of national self-determination and democracy—understood in the abstract as a kind of popular sovereignty—made the idea of the collective nation somehow the embodiment of democracy. Even a cursory glance at the subsequent history of this region shows us that in fact, the individual was far more constrained by the demands of national belonging after 1918 than she or he had been by the demands of belonging to an empire. To put it crudely: whereas the Empire had largely avoided the question of national ascription, the nation-state adopted it with fervor.[36]

Polities that asserted their state identity in narrowly ethnic, linguistic, or nationalist terms, terms that approached racialism in their strong insistence on difference, had replaced the Empire. This change also required that individuals had to be treated primarily as members of national groups. The enjoyment of citizenship and civil rights depended on group membership now, rather than on an individual's relationship to a state.

Conclusion

National self-determination did not contradict empire. In many ways the concept, defined in terms of language use, was both a product and served as a guiding principle of Habsburg institutions, administrative practices, and legal decisions in the nineteenth century. This was true for the post-1867 Austrian half of the Dual Monarchy, for the Dual Monarchy's joint institutions, and in the 1910 statute for Bosnia Herzegovina. But beyond the apparent simplicity of the term "national self-determination" lurked key questions of scale. What was the unit of self-determination? The individual? The nation? Who determines what for whom? And what happens to those who, in the abstract, were rendered invisible, those who were relegated to minority status, those who did not fit the allowable categories of the nation-state? Some have argued that a range of international and humanitarian organizations—in particular through the League of Nations—replaced empire to guard the interests of these new minorities.[37] But it also seems clear that those same international organizations, however unwittingly, also abetted the inevitable tragedies produced by the creation or enlargement of the successor states. After all, their humanitarian purpose was to stabilize the new nation-state order by attempting to alleviate many of the very social problems—refugees, statelessness—that the nation-state solution had caused in the first place.

Many of us have argued that the states that replaced Austria-Hungary were themselves more the products of imperial continuities than their propagandists liked to admit. I have often referred to them as "little empires." Precisely the institutions that regulated questions of nationhood, citizenship status, and cultural difference in these states were adapted from administrative and legal practices in both halves of the Habsburg Monarchy. Only now these institutions and practices existed in constitutional frameworks that validated and privileged belonging to particular nations. In some instances, as Emily Greble has shown with regard to the Muslims of Yugoslavia, this in fact produced a differentiated form of citizenship precisely of the type that nation-states generally claim to reject.[38] In other instances, as Dominique Reill has shown with regard to the city of Fiume, the choice to attach to a nation-state constituted an attempt to maintain the privileges of imperial citizenship.[39] However, the interwar constitutional frameworks also differentiated these states radically from the old Empire. Legally, as I have argued, in Habsburg Austria, there had been no linguistic majorities or minorities at the imperial state level. These had only existed in an administrative sense at the level of the crownland (province) or district. Under empire, the fact of belonging to a particular language group had not conferred particular privileges of citizenship or changed one's access to civil rights, the way it did under the successor states. There were certainly technically privileged *languages* in Austria and its crownlands, but not privileged *language groups* or nations. An illiterate peasant from the Gottschee region of largely Slovene-speaking Carniola who spoke German enjoyed no social or legal privileges over a Slovene-speaking merchant in Ljubljana, for example. And in most regions, neither individuals nor families were tied to a specific language group by law, the way they would be under the successor states. None of this argues for the relative benefits of empire nor does it seek to contribute to the unfortunate phenomenon of imperial nostalgia. It is, however, an attempt to argue what should be obvious: first, that ethnic nation-statehood is not the only possible internal organization of states; secondly, that the experience of the twentieth century hardly suggests that ethnic nation-statehood is a form somehow more stable, more democratic in its behavior toward its legal minorities, or, despite Masaryk, less susceptible to exercising force to keep its citizens in line.

Notes

1   The official name of the Austrian half of Austria-Hungary was "The Kingdoms and principalities represented in the imperial parliament." It was also referred to as "Cisleithania" while Hungary became "Transleithania." I use "Austria" to denote this state even though this was not its name until 1916. According to the Austrian and Hungarian censuses of 1910, German speakers constituted the largest single linguistic group (at 35.58 percent) of the Austrian population and 23.36 percent of Austria-Hungary as a whole, while Hungarian speakers made up 19.57 percent of the whole and 48.1 percent of Hungary (without the Kingdom of Croatia the number was 54.4 percent). However, these formal numbers tell us little about national identification, since the Austrian census asked people to report their normal "language of use" [*Umgangssprache* in German], not a "mother tongue" or "national language." The Hungarian census asked for mother tongue and it took some account of bilingualism, partly to track the success of the state's Magyarization policies. *Die Habsburgermonarchie 1848–1918*. Vol. 3, *Die Völker des Reiches*, ed. Adam Wandruszka and Peter Urbanitsch (Vienna: Verlag der österreichischen Akademie der Wissenschaften, 1980), Tables 1 and 29, 36, 414.
2   Thomas Garrigue Masaryk, "The Problem of Small Nations and States," in *We Were and We Shall Be: The Czechoslovak Spirit through the Centuries*, ed. Zdenka and Jan Muzner (New York: Frederick Unger, 1941), 153.
3   Andrea Orzoff and Chad Bryant have each analyzed the ways that discursive efforts to promote the legitimizing mythology of a democratic Czechoslovakia "involved the demonization of the Habsburg Monarchy, which was now cast as a reactionary, repressive, and antinational regime." Chad Bryant, *Prague. Belonging in the Modern City* (Cambridge, MA: Harvard University Press, 2021), 126. Also, Andrea Orzoff, *The Battle for the Castle. The Myth of Czechoslovakia in Europe, 1914–1948* (New York: Oxford University Press, 2009).

4   Austria's "December Laws" (or constitution) of 1867 defined nationhood largely in linguistic terms for the Austrian half of Austria-Hungary. The Hungarian "Law of Nationalities" of 1868 did the same. In practice, however, religious difference could play a role in national self-definition, especially regarding how Ruthene or Ukrainian nationalists defined themselves in opposition to Polish nationality. Jewish Nationalists sought to establish a Jewish nationality in Austria but the Austrian Supreme Court ruled twice that because language use defined nationality, Jews (who spoke several languages in the Empire) could not be considered a nation. For the different and changing understandings of nationhood in the Ottoman Empire, see Erol Ülker's chapter in this volume.
5   Ágoston Berecz, "Top-down and Bottom-up Magyarization in Multiethnic Banat Towns under Dualist Hungary (1867–1914)," *European Review of History: Revue Européenne d'histoire* 28, no. 3 (2021): 422–40.
6   After 1918, even the nationalist censuses (with all their manipulations and their amalgamated categories that later broke down, such as Czecho-Slovak or Serbo-Croat) only documented 65.5 percent Czechoslovaks for Czechoslovakia, 69.2 percent Poles in Poland, 71.9 percent Romanians for Romania, 74.3 percent "Serbo-Croat" for Yugoslavia. Statistics from Joseph Rothschild, *East Central Europe between the Two World Wars* (Seattle and London: University of Washington Press, 1974), 36, 89, 203, 284.
7   This was the case, for example, among Ukrainian or Ruthene speakers and Hungarian-speaking Szeklers in post-1918 Greater Romania. Irina Livezeanu, *Cultural Politics in Greater Romania* (Ithaca, NY: Cornell University Press, 1995), 63–7; 136–9. This belief in de-nationalization dominated radical Czech- and German nationalist discourse in pre- and interwar Bohemia, as Tara Zahra demonstrates superbly in *Kidnapped Souls. National Indifference and the Battle for Children in the Bohemian Lands, 1900–1948* (Ithaca, NY: Cornell University Press, 2007), and is also a common trope in post-1918 Slovenia. Zahra argues that this belief underlay nationalist frustration with national indifference, and that it radicalized nationalists who often competed for the same children for their national schools.
8   On the very late date at which Wilson abandoned Austria-Hungary, see most recently, Larry Wolff, *Woodrow Wilson and the Reimagining of Eastern Europe* (Palo Alto: Stanford University Press, 2020), 90–6.
9   South African President Jan Smuts wondered, for example, whether it would not be wiser to create protectorates comparable to those in the Middle East in Habsburg Central Europe. "The peoples left behind by the decomposition of Russia, Austria, and Turkey are mostly untrained politically; many of them are either incapable or deficient in the power of self-government." Quoted in Margaret MacMillan, *Paris 1919. Six Months That Changed the World* (New York: Random House, 2002), 99.
10 Erez Manela, "Imagining Woodrow Wilson in Asia: Dreams of East-West Harmony and the Revolt against Empire in 1919," *American Historical Review* 111, no. 5 (2006): 1327–51.
11 Tomasz Kamusella, *The Politics of Language and Nationalism in Modern Central Europe* (London: Palgrave Macmillan 2008), gives an exhausting account of the developing politics of language among several regions of Central, Eastern, and Southeastern Europe. On Herder, see page 495. For other excellent studies on language use and developing nationalism, see Alexander Maxwell, *Choosing Slovakia. Slavic Hungary, the Czechoslovak Language and Accidental Nationalism*

(London: I.B. Taurus) and Edin Hajdarpasic, *Whose Bosnia? Nationalism and Political Imagination in the Balkans 1840–1914* (Ithaca, NY: Cornell University Press, 2015). On Slovene language and nationhood, see the excellent work by Joachim Hösler, *Von Krain Zu Slowenien. Die Anfänge der nationalen Differenzierungsprozesse in Krain und der Untersteiermark von der Aufklärung bis zur Revolution 1768–1848* (Munich: Oldenbourg, 2006).

12   Gerald Stourzh and others also point out that the language policies of the 1850s did not constitute an attempt to effect a *germanization* of the population, despite claims to the contrary by Hungarian or Czech politicians of the time. Gerald Stourzh, *Die Gleichberechtigung der Nationalitäten in der Verfassung und Verwaltung Österreichs, 1848–1918* (Vienna: Verlag der österreichischen Akademie der Wissenschaften, 1985), 42, 49.

13   On the Hungarian Diet's change from Latin to Hungarian, see István Deák, *The Lawful Revolution. Louis Kossuth and the Hungarians* (New York: Columbia University Press, 1979). On the varied significations of multilingualism, see Pieter M. Judson, "Encounters with Language Diversity in Late Habsburg Austria," in *Language Diversity in the Late Habsburg Empire*, ed. Markian Prokopovych, Carl Bethke, and Tamara Scheer (Leiden and Boston: Brill, 2019), 12–25.

14   *Verfassungsurkunde des österreichischen Kaiserstaates*, http://verfassungen.at/at-18/verfassung48-i.htm (accessed June 27, 2021).

15   *Stenographische Protokolle des Hauses der Abgeordneten*, 8.10.1867, 1, p. 784.

16   Jürgen Pirker, "*Kollektive Rechte. Strukturfragen und Entwicklung in der Rechtsprechung zu den Freiheiten der Assoziation, Nationalität und Religion im Staatsgrundgesetz von 1869 bis 2019*" (Habilitationsschrift, Institut für öffentliches Recht und Politikwissenschaft, Karl-Franzens-Universität Graz, 2019), 104.

17   Joachim von Puttkamer, *Schulalltag und nationale Integration in Ungarn. Slowaken, Rumänen und Siebenbürger Sachsen in der Auseinandersetzung mit der ungarischen Staatsidee 1867–1914* (Munich: R. Oldenbourg Verlag, 2003), 36; Ágoston Berecz, *The Politics of Early Language Teaching: Hungarian in the Primary Schools of the Late Dual Monarchy* (Budapest: Central European University Press, 2013), 60.

18   On the court cases generally, see Stourzh, *Die Gleichberechtigung*. On the courts and school policy, Hannelore Burger, *Sprachenrecht und Sprachengerechtigkeit im österreichischen Unterrichtswesen 1867–1918* (Vienna: Verlag der österreichischen Akademie der Wissenschaften, 1995).

19   This was the case, for example, with Czechoslovak law regarding the minimum population requirements for the state to provide schools in a minority language. Zahra, *Kidnapped Souls*, especially 106–33.

20   Burger, *Sprachenrecht und Sprachengerechtigkeit*. This forty-child requirement for the establishment of a state school remained a standard used in some of the states to which the minority treaties applied after 1918.

21   Stourzh, *Die Gleichberechtigung*. The situation in the military was interesting in this regard because often even the German-speaking recruits did not know or understand many of the eighty or so German language commands all recruits had to learn. On the military, Tamara Scheer, *Language Diversity and Loyalty in the Habsburg Army, 1868–1918* (Habilitation: University of Vienna, 2020).

22   On the Austrian census and its uses by nationalists, see Pieter M. Judson, *Guardians of the Nation. Activists on the Language Frontiers of Imperial Austria* (Cambridge, MA: Harvard University Press, 2006), 14–16; Emil Brix, *Die Umgangssprachen in Altösterreich zwischen Agitation und Assimilation: die Sprachenstatistik in der*

zisleithanischen Volkszählungen, 1880 bis 1910 (Vienna: Verlag der österreichischen Akademie der Wissenschaften, 1982); and Wolfgang Göderle, *Zensus und Ethnizität: zur Herstellung von Wissen und soziale Wirklichkeiten im Habsburgerreich zwischen 1848 und 1910* (Göttingen: Wallstein, 2016).

23 As Zahra points out, this was common practice even in Czechoslovakia, arguably the most politically democratic of the successor states. Officials who took the census in Czechoslovakia were empowered to dispute a person's answer and to carry out an investigation if they believed the person had given the "wrong answer" about nationality. If the investigation confirmed the suspicions of the official, the individual was subjected to a fine or even to a jail sentence. Zahra, *Kidnapped Souls*, 106; 118–26.

24 Lothar Höbelt, "Bohemia 1913—A Consensual Coup d'état?" *Estates and Representation* 20, no. 1 (2000): 207–14; Gerald Stourzh, "Verfassungsbruch im Königreich Böhmen. Ein unbekanntes Kapitel zur Geschichte des richterlichen Prüfungsrechts im alten Österreich," in *Der Umfang der österreichischen Geschichte. Ausgewählte Studien 1990–2010*, ed. Gerald Stourzh (Vienna: Böhlau, 2011), 139–55.

25 Austria's administrative structures assigned considerable political and economic autonomy to individual communes and this also created considerable space for local initiative and autonomous decision-making. Jeremy King, "The Municipal and the National in the Bohemian Lands, 1848–1914," *Austrian History Yearbook* 42 (2011): 89–109.

26 Pieter M. Judson, *The Habsburg Empire. A New History* (Cambridge, MA: Harvard University Press, 2016), 327–8. There is now a rich literature on the *Kronprinzenswerk*. For the ways in which Habsburg scientists conceptualized nature in terms of empire, see Deborah Coen, *Climate in Motion. Science, Empire, and the Problem of Scale* (Chicago: University of Chicago Press, 2018). On the circulation of imperial knowledge within empire and the organization of universities, see Jan Surman, *Universities in Imperial Austria 1848–1918. A Social History of a Multilingual Space* (West Lafayette, IN: Purdue University Press, 2018).

27 Judson, *Guardians*, 1–3.

28 Tara Zahra, "Imagined Non-Communities: National Indifference as a Category of Analysis," *Slavic Review* 69, no. 1 (2010): 93–119; Rogers Brubaker, *Ethnicity without Groups* (Cambridge, MA: Harvard University Press, 2006); Pieter M. Judson, "Nationalism and Indifference" in *Habsburg Neu Denken. Vielfalt und Ambivalenz in Zentraleuropa. 30 kulturwissenschaftliche Stichworte*, ed. Johannes Feichtinger and Heidemarie Uhl (Vienna: Böhlau, 2016), 148–55; Martin Van Ginderachter and Jon Fox, eds., *National Indifference and the History of Nationalism in Modern Europe* (London: Routledge, 2019).

29 This puzzling lack of bilingual schools in multilingual regions resulted from several court cases in which nationalists successfully cited the constitutional provision that no one would have to learn the second provincial language. Using that constitutional argument, nationalists succeeded in closing many traditionally bilingual or "utraquist" schools in Styria, Bohemia, and Moravia.

30 This is the compelling argument in Zahra's *Kidnapped Souls*.

31 Laurence Cole, *Military Culture and Popular Patriotism in Late Imperial Austria* (Oxford: Oxford University Press, 2014).

32 See especially, Martin Moll, *Kein Burgfrieden. Der deutsch-slowenische Nationalitätenkonflikt in der Steiermark 1900–1918* (Innsbruck: Studienverlag, 2007). Other examples are given in József Galántai, *Hungary in the First World War*

(Budapest: Akadémia Kiadó, 1989), 95–8; Irina Marin, "World War I and Internal Repression. The Case of Major General Nikolaus Cena," *Austrian History Yearbook* 44 (2013): 195–208; Christoph Führ, *Das K u K Oberarmeekommando und die Innenpolitik in Österreich 1914–1917* (Vienna: Böhlau, 1968), 181.

33 On the position of Ireland within the United Kingdom until independence, see Alvin Jackson's chapter in this volume. For the treatment of Irish loyalists within the Irish Free State and their ambivalent forms of identification during the interwar period, see Brian Hughes's chapter in this volume.

34 Tara Zahra, "'Each Nation Cares Only for Its Own': Empire, Nation, and Child Welfare Activism in the Bohemian Lands, 1900–1918," *American Historical Review* 111, no. 5 (2006): 1378–402.

35 Gábor Egry, "Negotiating Postimperial Transitions. Local Societies and Nationalizing states in East Central Europe," in *Embers of Empire. Continuity and Rupture in the Habsburg Successor States after 1918*, ed. Paul Miller and Claire Morelon (New York: Berghahn, 2019).

36 It is possible to argue that after 1905 ascription was becoming a legal norm for the first time in the crownland of Moravia, because of specific conditions in the Moravian Compromise of 1905. This compromise between the imperial state and the Czech and German nationalist parties in Moravia divided the population in an arrangement that gave the Czech and German "nations" a kind of non-territorial autonomy. In order to function, the compromise required all citizens who did not belong to the landholding nobility to register in one national cadaster or the other. They then could not change cadasters at a later date. Stourzh, King, Zahra, and others have all argued persuasively that this attempt to diffuse nationalist conflict unintentionally became a harbinger of dangerous developments to come, because it wrote ascription into provincial law for the first time in Austria. See especially Gerald Stourzh, "Ethnic Attribution in Late Imperial Austria: Good Intentions, Evil Consequences," in *From Vienna to Chicago and Back. Essays on Intellectual History and Political Thought in Europe and America*, ed. Gerald Stourzh (Chicago: University of Chicago Press, 2007); Zahra, *Kidnapped Souls*.

37 See most recently the excellent essays in Peter Becker and Natasha Wheatley, eds., *Remaking Central Europe. The League of Nations and the Former Habsburg Lands* (Oxford: Oxford University Press 2021).

38 Emily Greble, *Muslims and the Making of Modern Europe* (Oxford: Oxford University Press, 2021).

39 Dominique Kirchner Reill, *The Fiume Crisis. Life in the Wake of the Habsburg Empire* (Cambridge, MA: Harvard University Press, 2020).

3

"Prison of the Nations?" Union and Nationality in the United Kingdom, 1870–1925*

Alvin Jackson

The United Kingdom of the late nineteenth century was, and is, frequently seen as a unitary state, and sometimes even (at least in terms of the island of Britain) as a relatively homogeneous national territory. At different times successive central governments of the kingdom pursued integrationist or assimilationist projects toward this end; and indeed, the different "acts" of union (1535, 1542 for Wales, 1707 for Scotland, 1801 for Ireland) may credibly be seen in this light.[1]

Parliamentary union in 1707 and 1801 was effectively (if not explicitly) a device for converting the hard power of a militarily, economically, and demographically preeminent nation, England, into nominally voluntary forms of soft power over weaker, neighboring polities and peoples. The precise vocabulary of "majority" and "minority," in these applications, would not gain significant currency until the twentieth century, but there was still a related language of authority, influence, and interest, which in turn was bound with military, economic, and demographic strength. The latter of course was being defined with increasing precision through the census data which were being accumulated in Britain from 1801. Moreover, if the language of majority and minority was not yet explicit, then the union intentionally recast a predominantly Catholic Ireland within a new, and predominantly Anglican and British, state.

Some additional reflection on vocabulary and definitions needs to be briefly offered at this stage. This chapter deploys the idea of "minority nationality"—though it does so with caution, and with the recognition that there is a temptation here toward (debatable) normative assumptions. Of course, the notion of "nationality" is generally recognized and understood as a nineteenth-century construct, while (as noted) that of "minority" came later: thus, the overall idea of "minority nationalities" gained traction in the early twentieth century. Equally, the specific language of "subject" or "subsidiary" nationalities was applied in the later twentieth century, not least in terms

---

* The chapter generally focuses on the late nineteenth and early twentieth centuries. The dates in the title refer to the period spanning from the disestablishment of the Church of Ireland (and the first significant modification of the Irish union) to the conclusion of the Boundary Commission between the United Kingdom and the new Irish Free State (and the effective toleration of the land border between Northern Ireland and the Free State).

of those Central and Eastern European states bound to the USSR. It should also be emphasized that nationalist movements within wider empires did not see themselves as "minorities" within their own perceived national territory. However, while the specific vocabulary has evolved, and has also been contested, the related idea that unions and empires have embraced hierarchies of power and privilege in terms of their component peoples was very firmly rooted in the late nineteenth century, and indeed long before. As an extensive literature now recognizes, nineteenth-century empires (and unions) were predicated on the basis of an array of—supposedly—scientifically constructed ethnic and other rankings.

With the establishment of union, successive central governments often treated or imagined the "minority" peoples of the United Kingdom as undifferentiated extensions of (southeast) England. Wales was certainly enfolded within the structures of English government until at least the late nineteenth century. To a lesser extent, so too was Scotland. The union of 1707 permitted the continuation of a range of distinctive institutions, and (as in Ireland) there was much use by Westminster of delegated authority, but otherwise Scotland was well integrated within a centralizing and (imagined) unitary state: indeed, until the early twentieth century (and sometimes beyond) Scotland was regularly designated, for postal and other purposes, as "North Britain." Ireland (like Scotland and Wales) was governed inconsistently and without any grand plan, but assimilationist strategies were periodically deployed until 1921— and indeed afterward, within Northern Ireland.[2] Northern Irish devolution was suspended in 1972 under the (generally) assimilationist "direct rule" regime. One telling instance of the associated mindset, much misquoted, was Mrs. Thatcher's provocative declaration in 1981 that Northern Ireland was "part of the United Kingdom—as much as my constituency is" (her constituency being Finchley in northwest London). But Thatcher's dictum (while contradicted by some of her government's subsequent actions) certainly reflected a centralist and undifferentiated view of the union state.

Scholars, too, for long defined the nineteenth-century United Kingdom, or rather nineteenth-century Britain, in terms of a unitary model, and alongside other centralized and homogenizing nation-states. While it is obvious that the national histories of Ireland, Scotland, and Wales have stimulated much distinctive scholarship, the historical literature on the detailed functioning of the United Kingdom as a complex multinational union state remains relatively underdeveloped, as does any sustained comparison between it and other multinational unions and empires across late-nineteenth- and early-twentieth-century Europe.[3]

This chapter suggests a range of alternative approaches to understanding the relationship between the component nationalities of the unions and the survival of the latter. First, it looks to identify some of the limits to the vision and substance of the asymmetrical unions of the United Kingdom, which were forged in 1707 (between England and Scotland) and in 1801 (between Great Britain and Ireland). That is to say, it seeks to establish some of the practical limits to any homogenizing tendency—some of the "centrifugal" pressures upon the unions of the United Kingdom and their related hold (or lack of it) upon the "minority" nationalities.

Yet the union between England and Wales has lasted for over 500 years, if one takes the legislation of 1535 and 1542 as starting points. The union of England and Scotland has survived for over 300 years; and the union of Great Britain and Ireland survived from 1801 to 1922 and has continued in a truncated form from 1922 to the present day as the union of Great Britain and Northern Ireland. So, a second major theme of the chapter is longevity: while there were some constraints and some oppression, the union managed for long to hold the different nations of Britain and Ireland together within one complex multinational state. Again, the chapter seeks to identify some of the "centripetal" dimensions to the unions of the United Kingdom—some of the agencies and institutions binding the minority nationalities to union.[4]

It may be immediately clear to some readers that the chapter deploys an analytical schema used originally for other forms of (federal) union by James Bryce, and adapted by the historian of Habsburg "dissolution," Oszkár Jászi. Each of these sought to identify the "centripetal" and "centrifugal" (or "aggregative" and "segregative") forces at play in the making and unmaking of, respectively, federal polities, and the great composite monarchy of Central Europe, that of the Habsburgs.[5] But, critically, for Jászi at least, there could not always be a neat taxonomy of union, since centripetal forces might also function in a centrifugal manner.[6] Bearing this caution in mind, the chapter sets out some of the centrifugal aspects of the union state, especially in terms of its different national constituents, while then shifting the focus and emphasis to the centripetal.

Linked with this, an additional, and third, central theme of the chapter is comparison. However, the comparisons suggested here are not between Britain and contemporary European nation-states (or aspirant nation-states), but rather between the multinational United Kingdom and other multinational European unions and empires such as (primarily) Austria-Hungary. In particular, these comparisons focus largely on the relationship between the dominant nationalities of these polities, the *Staatsvölker*, and the "subsidiary" (or "minority") nationalities.

There is obviously a case for caution in pursuing any comparison.[7] These polities could certainly be different forms of union—personal, accessory, and imperial—and they often sat in very different places on a spectrum of intensity. But the analytical challenge here is not so much in comparing wholly different types of union—constitutional "apples" and "oranges." It rather rests with comparing different types of hybrids, which (at the same time) were each relentlessly evolving. Moreover, the United Kingdom merits comparison with other "unions" partly because they were all contemporary or near-contemporary creations, rooted in continental warfare, and rooted too in traditions of personal union. Each was an asymmetrical union of large and small partners, and much of the resultant chemistry arose from these imbalances. Each was a mix of contemporary strategic or geo-political exigency and historic linkage. And, finally, contemporaries frequently made comparisons. It is true that some British unionists (like Albert Venn Dicey) gloried in the supposedly unique brilliance of the British constitution, but many Liberals (pre-eminently Gladstone) and Irish constitutional nationalists (like John Redmond) looked to the Dual Monarchy both for analogies with the United Kingdom of Britain and Ireland as well as possible models of reform.[8] In addition, Arthur Griffith, the patriarch of the Sinn Féin movement in early-twentieth-century Ireland, famously invoked "the resurrection of Hungary."[9] The *Ausgleich* relationship between Austria and Hungary—and also the *Nagodba* between Croatia and Hungary—were much discussed in the context of Britain's successive Irish home rule crises.[10] Comparing the United Kingdom of the nineteenth century, and its minority nationalities, with other multinational unions and their peoples makes sense because Victorians envisioned their polity, and its reform, in comparative terms.

The Limits of Union

The late-nineteenth-century United Kingdom was ostensibly a unitary state, with a union parliament at Westminster for all of the constituent nationalities, and an overarching monarchy and crown forces, together with a (sometimes) shared external imperial project. However, in numerous respects the union state was problematic either in terms of structure and homogeneity, or in terms of its conceptualization; and this in turn created space for (or indeed provoked) the articulation of "minority" national identities, evidently at odds with the British enterprise, but in practice sometimes either partly assimilated within it, or locked into a mutual dependency. Here, I want to review an array of arguments reflecting on the conceptualization and operation of union in Britain and Ireland, although constraints of space have necessitated some tough choices about those areas which have received attention and emphasis.

The nineteenth-century United Kingdom state of Great Britain and Ireland was "under-imagined": it lacked an origins myth, a statement of principle or purpose, and it also lacked an associated commemorative culture.[11] The United Kingdom, forged in 1707 and 1801, did not at the beginning reflect a coherent vision or an ideal—in comparison with some nation-states or federal unions. It was originally a set of pragmatic bargains binding the English parliament and its Scots counterpart (in 1707), as well as the British and the Irish ascendancy elite (in 1801), and it was principally concerned with immediate commercial and military realities. Financial crisis and international warfare were critical contexts and drivers to union in 1707 and 1801. The Scots and Irish economies, especially the public finances, were in disarray in the context of war and (in the Irish case) rebellion. Furthermore, continental European warfare constituted a significant threat to English stability at both times. This is not to say, of course, that the origins of other forms of state may not be situated in warfare or economic upheaval. But it is to suggest that the formation of the United Kingdom may be distinguished from the elaborate or abstract ideals such as partly impelled (for example) the American or French (or Irish) revolutions.[12]

It is true that Great Britain, created in 1707, and to a much lesser extent the United Kingdom, created in 1801, built upon an older set of British identities imagined from at least the sixteenth century. But there was no model transition from intellectual propagation through elite conversion to popular conversion: the promotion of any British project, whether by King James VI and I at the beginning of the seventeenth century, or by Oliver Cromwell in the 1650s, involved top-down initiatives which met resistance even in the metropolitan center.[13] The development of a more popular Britishness had to wait until the eighteenth century, as will be discussed below, though whether this constituted a national identity as opposed to an overarching dynastic identity, as with *Habsburgtreue* in the Dual Monarchy, is (at the very least) open to debate.[14] There are in fact some comparisons to be made here with other multinational union states or empires, such as indeed the Dual Monarchy, or the United Kingdoms of Sweden-Norway (1814–1905), or the United Kingdom of the Netherlands (1815–30)— all of which were essentially pragmatic arrangements which reflected a set of economic, strategic, and geopolitical realities and which were vulnerable to their revision.

Closely linked with this, the United Kingdom lacked a unifying moral imperative— in contradistinction to several of the emergent nation-states of the nineteenth and twentieth centuries. Indeed, the perennial problem with many unions is that, given their often contingent and opportunistic origins, they have lacked either a founding expression of aspiration or an overall vision binding component nationalities. Many constitutional scholars have emphasized that constitutions are not merely sets of rules, but also an embodiment of a nation or society's values: as Vernon Bogdanor has remarked, "almost all codified constitutions are enacted to mark a new beginning."[15] But, however much the formation of the United Kingdom may have marked "a new beginning," its lack of a formally codified constitution underlined the absence of a vision of purpose.

Moreover, in the case of both Scotland and Ireland, the birth of their respective unions has been lastingly associated with corruption, the black arts of political management, and the specter of military threat. Each of the unions was attained in the context of expressions of English or British military ascendancy (in the Irish case in the immediate aftermath of the epically bloody suppression of the 1798 Rising). The negotiations accompanying each of these unions were characterized by an extraordinarily lavish (judged by contemporary norms) distribution of official patronage in the form of the distribution of aristocratic titles, government office and cash. The skillful historical interrogation and contextualization of these origins have not substantially affected their negative popular standing amongst the constituent— "minority"—nationalities of the union state.[16] It is true that the wider envisioning of Britishness by Scots from the sixteenth century onward sometimes helped to counterbalance this otherwise bleak reckoning of union. But on the whole, the dubious nativity of both the Scots and Irish unions has been a central and sustained aspect of the popular "under-imagining" of the United Kingdom.

These complex origins narratives were also, however, a feature of other contemporary unions. This was clearly the case with Austria-Hungary: no amount of self-congratulation could disguise the fact that the great redesign of the Habsburg lands achieved through the *Ausgleich* of 1867 was precipitated by the Empire's defeat by Prussia at Königgrätz/Sadowa in July 1866.[17] As with the United Kingdom of Britain and Ireland, Austria-Hungary was born in the context of not only military challenge, but also financial threat.[18]

In addition, the United Kingdom lacked an overarching culture of state commemoration. Apart from occasional short-lived initiatives, there was (and is) remarkably little celebration of the anniversaries of the creation of Great Britain or the United Kingdom. The coronations, birthdays, marriages, and jubilees of the monarch, as head of the union state, have been routinely celebrated, but not the birthday or anniversaries of the state itself. Linda Colley has famously commented on the importance of George III (r.1760–1820) to the formation of Britishness. Similarly, Victoria (r.1837–1901) was central to the elaboration of British imperialism, while Elizabeth II (r.1952–2022) may well be viewed as critical to the sustaining of union.[19] There was no Union Day, but between 1902 and 1958 there was instead an increasingly desultory commemoration of "Empire Day," held on Victoria's birthday, 24 May, each year.[20]. More recently, Gordon Brown broached the idea of a "British Day" in 2006 and instituted "Armed Forces Day" in that year: he also sanctioned some commemoration of the tercentenary of union in 2007. Boris Johnson appeared to be investigating similar unifying stratagems during his premiership. But this has all been a matter of starting late in the day, and largely from scratch. There remains no equivalent in the United Kingdom of Independence Day or Bastille Day or the Russian Victory Day—or indeed any equivalent of the individual national days and focused national celebrations of the constituent polities of the United Kingdom.

This deficit was a feature of other union polities. In general, the foundation of union states was vastly overshadowed by the celebration of the related ruling dynasty—Habsburg, Orange-Nassau, or Hanover and Saxe-Coburg-Gotha.[21] Supranational commemoration in the Dual Monarchy focused largely upon the Habsburgs, and in particular (by the end of the nineteenth century) upon the aging patriarch of empire, Franz Joseph. There was also some memorialization at this time, often by German liberals, of the reforming and centralizing emperor, Joseph II.[22] However, much of the commemorative culture of the Dual Monarchy centered on the ruling emperor-king, whose golden jubilee (in 1898) and diamond jubilee (in 1908) stimulated elaborate celebrations. In addition, Franz Joseph's periodic tours of his domains were associated with carefully choreographed displays of loyalty to the supranational monarchy. In both Austria and the United Kingdom, there was a shared absence of what Jászi called "civic education"; and in particular there was a relative absence of any overarching propagation, commemoration, or celebration of the values and purpose of the state.[23] Generally speaking, therefore, multinational union states have facilitated the creation of dynastic loyalty, rather than any supranational loyalty to the polity itself. Generally speaking, too, unions have sustained a riskily high symbolic investment in monarchy.

This leads to a further argument: the nineteenth-century United Kingdom did not possess a strong national identity which was able to thoroughly unify all of the "minority" nationalities. Britain and Britishness were of course conceptualized at an elite level long before 1707. But—in Dicey's terms—"the Union did not originate in the sort of feeling which is now called 'nationalism,' though it resulted in the creation of a new State of Great Britain."[24] A complex popular British national identity arose only in the wake of the union between England and Scotland in 1707, drawing strength (in the argument of Colley) from Protestantism, the monarchy, and foreign wars.[25] In some arguments, this identity was critically bolstered in the late nineteenth century through the consolidation of a global empire, and the fabrication of a popular British imperialism.[26]

British national identity clearly continues to be a tenacious and significant—if declining—phenomenon amongst both the Scots and other, "minority," nationalities of the union. But this Britishness had been largely established before the union with

Ireland in 1801. Moreover, in the eighteenth century, Britishness had been defined partly against the Catholic "Other" in terms of the wars against continental enemies such as France. This created a workably inclusive, overarching identity for the primarily Presbyterian Scots, as well as for the Welsh, who were shifting decisively from Anglican to non-conformist Protestantism in the late eighteenth and nineteenth centuries. Yet in 1801 Britain and Britishness became bound, through union, with a primarily Catholic polity, Ireland. After 1801 the United Kingdom state and Britishness somehow had to accommodate this Catholic "Other," at least in its Irish formulation. There was thus an ongoing tension between the state and its supposedly unifying political identity; and this was fateful so far as the relationship between union and constituent nationalities was concerned.

However, union did not obliterate the component minority national identities of the state. Indeed, in certain senses the union state may even have helped to define the shape and content of its component nationalities. Scottishness was largely accommodated within the United Kingdom in the nineteenth century by various agencies, including the Presbyterian Church of Scotland, as well as the distinctive national legal system and civil society.[27] Welshness was similarly accommodated, and Welsh historians have laid emphasis both on the overwhelmingly cultural (as opposed to political) definition of Welsh nationality, and on the assimilationist impact of empire on Welsh patriotism at the end of the nineteenth century.[28] But on the whole Irishness was much less effectively embraced, although there is evidence of impact in terms of not only Irish unionists but also imperially minded nationalists like John Redmond and his followers.[29] English national identity was resurgent in the late nineteenth century but, as the *Staatsvolk* of the United Kingdom, the English were largely indistinguishable from, and interchangeable with, Britain and Britishness. However, this consolidation of Englishness was clearly linked to the expression of other (Irish, Scots, Welsh) national identities in the union state. Indeed, it was reciprocally bound with their consolidation in the late nineteenth and early twentieth centuries (as well as in the early twenty-first century). Moreover, threats to the United Kingdom have come not only from the "minority" nationalities, but also (occasionally, as in the late nineteenth and early twenty-first centuries) from this resurgent Englishness. And in a similar way, perhaps, Austria-Hungary was periodically threatened, not only by Czech or Italian nationalist claims on the periphery, but rather by the reinforcement of German Austrian and Magyar identities within the political core (as during the First World War). For Oszkár Jászi, famously, "the Austrian system was entirely incapable of establishing any kind of a popular state consciousness whereas the Hungarian civic education was overdoing Magyar national consciousness."[30] Ultimately—in Jászi's argument—the dynastic patriotism of the Habsburg state proved to be "powerless against the popular enthusiasm of the exuberant national individualities," including those at the heart of the *Ausgleich*.[31]

The issue of British (and indeed Habsburg) identity was deeply intertwined with that of religious profession. And these links between supranational identities and the churches broach, in turn, the wider relationship between religion and the United Kingdom (and other multinational unions) in the nineteenth century. The British and Irish union was associated with, originally underpinned and ultimately curtailed by, religion—by Protestantism, especially in the sense of the two national churches, the United Church of England and Ireland, and the Church of Scotland. The argument for union in 1707 was originally associated, of course, with the acceptance of a Protestant Hanoverian royal succession, and it was bolstered by the contemporary guarantees given to the Church of Scotland. And indeed, in the case of Britain and Ireland, the new United Kingdom of 1801 was (as Stewart J. Brown has deemed it) "a semi-confessional state," endowed with an ostensibly new enterprise, the United Church of England and Ireland, even if in practice the two Churches of England and Ireland continued pretty much as before.[32] The United Church of the union state was funded in part by tithe, or taxation, payments, levied on various forms of agricultural income, and imposed on all, regardless of whether they were members of the Church or (as in the majority of cases beyond England) not.[33]

Religion worked across the United Kingdom as a centrifugal and a centripetal force at once. Calvinism in Scotland and Wales, associated with the Church of Scotland and Welsh Methodism, was linked with both national distinctiveness, and with a degree of separation from the "semi-confessional" Anglican union state. In Wales, in particular, Protestant non-conformity was associated with Welsh radical liberalism and patriotism at the end of the nineteenth century. But Scots Presbyterianism and Welsh non-conformity in general were simultaneously distinctive markers of their respective peoples, while also being highly fissiparous phenomena. In both polities Presbyterianism, whether of the Kirk or Free Church or Calvinistic Methodism, was certainly a shared badge of difference, but this was mitigated in various ways—not least in Scotland because, while the Presbyterian Kirk was clearly not the Church of England, it was nonetheless an established church and thus entangled within the British union state. Moreover, in general terms Protestantism and Britishness were co-related. Thus, while Welsh non-conformism and the Scottish Kirk might not have been part of the union church (the United Church of England and Ireland), they were still embraced within British Protestant identity. In short, both Scots and Welsh Calvinism served simultaneously to express "minority" national difference, as well as some of the limits of that difference.

In Ireland, union became effectively associated with Protestant ascendancy in 1801, in the context of the absence of the promised Catholic emancipation. The key point here is that in Scotland the Presbyterian faith of the majority of the Scots population was effectively reconciled with union through careful diplomacy in 1707, while in Wales Protestant non-conformity broadly helped to bind a Welsh patriotic identity within a set of British and imperial frameworks. In Ireland, however, union was achieved on the back of a negotiation between the British government and the dominant Irish Ascendancy elite within the exclusively Protestant Irish parliament and the suggested linking of union with Catholic civil rights, or Catholic emancipation, never materialized. Thus, where union and religious faith were broadly reconciled in Scotland and Wales, union and faith were separated by a gulf of perceived betrayal and oppression in Ireland.

In short, the British union state of the nineteenth century had some significant confessional features which excluded large sections of the population, and in particular Irish Catholics. Religious distinctiveness in Ireland, Wales, and Scotland was associated in each case with well-defined national identities. But only in Ireland did this ultimately prove incompatible with the union and wider empire.

Just as the effort to link religion with union state-building ultimately proved problematic in Britain, so this was the case in central Europe and elsewhere. Just as Anglican Protestantism was promoted as the established church of the union state in the early nineteenth century, so the Roman Catholic Church was famously one of the most solid pillars of the Habsburg dynasty.[34] Indeed, the relationship between the dynasty and the Church was peculiarly and lastingly intimate. It has also been conventionally acknowledged that "it was their [Habsburg] task to uphold the true faith against the two threats of the infidel and heretic."[35] The ceremonial associated with the Habsburg monarchy emphasized its Catholic fidelity (for example in the annual Corpus Christi processions) and the Austrian episcopal hierarchy responded to imperial and royal patronage with a lavish reciprocal loyalty. However, complementing this relationship was a parallel association between national sentiment and those subjects of the Dual Monarchy who were not Catholics: Lutherans and Calvinists, for example, assumed disproportionate influence within the leadership of Slav and Magyar nationalism.[36] Slovak nationalism gestated within the Lutheran lycée system.[37] Czechs—Catholics and Lutherans—signified their repudiation of Habsburg dominance through the memorialization of the reformer Jan Hus, while the corollary of celebrating Hus was the overthrow of Catholic imagery specifically associated with the suppression of Bohemian autonomy.

In short, the multinational states of the nineteenth century were associated with the imposition of legally privileged or state churches, whether the United Church of England and Ireland, or the Church of Scotland, or the Catholic Church in Austria. Those excluded from this sanction constituted a potential base for opposition—whether in terms of covenanters, Episcopalians and the Free Church in Scotland, Catholics in Ireland, Lutherans in Bohemia, Calvinists in Hungary. Only in the later decades of the nineteenth century were these threats partly addressed, whether in terms of disestablishment in both Ireland (1869) and Wales (1914–20), or through the enhanced religious freedoms associated with the new Dual Monarchy after 1867.

Centripetal Forces and Union

Thus far the emphasis has been on some of the limitations of the unions of the United Kingdom in the nineteenth century, as well as on the related imaginative and conceptual space available to the component nationalities of the kingdom. But it also needs to be emphasized that (with one major secession, in 1921) the United Kingdom has survived.

Given the emphases on the consolidation of nationalism in Scotland and Wales, and the attainment of statehood in Ireland, this obvious longevity is often overlooked in Irish and British historiography, where the teleology is (generally and understandably) one of decline and disunity. Yet there are other approaches and I have sought elsewhere to examine the theme of longevity in the context of the Irish and Scottish unions.[38] There are parallels in the historiographies of other polities, too. The Habsburg Dual

Monarchy survived for over half a century and the analytical focus over the past thirty years or so has shifted from the preordained "doom of the Habsburgs" toward health, strength, and contingency.[39] How, then, can the longevity of the unions of the United Kingdom of Great Britain and Ireland—their apparent hold over a range of subsidiary and minority nationalities—be illuminated?

This longevity can certainly be understood in terms of a range of overarching institutions supporting the United Kingdom. Thinking about the Dual Monarchy, Jászi identified a range of "centripetal" institutions and agencies. Jászi's view overlapped with the earlier, more demotic, view of the physician and revolutionary, Adolf Fischof, who famously envisioned a Dual Monarchy supported by four "armies"—standing (the military), sitting (the bureaucracy), kneeling (the Church), and crawling (the secret police). All of these were relevant to the United Kingdom, but, while the role of the "crawlers" (the active intelligence gathering of the Royal Irish Constabulary) should be mentioned, as well as the importance of the "sitters" (the expanding union bureaucracy of the later nineteenth century), the focus here is on the monarchy, as well as its "standers" and "kneelers."

The monarchy has been a central unifying institution within the United Kingdom, though it has not functioned in a uniform manner across all of its constituent polities. The institution itself played an important role in the construction of the early medieval English kingdom, and it was associated with periodic assertions of authority over the whole of Britain. However, the parallel creation of a relatively unified Scottish state together with its own monarchy in the early Middle Ages ultimately created the basis for a wider "British" crown. The two thrones were connected by periodic intermarriage, and were finally unified in 1603, when the Scottish king acceded by right of inheritance to the crown of England. The Scottish royal house, the Stuarts, ruled Britain until 1714. The subsequent Hanoverian and Saxe-Coburg-Gotha dynasties came to identify very strongly with Scotland, a critical development being improved transportation and mobility, and the establishment (by 1856) of a royal residence at Balmoral, in the Cairngorms. There has continued to be a sustained tradition of intermarriage between the royal family and the Scottish aristocracy. Queen Victoria's daughter, Louise, married Lord Lorne, later ninth Duke of Argyll, while King George VI, as Duke of York, married Lady Elizabeth Bowes-Lyon, daughter of the thirteenth Earl of Strathmore.

However, the relationship between the British monarchy and the Irish and Welsh had other complexities.[40] Royalist sympathies or frameworks of thought were deeply embedded within the Catholic Jacobite and Gaelic traditions in Ireland. And there is plenty of evidence for the period up to the 1880s to suggest that the monarchy had at least the potential to serve as a reconciling force between Catholic Ireland and a reformed union state (as with the clear loyalty of successive generations of constitutional nationalist politician to the crown—from Daniel O'Connell to John Redmond). It is also evident that the monarchy retained the sympathetic interest of many Irish people until the eve of the Great War: George V (r.1910–36), for example, undertook a successful coronation visit to Ireland as late as July 1911, less than five years ahead of the Easter Rising.

At the same time, however, the British monarchy did not make the same sustained effort with Ireland as it had done with Scotland. There were certainly occasional royal tours in Ireland under the union: Queen Victoria visited four times, and her successor, Edward VII (r.1901–10), visited three times. But, critically, there was no permanent royal residence in Ireland (unlike Scotland), and therefore no established pattern of travel and engagement. Moreover, there was no sustained royal identification with Irish culture in the same way that there has been with Scottish culture: there was no Irish equivalent of Queen Victoria's best-selling rhapsody on her Scottish life, *Leaves from the Journal of Our Life in the Highlands* (1868), no Irish equivalent of her embrace of the tartan and of the Presbyterian Kirk.[41]

The Welsh, like the Scots, but unlike the Irish, had part-ownership of the British monarchy and its associated institutions. Wales was associated with a loyalism, which was in part linked to the Welsh origins of the Tudor royal dynasty (1485–1603). On the other hand, it would be wrong to suggest that an uncomplicatedly rosy set of relationships prevailed between the Welsh and Scots and monarchy, and an uncomplicatedly bleak set of relationships between it and the Irish. The royal coat of arms, for example, incorporated heraldic references to Scotland and Ireland, but not to Wales (and the disputes within other European multinational monarchies on perceived heraldic slights—in Austria-Hungary and also Sweden-Norway—illustrate the potential combustibility of such apparently marginal issues).[42] It is notable, too, in terms of the key area of titles and honors, that while there were distinctive Scots and Irish orders of chivalry (the orders of the Thistle and St. Patrick, respectively), there was no Welsh equivalent (though it is true, of course, that the Order of St. Patrick was yet another Irish national institution which exclusively served the interests of the ascendancy elite in the years of union).

Moreover, judged purely from the perspective of Victoria's reign, the Welsh came off worse, in terms of royal handling, than even the Irish. Victoria embraced Scotland and the Stuarts, while barely doing her duty in Ireland, and scarcely setting foot at all in Wales: the calculation is that, through her long reign, she spent a total of seven years in Scotland and managed only seven days in Wales.[43] Victoria, supreme governor of the Church of England, enthusiastically embraced Presbyterianism while in Scotland; but she regarded the non-conformity of her Welsh subjects and the Catholicism of the Irish with much less comprehension or sympathy.

In terms of the Welsh, however, there was a critical counterweight. The Welsh had ownership of monarchy, not simply through dynastic antiquity, but also through the princes of Wales. The designation of the heir apparent to the monarch as "Prince of Wales" from the time of Edward I ultimately created a direct association between Wales and the crown. This of course was cemented by the invention of the tradition of investiture, first deployed for Prince Edward (the future Edward VIII) at Caernarfon Castle in 1911, and revived for Prince Charles in 1969. The ceremony at Caernarfon in 1911 has been seen as sealing an alliance between middle-class Welsh non-conformity and the British royal establishment.[44] Indeed, as in Scotland, so in Wales, contentious and divisive national histories were reframed in more ecumenical terms by successive monarchs: just as the house of Hanover annexed and detoxified its Stuart heritage, so its successors performed a similar function in Wales, turning (what was) an appropriated historical title into an expression of national unity.

In short, if Scotland and Wales were effectively bound within Britishness, then they were also effectively bound within, and possessed part ownership of, key institutions of Britishness such as the monarchy. This was less true for Ireland, but even here the monarchy was capable of generating some dynastic loyalty. Indeed, just as a widespread attachment to the Habsburg monarchy, or *Habsburgtreue*, constituted a key supranational bond within Austria-Hungary, so there was always a similar potential with the House of Saxe-Coburg-Gotha in all of the Celtic nations of the Atlantic archipelago.[45]

Moreover, an array of institutions associated with the monarchy served to consolidate these binding functions.[46] The crown forces, especially the army, could (and did) serve to suppress dissent, whether in Scotland (as with the Jacobite risings of 1715 and 1745–6) or in Ireland (as with separatist insurgency in 1798, 1848, 1867, and 1916), but these forces also helped to tie Scots to the cause of monarchy and union in particular in the second half of the eighteenth century and afterward.[47] In fact, both the Scots and the Irish served in disproportionately strong numbers in the army during the French Revolutionary and Napoleonic Wars. Both the Scots and the Irish were distinctive and disproportionate presences in the nineteenth-century British army (the Irish comprised 42 percent of the army in 1830, when they were only one-third of the United Kingdom's population). However, the Scottish military tradition was much more comprehensively celebrated in the Victorian army than its Irish equivalent—under the patronage of key Scottish commanders such as Sir Colin Campbell and Lord Clyde.[48] Moreover, with the death of Jacobitism, and despite the large numbers of Irishmen in its ranks, the army was more frequently in direct conflict with the Irish population than with the Scots or Welsh. Historically the strength of Scottish support for the crown and for the crown forces has represented an argument or a bolster for union.

Loyalty to the monarchy proved to be a binding sentiment both in the United Kingdom and in Austria-Hungary. Yet the loyalist cultures which were thereby generated naturally focused on the person of the monarch—particularly so in the cases of Franz Joseph and of Victoria—and there is a distinction to be drawn between loyalty to individual rulers and loyalty to the wider institution of monarchy. In other words, the transition from long-lived monarchs like Victoria or Franz Joseph to their respective successors made a difference. Moreover, the complex and composite nature of each crown meant that there was no automatic equation between a unifying loyalism and a unifying statist sentiment: Austro-Hungarianness or United Kingdomness was not the obvious by-products of these dynastic sympathies.[49] Jászi pointed out nearly a century ago that there could not always be a neat taxonomy of union, since centripetal forces might also function in a centrifugal manner. In fact, in both the Habsburg Empire and the United Kingdom, the respective monarchies have served simultaneously to bind and subvert the two states. On the one hand, as has been rightly observed, "the symbolic language of monarchy often cloaked new forms of governance and government obligation in reassuringly familiar terms."[50] On the other hand, this reassurance wilted somewhat when "familiar" royal faces disappeared.

Multinational unions survived partly through active agencies, institutions, and loyalties (and force). They also survived because of indifference. Here one can scarcely do better than to look to the reflection on this question offered within recent Habsburg scholarship in terms of the identification of "national indifference": "in studying nationalism in this period," Pieter Judson has argued, "it helps to avoid seeing people as consistently belonging to one or another defined nation in the way that nationalists did … it helps to approach questions of identification by thinking more in terms of particular practices that expressed feelings of loyalty or commitment rather than in terms of people's fixed identities."[51] In his contribution to this volume, Judson adds that such an approach "moves us away from ideas of fixed, authentic, or even fluid identities. Instead, it invites us to evaluate *why* the idea of nation might be important in one situation and not in another?"[52] While it is clearly possible to take these insights too far with the United Kingdom, it is also the case that they chime with a disparate array of Irish historical scholarship, embracing work on Irish local electoral politics in the nineteenth century, as well as with some more recent studies of the 1916 Rising and the revolution.[53]

In highlighting new approaches to the understanding of the Dual Monarchy and other nineteenth-century multinational unions, such work implicitly broaches the case for considering a wider reconceptualization of the United Kingdom. In essence this involves reintroducing into the history of the United Kingdom (and other unions) the notion of the citizen who (in the context of seismic political or economic events) was primarily concerned with negotiating her or his own daily life rather than with the activation of any of the constituent, minority, or majority, nationalisms of the union. In both the Habsburg Empire and the United Kingdom the proliferation and pragmatism of such individuals help to illuminate the otherwise paradoxical survival of these "prisons of the nations."

In fact, this is already an implicit, if unremarked, theme across much Irish historical scholarship on the union. Thus, Theo Hoppen's work on Irish elections and society in the mid-nineteenth century has, as a subsidiary theme, an emphasis upon the extent to which Irish politics remained highly localized—this in an age of national mobilization.[54] The research of numerous scholars, based partly on new material from the Bureau of Military History archives in Dublin, has identified many striking new themes, but not least the impatience of some national activists with their more relaxed or passive compatriots, as well as the vocabulary of indifference ("shoneen," "West Brit").[55] Brian Hughes's study of the ways in which the Irish Republican Army sought to enforce its authority between 1919 and 1921 usefully underlines the "indifference, indecision or cynicism" that often prevailed beyond the communities of separatist activism. Indeed, Hughes presents case studies on Ireland which effectively chime with Jeremy King's work on Budweis/České Budějovice in terms of the contingent—or "situational"— nature of political choices: particularly striking in this respect is Hughes' evocation of those who simultaneously applied to both the Irish Free State and the British authorities for compensation arising out of the struggle of 1919–21. His work illustrates crisply the kinds of ambiguous, alternate, or sequential loyalties—or, alternatively, survival instincts—which characterized many as the first Irish union came to an end.[56]

Such pragmatists made judgments based upon personal or wider economic advantage. More generally, economic growth has clearly helped to underpin pragmatic support for the union between England and Scotland in the eighteenth century. The economic plight of Scotland in the 1690s and in the aftermath of the Darien adventure in Panama (1698–9) provided a compelling argument for union in 1706–7, as did the chaotic public finances of Ireland in the 1790s.

The substantial growth of the Scottish economy and of urban Scotland after the mid-eighteenth century was credited by Scots to the tariff and parliamentary union with England. Equally, Wales' economic and industrial growth in the same period owed much to its close relationship with England, and to both English capital and English labor. There was no simple correlation, however, between wealth and unionism: spatial and temporal relativities were also important insofar as (for example) rivalries between the condition and treatment of individual polities, as well as between different regions of individual polities, fed into national and regional resentments, even though economic conditions overall might have been buoyant. In the case of both south Wales and the northeast of Ireland economic growth was associated not merely with prosperity, but also with immigration from England, which simultaneously promoted unionism as well as stimulating patriotic and particularist responses.

However, taken in the round, Scotland and Wales' economic growth and industrialization in the nineteenth century were convincingly ascribed to union, where Ireland's condition was quite different. Here, outside eastern Ulster, the union did not bring spectacular economic gains. Indeed, the reverse was emphatically the case, given the devastating failure of the potato crop in 1845 and succeeding years. The Great Famine (1845–52), which resulted in more than 1 million deaths through starvation and disease, and an even greater number of additional migrants, was almost from the start ascribed to the limitations of government policy under Lord John Russell—and indeed the broader failure of the union state to effectively redistribute resource from areas of plenty to the starving Irish cottier class. Union, growth, and prosperity—and "modernization"—were conventionally interlinked for much of Scotland and Wales: union, famine, and migration were just as readily interlinked for most of Ireland beyond the industrialized northeast.

The economic experience of complex multinational states like the United Kingdom was therefore variegated. Of course, it is not possible to argue that there was a simple equation between stability in union states and economic success. It has been persuasively suggested that the political crises of the Habsburg monarchy—and (it might be said) also of the United Kingdom of Britain and Ireland—were not "the result of stagnation, but [rather] of lop-sided development."[57] By the later nineteenth century, despite widespread growth, some Hungarians (like many Irish in relation to Britain) argued that they were kept in semi-colonial servitude through their tariff union with Austria. At the same time, however, the north-east of Ireland enjoyed growth driven by heavy industry and textiles which was dependent upon access to British and imperial markets, and which was linked with an increasingly organized unionist movement. These Irish unionists complained about the agrarian preoccupations and outlook of nationalists in the south and west of the island. And if Ireland complained about Britain, and the north of Ireland complained about the south, then Hungary complained about Austria, and Croatia in turn complained against Hungary. The Scots student of the Dual Monarchy, Robert Seton-Watson, expressed some of this anger in arguing against the chauvinism of Budapest's railway development policies: "The railway policy which Budapest has advocated and enforced for many years past is the chief factor in checking Croatia's natural economic development and hence also the political development of the southern Slavs."[58] He also believed that "the whole southern Slav world is at present the victim of a selfish policy of monopoly and favoritism directed from Budapest."[59]

It need hardly be emphasized that similarly contentious issues of taxation and benefit, and of asymmetric economic development, have plagued the histories of Britain and Ireland since the formation of the two unions in 1707 and 1801. Here too, union has meant the controversial sharing of large national debts, disputes about the withholding of resource (again, most controversially during the catastrophic Great Famine in Ireland), and arguments over the appropriate levels of taxation (most clearly during the Irish financial relations controversy of the mid-1890s). The funding algorithm, the Goschen formula (1888–1978), through which public funds were distributed across the constituent nations of the United Kingdom, was disputed—and indeed it initially privileged England and Wales at the expense of Ireland. Equally, issues of taxation and resource have had traction in Scotland, and in particular since the discovery and successful extraction of North Sea gas and oil from the mid and late 1960s.[60]

On the whole, therefore, while there has been an association between the economic benefits of union and its stability, these benefits have always been mitigated by evidence (real or sometimes exaggerated) of inequality or disparity. Union polities such as the United Kingdom have long been characterized by regional disputes over the allocation of resource, or the balance between taxation and benefit, which have frequently served to fuel national resentments, and which have occurred in the context of wider prosperity. Here, again, following Jászi's famous insight, the centripetal may be simultaneously, or sequentially, the centrifugal.

Last, in terms of this taxonomy of cohesion within the union state, the unions of the United Kingdom were relatively flexible and relatively incomplete and therefore offered space for the expression of "minority" patriotism. The historian Richard Lodge argued that the "Scots union was at its origin illogical, and will probably be illogical at its end. It may well be that this is the secret of its success."[61] The success certainly of the union of England and Scotland arose partly from the fact that it was parliamentary and fiscal. But it was not a judicial, educational, or religious union: the distinctive educational, judicial, and fiscal establishments in Edinburgh survived 1707 and provided a vehicle for Scottish national pride within the union. Much of civil society in nineteenth- and twentieth-century Scotland functioned in fact as a vehicle for patriotism inside the union.[62]

Thus, the Scots and Welsh unions were able to embrace their respective patriotisms. The Irish largely did not. After the promulgation of the Irish union in 1801 distinctive Irish institutions remained, but—in the absence of full Catholic civil rights—these continued for long to rest in the hands of the Irish Protestant ascendancy (the Castle administration, the judiciary, the privy council, ministerial positions). They therefore did not wholly function as a medium of assimilation for the mass of the people. In Scotland there were key local institutional focuses for patriotic feeling, while it was still possible to participate fully in the union state.

In addition, the United Kingdom state did not consistently or systematically seek homogeneity through the "British Isles." As has been stressed, the union settlements between England and Scotland and between Britain and Ireland (1801) were negotiated compromises which from the start failed to deliver exactly symmetrical unions or a wholly unitary state. At the beginning of the nineteenth century, it is true, British policy aimed at the creation of a more uniform polity, with (for example) the maintenance of an Anglican state church in England, Wales, and Ireland and, of course, a unitary parliament and executive. But intermittently, from the 1830s onward in Ireland and especially in the last quarter of the nineteenth century throughout the "British Isles," successive union governments strove to create a polity which reflected the particular circumstances of each of the constituent nations. The Anglican Church was disestablished in Ireland in 1869–70, while land legislation and other reforms were tailored to meet the specifics of the Irish case, especially after 1881. This malleability extended as far as the issue of administrative devolution, which was cautiously and incrementally pursued in Ireland and Scotland by both conservative and liberal governments, as well as wider legislative autonomy, which was attempted by the liberals for the benefit of Ireland in 1886, 1893, and 1912. In Scotland, distinctive land legislation, modeled on Irish precedents, was applied in the 1880s to the western highlands and islands. Ultimately, home rule was seriously considered for Scotland, as in Ireland, in the years immediately before the First World War.

Wales was more thoroughly assimilated into England. Here too, however, the union state responded flexibly and effectively to the growing Welsh patriotism of the second half of the nineteenth century through special legislation and the foundation of Welsh national institutions. Where both Ireland and Scotland were long used to separate legislative and administrative treatment, Wales had to wait until the 1880s for the first specifically Welsh legislation since the mid-seventeenth century, achieved (like Irish disestablishment) on the back of denominational mobilization—the Sunday Closing (Wales) Act (1881) and the Wales Intermediate Education Act (1889). The gradual creation, from the late nineteenth century onward, of a swathe of grand national institutions—the University of Wales (1893), the National Museum of Wales in Cardiff (1905–7), the National Library of Wales in Aberystwyth (1907) together with Welsh local government (1889), the Central Welsh (Education) Board (1896), the Welsh Department of the Board of Education (1907)—sent mixed messages. While these were props of a Welsh national infrastructure, they also signaled the extent to which Welsh national identity was bound in with the British state. Certainly, one of the key advocates of each of these enterprises was David Lloyd George, who had securely anchored Welshness, indeed Welsh non-conformist radicalism, to the heart of the British establishment.[63]

But this issue of flexibility is also linked to the fact that the unions of the United Kingdom were not part of, or bolstered by, a codified written constitution.[64] The question of the flexibility of union therefore broaches the benefits or otherwise of a codified British constitution in terms of the overall stability of the United Kingdom, as well as the relationship between "minority" nationalities and the union state.

On the one hand, the fact that the basis of union in the United Kingdom was regular parliamentary legislation, capable of easy review and easy supersession, has permitted a political mobility which (on balance) has helped to sustain the union. There was no legal obstacle to (for example) Gladstone modifying the constitution of the union—whether through disestablishing the Church of Ireland in 1869–70, or seeking to legislate for home rule in 1885–6 and 1893. Equally, there was no legal impediment to parliament voting for the devolution and partition settlement of 1920, or (in effect) the termination of the first United Kingdom through Irish independence in 1921. Nor has there been any legal obstacle to parliamentary majorities enacting many other constitutional refinements, including devolution, since the 1990s. Flexibility has been one factor in the periodic revision and renewal of the unions of the United Kingdom.

On the other hand, there were obvious costs to this flexibility. It was not employed consistently against a clear set of principles. Instead, either it has been invoked sometimes by narrow political considerations or it has been brought about by popular mobilization against an otherwise resistant parliament. Indeed, if significant constitutional change hinged upon a simple parliamentary vote, then pressure politics, including militant mobilization, was effectively incentivized. In some senses this— the achievement of reform, but only after mass mobilization—is the essence of the history of Ireland under the union, and it is a history which has not been lost upon later Scottish nationalists.[65]

Conclusion

Why then have the unions of the United Kingdom either failed to embrace their constituent nationalities (in the case of Ireland) or faltered (as in the case of Scotland and Wales)? The Scottish and Welsh unions have survived so far because they have in fact been able to contain and represent much of the patriotic feeling which has been expressed by these "minority" nationalities. The compromises demanded by the reconciliation of an Anglican monarchy, an English-dominated British state, the vested interests within Scottish and Welsh society, and the claims and rights of the Scottish and Welsh people have hitherto proved manageable within the flexible structures of the union state. Equally, the Irish union of 1801 lasted for as long as it did (until 1921) partly because the accommodating influences relevant to Scotland and Wales were sometimes relevant to some of the Irish as well. It ultimately failed, however, because it could neither lastingly accommodate nor wholly overwhelm a distinctive Irish national sentiment.

The union itself was incomplete, vitiated, pragmatic, and confessional—rather than visionary or aspirational or wholly civic. These were not fatal difficulties, however, since the union (like the Dual Monarchy) was also relatively malleable. By the later nineteenth century, led by Gladstone (who in turn borrowed from earlier exemplars), there was a transition toward greater responsiveness and flexibility concerning the Irish—a transition reflected in the disestablishment of the union church in Ireland, special land legislation, and ultimately in the Liberal party's embrace of home rule for Ireland. Moreover, while addressing originally the sectional needs of the Irish Protestant landed classes, the central institutions of union (such as the monarchy or the army) also sometimes accommodated some majority Catholic conviction and ambition.

Linked with this, the notion of "national indifference" within Habsburg historiography is conceptually relevant to Ireland and the other constituent nations of the United Kingdom. It is of course true that both Irish nationalists and their minority unionist opponents swiftly came to define their politics primarily in terms of nationality, and specifically that by 1913 the notion of "two Irish nations" had begun to gain traction.[66] In reality, however, there was a strong Irish tradition of accommodation to the British state which was not simply a matter of Irish Protestantism and unionism. This was most clearly expressed in terms of Irish service in the army, within the police force (the Royal Irish Constabulary) and within the Empire. Different forms of Irishness were loosely linked by a form of dynastic loyalty, which was clearly evident within some aspects of constitutional Catholic and nationalist politics.[67]

Of course, the compromises demanded by reconciling a semi-confessional "majority" British Protestant state with the claims and rights of its "minority" Irish Catholic population ultimately proved overwhelming. But, just as with the Dual Monarchy, so it took the First World War to expose the wheezes and dodges inherent in the Irish union—and thereby to deliver the death of the "first" United Kingdom.[68]

Notes

1 For the oscillations of British policy in Ireland, see K. Theodore Hoppen, *Governing Hibernia: British Politicians and Ireland, 1800–1921* (Oxford: Oxford University Press, 2016). The Welsh measures came, by the late nineteenth century, to be defined as "acts of union," comparable to their Scots and Irish counterparts: see, for example, William Llewellyn Williams, *The Union of England and Wales, Transactions of the Honourable Society of Cymmrodorion: Session 1907-8* (London: Cymmrodorion Society, 1909).

2 Hoppen, *Governing Hibernia*. See also Alvin Jackson, *Home Rule: An Irish History, 1800-2000* (London and New York: Weidenfeld and Oxford University Press, 2003).

3 Steve Beller, *The Habsburg Monarchy, 1815-1918* (Cambridge: Cambridge University Press, 2018), 212. Comparison has, however, been much broached—see, for example, Laurence Brockliss and David Eastwood, eds., *A Union of Multiple Identities: The British Isles, 1750-1850* (Manchester: Manchester University Press, 1997), 3.

4 See Alvin Jackson, *The Two Unions: Ireland, Scotland and the Survival of the United Kingdom, 1707-2007* (Oxford: Oxford University Press, 2012).

5 Oszkár Jászi, *The Dissolution of the Habsburg Monarchy* (Chicago: Chicago University Press, 1929); James Bryce, *Studies in History and Jurisprudence* (Oxford: Oxford University Press, 1901).

6 Often highlighted, but see most recently Beller, *Habsburg Monarchy*.

7   Deborah Cohen, "Comparative History: Buyer Beware," in *Comparison and History: Europe in Cross-National Perspective*, ed. Deborah Cohen and Maura O'Connor (New York: Routledge, 2004).
8   For Redmond see John Redmond, *Historical and Political Addresses* (Dublin: Sealy, Bryers & Walker, 1898), 191, 237–8. See also Albert V. Dicey, *England's Case against Home Rule*, 3rd ed. (London: John Murray, 1887); A. V. Dicey, *A Leap into the Dark: Or Our New Constitution* (London: John Murray, 1893), 161.
9   Arthur Griffith, *The Resurrection of Hungary: A Parallel for Ireland*, 3rd ed. (Dublin: Whelan, 1918).
10 For example, British Library, Gladstone Mss, Add.MS. 44148, f.127: Gladstone to Hartington, September 8, 1885; Richard Shannon, *Gladstone: Heroic Minister, 1865–98* (London: Penguin, 1999), 378; Robert W. Seton-Watson, *The Southern Slav Question and the Hapsburg Monarchy* (London: Constable, 1911).
11 Colin Kidd, *Union and Unionisms: Political thought in Scotland, 1500–2000* (Cambridge: Cambridge University Press, 2008).
12 Jackson, *Two Unions*.
13 See Bruce Galloway, *The Union of England and Scotland, 1603–1608* (Edinburgh: John Donald, 1986); Miroslav Hroch, *Social Conditions of National Revival in Europe: A Comparative Analysis of the Social Composition of Patriotic Groups among the Smaller European Nations* (New York: Columbia University Press, 2000); Hroch, *European Nations: Explaining their Formation* (London: Verso, 2015).
14 The classic text is Linda Colley, *Britons: Forging the Nation, 1707–1837* (New Haven: Yale University Press, 1992).
15 Vernon Bogdanor, *The New British Constitution* (Oxford: Hart, 2009).
16 G. C. Bolton, *The Passing of the Irish Act of Union: A Study in Parliamentary Politics* (Oxford: Oxford University Press, 1966); Patrick Geoghegan, *The Irish Act of Union: A Study in High Politics, 1798–1801* (Dublin: Gill & Macmillan, 1999); Christopher Whatley, *Bought and Sold for English Gold: Explaining the Union of 1707*, 2nd ed. (Edinburgh: Edinburgh University Press, 2001).
17 In terms of other union states, the birth-narrative of the United Kingdom of the Netherlands is discussed in Friso Wielenga, *A History of the Netherlands, from the Sixteenth Century to the Present Day* (London: Bloomsbury, 2015); see also Joep Leersen, "Retro-fitting the Past: Literary Historicism between the Golden Spurs and Waterloo," in *The Historical Imagination in Nineteenth Century Britain and the Low Countries*, ed. Hugh Dunthorne and Michael Wintle (Leiden: Brill, 2013), 111–31.
18 Pieter Judson, *The Habsburg Empire: A New History* (Cambridge: Harvard University Press, 2016), 121.
19 See Colley, *Britons*.
20 Jim English, "Empire Day in Britain, 1904–58," *Historical Journal* 46, no. 1 (2006): 247–76.
21 For the Bernadotte monarchy see, for example, Thomas K. Derry, *A History of Modern Norway, 1814–1972* (Oxford: Oxford University Press, 1972), 92; Raymond Lindgren, *Norway-Sweden: Union, Disunion and Scandinavian Integration* (Princeton: Princeton University Press, 1959), 49.
22 See, for example, Nancy Wingfield, "Emperor Joseph II in the Austrian Imagination to 1914," in *The Limits of Loyalty: Imperial Symbolism, Popular Allegiances, and State Patriotism in the Late Habsburg Monarchy*, ed. Laurence Cole and Daniel Unowsky (New York: Berghahn, 2007), 62–85.

23 Jászi, *Dissolution*, 435, 438, 447, 449. Jászi's critique of Austrian civic education (through the schools) was juxtaposed against his portrayal of the very different Hungarian system: in the former the school system was "permeated by the old dynastic and patrimonial conception of the state," whereas in the latter Hungarian civic education repeatedly hammered home Magyar national consciousness. Ibid., 435. As a result "the strangeness of the people to each other was the cause of the downfall of the old Austria and our school system did nothing to prevent it." Ibid., 438.
24 Albert V. Dicey and Robert S. Rait, *Thoughts on the Union between England and Scotland* (London: Macmillan, 1920), 112.
25 Colley, *Britons*.
26 Tom Nairn, *The Break-up of Britain: Crisis and Neo-nationalism* (London: Verso, 1977); Tom Nairn, *After Britain: New Labour and the Return of Scotland* (London: Granta, 2000).
27 Graeme Morton, *Unionist Nationalism: Governing Urban Scotland, 1830–60* (East Linton: Tuckwell, 1999).
28 Much discussed but see, for example, Thomas E. Ellis and Annie J. Ellis, *Speeches and Addresses by the Late T. E. Ellis* (Wrexham: Hughes, 1912), 85–118; Kenneth O. Morgan, *Rebirth of a Nation: Wales, 1880–1980* (Oxford: Oxford University Press, 1981), 33–4.
29 For a discussion of the anti-imperial theme within the formation of modern constitutional nationalism see Paul Townend, *The Road to Home Rule: Anti-Imperialism and the Irish Nationalist Movement* (Madison: Wisconsin University Press, 2006).
30 Jászi, *Dissolution*, 435, 447.
31 Ibid., 449.
32 Stewart J. Brown, *Providence and Empire, 1815–1914* (Harlow: Routledge, 2008).
33 Stewart J. Brown, *The National Churches of England, Scotland and Ireland, 1801–46* (Oxford: Oxford University Press, 2001).
34 Jászi, *Dissolution*, 163.
35 Hugh Seton-Watson and Christopher Seton-Watson, *The Making of a New Europe: R.W. Seton-Watson and the Last Years of Austria-Hungary* (Seattle: Washington University Press, 1981), 23.
36 Robin Okey, *The Habsburg Empire, c.1765–1918: From Enlightenment to Eclipse* (Basingstoke: Macmillan, 2001), 101; Beller, *Habsburg Monarchy*, 16.
37 Okey, *Habsburg Empire*, 108.
38 Jackson, *Two Unions*.
39 The acme of new approaches of this kind has been Judson, *Habsburg Empire*. The notion of "doom of the Habsburgs" comes from the eponymous work by Henry Wickham Steed (London: Arrowsmith, [1937]).
40 James H. Murphy, *Abject Loyalty: Nationalism and Monarchy during the Reign of Queen Victoria* (Cork: Cork University Press, 2001); James Loughlin, *The British Monarchy and Ireland: 1800 to the Present* (Cambridge: Cambridge University Press, 2007); James Loughlin, "Royal Agency and State Integration: Ireland, Wales and Scotland in a Monarchical Context, 1840s–1921," *Journal of Imperial and Commonwealth History* 41, no. 3 (2013): 1–26.
41 Queen Victoria, *Leaves from the Journal of Our Life in the Highlands from 1848 to 1861* (London: Smith Elder, 1868). For Scotland and the monarchy, see the work of Richard Finlay, "Queen Victoria and the Cult of Scottish Monarchy," in *Scottish History: The Power of the Past*, ed. Edward J. Cowan and Richard J. Finlay

42 Alvin Jackson, "Union States, Civil Society and National Symbols in the Nineteenth Century: Comparing United Kingdoms," *Scandinavica: an International Journal of Scandinavian Studies* 58, no. 2 (2019): 58–75.
43 Loughlin, "Royal Agency and State Integration," 383.
44 John S. Ellis, "The Prince and the Dragon: Welsh National Identity and the 1911 Investiture of the Prince of Wales," *Welsh History Review* 18, no. 2 (1996): 272–94; Ellis, "Reconciling the Celt: British National Identity, Empire and the 1911 Investiture of the Prince of Wales," *Journal of British Studies* 37, no. 4 (1998): 391–418. See also John Ellis, *Investiture: Royal Ceremony and National Identity in Wales, 1911–1969* (Cardiff: University of Wales Press, 2008).
45 For different assessments of the role of *Habsburgtreue* see, for example, Judson, *Habsburg Empire*; Jeremy King, *Budweisers into Czechs and Germans? A Local History of Bohemian Politics, 1848–1948* (Princeton: Princeton University Press, 2002).
46 Though see Jackson, *Two Unions*, 121–215 for a fuller exploration.
47 See, for example, Andrew Mackillop, *More Fruitful than the Soil: Army, Empire and the Scottish Highlands, 1715–1815* (Edinburgh: Tuckwell, 2000).
48 See, for example, Edward Spiers, *The Scottish Soldier and Empire, 1854–1902* (Edinburgh: Edinburgh University Press, 2006).
49 Though "Ukania," echoing Robert Musil's "Kakania" (from "*k(aiserlich) und k(öniglich)*"), has been suggested by Tom Nairn: see Krishan Kumar, *The Making of English National Identity* (Cambridge: Cambridge University Press, 2003), 3.
50 Judson, *Habsburg Empire*, 341.
51 Judson, *Habsburg Empire*, 312; Tara Zahra, *National Indifference and the Battle for Children in the Bohemian Lands, 1900–48* (Ithaca: Cornell University Press, 2008); Tara Zahra, "Imagined Non-communities: National Indifference as a Category of Analysis," *Slavic Review* 69, no. 1 (2010): 93–119.
52 See Pieter Judson's chapter in this volume, 29.
53 See, for example, Hoppen *Elections, Politics and Society*; Jackson, *Home Rule*; Fearghal McGarry, *The Rising: Ireland, Easter 1916*, updated edition (Oxford: Oxford University Press, 2017); Brian Hughes, *Defying the IRA: Intimidation, Coercion and Communities during the Irish Revolution* (Liverpool: Liverpool University Press, 2016).
54 Hoppen *Elections, Politics and Society*.
55 For example, McGarry, *The Rising*.
56 Hughes, *Defying the IRA*; King, *Budweisers into Czechs and Germans?*. See also Brian Hughes' chapter in this volume.
57 Okey, *Habsburg Empire*, 335, 360.
58 Seton-Watson, *The Southern Slav Question*, 329.
59 Ibid., 334.
60 See Christopher Harvie, *Fool's Gold: The Story of North Sea Oil* (London: Hamish Hamilton, 1994).
61 In Peter Hume Brown, ed., *The Union of 1707: A Survey of Events* (Glasgow: Glasgow Herald, 1907), 173–4.
62 Morton, *Unionist Nationalism*.
63 Brian Harrison, *The Transformation of British Politics, 1860–1995* (Oxford: Oxford University Press, 1996), 112.

64 Linda Colley, "Empires of Writing: Britain, America and Constitutions, 1776–1848," *Law & History Review* 32, no. 2 (2014): 237–66.
65 Alvin Jackson, "Shamrock and Saltire: Irish Home Rule, Independence, and the Scottish Referendum, 1914–2004," in *Uncertain Futures: Essays about the Irish Past for Roy Foster*, ed. Senia Paseta (Oxford: Oxford University Press, 2016), 257–69.
66 William F. Monypenny, *The Two Irish Nations: An Essay on Home Rule* (London: John Murray, 1913).
67 For more detail on loyalism in the Irish Republic, see Brian Hughes' chapter in this volume.
68 I am grateful to the Leverhulme Trust for its support of my research, reading, and reflection on the theme of multinational union states.

4

Nationalism, Religion, and Minorities from the Ottoman Empire to the Republic of Turkey

Erol Ülker

This chapter deals with the transition from the Ottoman Empire to the Republic of Turkey focusing on the question of nationalism and ethnoreligious minorities. It examines how the category of national minority was defined during the formation of Turkey as a new nation-state and how ethnic and religious minorities were treated in the process. To address these issues, I will, first, explore the rise of Turkish nationalism and its impact on the Young Turks' nationality policies in the Second Constitutional Period (1908–18). I will, then, concentrate on the Armistice Period (1918–23) to discuss the nation-building policies of the Turkish government formed in Ankara during the Greco-Turkish War (1919–22). Much of the Ottoman Empire's Greek Orthodox population was driven out of Asia Minor at the end of this war, which was a decisive stage in the ethnoreligious homogenization of Anatolia. Not only did the Turkish national regime gain international recognition with the Lausanne Treaty, signed in July 1923, but it also legitimized the deportation of a great number of Greek Orthodox people through a convention legislating the exchange of minority populations with Greece. In the Lausanne Congress, Turkey was incorporated into the minority protection system associated with the League of Nations, but minority status was provided only for non-Muslim communities, whereas non-Turkish Muslim nationalities were excluded from the League's minority protection regime. In the concluding part of this chapter, I will discuss the implications of this international arrangement for the nation-building policies of post-Lausanne Turkey.

The rise of Turkish nationalism in the late Ottoman period and the construction of Turkish national identity in this process has been one of the most examined topics in Ottoman-Turkish studies. It is not possible to explore this comprehensive literature exhaustively in this chapter. However, a relatively recent trend in the study of the late Ottoman period is directly related to the discussion below. It focuses on the role of religion in nationalism and nation-building during this period.[1] Islam, in this context, signifies a national (or proto-national) identification as an ideological and cultural phenomenon rather than the faith of individuals or a religious doctrine. Kemal Karpat's *Politicization of Islam* provides one of the most systematic analyses in this respect focusing on the Hamidian Period (1876–1909) and its aftermath.[2] More recently, Barış Ünlü has employed a different conceptual terminology to deal with a similar question. In his widely read book, *Turkishness Contract*, published in 2018, he accounts for the categories of Turkishness (*Türklük*) and Muslimness (*Müslümanlık*) as worlds of privileges not recognized for non-Turks and non-Muslims. According to Ünlü, the Muslimness contract was born in the Hamidian Period, after the Ottomanism contract formulated by the *Tanzimat* reformers had failed.[3] It relied on a tacit agreement between the state and society, which required that persecution and discrimination of non-Muslim communities should not be questioned and not, even, publicly spoken about. For Ünlü, this contract remained in force until the Greco-Turkish War ended. Thereafter a transition to the Turkishness contract gradually occurred, leading to the exclusion of those Muslims resisting Turkification, above all the Kurdish people.

From a different perspective, Eric Jan Zürcher engages with the role of religion in nationalism and national identification as well. He argues that the oft-cited discussion in late Ottoman history referring to a competition among Ottomanism, Islamism, and Turkism does not explain the Young Turks' ideological motive. According to Zürcher, the Unionists, that is, the leading cadre of the Committee of Union and Progress (CUP), "were motivated by a peculiar brand of Ottoman Muslim nationalism."[4] For Zürcher, the Young Turks' nationalism appealed to the Ottoman Muslim nation, not to the Turkish nation, during the formative phase of modern Turkey, which includes the years of the Balkan War, the First World War, and the war for national independence. There are, of course, important differences between Zürcher's concept of Muslim nationalism and Ünlü's Muslimness contract, but they both argue that developments such as the Armenian genocide, the mobilization of the Anatolian Muslims during the National Struggle led by the Turkish national movement in the Armistice Period, and the population exchange between Turkey and Greece attest to a sharp division between Muslims and non-Muslims. They, thus, agree on the determining role of religion in separating "us" from "them" in late Ottoman history. To be sure, there is a broader literature analyzing how Islam became the core element of Ottoman national or proto-national identification,[5] but much of the existing research on this topic concentrates on the reign of Abdülhamid II (1876–1909), the Hamidian Period, during which Islam and pan-Islamism received more emphasis in the official Ottoman ideology.[6] Until the 1990s, however, it was not very common to associate the Young Turks' nationality policies with the idea of a Muslim nation and Muslim nationalism.[7] The Young Turks were considered to have been Turkish nationalists, who had resorted to Islam as a tactical instrument or out of obligation.[8]

In this chapter, I emphasize the importance of religion too, but I employ the term Turkish nationalism, instead of Muslim nationalism or the Muslimness contract, to discuss the question of minorities and nation-building during the transition from empire to nation-state.[9] This is not just a terminological choice. I argue that the Young Turks, who ruled the Ottoman Empire during much of the Second Constitutional Period, who led the National Struggle in the Armistice Period, and who became the founders of the Republic of Turkey, were concerned with not only the non-Muslim minorities but also the heterogeneity of the Muslim population in terms of culture, language, and ethnicity. This makes them Turkish nationalists. Studying the persecution of non-Muslims should not prevent us from identifying the Young Turks' assimilationist policies toward non-Turkish Muslim peoples. These were different but related aspects of nation-building in the late Ottoman and early republican Turkish context.

Background

The Ottoman Empire was a multi-ethnic and multi-religious polity from the outset.[10] Ottoman rulers recognized this ethnoreligious diversity from the early stages of the imperial state formation, allowing the organization of Christian and Jewish elements into "culturally autonomous and self-regulating communities with religious leaders acting as the intermediaries between the state and community," the so-called millets.[11] Starting in the late eighteenth century, Ottoman statesmen embarked on modernization and centralization efforts to restructure the Empire based on the model of centralized European states. This trend culminated in the *Tanzimat* reforms, which were launched with the Gülhane Rescript of 1839. In the context of rising national movements especially among the Christian peoples inhabiting the Empire's western borderlands, the ethnoreligious heterogeneity of the Empire's population was one of the questions the Ottoman reformers had to deal with. During the nineteenth-century *Tanzimat* reforms, the Ottoman ruling elite sought to integrate the Empire's non-Muslim communities through the Ottomanist ideal of common citizenship.[12] Ottomanism referred to the unity of all Muslim and non-Muslim peoples in Ottoman domains and this principle was expressed in various official texts, including the Reform Edict of Islahat in 1856, the Ottoman Nationality Law of 1869, and the Constitution of 1876 (*Kânun-ı Esâsî*).[13] However, the Ottoman Empire lost control of much of its territory in Europe as a result of the 1877–8 war with Russia, which meant that the number and proportion of Christians in the Ottoman population significantly declined. Thereafter, the integration of the non-Turkish Muslim peoples, like the Arabs and Kurds, came to be seen as all the more important for the unity of the Empire. During the reign of Abdülhamid II, the so-called Hamidian Period, Ottomanism was re-interpreted from an Islamist point of view, emphasizing and appealing to the unity of the Muslim communities rather than the equality of Muslims and non-Muslims.[14]

The Constitutional Revolution of July 1908 was a crucial turning point for the Ottoman Empire's nationality policies. At the outset, the leaders of the Committee of Union and Progress (CUP), which led the Revolution, seemed attached to the Ottomanist ideal of *İttihad-ı Anasır* (Unity of Elements), that is, the unity of all ethnoreligious communities in the Empire, whether they were Muslim, Christian, or Jewish.[15] This attitude was, partly, a reaction to the Islamist policies of Abdülhamid II. Nevertheless, Turkish nationalism became one of the major intellectual and ideological trends from the beginning of the Second Constitutional Period.[16] Before and after the Revolution, The Young Turks flirted with nationalist ideas as well; their journals appealed to the idea that the Turks formed the dominant nation of the Ottoman Empire.[17] The CUP remained loyal to Ottomanism in its public discourse, but the Young Turks interpreted Ottomanism in a more aggressive manner. Their brand emphasized that the integrity of the Ottoman state as a multinational empire should be maintained, but the other nationalities should be subordinated to the nation of the Turks.[18] During the initial years of the Second Constitutional Period, even the most important ideologues of Turkish nationalism, such as Ziya Gökalp, promulgated their adherence to Ottomanism, but their formulation of Ottomanism differed from that of *Tanzimat* reformers in its appeal to the dominant position of the Turkish nationality.[19] Only a relatively narrow group of Turkish nationalists, composed mainly of Tatar-Turkish immigrants from Russia, like Yusuf Akçura, repudiated Ottomanism in favor of a pan-Turkist project.[20]

With the Albanian revolt of 1912 and the Balkan Wars (1912–13), Turkish nationalism became increasingly more important for the CUP's nationality policies.[21] Albanian independence, together with the end of Ottoman presence in Macedonia and much of Thrace, left the Empire as a conglomerate of today's Anatolia and the Arab provinces. As a result, the idea of achieving a unified empire through Ottomanist policies was discredited in the eyes of the CUP leaders, the Unionists. The nationalist project of Turkification was put into practice after the CUP monopolized political power with the coup of January 1913,[22] which was carried out following a period of approximately six months during which the CUP had been removed from power. A part of the Turkification policy was the nationalization of the economy through the elimination of the Greek and Armenian commercial classes that had long dominated the trade and financial sectors and their replacement with a Muslim-Turkish commercial class. This policy was connected to the idea of Turkish domination in the Empire that had been on the Young Turks' political agenda since the initial phase of the Second Constitutional Period. The economic boycotts that had targeted the non-Muslim communities had been earlier experimentations with economic nationalism at the grassroots level.[23] Various social and economic agents from the CUP's local branches to the artisan and labor association as well as autonomous boycott committees had been involved. When the CUP fully seized political power, this policy came to be implemented in a more determined manner with various state departments, including the Ministry of War, put at the disposal of the efforts of creating a class of Muslim-Turkish businessmen.

Nationalism, Assimilation, Dissimilation

More importantly, the Unionists embarked on a policy of demographic and territorial nationalization, or Turkification, especially after the Ottoman Empire participated in the Great War on the side of Germany and Austria-Hungary. Ziya Gökalp, one of the prominent nationalist ideologues associated with the Young Turks, most clearly expressed the ideological background of the Turkification project carried out during the First World War period.[24] He refers to the principles under which individuals constitute the nation as follows:

> Individuals actually constituting a nation are not the only members of a nation. All those who may speak that language in the future will also be members of that nation. Thus, for example, the Pomaks [Bulgarian Muslims] now speaking

Bulgarian and the Cretan Muslims now speaking Greek may learn Turkish in the future and cease to be Bulgarian- or Greek- speaking peoples. This means that nationality is not determined by language alone but also by religion.[25]

Ziya Gökalp makes this statement in an article published in 1914, on the eve of the Great War. He goes on to argue that, "as language plays a part in deciding religious affiliation, so religion plays a part in determining membership in a nationality." He elaborates on this argument with examples:

The Protestant French became Germanized when they were expelled from France and settled in Germany. The Turkish aristocracy of old Bulgars became Slavicized following their conversion to Christianity. And today, the non-Turkish Muslims migrating to Turkey in a scattered way are becoming Turkified because of their religious affiliation. We may conclude, therefore, that there is a close relationship between linguistic and religious association.[26]

Attributing a crucial role to religious affiliation, Ziya Gökalp apparently rejects the inclusion of non-Muslims into the national category of Turkishness. In other words, there could be no Christian or Jewish Turk. At the same time, he opens the doors of Turkishness to non-Turkish-speaking Muslims. However, they cannot be regarded as part of the Turkish nation with the cultural and linguistic traits they had. Ziya Gökalp expects their assimilation, or Turkification:

In order for an ideal to arise in the future, it must spring from the intensification of one of the existing groups. Therefore, a great ideal should be born out of the intensification of only that group, which, in addition to being richest and most powerfully organized, is in a position to bring together and assimilate all other groups in its own organization. Which, then, is this inclusive group? Among the existing ones it is the language group-that is, the nationality group-which is most capable of fulfilling such a function.[27]

In his important study on nationalism and nationhood in Europe, Rogers Brubaker points out that terms like nationalization, homogenization (or Turkification for that matter) are generally not sufficient concepts to explain different dimensions of nation-building policies.[28] These terms can refer to two different, even antithetical processes. On the one hand, they can designate an attempt to nationalize a citizenry by turning, for example, Ukrainians into Poles, which occurred in the Polish state during the interwar period.[29] In this sense, the term homogenization or nationalization refers to a form of assimilation, in other words, to an attempt of "making similar." On the other hand, the same terms can refer to policies involving dissimilation rather than assimilation. Instead of making people similar to the putative characteristics of the core nation, perceived as the legitimate owner of the state, such terms prescribe differential treatment on the basis of their presumed difference. In other words, instead of seeking to alter different identities, such efforts take them as given. According to Brubaker, "assimilationist nationalization seeks to eradicate difference, while dissimilationist nationalization takes difference as axiomatic and foundational."[30]

Apparently, Ziya Gökalp's vision of the Turkish nation involves the ideological roots of assimilation and dissimilation at the same time. Both of these strategies were reflected in the CUP's nationality policies during, especially, the First World War. The Young Turk government attempted to homogenize the ethnoreligious and cultural composition of the population in Anatolia through both dissimilation and assimilation. There was no intention of assimilating non-Muslim subjects. On the contrary, the Young Turks aimed to "purify" Anatolia from the Armenian and Greek Orthodox elements. The deportation of Armenians was a crucial phase of this process. It was legislated by the infamous law of relocation (*Tehcir Yasası*), adopted in May 1915, and led to the extermination of thousands. The elimination of the Armenian population in this process is regarded as one of the first genocides of the twentieth century.[31] Also, the Orthodox Greek population of Asia Minor was exposed to deportation from the Aegean coastal regions to the interior of Anatolia.[32] Thousands of Greeks fled to the shores of Greece because of this policy. On the other hand, the CUP government employed demographic measures to assimilate non-Turkish ethnic Muslims, especially Kurds and immigrants from the Balkans and Caucasus.[33] The goal was to settle or relocate them in a way to promote their assimilation to Turkish culture and language, although it is difficult to estimate how successfully this strategy was effectively put into practice. Theoretically, at least, the total number of immigrants should be kept below 10 percent of the total number of the inhabitants where they were settled. Kurdish refugees were to be treated similarly. The government attempted to resettle many Kurds from the southeast of Anatolia, such as Urfa and Zor, to prevent their "Arabisation."[34] The Kurds resettled in the interiors of Anatolia should not have clustered in the same region. It was thought that they could be assimilated only if they were mixed with the local population.

The CUP's Turkification policies rested on a clear taxonomy of the Empire's ethnoreligious communities, but there was no official category for national and religious minorities yet.[35] Ottomanism and the idea of Ottoman citizenship, encompassing all subjects regardless of their religious and ethnic background, remained to be the official discourse of national identification up until the collapse of the Ottoman Empire. Yet, despite the official discourse, the Young Turks were de facto engaging in the homogenization of the population. The question of national minorities was introduced to public debates during the National Struggle, which was launched after the Ottoman defeat in the Great War. National minorities were officially recognized with the Lausanne Treaty of 1923, the foundational text of the Republic of Turkey. However, the terms of this treaty concerning minorities and minority rights were very problematic.

National Struggle, Treaty of Sèvres, and Minorities

The Ottoman Empire was on the side of the defeated belligerents at the end of the Great War. Shortly after Bulgaria surrendered and when the dissolution of the Austro-Hungarian Empire became clear, an Ottoman mission signed the Armistice of Mudros at the end of October 1918. The CUP government fell from power with the Ottoman capitulation. What followed was the occupation of the Ottoman territory by the Allied powers. This was accompanied by the gradual formation of the Turkish national movement relying on and claiming to represent the Muslim population of Anatolia and Thrace.[36] Although the CUP was disbanded after the Armistice, its former members, that is, the Unionists, played a key role in the rise of the Turkish national movement, which launched the so-called National Struggle against the partition of the Ottoman Empire. The headquarters of this movement was installed in the central Anatolian town of Ankara, where the Turkish National Grand Assembly was inaugurated in April 1920. Led by the national government in Ankara, the success of the National Struggle, which focused largely on the Greco-Turkish War in Anatolia, was dependent on the unity of all the Muslim elements, regardless of their language and ethnic backgrounds. Therefore, the National Struggle was presented to be the struggle of the Muslim nation against the Allied powers and their Christian supporters in the Empire.[37] Assimilating the non-Turkish Muslim communities was not an option in this context.

While the Turkish national movement was in the making, the Allied powers were engaged in postwar settlements. One of the issues that preoccupied them over the course of the Paris Peace Conference was the question of national minorities. Their interest in minority rights stemmed partly from problems in putting Woodrow Wilson's principle of national self-determination into practice. In Wilson's perspective, territorial changes and border revisions should be undertaken based on the interests and benefits of the peoples.[38] But this was not an easy goal. Europe's demographic and ethnic structure was too complex to fully implement the principle of national self-determination.[39] This principle was put into practice unless it contradicted the victors' geopolitical, economic, and strategic interests.[40] Consistent application of national self-determination would have resulted in more dramatic changes in the map of Europe than what Wilson must have estimated.[41] Thus it was clear that the minorities problem would persist as a serious challenge to the seemingly national states and the new world order to be created.[42] This is why a minority protection system associated with the League of Nations was set up at the Paris Peace Conference.

The leaders of the Turkish National Struggle were certainly aware of the developments concerning minority rights. In January 1920, the proponents of the national movement in the Ottoman Parliament accepted an important charter, called the National Pact, which consisted of six points (or decisions). Proclaimed in February 1920, it became the National Struggle's basic program. Article 5 of the National Pact emphasized the national movement's commitment to minority protection:

> The rights of minorities as defined in the treaties concluded between Entente Powers and their enemies and certain of their associates shall be confirmed and assured by us—in reliance on the belief that the Muslim minorities in neighboring countries also will have the benefit of the same rights.

On the other hand, Article 1 identifies an "Ottoman-Islamic majority" that is unified in religion, race, and hope. This implies that only non-Muslim communities were seen as minority to be provided with certain minority rights determined by the

Allied powers. Nonetheless, the conditions imposed on the Ottoman Empire with the Treaty of Sèvres did not satisfy the expectations of the leaders of the Turkish national movement.

The structure of the League's minority protection system relied on provisions to be accepted by individual states with respect to the treatment of national minorities and the League was recognized as the guarantor of minority rights.[43] There were different categories of states that were incorporated differently into the system. Some of them accepted minority rights as a result of negotiations and bargains over independence and the extension of territory. This was the case with five newly created or enlarged states: Poland, Czechoslovakia, Yugoslavia, Romania, and Greece. They undertook responsibilities concerning minority protection by signing special minority treaties. Some other states were admitted to the League of Nations on the condition of accepting minority protection. Albania, Lithuania, Latvia, Estonia, and Iraq made declarations about minority protection when they applied for membership to the League of Nations. There was also the category of states defeated in the Great War. The peace treaties signed with those states and their followers included specific provisions about minority rights. The Ottoman Empire was one of them alongside Austria, Hungary, and Bulgaria.

The Treaty of Sèvres was signed by the representatives of the Ottoman Empire and the Allied powers on August 20, 1920. This treaty included substantial conditions for the Ottoman Empire. It provided independence for Armenia and autonomy for Kurdistan. Smyrna and its surroundings were left to Greece. Articles 140–151 were concerned specifically with the protection of minorities. In addition to general statements about minorities and minority protection, the treaty included specific provisions targeting the demographic policies of the CUP government during the Great War. Article 142 states that no conversions to Islam after November 1, 1914, would be accepted as valid. Article 144 declared the Law of 1915 relating to Abandoned Properties null and void. This article states:

> The Turkish Government solemnly undertakes to facilitate to the greatest extent the return to their homes and re-establishment in their businesses of the Turkish subjects of non-Turkish race who have been forcibly driven from their homes by fear of massacre or any other form of pressure since January 1, 1914. It recognizes that any immovable or movable property of the said Turkish subjects or of the communities to which they belong, which can be recovered, must be restored to them as soon as possible, in whatever hands it may be found. Such property shall be restored free of all charges or servitudes with which it may have been burdened and without compensation of any kind to the present owners or occupiers, subject to any action which they may be able to bring against the persons from whom they derived title.[44]

With such provisions the Ottoman mission accepted not only the safe return of deported Christians but also the restoration of their properties. Also accepted was the authority of the Council of the League of Nations and the commissions to be appointed by the Council in the application of those provisions.

However, the Ankara government repudiated the Sèvres Treaty. As Volker Prott's chapter discusses in more detail in this volume, the Greek forces of occupation were defeated and expelled from Smyrna by September 1922. Thereafter, thousands of Christians fled from Asia Minor ahead of the advancing Turkish army. In Anatolia and Thrace, some 900,000 Greek Orthodox people became refugees in a few months that followed the beginning of the Turkish offensive in August 1922.[45] The Greek exodus spread to the Ottoman capital Istanbul as well. Although the city was under Allied occupation and away from the battle zone, news of atrocities inflicted on the Christian communities of Asia Minor and the ongoing mobilization of the Muslim masses created a sense of panic among Greeks as well as Armenians causing many of them to flee from the city at all costs.[46] There was strong pressure to nationalize the economy while purging it of its Christian elements. Nationalist labor and artisan unions were involved in this xenophobic campaign.

Lausanne Treaty

It was in this context that the Ankara government dispatched a diplomatic mission to Lausanne to take part in the international conference for the renegotiation of the conditions of peace. In the meantime, the Ottoman sultanate was abolished by the Turkish Grand National Assembly. The Lausanne Peace Treaty was signed in July 1923, after a long period of negotiations that had begun in November 1922. The Republic of Turkey, promulgated in October 1923, relied on the provisions of the Lausanne Treaty. The borders of the new regime were drawn over the course of the Lausanne conference, the questions concerning capitulations, war reparations, and Ottoman debts were settled there, and the international status of the Straits was decided. One of the most important matters discussed in Lausanne was national minorities. In the end, the Lausanne Treaty included specific articles concerning the definition, status, and protection of national minorities, by which Turkey was incorporated into the League of Nations' minority protection regime.[47] In terms of the definition of national minorities, however, the clauses of the Lausanne Treaty were quite different from those outlined in the Sèvres Treaty.

The League of Nations' minority protection system did not rely on objective criteria identifying national minorities once and for all. The phrase "racial, religious or linguistic minorities" was often used as synonymous with national minorities,[48] but the Lausanne Treaty proves that such terms fell short of defining which groups and peoples would be recognized as minorities and, thus, provided with minority protection. As noted above, the League's minority protection regime was dependent on the peace treaties to be signed with individual states or their declarations. During the Lausanne Conference, in particular, this left the definition of minorities open to negotiations and bargaining of the contracting parties. The Allied powers urged the Turkish mission to recognize the existence of linguistic and ethnic minorities along with non-Muslim religious minorities. The Turkish side, on the other hand, insisted on the argument that the question of minorities always had reference to non-Muslims in Turkey; there was a cultural and historical unity among the Muslim population of Turkey, so only non-Muslims would be accepted as minority.[49] Yet the rulers of the Republic of Turkey, which was proclaimed in October 1923, exerted the policy of assimilating non-Turkish Muslims, like the Young Turks had done in the Second Constitutional Period, especially during the Great War. It is interesting that many of those who designed the Republic's assimilative policies had been involved in the Young Turks movement.

By the time the Lausanne Conference convened, the Greek army of occupation had been driven out of Asia Minor and the Ankara government had seized de facto control of Istanbul. Therefore, the Turkish mission had an upper hand in the negotiations over the definition of national minorities. Eventually, unlike the Treaty of Sèvres, the Lausanne Treaty referred only to non-Muslim minorities and minority rights were recognized only for them.[50] None of the non-Turkish Muslim peoples were categorized as such. With the Lausanne Treaty, Turkey accepted to provide negative and positive rights for the non-Muslim minorities. Negative rights include "full and complete protection of life and liberty for all inhabitants of Turkey without distinction of birth, nationality, language, race or religion" (Article 38).[51] "Turkish nationals belonging to the non-Muslim minorities shall enjoy the same civil and political rights as Muslims" (Article 39). Regarding positive rights, Turkey accepted the settlement of questions about the personal status and family law of non-Muslim minorities in accordance with their own customs (Article 42). Non-Muslim minorities "shall have an equal right to establish, manage and control charitable religious, social and educational institutions at their own expense and with the right to use their own language and exercise their own religion freely therein" (Article 40). All the articles of the Lausanne Treaty concerning the protection of minorities were recognized as fundamental laws not subject to variation and interference by or under any law, regulation, or official action (Article 37). The Turkish government accepted the international guarantee of the League of Nations and the authority of the Permanent Court of International Justice concerning any issues about minorities in Turkey; "any Member of the Council of the League of Nations shall have the right to bring to the attention of the Council any infraction or danger of infraction of any of these obligations" (Article 44).

Population Exchange[52]

The recognition of minority status only for the Jewish and Christian communities points out the importance of religion in Turkish national identification. Another important development confirming the role of religion in this respect was the compulsory exchange of minority populations between Greece and Turkey. Signed on January 30, 1923, during the Lausanne Conference, the Convention and Protocol concerning the Exchange of Greek and Turkish Populations took religion as the main element of national identification for both sides.[53] The population exchange was a decisive stage in the Turkish government's nation-building policies and was carried out under the auspices of the League of Nations.

The first experience with population exchange had involved the Ottoman Empire and Bulgaria. In November 1913, after the Second Balkan War, a mixed commission consisting of Ottoman and Bulgarian delegates signed a protocol to carry out a population exchange.[54] It set the conditions for the voluntary exchange of Bulgarians and Muslims within a fifteen-kilometer-wide zone along the Ottoman-Bulgarian frontier.[55] In effect, the protocol recognized a de facto situation since the populations concerned had almost already migrated during the Balkan Wars.[56] As a result, 9,714 Muslim families (48,570 persons) from the Bulgarian territory were exchanged with 9,472 Bulgarian families (46,764 persons) from Ottoman's Thrace region.[57] Another attempt of population exchange was negotiated by the Ottoman and Greek governments in May 1914. The plan was to exchange the Orthodox Greek population of the Ottoman Empire for the Muslim population of Greece.[58] The Ottoman and Greek governments agreed on a voluntary exchange.[59] A mixed commission was established in June 1914 to do so, and it held a number of meetings. But, shortly thereafter, the Ottoman Empire entered the First World War on the side of the Central Powers, so the commission's work was suspended before the population exchange was implemented.

While this first attempt was not successful due to the war, the possibility of an exchange of the Orthodox Greek and Muslim populations came back onto the governments' agenda during the Lausanne Conference. It seems that the proposal for a separate convention to exchange minorities was made by Dr. Fridtjof Nansen, who had been appointed by the League of Nations to deal with the refugees from Asia Minor.[60] After long discussions, "the Convention and Protocol concerning the Exchange of Greek and Turkish Populations" and the annexed protocol was signed on January 30, 1923. Article 1 of the convention established the compulsory character of the exchange as well as defined the exchangeable persons.

> As from May 1, 1923, there shall take place a compulsory exchange of Turkish nationals of the Greek Orthodox religion established in Turkish territory, and of Greek nationals of the Muslim religion established in Greek territory. These persons shall not return to live in Turkey or Greece respectively without the authorization of the Turkish Government or of the Greek Government respectively.[61]

Whereas the former attempt of population exchange had been designed by a bilateral arrangement on a voluntary basis, the January 1923 Convention set the conditions for a compulsory exchange to be carried out under the auspices of the League of Nations. In effect, the population exchange was concerned with two distinct categories. According to Article 3, those who had already migrated constituted the first category. This included the Orthodox Greeks of the Ottoman Empire and the Muslims of Greece who had left their home and migrated between October 18, 1912 (beginning of the First Balkan War), and January 30, 1923 (the date the Convention was signed). In this category, as noted above, there were nearly 900,000 Greeks who had fled from Asia Minor alongside the withdrawing Greek troops. The second category consisted of the Greek Orthodox and Muslim populations who had not migrated yet. They were to be exchanged and resettled in the framework outlined in the Convention. More than 190,000 Greeks and 380,000 Muslims were exchanged in 1923–4, after the Convention was signed.[62]

National Identity and Population Exchange

It is apparently true that not only the definition of minorities in the Lausanne Treaty but also the Convention and Protocol concerning the Exchange of Greek and Turkish Populations drew on religion as a major component of national identification. Regardless of what language they spoke, which ethnicity they belonged to, or which national culture they identified with, no Muslims were categorized as national minorities, and that was a deliberate policy pursued by the founders of the Republic of Turkey. Nevertheless, there were certain limits to religion in the identification of who belonged to the core nation and who did not. The compulsory population exchange was not free from ethnoreligious concerns. As correctly observed by Koufa and Svolopoulos, even the phrase "Greek and Turkish populations" in the title of the Convention ("Convention concerning the Exchange of Greek and Turkish Populations") shows that the religious affiliation of the people to be exchanged (exchangees) was associated with their ethnic and national consciousness.[63] The terms "Muslim" and "Turk" were used interchangeably throughout the discussions that took place in the sub-commission of the exchange of populations in Lausanne.[64] The Turkish delegation proposed the term "Muslim Turks" to specify the persons who shall migrate to Turkey.[65] This term was apparently considered analogous to "Greek Orthodox" and introduced an ethnoreligious criterion.[66]

Turkey was interested in bringing the Muslims of Turkish origin to the country and this concern was made clear in a governmental decree dealing with the implementation of population exchange and adopted in July 1923.[67] Article 8 of this decree stated:

> As the Government of the Turkish Grand National Assembly aims only to save the Turks in Greece from pressure and increase the population in our country by accepting the population exchange, if it is intended to eject from Greece those who are citizens of another state based on the Lausanne Treaty, the Turkish delegation will defend in the Mixed Commission that they be sent to the state to which they racially belong, not to Turkey.[68]

In this statement the term race refers to a concept of nationality based on culture rather than to a biological understanding of the term. The Turkish government emphasized its determination to deny immigration to non-Turkish Muslim elements and this attitude was repeated in Article 16 of the same decree, according to which those immigrants associated with another state would be sent to the country to which they are racially and emotionally attached.[69]

The Albanian population of Greece formed the major group to be excluded from the population exchange. This was because of the existence of Albania as an independent state that had split from the Ottoman Empire. Albanians were more likely to develop national consciousness than Muslim peoples without a state, like Bosnians and Pomaks. This rendered Albanians more difficult to assimilate so the arrival of Albanian exchangees and immigrants was sharply criticized in the Turkish

National Assembly. In the sub-commission of population exchange it was pointed out that Albanian Muslims were sharing the same faith as Turkish Muslims, but they were not of the same nationality.⁷⁰ Discussions concerning the status of Albanians continued during the implementation of the population exchange and in the Mixed Commission charged with regulating this process. At the center of such disputes were Çams, the Albanian-speaking Muslims of Chamuria (or Çamlık in Turkish), a region located at the coast of Epirus. According to Dimitris Michalopoulos, this was the only area of Epirus where Muslims resided.⁷¹ Michalopoulos estimates that they numbered around 20,000 in 1923.⁷² The forced migration of these people in the framework of population exchange became a diplomatic matter between Greece and Albania; it was discussed in the League of Nations in December 1923 and then forwarded to the Mixed Commission. In the end, they were exempted from the population exchange.⁷³ The Turkish government's position in this controversy was clear from the outset. A governmental decree signed by Mustafa Kemal in September 1924 states clearly that the Albanian Muslims of Çamlık could not be exchanged and thus they would not be accepted in Turkey.⁷⁴ In January 1927, Greece once again approached Turkey concerning the migration of the Albanians of Çamlık, but the Turkish government refused to change its position.⁷⁵

The population exchange centered around the nationality not the religious affiliation of the exchangees. To be sure, religion was an important element of national identification on both the Greek and Turkish sides, but it was not a sufficient criterion to determine an individual's national attachment. Nevertheless, there was a considerable number of Muslim exchangees who spoke Greek or Albanian as a mother tongue. The Turkish government treated incoming Muslims differently based on their nationality. According to Article 17 of the aforementioned governmental decree, Turkish exchangees were free to choose wherein they would settle as long as they could afford the required costs without any demand from the government. Article 18, however, specified that non-Turkish (*gayr-ı Türk*) immigrants were supposed to settle in the regions assigned by the government; otherwise, they would be deported.⁷⁶ Article 29 clarifies the conditions based on which non-Turk immigrants would be settled:

> Taking into account that the most difficult obstacle to the civil and social improvement is the dissimilarity in the language and customs, the proportion of the immigrants, regardless of race or nationality, whose language and customs belong to another race shall never be over 20 percent in any Turkish [Türk] town and village.⁷⁷

The national government in Ankara was willing to carry on with the assimilationist policies of the Second Constitutional Period. The great proportion of Armenian and Greek Orthodox communities had mostly been eliminated through the demographic measures of deportation, forced migration, and population exchange before the Republic was proclaimed in October 1923. Hence, thereafter, Turkey's nation-building policies focused more explicitly on the assimilation of Muslims.

Concluding Remarks

This chapter has dealt with the subject of nationalism and ethnoreligious minorities during the transition of the Ottoman Empire to the Republic of Turkey. More specifically, the relationship between the implementation of nation-building policies and the determination of national minorities in this process has been examined. There was no official category of national minority recognized by the Young Turks. However, the distinction between Muslims and non-Muslims had been consolidated as the main dividing line in Ottoman society, setting apart the Empire's dominant identity from the rest of the population since the Hamidian Period. This dichotomy also marked the Young Turks' nationality policies in the Second Constitutional Period, aside from a short interlude after the Constitutional Revolution, during which they seemed committed to the ideal of unity of all Ottoman subjects regardless of their nationality or faith. Especially during the First World War, the Young Turks embarked on the Turkification, that is, ethnoreligious homogenization of Anatolia by eliminating the Armenian and Greek communities. However, being of a Muslim background was a necessary, albeit not sufficient, condition to be regarded as part of the Turkish nation, the Empire's dominant nationality. The CUP government intended to assimilate non-Turkish Muslim subjects and immigrants while dissimilating the Christian communities, to use Rogers Brubaker's terminology. Considering the devastating results of the Armenian and Greek deportations, it is clear that there was a drastic difference between the human costs of these two demographic engineering strategies. Nevertheless, assimilation and dissimilation were two different yet related aspects of the same nation-building project carried out in an imperial context. This nationalist project also affected the way in which the Turkish national movement tackled the question of national minorities. At the Lausanne Conference, the Turkish mission sought to recognize only the non-Muslim communities as national minorities; in their eyes it was not acceptable to categorize Muslim peoples this way, because they could potentially be assimilated into Turkishness. But this attitude did not prevent them from objecting to the immigration of Muslim Albanians to Turkey or undertaking assimilative measures while settling non-Turk immigrants.

The efforts of the national government to homogenize the population of Turkey continued after the promulgation of the Republic in October 1923. During the interwar period, the founders of the Republic continued to implement assimilationist and dissimilationist measures drawing on the model of the Young Turks' nation-building policies. The general attitude toward non-Muslim minorities remained dissimilationist throughout this period and beyond, although the non-Muslim population, and through extension their proportion within the population, had significantly declined.[78] The 1924 Constitution builds on a civic and territorial notion of identity, but it also shows the limits of citizenship in defining what Turkishness stands for. Article 88 of the 1924 Constitution states that "the people of Turkey regardless of their religion and race are, in terms of citizenship, to be Turkish."[79] This definition shows that Turkish citizenship as a civic-territorial category, and the Turkish nation, as an entity defined in ethnoreligious terms, did not coincide in the Republic's official discourse and identity policies.[80] Christian or Jewish subjects were categorized as people of Turkish nationality, but only "in terms of citizenship." Non-Muslims were not considered part of the Turkish nation, which was identified as an ethnoreligious category and seen as the core nation on which the Republic rested. This division between the citizens of Muslim and non-Muslim background was continuously highlighted. Members of Christian and Jewish communities were exposed to xenophobic "Citizen Speak Turkish!" campaigns; they were discriminated in job markets, and unable to apply for specific administrative positions and in the service sector.[81] Discrimination evolved into persecution from time to time, with the antisemitic pogroms that broke out in 1934.[82] In 1942, due to the Wealth Tax, many non-Muslims, especially the members of the Jewish community, were sent to Aşkale, where they were forced to work in labor camps.[83] Persecution of the non-Muslim minorities culminated in 1955 with the September 6–7 pogroms, which left Istanbul an essentially Turkish city as most non-Muslims were driven out.[84]

However, religion was not the only component of Turkish national identity. It became clear from the outset that the Republic of Turkey was a nation-state that relied on the hegemony of Turks more than the fraternity of Muslims. Hence, Turkification involved the assimilation non-Turkish Muslims as well, who were not recognized as minorities and, therefore, were not protected by the League of Nations. The Kurdish leaders who had supported the National Struggle were disappointed with the national and secular character of the republican regime, one of whose first actions was to abolish the Caliphate, the symbol of Muslim fraternity. Turkish hegemony in the new regime was decisively challenged for the first time by the Seyh Sait rebellion that erupted in February 1925 and that spread to much of Turkey's Kurdish populated southeast.[85] Especially after this rebellion, the government carried out systematic demographic polices of migration, deportation, and resettlement as the main instruments of nation-building.[86] To that end, the executive planned to resettle the rebellious Kurds elsewhere in the interior of Anatolia in a scattered way, so that they could be assimilated. At the same time, Turkey accepted and even promoted Muslim immigration from the Balkans and the Caucasus. According to the legislation adopted in the 1920s and 1930s, non-Turkish Muslim immigrants were to be settled in accordance with the government's assimilative plans.[87] Domestic laws, rather than international agreements, notably the laws on settlement of 1926 and 1934 were the main legal instruments for these nationalist demographic policies.[88] Not only did these laws enable government authorities to cope with the immigrant influx of the 1920s and 1930s, but they also contained specific provisions that granted the Ministry of the Interior sweeping powers to manage the settlement and relocation of the population. The Settlement Law of 1934 clearly expresses the assimilative mentality of the Republic's demographic policies.[89] According to Şükrü Kaya, the Minister of the Interior, this law was designed to make Turkey a country "speaking one language, thinking in the same way, and sharing the same sentiment."[90]

Notes

1 See, for example, Gökhan Çetinsaya, "Rethinking Nationalism and Islam: Some Preliminary Notes on the Roots of 'Turkish-Islamic' Synthesis in Modern Turkish Political Thought," *The Muslim World* 89, no. 3–4 (1999): 350–76.

2   Kemal Karpat, *The Politicization of Islam: Reconstructing Identity, State, Faith, and Community in the Late Ottoman State* (Oxford and New York: Oxford University Press, 2001).
3   Barış Ünlü, *Türklük Sözleşmesi. Oluşumu, İşleyişi ve Krizi* (Ankara: Dipnot Yayınları, 2018), 82–158.
4   Eric J. Zürcher, *The Young Turk Legacy and Nation-building. From the Ottoman Empire to Atatürk's Turkey* (London and New York: I.B. Tauris), 230–1. For the implications of Muslim nationalism for the Turkish resistance movement in the Armistice Period, see also Eric J. Zürcher, "Contextualizing the Ideology of the Turkish National Resistance Movement," *Middle Eastern Studies*, no. 57 (2021): 265–78.
5   See for example Y. Doğan Çetinkaya, *The Young Turks and the Boycott Movement: Nationalism, Protest and the Working Classes in the Formation of Modern Turkey* (London and New York: I.B. Tauris, 2014). Çetinkaya prefers the term Muslim/Turkish nationalism to Turkish nationalism. Based on his study of boycott movements, he argues that Islam and Muslim identity formed the main frame of reference for the nationalist movement. For Çetinkaya, "Islam was a distinct marker of communal identity" in the Second Constitutional Period.
6   See, for example, Nikki R. Keddie, "Pan-Islamism as Proto-Nationalism," *The Journal of Modern History*, no. 41 (1969): 17–28. See also Selim Deringil, "The Invention of Tradition in the Ottoman Empire 1808–1908," *Comparative Studies in Society and History*, no. 35 (1993): 3–29; *The Well-protected Domains: Ideology and the Legitimation of Power in the Ottoman Empire 1876–1909* (London and New York: I.B. Tauris, 1998); "'They Live in a State of Nomadism and Savagery': The Late Ottoman Empire and the Post-Colonial Debate," *Comparative Studies in Society and History*, no. 45 (2003): 311–42.
7   One of the pioneering works dealing with the Young Turks' Islamist policies belongs to Hasan Kayalı, *Arabs and Young Turks: Ottomanism, Arabism, and Islamism in the Ottoman Empire, 1908–1918* (Berkeley: University of California Press, 1997).
8   Zürcher, *The Young Turk Legacy*, 222–3.
9   For the relationship between empire and nation in the context of Habsburg Central Europe, see Pieter Judson in this volume. This relationship is also explored by Alvin Jackson in this volume with reference to the United Kingdom, which is compared with the case of Austria-Hungary.
10 For a concise discussion on the formation of the Ottoman Empire, see Jane Burbank and Frederick Cooper, *Empires in World History. Power and the Politics of Difference* (Princeton and Oxford: Princeton University Press, 2010), 128–48.
11 Karen Barkey and George Gavrillis, "The Ottoman Millet System: Non-Territorial Autonomy and Its Contemporary Legacy," *Ethnopolitics*, no. 15-1 (2016): 26. On the millet system, see also Kemal Karpat, "Millets and Nationality: The Roots of the Incongruity of Nation and State in the Post-Ottoman Era," in *Christians and Jews in the Ottoman Empire Volume 1: The Central Lands*, ed. Benjamin Braude and Bernard Lewis (New York and London: Holmes & Meier Publishers, 1982), 141–69. Benjamin Braude argues that there was no institutionalized millet system in the Ottoman Empire until the nineteenth century. Benjamin Braude, "Foundation Myths of the Millet System," in ibid., 69–88. Karen Barkey takes issue with this argument of Bruade in her book *Empire of Difference. The Ottomans in Comparative Perspective* (Cambridge: Cambridge University Press, 2008), 115–16.
12 This policy is conceptualized as "Ottomanness Contract" by Ünlü, *Türklük Sözleşmesi*, 83–92.

13 Ariel Salzmann, "Citizens in Search of a State: The Limits of Political Participation in the Late Ottoman Empire, 1808–1914," in *Extending Citizenship, Reconfiguring States*, ed. Michael Hanagan and Charles Tilly (Maryland: Rowman and Littlefield Publishers, 1999), 39–45.
14 Karpat, *The Politicization of Islam*, 320–7.
15 Ahmet Yıldız, *Ne Mutlu Türküm Diyebilene: Türk Ulusal Kimliğinin Etno-Seküler Sınırları (1919-1938)* (Istanbul: İletişim Yayınları, 2001), 73–6; Feroz Ahmad, "Unionist Relations with the Greek, Armenian and Jewish Communities," in *Christians and Jews*, ed. Braude and Lewis, 401.
16 For a comprehensive study of Turkish nationalist ideas and journals in the Second Constitutional Period, see Masami Arai, *Jön Türk Dönemi Türk Milliyetçiliği* (Istanbul: İletişim Yayınları, 2003).
17 Şükrü Hanioğlu, *Preparation for a Revolution: The Young Turks, 1902-1908* (Oxford: Oxford University Press, 2001), 295–302.
18 Erol Ülker, "Contextualizing Turkification: Nation-building in the Late Ottoman Empire," *Nations and Nationalism*, no. 11–14 (2005): 617–21.
19 Arai, *Jön Türk Dönemi*, 92–103, 145–7.
20 François Georgeon, *Türk Milliyetçiliği'nin Kökenleri. Yusuf Akçura (1876-1935)* (Istanbul: Tarih Vakfı Yurt Yayınları, 1999), 51–113.
21 Ülker, "Contextualizing Turkification," 621–2.
22 Previously I have discussed the concept of Turkification and its imperial context in Ibid., 621–30. In this chapter I refer to this earlier article in my conceptualization of Turkification.
23 Çetinkaya, *The Young Turks and the Boycott Movement*, 89–159.
24 For a study of Ziya Gökalp and his ideas, see Taha Parla, *The Social and Political Thought of Ziya Gökalp, 1876-1924* (Leiden: E. J. Brill, 1985).
25 Ziya Gökalp, "Nation and Fatherland," in *Ziya Gökalp, Turkish Nationalism and Western Civilization Selected Essays of Ziya Gökalp*, ed. Niyazi Berkes (London: George Allen and Unwin Ltd., 1959), 78.
26 Ziya Gökalp, "The Ideal of Nationalism," in ibid., 80–1.
27 Ibid., 80.
28 Rogers Brubaker, *Nationalism Reframed: Nationhood and the National Question in the New Europe* (Cambridge: Cambridge University Press, 1996), 88.
29 Ibid., 84–6.
30 Ibid., 88. Harris Mylonas proposes a tripartite classification about nation-building policies: assimilation, accommodation, and exclusion. He examines the implementation of these policies in the Balkan states, including Turkey, after the First World War. Harris Mylonas, *The Politics of Nation-building. Making Co-Nationals, Refugees, and Minorities* (Cambridge: Cambridge University Press, 2012).
31 For the literature on the Armenian genocide, see, for example, Taner Akçam, *The Young Turks' Crime against Humanity. The Armenian Genocide and Ethnic Cleansing in the Ottoman Empire* (Princeton and Oxford: Oxford University Press, 2012); Donald Bloxham, *The Great Game of Genocide. Imperialism, Nationalism, and the Destruction of the Ottoman Armenians* (Oxford: Oxford University Press, 2005). For the genocidal processes carried out in particular localities, see Uğur Ümit Güngör, *The Making of Modern Turkey. Nation and State in Eastern Anatolia, 1913-1950* (Oxford: Oxford University Press, 2012), 55–106; Ümit Kurt, *The Armenians of Aintab. The Economics of Genocide in an Ottoman Province* (Cambridge and London: Harvard University Press, 2021).

32 Ellinor Morack shows that the Young Turks embarked on the forced migration of the Orthodox Greek population in western Anatolia starting in 1913. After an attempt of population exchange in 1914, to which I refer below, the deportations of the Ottoman Greeks continued in 1915–16. Ellinor Morack, *The Dowry of the State? The Politics of Abandoned Property and the Population Exchange in Turkey, 1921–1945* (Bamberg: The University of Bamberg Press, 2017), 74–83. For a more specific study focusing on the western Anatolian town of Foçateyn, located on the Aegean coast of today's İzmir, and its demographic and social transformation in the context of transition from empire to nation-state, see Emre Erol, *The Ottoman Crisis in Western Anatolia. Turkey's Belle Époque and the Transition to a Modern Nation State* (London and New York: I.B. Tauris, 2016).

33 For a seminal study on the CUP's demographic policies of settlement and migration intended to assimilate Muslim communities see Fuat Dündar, *İttihat ve Terakki'nin Müslümanları İskân Politikası (1913-1918)* (Istanbul: İletişim Yayınları, 2001), 39–173. On this topic see also Ülker, *Contextualizing Turkification*, 626–30.

34 Dündar, *İttihat ve Terakki'nin Müslümanları İskân Politikası*, 141.

35 Baskın Oran indicates that the term minority (*azınlık*) did not exist in the Ottoman period. The term *ekalliyet* (which can be translated as minority) came to be referred to non-Muslims under the CUP rule. The National Pact, accepted by the patriotic members of the Ottoman Parliament in 1920, employed the expression *ekalliyetler hukuku* for the "rights of minorities." Baskın Oran, *Etnik ve Dinsel Azınlıklar. Tarih, Teori, Hukuk, Türkiye. Gayrimüslimler, Kürt Hakları, Alevi Hakları, OHAL Rejimi* (Istanbul: Literatür Yayınları, 2018), 171.

36 Eric Jan Zürcher, *The Unionist Factor, The Role of the Committee of Union and Progress in the Turkish National Movement, 1908–1926* (Leiden: E. J. Brill, 1984), 68–105.

37 Yıldız, *Ne Mutlu Türküm Diyebilene*, 87–100.

38 Antonio Cassese, *Self Determination of Peoples: A Legal Appraisal* (Cambridge: Cambridge University Press, 1996), 19–22.

39 Inis L. Claude, Jr., *National Minorities: An International Problem* (Cambridge: Harvard University Press, 1955), 12.

40 Cassese, *Self Determination of Peoples*, 25.

41 Claude, *National Minorities*, 11.

42 It is estimated that 60 million Europeans lived as minority before the First World War. This number fell to 20–25 million after the war, which is still serious enough. Michael R. Marrus, *The Unwanted: European Refugees from the First World War through the Cold War* (Philadelphia: Temple University Press, 2002), 69–70.

43 Claude, *National Minorities*, 16.

44 Treaty of Peace between the Allied and Associated Powers and Turkey Signed at Sèvres, August 10, 1920, 33, https://archive.org/stream/TS00113/TS0011_djvu.txt (accessed June 27, 2022).

45 Onur Yıldırım, *Diplomacy and Displacement. Reconsidering the Turco-Greek Exchange of Populations, 1922–1934* (New York and London: Routledge, 2006), 88–92. See also Volker Prott's chapter in this volume.

46 Erol Ülker, "Turkish National Movement, Mass Mobilization, and Demographic Change in Istanbul, 1922–1923," in *Contemporary Turkey at a Glance II. Turkey Transformed? Power, History, Culture*, ed. Meltem Ersoy and Esra Özyürek (Wiesbaden: Springer VS, 2017), 177–92.

47 There is a growing literature on the relationship between Turkey's nation-building policies in the interwar period and the League of Nations. This literature focuses on

the League's minority protection regime, its role in the determination of minorities in Turkey, and the exchange of minority populations between Turkey and Greece. In addition to Yıldırım, *Diplomacy and Displacement,* see, for example, Umut Özsu, "Fabricating Fidelity: Nation-Building, International Law, and the Greek-Turkish Population Exchange," *Leiden Journal of International Law,* no. 24 (2011): 823–47; Umut Özsu, *Formalizing Displacement. International Law and Population Transfers* (Oxford: Oxford University Press, 2015); Lerna Ekmekçioğlu, "Republic of Paradox: The League of Nations Minority Protection Regime and the new Turkey's Step-Citizens," *International Journal of Middle East Studies,* no. 46 (2014): 657–79; Caroline Liebisch-Gümüş, "Embedded Turkification: Nation-building and Violence within the Framework of the League of Nations 1919–1937," *International Journal of Middle East Studies,* no. 52 (2020): 229–44.

48   Claude, *National Minorities,* 16.
49   Discussions and negotiations about the question of minorities in Turkey took place in the Commission of Territorial and Military Problems and the Subcomission of Minorities in the Lausanne Conference. For the Minutes of the meeting of these commissions, see Seha L. Meray, trans., *Lozan Barış Konferansı: Tutanaklar, Belgeler. Takım I, Cilt 1, Kitap 1* (Ankara: Ankara Üniversitesi Basımevi, 1969); *Lozan Barış Konferansı: Tutanaklar, Belgeler. Takım I, Cilt 1, Kitap 2* (Ankara: Ankara Üniversitesi Basımevi, 1970). The Turkish position regarding minorities becomes clear in the speeches and statements by the Turkish delegates İsmet İnönü and Rıza Nur in those meetings.
50   For the definition and rights of national minorities in the context the Lausanne Treaty in Turkey, see Oran, *Etnik ve Dinsel Azınlıklar,* 231–50.
51   For the Part 1—Political Clauses of the Lausanne Treaty, which includes forty-five articles, see http://www.hri.org/docs/lausanne/part1.html and https://www.mfa.gov.tr/lausanne-peace-treaty-part-i_-political-clauses.en.mfa (accessed June 27, 2022).
52   This term reflects the terminology used in the agreement and the Turkish term for it is "*Mübadele.*"
53   For the text of the convention and the annexed protocol, see İsmail Soysal, *Türkiye'nin Siyasal Andlaşmaları: Tarihleri ve Açıklamaları ile Birlikte* (Ankara: Türk Tarih Kurumu Basımevi: 1989), 177–83.
54   Stephen P. Ladas, *The Exchange of Minorities: Bulgaria, Greece and Turkey* (New York: The Macmillan Company, 1932), 19.
55   Harry J. Psomiades, *The Eastern Question: The Last Phase—A Study in Greek-Turkish Diplomacy* (Thessaloniki: Institute for Balkan Studies, 1968), 60.
56   Y. G. Mourelos, "The 1914 Persecutions and the First Attempt at an Exchange of Minorities between Greece and Turkey," *Balkan Studies* 26, no. 2 (1985): 391.
57   Ladas, *The Exchange of Minorities,* 20.
58   Mourelos, *The 1914 Persecutions,* 393–4.
59   Ladas, *The Exchange of Minorities,* 21–2.
60   Yıldırım, *Diplomacy and Displacement,* 40.
61   Quoted from Kallipoli K. Koufa and Constantinos Svolopoulos, "The Compulsory Exchange of Populations between Greece and Turkey: The Settlement of Minority Questions at the Conference of Lausanne, 1923, and Its Impact on Greek-Turkish Relations," in *Comparative Studies on Governments and non-Governments Ethnic Groups in Europe, 1850–1940: Ethnic Groups in International Relations,* ed. P. Smith, K. Koufa, and A. Suppan (Dartmouth: European Science Foundation, New York University Press, 1991), 288.

62 Yıldırım, *Diplomacy and Displacement*, 90–1; Cevat Geray, *Türkiye'den ve Türkiye'ye Göçler ve Göçmenlerin İskanı* (Ankara: Siyasal Bilgiler Fakültesi-Maliye Enstitüsü, 1962), 11.
63 Koufa and Svolopoulos, *The Compulsory Exchange of Populations*, 288–9. I used the term "exchangee" in the sense of "*mübadil*."
64 For example, the sub-commission's report presented to the Committee of Territorial and Military Problems identified the subject of the population exchange as "Greek and Turkish minorities." Meray, *Lozan Barış Konferansı: Tutanaklar, Belgeler. Takım I, Cilt 1, Kitap 1*,321, 333, 335.
65 Meray, *Lozan Barış Konferansı: Tutanaklar, Belgeler. Takım I, Cilt 1, Kitap 2*, 368.
66 Ladas. *The Balkan Exchange of Minorities*, 380.
67 "30 Kanunisani 1923 Tarihinde Lozanda Yunan Murahhaslariyla Yapılan Mukavele Mucibince Tanzim Olunan Talimatnamenin Mer'iyete Vaz'ı Hakkında Kararname," no: 2600, 17/7/1339–17/7/1923, *Düstur*, Tertip: 4, Cilt: 3, 135–42.
68 Ibid., 136–7.
69 Ibid., 139.
70 Meray, *Lozan Barış Konferansı: Tutanaklar, Belgeler. Takım I, Cilt 1, Kitap 2*, 344.
71 Dimitris Michalopoulos, "The Muslims of Chamuria and the Exchange of Populations between Greece and Turkey," *Balkan Studies* 27, no. 2 (1986): 304.
72 Ibid.
73 Ibid., 305–8.
74 *Devlet Arşivleri Başkanlığı Cumhuriyet Arşivi* (BCA, Directorate of State Archives / The Republic Archive), Fon No: 30.18.1.1, Yer No: 8.39.3, 14/09/1924.
75 Michalopoulos, "The Muslims of Chamuria," 310.
76 "30 Kanunisani 1923 Tarihinde Lozanda Yunan Murahhaslariyla Yapılan Mukavele Mucibince Tanzim Olunan Talimatnamenin Mer'iyete Vaz'ı Hakkında Kararname," no: 2600, 17/7/1339–17/7/1923, *Düstur*, Tertip: 4, Cilt: 3, 138.
77 Ibid., 140.
78 Non-Muslims formed close to 20 percent of the population within the present-day borders of Turkey before the First World War. This rate declined to around 2.5 percent according to the population census of 1927. Ayhan Aktar, "Homogenizing the Nation, Turkifying the Economy: Turkish Experience of Populations Exchange Reconsidered," in *An Appraisal of the 1923 Compulsory Exchange between Greece and Turkey*, ed. Renee Hirschon (Oxford: Berghahn Books, 2003), 81; Zafer Toprak, "The Demographic Consequences of Lausanne Treaty in Turkey" paper presented at the conference on *The Exchange of Populations, The Refugee Studies Program* (Oxford: Quinn Elizabeth House, September, 1998), 3. For more statistics about the demographic structure of Turkey derived from the population censuses, see Fuat Dündar, *Türkiye Nüfus Sayımlarında Azınlıklar* (İstanbul: Doz Yayınları, 1999).
79 Yıldız, *Ne Mutlu Türküm Diyebilene*, 139–41; Mesut Yeğen, "Yurttaşlık ve Türklük," *Toplum Bilim* 93 (2002): 207–15.
80 At this point, we should remember Rogers Brubaker's distinction between citizenship and nationality, with the former being formal and abstract and the latter being informal and substantial. It is, thus, possible to hold legal citizenship while being considered of different nationality for ethnoreligious reasons. Rogers Brubaker, *Citizenship and Nationhood in France and Germany* (Cambridge: Harvard University Press, 1992), 21–34.

81 Ayhan Aktar, *Varlık Vergisi ve Türkleştirme Politikaları* (İstanbul: İletişim Yayınlar, 2001), 101–34. On the Turkification of the economy, see also Murat Koraltürk, *Erken Cumhuriyet Döneminde Ekonominin Türkleştirilmesi* (İstanbul: İletişim Yayınları, 2011).
82 About the Thrace affair, see Ayhan Aktar, *Varlık Vergisi ve Türkleştirme Politikaları*, 71–99; Erol Ülker, "Assimilation, Security and Geographical Nationalization in Interwar Turkey: The Settlement Law of 1934," *European Journal of Turkish Studies*, Thematic Issue: Demographic Engineering—Part I, no. 7 (2008), 9–12.
83 Aktar, *Varlık Vergisi ve Türkleştirme Politikaları*, 135–244.
84 Concerning the September 6–7 affairs, see Dilek Güven, *Cumhuriyet Dönemi Azınlık Politikaları ve Stratejileri Bağlamında 6-7 Eylül Olayları* (İstanbul: İletişim Yayınları, 2021); Rıfat N. Bali, *6–7 Eylül 1955 Olayları. Tanıklar-Hatıralar* (İstanbul: Libra Kitapçılık ve Yayıncılık, 2012).
85 For a concise and informative discussion on the development of Kurdish nationalism, the Şeyh Sait rebellion, and developments leading to this movement, see Hamit Bozarslan, "Türkiye'de Kürt Milliyetçiliği: Zımnî Sözleşmeden Ayaklanmaya (1919-1925)," in *İmparatorluktan Cumhuriyete Türkiye'de Etnik Çatışma*, ed. Eric Jan Zürcher (Istanbul: İletişim Yayınları, 2017), 89–121.
86 A pioneering work analyzing the relationship between Turkey's nation-building and migration-settlement policies belongs to Kemal Kirişçi, "Disaggregating Turkish Citizenship and Immigration Practices," *Middle Eastern Studies* 36, no. 3 (2000). See also Soner Çağaptay, "Kemalist Dönem'de Göç ve İskan Politikaları: Türk Kimliği Üzerine Bir Çalışma," *Toplum-Bilim*, no. 93 (2002): 218–41.
87 For a study of how the government employed migration and settlement policies for the assimilation of the non-Turkish Muslim communities, see Erol Ülker, "Assimilation of the Muslim communities in the first decade of the Turkish Republic (1923–1934)," *European Journal of Turkish Studies* (2007), https://doi.org/10.4000/ejts.822 (accessed June 27, 2022).
88 "İskan Kanunu," no: 885, 31/06/1926, *Düstur,* Tertip: 3, Cilt: 7, 1441–3; "İskan Kanunu," no: 2510, 14/06/1934, *Düstur*, Tertip: 3, Cilt: 15, 1156–75.
89 For a discussion on the transnational context of the Settlement Law of 1934, see Ramazan Hakkı Öztan, "Settlement Law of 1934: Turkish Nationalism in the Age of Revisionism," *Journal of Migration History*, no. 6 (2020): 82–103.
90 *Türkiye Büyük Millet Meclisi Zabıt Ceridesi* (TBMM, Minutes of the Grand National Assembly of Turkey), Devre: IV, Cilt: 23, İçtima: 3, 14/06/1934, 141.

Part Two

The Minority Question across Europe: Comparing Policies, Regimes, and Resistance

5

Assessing the "Paris System": Self-determination and Ethnic Violence in Alsace-Lorraine and Asia Minor, 1919–23

Volker Prott

The Alsatian capital Strasbourg is a long way from Smyrna (today's Izmir), the main seaport of western Asia Minor (Anatolia). Yet in the wake of the First World War, both cities were gripped by the same, powerful new historical force that tied national self-determination and minority rights to interstate conflict and ethnic violence. Across Europe and in several parts of Europe's colonial sphere, the quest for sovereignty and self-determination wound up with looting, deportations, massacres, and mass expulsions of minorities.[1] Robert Gerwarth, John Horne, and others have placed the violence following the armistice of November 1918 in the context of a "Greater War" that stretched from 1913 to 1923.[2] If seen from this perspective, the rhetoric of national self-determination had both a stabilizing and a destabilizing effect. On the one hand, it mobilized Allied forces and populations to bring the fighting to a successful end. But on the other, it infused international politics and nationalist movements with a powerful new idea with which to challenge the territorial status quo beyond the end of the war. As the cases of Alsace-Lorraine and Asia Minor indicate, the resulting dynamics of violence and political strife between 1918 and 1923 cut across simple divisions of a civic, politically unified, and peaceful "West" versus an ethnically fragmented and violent "East."[3]

Despite the growing number of studies on postwar violence and the "Greater War," we still lack a systematic comparative framework to assess and explain why the "Paris system" caused such regionally diverse dynamics.[4] Most of the above-cited studies focus on a single case, loosely placed in a wider postwar setting. While there are a few insightful works juxtaposing two regions affected by conflicts involving minorities, these are predominantly concerned with the cases at hand and only in passing, if at all, allude to more general factors, patterns, or mechanisms driving these conflicts.[5] Recent French and German accounts of the Paris Peace Conference of 1919 and its repercussions highlight the complexity, contradictions, and multiple limitations of the emerging international order; yet they offer little by way of analytical guidance and systematic comparison of different regional settings.[6] More recently, Roberta Pergher and Marcus Payk have provided an excellent and concise survey of territorial and domestic ethnic conflicts across several European and colonial settings in the aftermath of the Paris Peace Conference.[7] Yet they too touch upon the contours and inner workings of the "Paris system" only briefly and in general terms, defining the postwar order rather vaguely as "an informal, dynamic combination of various related promises, practices, and proclamations" that "provided a new language and understanding of nationalism and internationalism, sovereignty and territoriality, ethnicity and popular participation."[8]

A more promising approach is offered by the work of several international historians who have made important inroads toward a more systematic study of both the regional diversity and overall functioning of the Paris system. Thus, Carole Fink and Mark Mazower have demonstrated how the Great Powers used minority treaties as instruments to maintain their supremacy within the emerging international system of formally equal nation-states.[9] Erez Manela's work reveals the unintended consequences of self-determination as a transnational political idea and practice, revealing a broader pattern of frustrated expectations causing rebellions in four very different colonial settings.[10] In a much-cited article, Eric Weitz offered the first synthesis of this new strand of research on the Paris peace settlements, arguing that the entanglement—not the opposition, as Woodrow Wilson and the Allies claimed—of self-determination and minority rights with ethnic violence and deportations was the fundament of the "Paris system."[11] Weitz used the term "population politics" to capture the common thrust of ethnic violence and self-determination, which for him represented "two sides of the same coin."[12] Meanwhile, other scholars have explored the regional diversity of the "Paris system" and the crucial role of varying regional and local conditions as well as the transformative impact Allied decisions and the rhetoric of self-determination had on these regions.[13]

This chapter builds on these recent scholarly advances and takes further steps toward a systematic comparative examination of the peace order that followed the First World War. Comparing two different regions affected by the Paris peace settlements, Alsace-Lorraine and Asia Minor, it examines the respective local conjunctures of self-determination and ethnic violence. The central aim of the chapter is to determine which international, national, and local factors fueled the two conflicts, which more general mechanisms were at play, and how we can explain the diverging dynamics of violence in the two cases.

While Alsace-Lorraine and Asia Minor are not the only or even the most prominent examples of peacemaking and ethnic conflict after the First World War, they effectively reveal the crucial facets of the Paris system. The comparison of these two postwar conflicts, which are highly diverse in their outcomes and intensity but surprisingly similar in the mechanisms that drove them, allows us to examine how the new international order operated in different regional settings and where and why it failed. Both regions were marked by competing national claims, disputes about self-determination, and, following territorial changes after the war, they both saw ethnic violence and forced removal on a comparatively large scale. In Alsace-Lorraine, French authorities carried out a "triage" of the local population and expelled a significant proportion of the remaining German population, a policy that in its initial fervor differed markedly from other postwar disputes in Western Europe such as

Eupen-Malmedy, Schleswig, or South Tyrol.[14] Asia Minor, in turn, plunged into a full-blown war accompanied by large-scale deportations and mass killings of civilians. In contrast to Alsace-Lorraine, where the new border prevailed throughout the interwar period, the conflict in Asia Minor ended in a major caesura for the Paris system: when the Allies and the rulers of the new state of Turkey signed the Treaty of Lausanne in July 1923, they effectively declared defunct the earlier Treaty of Sèvres that had been concluded with the Ottoman Empire in August 1920. It was the first reversal of the Paris peace treaties caused by violent revisionism.

The comparison of Alsace-Lorraine and Asia Minor also helps us bridge the divide between "Western" and "Eastern" European regions, which is one of the central aims of this volume. Comparing cases from different parts of the continent, this chapter seeks to overcome older notions of a "civilized" West and a "violent" East. Instead, examining the two cases at multiple levels, ranging from the local and national to the international, the chapter explores regional variations of the Paris system that frequently cut across a simple East-West dichotomy while at other times reaffirming wider regional differences in often surprising ways.

In view of the striking similarities between Alsace-Lorraine and Asia Minor, the chapter argues that the "Paris system" was indeed a common ideological and political framework that generated a transnational set of concepts, incentives, and mechanisms that operated across diverse regional settings. Yet the chapter also finds that the same mechanisms and incentives functioned in highly diverse ways depending on different international, national, and local circumstances. The incentive to use ethnic violence to legitimize and strengthen territorial control, for instance, was nearly ubiquitous in disputed border zones in postwar Europe. Upon closer inspection, however, we find that cases ranged from comparatively peaceful settlements such as Eupen-Malmedy or Schleswig right up to civil war-like situations as in Upper Silesia and the genocidal violence that shattered Asia Minor.

To disentangle and explain this regional divergence, the chapter identifies five key factors: (1) the (political, geographic, and economic) adequacy of territorial decisions with regard to local conditions; (2) the strength of state actors involved in the dispute; (3) the degree of international military, political, and economic commitment; (4) the nature and strength of local political identities; and (5) pre-existing traditions of ethnic violence and conflict resolution. Taken together, the five factors reflect the multi-level dynamic of the Paris system: two concern the broader international dimension (1 and 3), one deals with the specific national context (2), and two address the local context of the conflict (4 and 5). Further research would be needed to examine whether and to what extent the factors used here are applicable to other settings, how they operated there, and whether there are other mechanisms or categories that have greater explanatory power across a broader range of cases.

The two main sections of the chapter examine the two case studies, Asia Minor and Alsace-Lorraine, along the lines of the five factors mentioned above and place them in the wider context of the Paris system. The chapter concludes with a few reflections on the nature of the Paris system as an international order and perspectives for future research.

The Greek-Turkish Conflict, 1919–22

The Greek-Turkish war and the violence it generated must be understood in the context of violent nationalist policies in South-Eastern Europe and the late Ottoman Empire that predate the First World War.[15] The Young Turks, who assumed power in the Ottoman Empire in 1908, saw population exchanges and the promotion of a Turkish identity as a means to accelerate modernization and strengthen internal coherence in view of domestic weakness and external military threat.[16] The Balkan Wars of 1912–13 provided an indication of the devastation that ideas of national homogeneity or ethnic "unmixing," in Lord Curzon's infamous wording, could bring to villages and civilians across the warring states.[17] On the eve of the First World War, deportations of Christian minorities and negotiations for a first Greek-Turkish population exchange were well under way.[18]

The outbreak of the First World War raised the stakes and at the same time created a fundamentally different, open-ended situation. The decision of the Greek government under Prime Minister Eleftherios Venizelos to join the Entente in October 1916 suddenly made a national myth, the "Great Idea" of a resurrected Greek Empire in the Aegean, a diplomatic possibility.[19] In view of the crumbling Ottoman Empire, it seemed that Greece could, as a loyal ally of the alliance of liberal and democratic states, resume control of Constantinople and bring Western "civilization" to the alleged "backward" lands of the Ottoman rulers. Venizelos was particularly apt at cloaking Greek territorial aims in Asia Minor in the parlance of national self-determination. In a pamphlet on Greek territorial claims, hastily written up in Paris in January 1919 after numerous meetings with British, French, and American experts, Venizelos based Greek claims on population statistics and ethnicity, political will, and history, but also alluded to the allegedly superior degree of civilization of the Greek Orthodox inhabitants.[20]

Such language fell on fertile ground. It not only aligned with the Allies' geostrategic vision for a European-dominated Asia Minor, but it also resonated with Romantic notions of the ancient "Hellenic civilization" shared by many British, American, and French experts, diplomats, and policymakers.[21] Thanks to the existence of a sizeable minority of Greek Orthodox inhabitants in the city of Smyrna and along the Western coastline of Asia Minor, Greek claims also appeared to be rooted, at least to some extent, in ethnicity, which meant that they could be supported by government census data and visualized in persuasive ethnographic maps.[22] While doubts remained, the decision to award Greece with a portion of Ottoman territory resulted from a momentary conjuncture of inter-Allied rivalry, persistent pressure by the Greek delegation, and ambivalent recommendations emanating from the expert advisors.[23] On May 10, 1919, the "Big Three"—Georges Clemenceau, David Lloyd George, and Woodrow Wilson—used the temporary absence of the troublesome Italian allies to green-light the landing of Greek forces in the Ottoman city of Smyrna, ostensibly to protect Christian minorities, but in reality to set in motion the partition of the Ottoman Empire.

The Greek landing at Smyrna and its violent aftermath neither "civilized" the Muslim population of Asia Minor, nor did it anchor Western influence in the region. Instead, it was the spark that ignited the rise of modern Turkish nationalism. As the Turkish nationalist writer Halide Edib, who would soon join Mustafa Kemal in eastern

Asia Minor, remarked in her memoires: "Nothing mattered to me from that moment to the time of the extraordinary march to Smyrna in 1922. I suddenly ceased to exist as an individual: I worked, wrote, and lived as a unit of that magnificent national madness."[24] Kemal himself stated that without the Greek landing, the Turkish movement "might have gone on sleeping."[25] On the day of the Greek landing, Kemal, still in the service of the Sultan, was in the Black Sea region to inspect the eighth army and pacify the area.[26] In July 1919, Kemal was discharged from government service and began mobilizing the local Muslim population against the Greek occupation forces, thus setting the fundaments of a revisionist, anti-Allied Turkish nationalist government.[27]

Since their landing in Smyrna in May 1919, the Greek occupying forces found themselves trapped in a predominantly Muslim region without clear geographical, economic, or historical borders. Challenged by recurring attacks of Muslim bands of brigands and the growing force of Kemal's troops in the east, the Greek army soon pushed further inland in the quest to quell Turkish nationalist resistance and bring the Smyrna zone under control. As Arnold Toynbee and other Western observers noted, the Greek army engaged in mass deportations and attacks against local Muslims with the help of local brigands to change the demographics of the territories under their control.[28] A keen observer, Toynbee detected the systematic character of this violence. When he visited the military front between the Greek and Turkish forces near Gemlik in June 1921, Toynbee detected "a definite 'danger line'" that coincided with the northernmost expansion of the Greek army before it was forced to retreat: "The object of the atrocities, on this showing, was to exterminate the Turkish inhabitants of districts which it was no longer convenient for the Greek Army to hold."[29]

Meanwhile, the Turkish national forces, organized from the summer of 1919 by Mustafa Kemal, gained strength and began first to halt and finally to reverse the advances of the Greek army. Over the course of the war, they employed the same social engineering or "population politics" in reverse.[30] For the Turkish side, the Greek-Turkish war was as much a struggle for liberation as it was an exercise in violent nation-building responding to the new international order.[31] After the decisive defeat of Greek forces near Afyonkarahisar between August 26 and 28, 1922, and the subsequent collapse and disordered retreat of the Greek army, Turkish nationalist forces burned Greek and Armenian houses and deported and massacred thousands of Christian inhabitants on their way to Smyrna.[32] Already before, since the Greek landing in Smyrna and systematically from July 1921, the Turkish nationalists had joined forces with local Muslim brigands to terrorize, deport, and kill several tens of thousands of Greek and Armenian citizens in the Black Sea region.[33] The reports of Western observers, most often American relief workers and teachers, have strong reminiscences of the deportations and mass killings that occurred within the context of the Armenian Genocide during the First World War.[34]

The climax of this mass ethnic violence was the burning of Smyrna on September 13–14, 1922. While there is still scholarly dispute over who exactly started the fire and to what extent Kemal and his entourage were implicated,[35] the mass of archival evidence in French, British, and American archives points to the systematic spreading of the fire by Turkish soldiers and officers to destroy the Greek, Armenian, and European quarters of the city.[36] The result was the estimated death of at least 25,000 people in the night of the fire alone,[37] and the exodus of an estimated 1.6 million Greek Orthodox inhabitants of Asia Minor to mainland Greece, which was later reflected rather than stipulated by the Lausanne Agreement of 1923. The Treaty of Sèvres was the first of the Paris peace treaties to be successfully revised by the military might of a revisionist army fighting in the name of national self-determination. How can we explain this violent escalation of the conflict?

First, the Allied decision to award Greece with a zone of occupation around the city of Smyrna was untenable in geographic, economic, and political terms. As notably the American experts of the Inquiry had warned, the lack of a natural or historical border of the Greek zone destabilized it, while the new border cut important economic ties between the Aegean coast and its hinterland. Moreover, even Greek statistics indicated that the Greek Orthodox population was in a minority, with 33.3 percent Greeks, 57.4 percent Turks, and 3.9 percent Armenians residing in the area claimed by Greece.[38] Notably, this figure hardly reflected the actual desires of the local inhabitants, which are difficult to assess with any precision, but appeared to point to a preference for some form of mandate by a disinterested power, possibly the United States. On March 11, 1919, for instance, the American Commissioner in Constantinople, Lewis Heck, reported on his impressions of a recent visit of Smyrna to Secretary of State Robert Lansing: "All the Turks were united in declaring that they would welcome American control with open arms … In fact, the hopes placed in the United States and its disinterested policy are so high to be almost pitiful in their intensity."[39] Heck also warned of "bloody consequences" should the region be awarded to Greece.[40] Reports by local Western observers clearly indicated that like in so many other disputed regions, the equation of ethnicity—in this case derived from religious affiliation—with national identity was questionable to say the least. In late August 1922, shortly before the Smyrna fire, the British Lieutenant Intelligence Officer W. E. N. Hawksley Westall characterized the majority of "native" Orthodox and Muslim citizens as different only in religion, while only the upper classes had developed some sort of national identity.[41]

In addition to an ill-conceived territorial decision at Paris, a second destabilizing factor was the weakness of state actors directly involved in the conflict. While the influence of the Sultan in Constantinople was quickly fading, the Greek forces and civilian administration proved unable to provide for security and rule of law across their zone of occupation. Chronic banditry not just continued to plague the region, but the Greco-Turkish conflict further exacerbated the problem. As normal economic activity was severely disrupted or altogether collapsed due to the war, many people saw little choice but to join bands of brigands to survive.[42] Moreover, as mentioned above, both the Greek and the Turkish armies co-opted brigands in their attempts to establish control over disputed territories, which usually meant giving them a free hand in looting and destroying entire villages.[43] Much of the dynamic of ethnic violence in the Greek-Turkish conflict, including the mass killings and deportations of the Pontic Greeks and the burning of Smyrna, resulted from the interplay between weak state and military actors, on the one hand, and paramilitary units, on the other. The effect of the "Paris system" and its premium on nationally homogeneous territories was to politicize and ethnicize the activities of brigands, who began targeting members of a particular religious group, which most of them had not done before the war.[44]

The eroding international commitment to the Greek presence in Asia Minor was another crucial factor in the collapse of the Greek Army in August 1922. Even before, it undermined any attempt to enforce the Allied decision of May 1919 and the Treaty of Sèvres of August 1920. From the start, the decision to establish a Greek zone around Smyrna excluded the Italians, while the Americans and French gradually withdrew their support. Neither the Americans nor the Kemalists signed the Treaty of Sèvres, while the French government concluded an agreement with the Kemalists in October 1921 that practically amounted to diplomatic recognition.[45] Britain too gradually withdrew its support of the increasingly costly and desperate Greek endeavor.[46] Lacking legitimacy, funds, and commitment by the states and Great Powers directly involved, the Greek occupation was indeed highly vulnerable and fragile.

Two further factors—the nature and strength of local political identities and an existing tradition of state-led violence against religious minorities—help explain the large-scale ethnic violence that accompanied the collapse of the Greek army. As in many other parts of early twentieth-century Europe, the majority of the population in the late Ottoman Empire had little sense of a "national" identity. In such a situation of "fluid identities,"[47] religion became a powerful marker of difference, and ethnic violence was the most effective tool to mobilize and enforce these new "national identities." Moreover, as the systematic attacks by the Greek army against Muslim civilians, mass deportations of Pontic Greeks, and the burning of Smyrna demonstrate, both sides in the war were able to use established forms of state-led violence against religious minorities.[48]

Taken together, these five factors allowed strategies and decisions that involved mass ethnic violence to take the upper hand in Asia Minor and to determine the nature of the conflict. Deportations, looting and terror, massacres of religious minorities in specific territories, and genocidal violence were hardly held in check by effective state control, international commitment, or a wider legitimacy of Allied decisions. Instead, the Kemalist forces not just defeated the Greek army and revised the Treaty of Sèvres, but they also added the forced exchange of populations, sanctioned in the Lausanne Agreement of 1923, to the repertoire of international politics in an already weakened Paris system.[49]

The Return of Alsace-Lorraine to France, 1918–19

Contrary to Asia Minor, Alsace-Lorraine was a non-issue at the Paris Peace Conference. Toward the end of the war, the French government had successfully persuaded its British and American allies to accept its claim to the region as part of the armistice stipulations of November 11, 1918. From 1915, focusing predominantly on the United States, the French had launched numerous propaganda campaigns and sent several of their experts and diplomats abroad to prove the legitimacy of the French claim from the perspective of national self-determination.[50] Molding French claims to suit their American counterparts of the "Inquiry," French expert Emmanuel de Martonne visited Washington, DC and highlighted the deep-seated and unbroken attachment of the Alsatians and Lorrainers to the French Republic since the French Revolution, countering the (in his eyes) superficial and less important fact that the vast majority of the population spoke German or a Germanic dialect.[51] The French line of argument culminated in the claim that the Germans had not only violated the Alsatians' and Lorrainers' right to self-determination in 1871, but that they had also forfeited any possible claim to the region when they had attacked France yet again in 1914. This argument found expression, albeit in a somewhat ambivalent phrasing, in Woodrow Wilson's eighth point, according to which "the wrong done to France by Prussia in 1871 in the matter of Alsace-Lorraine, which has unsettled the peace of the world for nearly fifty years, should be righted, in order that peace may once more be made secure in the interest of all."[52]

Despite French efforts to align their territorial claim to the new language of self-determination, the silence over Alsace-Lorraine at the peace conference came as a surprise to many contemporaries. In the late nineteenth century, "Alsace-Lorraine" had become, and continued to be, the synonym of an unresolved national dispute. Usually referred to as the "question" of Alsace-Lorraine, the fate of the borderland was discussed controversially by French and German historians from the 1870s onward, leading Ernest Renan to his famous definition of the nation as an "everyday plebiscite."[53] The dispute over the national character of the region preoccupied socialists across Europe, who sought to find an amicable solution of the issue at the Stockholm peace conference in 1917, albeit with little tangible results.[54] A number of Alsatian writers and politicians such as René Schickele pursued a regional or rather transnational path to overcome the issue, placing emphasis on the benefits of the borderland's "double culture" and its important function as a bridge between France and Germany.[55]

The refusal of any form of self-determination for the Alsatians and Lorrainers caused uneasiness at the Paris Peace Conference and on the ground. At Paris, the young British historian and member of the British expert team at the conference, James Headlam-Morley, repeatedly expressed his concern over the silence around Alsace-Lorraine to his French colleagues. On one occasion, he remarked to French diplomat André Tardieu that he considered French policy toward the region to be "radically and completely wrong and unjustifiable."[56] His chief concern was that the people had had no say in the fate of their region. On the ground, the new French administrators sought ways to sidestep the issue. In early December 1918, French President Raymond Poincare declared in a speech in Alsace's capital of Strasbourg to the cheering masses that "the plebiscite is done."[57] While there is strong evidence that the majority of Alsatians and Lorrainers welcomed the arrival of the French troops, recent studies have found that in their enthusiasm, many people expressed relief over the end of the war and the lifting of martial law rather than a preference for French rule.[58] Contrary to the claims of French propagandists, therefore, the situation in the borderland remained confusing. Many Alsatians and Lorrainers had supported the German war effort.[59] And although many had departed before the arrival of French troops, there was still a sizeable minority of Germans from the interior, making up between 12 and 18 percent of the population.[60]

The French administrators sought to handle this, in their eyes, embarrassingly ambivalent situation by a policy of forced assimilation, ethno-political classification of the population, and mass expulsions of Germans and those Alsatians and Lorrainers who had been deemed politically untrustworthy.[61] Between November 1918 and June 1919, when the Versailles Treaty was signed, the French authorities expelled at least 100,000 Germans from Alsace-Lorraine.[62] There were cases of looting, denunciations, and sporadic violence against so-called "boches," a derogatory term for Germans from the interior. Local associations called for the arrest and mass expulsion of the entire German population of Alsace-Lorraine.[63]

The scene seemed set for an escalation of the conflict, yet the violence remained remarkably limited. Even before the Versailles Treaty came into force, French administrators began to allow exceptions in the classification scheme.[64] From March 1919, they slowed down the pace of expulsions, allowing persons deemed politically inoffensive or of eminent importance for the economy to remain in their homes and jobs. After the treaty of Versailles had been signed, the French government restored rule of law in the provinces, and expulsions almost subsided. In the case of Alsace-Lorraine, we therefore need to identify not just the factors that fueled the violence, but notably also those that worked to contain it.

In an international order defined by adherence to national self-determination and arbitration, the return of Alsace-Lorraine to France without consultation of the population undermined the legitimacy of the new border. As in western Asia Minor, moreover, the initial territorial decision of the Allies inadequately corresponded to local conditions in that it rested on the fiction of the national unity of an ethnically mixed region. Like in the Greek zone around Smyrna, the mismatch between the imperative of national homogeneity emanating from the Paris system, on the one hand, and a more complex mixture of ethnic and political identities in situ, on the other, produced a strong pull for administrators and parts of the local population to sort the "question" of national belonging out by use of violence. There were strong incentives for administrators and local Alsatians and Lorrainers to forge a new national unity around the expulsion of the German minority and the suppression of anything "German" more generally.

Nevertheless, and contrary to the Greek zone in Asia Minor, the new Franco-German border was firmly rooted in history and public debate around the "question" of Alsace-Lorraine. The return of the "lost provinces" was France's only public war aim, and there was little illusion among Germans or Alsatians and Lorrainers that French victory would mean the end of the short-lived experiments of local rule that had followed the collapse of the German army.[65] Although the Allied decision lacked legitimacy, therefore, it had a clear historical precedent and corresponded to the general expectations about Allied policy at the end of the war. Overall, the return of Alsace-Lorraine to France was therefore less disputed and considered less controversial than awarding Greece with territory in western Asia Minor.

With regard to the second factor, the power of the states immediately involved, we encounter a similar initial asymmetry between victors and defeated as in the Greek-Turkish case. The collapse of the German army not only forestalled popular consultation and negotiation over the fate of the region, but it also deprived German diplomacy and the German minority in Alsace-Lorraine of any real bargaining power. Letters written by Germans in the first couple of months after the end of the war express this feeling of being left at the mercy of the French administration. In one typical case, an inhabitant from Ars-sur-Moselle near Metz wrote that "we intend to stay, but this depends on how we will be treated. Our parents were not Lorrainers, but we are, because we were born in this country. I would regret much to leave it. Alas! We cannot do anything if they chase us away."[66] This asymmetry of state power allowed French administrators to ignore the recommendation of a gradual policy of integration developed by the central wartime body of experts and diplomats for the region, the *Conférence d'Alsace-Lorraine*.[67] Instead, acting under orders from Clemenceau, Under-Secretary of State Jules Jeanneney initially pursued a policy of accelerated and complete assimilation while pushing for the mass expulsion of the German minority.[68]

Yet the abrupt assimilation of the region into the French state coupled with economic difficulties generated growing resentment in the local population, giving rise to the so-called "malaise alsacien."[69] From the early spring of 1919, the initial euphoria over the end of the war and German military rule began to give way to a more sober assessment of the realities of life in a laical and centralized nation-state that seemed to have forgotten about its promises of respecting local customs and specificities. Many Alsatians and Lorrainers remembered the promises made by French General Joffre in November 1914, when he had solemnly declared to the inhabitants of Thann in French-occupied Upper Alsace: "Our return is definitive, you are French for good. With all the liberties it has always represented, France will treat your own liberties with respect: Alsatian liberties, your traditions, your convictions, your mores."[70]

Acting within the constraints of a liberal democratic state, the French government could hardly ignore this erosion of popular support. In an internal memo dated February 12, 1919, the legal advisor to the French Ministry of War, Paul Matter, demanded that French policy refrain from "acts of violence."[71] Instead, it should reclaim "this spirit of liberalism and goodwill that is our honor and our strength." By henceforth adopting a more accommodating policy toward the region, French policymakers sought to mitigate economic disruption and prevent the formation of a strong anti-French movement.[72] A significant national opposition to French rule in the region would not only have been costly to suppress, particularly in peacetime, but it would have been internationally embarrassing given France's outspoken claims about the fundamentally French character of its "lost provinces."

Facing no noteworthy local, national, or international opposition to their claim to the region, the French government was not only able to assert control quickly, but it could also afford to de-escalate its policy of ethnic classification and gradually slow down expulsions and measures of assimilation when they began to have a negative effect on the attitudes of the local population and the economy. After the signing of the treaty of Versailles in June 1919, the French government restored rule of law and democracy in its newly acquired provinces. In the following years, the French government was able to come to diplomatic terms with Germany over the new border in the Locarno agreements of 1925, an outcome that was diametrically opposed to the mass ethnic violence, large-scale population exchange, and reversal of the Paris peace treaties that resulted from the Greek landing at Smyrna.

At first sight, the lukewarm international commitment to the return of Alsace-Lorraine to France resembled the elusive alliance of the "Big Three" for a Greek zone in Asia Minor. The uneasiness mentioned above and much of the agitation surrounding the "question" of Alsace-Lorraine in the interwar period drew on the lack of explicit support that the decision had attracted from France's chief allies, the United States and Britain. Upon closer inspection, however, international commitment to the new border—even if it merely came in the form of acquiescing in taking the issue off the agenda of the Paris Peace Conference—was strong enough to stabilize Franco-German relations in the 1920s. For all its lack of legitimacy, the national and international commitment to the new border brought the benefit of clarity and, along with it, much-desired stability and peace. Indeed, the mixture of strong commitment and bilateral agreements between France and Germany anticipated the stabilization of Franco-German relations after the end of the Second World War.

In several ways, the fourth and the fifth factors—local identities and a tradition of ethnic violence—pushed for an escalation of the conflict. The war had polarized and politicized hitherto multilayered, predominantly regional, class-based, and religious identities of local inhabitants across Alsace-Lorraine. After the war, as Alison Carrol writes, it was "impossible (or at the very least very difficult)" for anyone who lived in this disputed borderland to remain indifferent to the issue of national identity.[73] The classification of the population into "native" Alsatians and Lorrainers and German "foreigners" exacerbated the tensions. Crucially, as the new authorities issued identity cards based on the classification scheme, they created clear markers of difference that lend themselves to discrimination and ethnic violence.[74] Likewise, the recent experiences of war and martial law established if not a tradition, then at least precedents of state-led violence against civilians.

While clear markers of difference and the wartime precedent of state-led violence against civilians increased the potential of ethnic violence, the region's long-standing tradition of democratic politics and rule of law worked to contain violent escalation. In marked contrast to Asia Minor, Alsace-Lorraine provided its new rulers with a tight-knit web of associations, trade unions, political parties, and a regional parliament that, despite the recent disturbances caused by the war, allowed the French administration to restore law and order comparatively quickly and without the support of paramilitary units and, at least in the longer run, nationalist zealots. While there was strong grassroots pressure to "cleanse" the region of its German minority, state control was effective in taking charge of the expulsion process and forestalling large-scale lawlessness and banditry—unlike the polycratic dynamic of the expulsion of the Greeks from Smyrna in September 1922. The complaints by the German delegation at the Interallied Armistice Commission at Spa, while vociferously decrying the "de-Germanization" of Alsace-Lorraine, rarely mentioned serious assaults against German citizens, let alone anything resembling the violence endured by both Christian and Muslim minorities during the Greek-Turkish war.[75]

Overall, in the case of Alsace-Lorraine, the five factors discussed here balanced each other out, leading to the mixed result of a brief and intense initial period of discrimination, dispossession, and expulsion of a significant part of the region's German minority that soon gave way to policies of stabilization and the restoration of rule of law and democratic procedures. Crucially, strong commitment by the French state coupled with the constraints of a liberal democratic framework and a generally expected and clear, if not fully legitimate, territorial decision meant that the signing of the treaty of Versailles effectively ended mass expulsions of German citizens and allowed for a process of normalization that culminated in the Locarno agreements six years later.

Conclusion

The comparison of Alsace-Lorraine and Asia Minor demonstrates that the same set of factors and mechanisms operated in these highly diverse and geographically disparate settings, albeit in a fundamentally different manner. In both cases, the initial territorial decisions by the Allies proved to be inadequate responses to the complex realities of ethnically mixed regions. The resulting discrepancy between the pretense of national homogeneity and an ambivalent situation on the ground generated incentives for state administrations and local citizens to use violent "population politics" to close the gap between their territorial claims and local reality. In both cases, moreover, there existed clear markers of difference among the population that lend themselves to discrimination and targeted ethnic violence. The (in)adequacy of the initial Allied decision and the nature of local identities, in combination with three other factors—state power, international commitment, and traditions of ethnic violence—go a long way in explaining why ethnic violence escalated in Asia Minor but was contained in Alsace-Lorraine (see Table 1).

Thus, the "Paris system" was neither merely a loose point of reference, nor was it a coherent international order. Rather, the period between 1917 and 1923 saw the emergence of a common—but highly uneven—global order organized around the ideal of ethnically homogeneous nation-states.[76] Compared to the period after 1945, the "Paris system" was indeed no rigid international order. Yet compared to the period before 1914, it certainly provided a meaningful political, legal, economic, and ideological framework that not only prompted politicians, experts, and local activists to rearrange territories along "national" lines, but also guided their political action and decision-making according to the same fusion of nationality, ethnic homogeneity, and state sovereignty. The Paris system is so hard to pinpoint because it was an emerging international order that was as much about redefining national territories and identities as it was about debating and fighting over the nature of sovereignty and legitimacy of political action.[77]

The contradictions in the system—notably between the universal emancipatory premise of "making the world safe for democracy", on the one hand, and the system's hierarchies and the limits of Allied power and commitment, on the other—created incentives for violent action, both at the level of diplomacy and on the ground. In disputed areas, depending on the specific local circumstances, politicians and military leaders often saw ethnic violence as an effective tool to create ethnically homogeneous spaces to legitimize their claims of territorial control and state sovereignty. Ethnic violence was less a consequence of "flawed" decision-making than a constitutive

Table 1 Comparison of Asia Minor and Alsace-Lorraine

	Asia Minor	Alsace-Lorraine
(1) **Adequacy of territorial decision**	Inadequate, severe lack of legitimacy	Inadequate and lack of legitimacy, but generally expected outcome of the war and based on well-established historical border
(2) **State power**	Weak, collaboration with warlords and brigands	Strong, within the constraints of a liberal democracy
(3) **International commitment**	Temporary and weak, Treaty of Sèvres not signed or accepted by national Turkish forces	Strong, although some ambivalence remained; Treaty of Versailles signed and accepted by both sides
(4) **Local identities and markers of difference**	Fluid identities, religion as clear marker of difference	Fluid but recently politicized identities, clear markers of difference
(5) **Tradition of ethnic violence**	Tradition of peaceful co-existence of religious groups, but also more recent episodes of genocidal violence against minorities; lack of rule of law and democratic traditions	Recent episodes of state-led violence against civilians, but longer tradition of rule of law, strong associations, and democratic procedures
Outcome	Gradual escalation: full-blown war, deportations, massacres, genocidal violence, forced removal of populations	Temporary escalation (mass expulsions, dispossession, sporadic physical violence) but quick containment of violence

element of the peace order. Diplomatic and in situ violence frequently resulted from the limitations and inconsistencies of self-determination and the subsequent frustration by local populations about decisions taken at Paris. More fundamentally, this same violence forced distant lands and politically detached populations into the new international order, both as a resource for politicians and military leaders and as agents who themselves shaped the system.

The conflicts in Alsace-Lorraine and Asia Minor emerged within the same international order that placed a premium on ethnic homogeneity, clear-cut national borders, and state sovereignty. Within this shared international order, the interplay of several factors and mechanisms determined whether and to what extent the conflicts escalated—not a simple dichotomy between an ethnically mixed and backward "East" and a nationally mature and progressive "West." As we have seen, several—but not all—of these factors cut across the East-West divide. We need further systematic comparisons of territorial and national conflicts in the aftermath of the Paris Peace Conference to map out the tectonics of the Paris system with greater precision. Such an endeavor promises to provide us with new answers to older but still very much open questions, most notably why and how exactly the interwar international order collapsed. This chapter has attempted to take a few tentative steps in this direction.

Notes

1   See Jochen Böhler, "Enduring Violence: The Postwar Struggles in East-Central Europe, 1917–21," *Journal of Contemporary History* 50, no. 1 (2015): 58–77; Julia Eichenberg and John Paul Newman, "Introduction: Aftershocks: Violence in Dissolving Empires after the First World War," *Contemporary European History* 19, no. 3 (2010): 183–94 (and the other articles in the same special issue); and Marcus M. Payk and Roberta Pergher, eds., *Beyond Versailles: Sovereignty, Legitimacy, and the Formation of New Polities after the Great War* (Bloomington: Indiana University Press, 2019).
2   Robert Gerwarth and John Horne, "The Great War and Paramilitarism in Europe, 1917–23," *Contemporary European History* 19, no. 3 (2010): 267–73; Robert Gerwarth and John Horne, "Vectors of Violence: Paramilitarism in Europe after the Great War, 1917–1923," *Journal of Modern History* 83, no. 3 (2011): 489–512; and most recently Robert Gerwarth, *The Vanquished: Why the First World War Failed to End* (New York: Farrar Straus and Giroux, 2016).
3   See the studies by Carlile Aylmer Macartney, *National States and National Minorities* (New York: Russell & Russell, 1968) and Richard Hartshorne, "A Survey of the Boundary Problems of Europe," in *Geographic Aspects of International Relations*, ed. Charles C. Colby (Port Washington: Kennikat Press, 1970). See also the excellent historiographical overview and discussion of the East–West divide in Tara Zahra, "The 'Minority Problem' and National Classification in the French and Czechoslovak Borderlands," *Contemporary European History* 17, no. 2 (2008): 137–65, here 141–4.
4   The term "Paris system" was coined by Eric D. Weitz, "From the Vienna to the Paris System: International Politics and the Entangled Histories of Human Rights, Forced Deportations, and Civilizing Missions," *American Historical Review* 113, no. 5 (2008): 1313–43.
5   See Zahra, "'Minority Problem'" and Timothy Wilson, *Frontiers of Violence: Conflict and Identity in Ulster and Upper Silesia, 1918-1922* (Oxford: Oxford University Press, 2010).
6   See, for example, the recent monographs by Georges-Henri Soutou, *La grande illusion: Quand la France perdait la paix, 1914–1920* (Paris: Tallandier, 2015); Klaus Schwabe, *Versailles: Das Wagnis eines demokratischen Friedens 1919–1923* (Paderborn: Schöningh, 2019); Jörn Leonhard, *Der überforderte Frieden: Versailles und die Welt 1918–1923* (Munich: C.H. Beck, 2018); and Eckart Conze, *Die grosse Illusion: Versailles 1919 und die Neuordnung der Welt* (Munich: Siedler, 2018).
7   Marcus M. Payk and Roberta Pergher, "Introduction," in *Beyond Versailles*, ed. Payk and Pergher.
8   Ibid., 5–6.
9   Mark Mazower, "Minorities and the League of Nations in Interwar Europe," *Daedalus* 126, no. 2 (1997): 47–63; Carole Fink, "The League of Nations and the Minorities Question," *World Affairs* 157, no. 4 (1995): 197–205; and Carole Fink, *Defending the Rights of Others: The Great Powers, the Jews, and International Minority Protection, 1878–1938* (Cambridge: Cambridge University Press, 2004).
10 Erez Manela, *The Wilsonian Moment: Self-determination and the International Origins of Anticolonial Nationalism* (Oxford: Oxford University Press, 2007).
11 Weitz, "Paris System"; see also Eric D. Weitz, "Self-determination: How a German Enlightenment Idea Became the Slogan of National Liberation and a Human Right," *American Historical Review* 120, no. 2 (2015): 462–96.
12 Weitz, "Paris System," 1313.

13   See, for example, Omer Bartov and Eric D. Weitz, eds., *Shatterzone of Empires: Coexistence and Violence in the German, Habsburg, Russian, and Ottoman Borderlands* (Bloomington: Indiana University Press, 2013).
14   On the cases of Eupen-Malmedy and South Tyrol see Emmanuel Dalle Mulle and Mona Bieling's chapter in this volume. On Schleswig see, for example, Peter Thaler, "A Tale of Three Communities: National Identification in the German-Danish Borderlands," *Scandinavian Journal of History* 32, no. 2 (2007): 141–66 and Jan Schlürmann, *1920—Eine Grenze für den Frieden: Die Volksabstimmungen zwischen Deutschland und Dänemark* (Kiel: Wachholtz, 2019).
15   For a concise outline of the historical background, see Erol Ülker's chapter in this volume.
16   See Tim Jacoby, "A Comparative Perspective on the Origins of Turkish Nationalism," *Studies in Ethnicity and Nationalism* 1, no. 2 (2001): 27–36, here 31; Erol Ülker, "Contextualising 'Turkification': Nation-building in the Late Ottoman Empire, 1908–18," *Nations and Nationalism* 11, no. 4 (2005): 613–36; Uğur Ümit Üngör, "Seeing like a Nation-state: Young Turk Social Engineering in Eastern Turkey, 1913–50," *Journal of Genocide Research* 10, no. 1 (2008): 15–39; Spyros A. Sofos, "Nationalism in Greece and Turkey: Modernity, Enlightenment, Westernization," in *Nationalism in the Troubled Triangle: Cyprus, Greece and Turkey*, ed. Ayhan Aktar, Niyazi Kızılyürek, and Umut Özkırımlı (Basingstoke: Palgrave Macmillan, 2010); Taner Akçam, *The Young Turks' Crime against Humanity: The Armenian Genocide and Ethnic Cleansing in the Ottoman Empire* (Princeton: Princeton University Press, 2012), ch. 3; and Taner Akçam, "The Young Turks and the Plans for the Ethnic Homogenization of Anatolia," in *Shatterzone of Empires*, ed. Bartov and Weitz.
17   On the Balkan Wars in this context, see Eyal Ginio, "Paving the Way for Ethnic Cleansing: Eastern Thrace during the Balkan Wars (1912–1913) and Their Aftermath," in *Shatterzone of Empires*, ed. Bartov and Weitz.
18   The most extensive studies on this issue are Yannis G. Mourelos, "The 1914 Persecutions and the First Attempt at an Exchange of Minorities between Greece and Turkey," *Balkan Studies* 26, no. 2 (1985): 389–413 and Matthias Bjørnlund, "The 1914 Cleansing of Aegean Greeks as a Case of Violent Turkification," *Journal of Genocide Research* 10, no. 1 (2008): 41–58. See also Mustafa Aksakal, "The Ottoman Empire," in *Empires at War: 1911–1923*, ed. Robert Gerwarth and Erez Manela (Oxford: Oxford University Press, 2014), 22; and Ellinor Morack, "The Ottoman Greeks and the Great War, 1912–1922," in *The World during the First World War*, ed. Helmut Bley and Anorthe Kremers (Essen: Klartext Verlag, 2014), 219–21.
19   On the "Great Idea" (Megali Idea) see Ioannis Zelepos, *Die Ethnisierung griechischer Identität 1870–1912: Staat und private Akteure vor dem Hintergrund der "Megali Idea"* (Munich: Oldenbourg, 2002); Marc Terrades, *Le drame de l'Hellénisme: Ion Dragoumis (1878–1920) et la question nationale en Grèce au début du XXe siècle* (Paris: L'Harmattan, 2005), 27–47; and Nicholas Doumanis, *A History of Greece* (Basingstoke: Palgrave Macmillan, 2010), 180–5. On the "Great Idea" and the specific diplomatic context in 1919, see Georgia Eglezou, *The Greek Media in World War I and Its Aftermath* (London: Tauris, 2009), 30 and Volker Prott, *The Politics of Self-Determination: Remaking Territories and National Identities in Europe, 1917–1923* (Oxford: Oxford University Press, 2016), ch. 3.
20   Eleftherios Venizelos, "Greece before the Peace Congress," in The National Archives, London (henceforth TNA), Foreign Office (henceforth FO) 608/37/1, file 19, pp. 1–15 (also available at http://www.archive.org/details/cu31924027901127, accessed June 27, 2022).

21   See David Ernest Roessel, *In Byron's Shadow: Modern Greece in the English & American Imagination* (Oxford: Oxford University Press, 2002).
22   See Jeremy W. Crampton, "The Cartographic Calculation of Space: Race Mapping and the Balkans at the Paris Peace Conference of 1919," *Social & Cultural Geography* 7, no. 5 (2006): 731–52.
23   See Michael John Llewellyn Smith, *Ionian Vision: Greece in Asia Minor, 1919–1922* (London: Hurst, 1998), 77–85 and Prott, *Politics of Self-Determination*, ch. 3.
24   Halidé Edib, *The Turkish Ordeal* (London: John Murray, 1928), 23.
25   Quoted in Philip Mansel, *Levant: Splendour and Catastrophe on the Mediterranean* (New Haven: Yale University Press, 2011), 207.
26   See Klaus Kreiser, *Atatürk: Eine Biographie* (Munich: C.H. Beck, 2014), 134–42.
27   On Kemal's activities in the Black Sea region, see Stéphane Yérasimos, "La Question du Pont-Euxin (1912–1923)," *Guerres mondiales et conflits contemporains* 153 (1989): 9–34, here 19–20.
28   On the Greek army's use of brigands, see ibid.; Nicholas Doumanis, *Before the Nation: Muslim-Christian Coexistence and Its Destruction in Late-Ottoman Anatolia* (Oxford: Oxford University Press, 2013), 161–3 and Prott, *Politics of Self-Determination*, ch. 6.
29   Arnold J. Toynbee, *The Western Question in Greece and Turkey: A Study in the Contact of Civilisations* (New York: Howard Fertig (reprint 1970), 1923), 315–16.
30   For a discussion of population politics, see Peter Holquist, "To Count, to Extract, and to Exterminate: Population Statistics and Population Politics in Late Imperial and Soviet Russia," in *A State of Nations: Empire and Nation-making in the Age of Lenin and Stalin*, ed. Ronald G. Suny and Terry Martin (Oxford: Oxford University Press, 2001); Weitz, "Paris System," and Prott, *Politics of Self-Determination*, 24.
31   Most recently, in a well-researched but also controversial study, the Israeli historians Benny Morris and Dror Ze'evi have argued that the entire period between the Armenian massacres of 1894 and the Greek-Turkish war constituted a single "thirty-year genocide" that formed the basis for the modern Turkish nation-state. See Benny Morris and Dror Ze'evi, *The Thirty-year Genocide: Turkey's Destruction of Its Christian Minorities, 1894–1924* (Cambridge: Harvard University Press, 2019). For more balanced views that examine the violence against Christian minorities in the context of the massacres and deportations of Muslims from the Balkans prior to the First World War and highlight the specificity of the period between 1912 and 1923, see the studies referenced in footnote 16 above.
32   See Smith, *Ionian Vision*, ch. 13 and Prott, *Politics of Self-Determination*, ch. 6.
33   On the Pontic Greeks see Tessa Hofmann, "Γενοκτονια εν Ροη - Cumulative Genocide: The Massacres and Deportations of the Greek Population of the Ottoman Empire (1912–1923)," in *The Genocide of the Ottoman Greeks: Studies on the State-sponsored Campaign of Extermination of the Christians of Asia Minor, 1912–1922 and Its Aftermath: History, Law, Memory*, ed. Tessa Hofmann, Matthias Bjørnlund, and Vasileios Meichanetsidis (New York: Aristide D. Caratzas, 2011); and Morris and Ze'evi, *Thirty-Year Genocide*, ch. 9.
34   See Prott, *Politics of Self-Determination*, ch. 6.
35   While some scholars have refrained from making a definite statement, the majority has placed the blame on the Turks. Only few Western scholars support the official Turkish position, according to which the Armenians and Greeks set fire to their own city. For an overview of the debate, see Biray Kolluoglu Kirli, "Forgetting the Smyrna

Fire," *History Workshop Journal* 60 (2005): 25–44 and Leyla Neyzi, "Remembering Smyrna/Izmir: Shared History, Shared Trauma," *History & Memory* 20, no. 2 (2008): 106–27.

36 See the British reports in TNA, FO 371/7886, 7894, 7898, 7902, 7949, 7950; French reports in the Archives du Ministère des affaires étrangères, Paris, Series E Levant (1918–1929), vol. 55 and American reports in National Archives and Records Administration, Washington (henceforth NARA), Record Group (henceforth RG) 59, file 867.4016/773. For published primary documents on the Smyrna fire, see Constantine G. Hatzidimitriou, "American Accounts Documenting the Destruction of Smyrna by the Kemalist Turkish Forces," in *American Accounts Documenting the Destruction of Smyrna by the Kemalist Turkish Forces, September 1922*, ed. Constantine G. Hatzidimitriou (New York: Caratzas, 2005); George Horton, *Report on Turkey: USA Consular Documents* (Athens: The Journalists' Union of the Athens Daily Newspapers, 1985), 180; and Dora Sakayan, *An Armenian Doctor in Turkey: Garabed Hatcherian: My Smyrna Ordeal of 1922* (Montreal: Arod Books, 1997), 10–11, 14.

37 According to the report by Percival Hadkinson, September 20, 1922, TNA, FO 371/7898, file no E10382/27/44, p. 48.

38 See Paul Masson, "Smyrne et l'Hellénisme en Asie Mineure: Rapport présenté à la séance du 2 décembre 1918," in *Tome Second: Questions européennes*, ed. Comité d'études (Paris: Imprimerie Nationale, 1919), 799. Masson used the statistics of the Greek Patriarchate of 1912.

39 Lewis Heck to Lansing, March 11, 1919, NARA, RG 59, file 867.00/859, p. 4 (in the report).

40 Ibid., 6.

41 Report by Hawksley Westall on the political situation in Smyrna, August 30, 1922, TNA, FO 371/7885, file no E8734/27/44. This ambivalent situation corresponds to widespread "national indifference" among European populations in this period. See Maarten van Ginderachter and Jon E. Fox, eds., *National Indifference and the History of Nationalism in Modern Europe* (London: Routledge, 2019) and the literature cited therein.

42 See, for example, Toynbee, *Western Question*, 157, Yérasimos, "Question du Pont-Euxin," and Smith, *Ionian Vision*, 210.

43 For examples see Prott, *Politics of Self-Determination*, ch. 6.

44 See Resat Kasaba, "Greek and Turkish Nationalism in Formation: Western Anatolia 1919–1922" (EUI Working Papers, RSC No. 2002/17, Robert Schuman Centre for Advanced Studies, European University Institute, Florence, 2002).

45 See Soutou, *La grande illusion*, 344–5.

46 See Smith, *Ionian Vision*, ch. 12.

47 On "fluid" identities see Peter Thaler, "Fluid Identities in Central European Borderlands," *European History Quarterly* 31, no. 4 (2001): 519–48 and Alison Carrol and Louisa Zanoun, "The View from the Border: A Comparative Study of Autonomism in Alsace and the Moselle, 1918–29," *European Review of History* 18, no. 4 (2011): 465–86.

48 See notably Üngör, "Seeing like a Nation-state," 16; Erik Jan Zürcher, *The Young Turk Legacy and Nation Building: From the Ottoman Empire to Atatürk's Turkey* (London: I.B. Tauris, 2010), 96, 108; Akçam, *Young Turks' Crime against Humanity* and Morack, "Ottoman Greeks and the Great War."

49 On the role of the Lausanne agreement as a positive model for the deportations during and after the Second World War, see Bruce Clark, *Twice a Stranger: The Mass Expulsions That Forged Modern Greece and Turkey* (Cambridge, MA: Harvard University Press, 2006); and Matthew Frank, *Expelling the Germans: British Opinion and Post-1945 Population Transfer in Context* (Oxford: Oxford University Press, 2007), ch. 1.
50 See Prott, *Politics of Self-Determination*, 69–72.
51 On de Martonne's visit to the United States, see Taline Ter Minassian, "Les géographes français et la délimitation des frontières balkaniques à la Conférence de la Paix en 1919," *Revue d'histoire moderne et contemporaine* 44, no. 2 (1997): 252–86 and Prott, *Politics of Self-Determination*, ch. 2.
52 See https://en.wikipedia.org/wiki/Fourteen_Points#Text (accessed June 27, 2022). Adopting passive voice, Wilson's eighth point does not specify *by whom* or *how* the "wrong" shall be "righted"—it could still mean a plebiscite. See also the discussion in Prott, *Politics of Self-Determination*, 55.
53 Ernest Renan, *Qu'est-ce qu'une nation? Et autres essais politiques: Textes choisis et présentés par Joël Roman* (Paris: Presses pocket, 1992), 55. On the Franco-German dispute over Alsace-Lorraine and what constitutes a nation, see Michael Heffernan, "History, Geography and the French National Space: The Question of Alsace-Lorraine, 1914–18," *Space & Polity* 5, no. 1 (2001): 27–48, here 28-30 and Laurence Turetti, *Quand la France pleurait l'Alsace-Lorraine: Les "provinces perdues" aux sources du patriotisme républicain, 1870–1914* (Strasbourg: La Nuée Bleue, 2008), ch. 1.
54 See Jürgen Stillig, "Das Problem Elsass-Lothringen und die sozialistische Internationale," *Vierteljahrshefte für Zeitgeschichte* 23, no. 1 (1975): 62–76 and Prott, *Politics of Self-Determination*, 65–8.
55 On Schickele, see Dieter Lamping, *Über Grenzen: Eine literarische Topographie* (Göttingen: Vandenhoeck & Ruprecht, 2001), ch. 2.
56 James Headlam-Morley to George Saunders, June 12, 1919, in James Headlam-Morley, *A Memoir of the Paris Peace Conference 1919: Edited by Agnes Headlam-Morley, Russell Bryant, Anna Cienciala* (London: Methuen, 1972), 143.
57 As quoted in *Le Temps*, December 10, 1918, 2.
58 See Christopher J. Fischer, *Alsace to the Alsatians? Visions and Divisions of Alsatian Regionalism, 1870–1939*, vol. 5 (New York: Berghahn Books, 2010), 121, 128; and Francis Grandhomme, "Retrouver la frontière du Rhin en 1918: L'entrée des poilus en Alsace et le retour à la France," *Revue d'Alsace*, no. 139 (2013): 237–58. For a more sceptical account cf. Alfred Wahl and Jean-Claude Richez, *L'Alsace entre France et Allemagne, 1850–1950* (Paris: Hachette, 1993), 251–2.
59 On the situation of the local population in Alsace-Lorraine during the First World War, see Volker Prott, "Challenging the German Empire: Strategic Nationalism in Alsace-Lorraine in the First World War," *Nations and Nationalism* 27, no. 4 (2021): 1009–25 and Volker Prott, "A Stress Test for German Nationalism: Protective Custody in Alsace-Lorraine during the First World War," *German History* 39, no. 4 (2021): 542–59.
60 The 1910 census specified the number of Germans from the interior resident in Alsace-Lorraine at 295,436, corresponding to 15.8 percent of the total population of 1,874,014. See Joseph Rossé et al., *Das Elsass von 1870–1932: IV. Band: Karten, Graphiken, Tabellen, Dokumente, Sach- und Namenregister* (Colmar: Alsatia, 1938), 37, 46.
61 See David Allen Harvey, "Lost Children or Enemy Aliens? Classifying the Population of Alsace after the First World War," *Journal of Contemporary History* 34, no. 4

(1999): 537–54; Laird Boswell, "From Liberation to Purge Trials in the 'Mythic Provinces': Recasting French Identities in Alsace and Lorraine, 1918–1920," *French Historical Studies* 23, no. 1 (2000): 129–62; Carolyn Grohmann, "From Lothringen to Lorraine: Expulsion and Voluntary Repatriation," *Diplomacy and Statecraft* 16, no. 3 (2005): 571–87 and Prott, *Politics of Self-Determination*, ch. 5.

62 By contrast, expulsions of "native" Alsatians and Lorrainers probably amounted to less than 100 cases. For numbers see Prott, *Politics of Self-Determination*, 169–70.
63 Ibid., 159.
64 Ibid., ch. 5, also for the following.
65 On the brief period between the armistice and the arrival of French troops in Alsace-Lorraine, see Joseph Rossé et al., *Das Elsass von 1870–1932: I. Band: Politische Geschichte* (Colmar: Alsatia, 1936), 488–505 and Stefan Fisch, "Der Übergang des Elsass vom Deutschen Reich an Frankreich 1918/19," in *Das Elsass: Historische Landschaft im Wandel der Zeiten*, ed. Michael Erbe (Stuttgart: Kohlhammer, 2002).
66 Report of French postal control (Metz) on the period of December 1–7, 1918, December 8, 1918, Service historique de la défense, Paris, 16 N 1464.
67 See Joseph Schmauch, "Préparer la réintégration des provinces perdues: La Conférence d'Alsace-Lorraine et les services d'Alsace-Lorraine à Paris," in *Boches ou tricolores: Les Alsaciens-Lorrains dans la Grande Guerre*, ed. Jean-Noël Grandhomme (Strasbourg: La Nuée Bleue, 2008) and Prott, *Politics of Self-Determination*, ch. 2.
68 See Rossé et al., *Das Elsass vol. I*, 559–71; Fischer, *Alsace to the Alsatians*, ch. 5; and Prott, *Politics of Self-Determination*, ch. 5.
69 See Rossé et al., *Das Elsass vol. I*, 543–50, 563–5; Joseph Schmauch, "Les services d'Alsace-Lorraine face à la réintégration des départements de l'est (1914–1919)" (PhD diss., École Nationale des Chartes, Paris, 2004), 495–532; and Fischer, *Alsace to the Alsatians*, 134.
70 Quoted in Prott, *Politics of Self-Determination*, 148.
71 Paul Matter, "Note sur le rapport de M. J. Kastler," 4, February 12, 1919, Archives départementales du Bas-Rhin, Strasbourg, 121 AL 902, also for the following quotation.
72 As Alison Carrol's chapter in this volume demonstrates, French policy continued to oscillate between more rigid and more tolerant approaches toward regional particularities throughout the interwar period.
73 Alison Carrol, *The Return of Alsace to France, 1918–1939* (Oxford: Oxford University Press, 2018), 17. See also Carrol's chapter in this volume.
74 On the classification scheme and identity cards, see, among many others, Harvey, "Lost Children or Enemy Aliens," 548; Boswell, "Purge Trials," 144; Fischer, *Alsace to the Alsatians*, 149; and Prott, *Politics of Self-Determination*, 154–6.
75 On the work of the interallied peace commission at Spa, see ibid., 172–4.
76 The quantitative dimensions of this fundamental shift to an inter-national order are captured well in Figure I.I in Andreas Wimmer, *Waves of War: Nationalism, State Formation, and Ethnic Exclusion in the Modern World* (Cambridge: Cambridge University Press, 2013), 2.
77 See Leonard V. Smith, *Sovereignty at the Paris Peace Conference of 1919* (Oxford: Oxford University Press, 2018).

6

Sovereignty and Homogeneity: A History of Majority-Minority Relations in Interwar Western Europe

Emmanuel Dalle Mulle and Mona Bieling

At the 1919 Paris Peace Conference, the Great Powers set up a new international order whose priority was to maintain peace in Europe. This system was centered around the principle of self-determination for all peoples and "focused on populations and an ideal of state sovereignty rooted in national homogeneity."[1] The new order opposed the dynastic principles that underpinned multi-ethnic empires, but it was hampered because the creation of homogeneous nation-states was not realistically possible. Conscious of this problem, the Great Powers resorted to a new system of minority protection whose objective was to shield minorities from a wide range of homogenizing and discriminatory policies that varied from genocidal violence to milder forms of linguistic assimilation and socioeconomic discrimination.

Notwithstanding some major shortcomings, the minority protection system introduced during the peace treaties and supervised by the League of Nations represented a fundamental change with respect to nineteenth-century international practices. The Great Powers were inconsistent in applying this system since it was enforced only in the newly independent states of Eastern Europe and within some older states in the region such as Bulgaria, Greece, and Romania. Western European countries, as well as most non-European ones, remained outside the jurisdiction of the League's Minorities Section. More powerful Western European states preferred this solution, as this inconsistency allowed for less interference within their own sovereign territories. Furthermore, in accordance with lingering civilizational stereotypes, Western politicians considered the populations of Eastern Europe to be less civilized and therefore in need of a lesson in "international deportment."[2]

The Great Powers cast the minority issue as an Eastern European problem.[3] This political decision was clearly reflected in contemporary studies on the subject. In a work that became a standard reference on the topic, the French ambassador Jacques Fouques Duparc located the origins of the minority problem in differences of language, race, and religion that, he stressed, were immense in Eastern Europe. In contrast, he claimed that Western Europe was "more stable in its political organization" and "had lost even the memory" of such "barriers" between groups.⁴ A decade later, in an article that appeared in *Foreign Affairs* with the telling title "Minorities: A Problem of Eastern Europe," Carlile Aylmer Macartney, one of the most influential interwar experts on the subject, consolidated this idea by claiming that "the minorities question" originated in large-scale national migrations that had ended in Western Europe in the Middle Ages, whereas they were still taking place in the East.⁵

Contrary to the widespread view of contemporaries that the minority question concerned Eastern Europe alone, in this chapter we argue that Western European political elites did confront salient minority issues and sometimes behaved in more repressive ways than their Eastern European counterparts. This is relevant for the study of minority questions in interwar Europe because most of the current historiography focuses on the system that the League of Nations supervised and, therefore, on the states located in the strip of land that stretches from the Baltic states to Turkey.⁶ The purpose of our contribution is to shift the historiographical focus from East to West through comparatively examining majority-minority relations in interwar Belgium, Italy, and Spain.⁷

As we employ a top-down comparative approach, for the sake of simplicity we use the terms minorities and majorities to describe segments of the population. However, with these expressions, we do not intend to suggest that these were monolithic entities. Identities in minority regions were often fluid and many of the people that nationalist leaders claimed to represent, or that state authorities deemed as belonging to a minority, did not identify with the alleged minority group.⁸ However, political elites in all three countries perceived the minority question as entailing two key elements: a claim of difference in national terms⁹ voiced by a sizable share of the population identified as a minority, and an asymmetric power relation between the supposed minority and the rest of the inhabitants of the state whereby the minority would be in a non-dominant position. This claim of difference was of course a political stand rather than an objective reality, but it still had very real consequences for a number of political actors and, by extension, an impact on ordinary people.

Between the two World Wars, the countries in our study, Belgium, Italy, and Spain, underwent important processes of sub-state national mobilization which posed a formidable challenge to state authorities. The governments that ruled these states during the interwar years adopted different policies to deal with national heterogeneity within their borders. Generally, liberal regimes granted minority populations greater protection than authoritarian governments, which often implemented harsh assimilative policies. Yet, even liberal regimes that remained democratic throughout the period, such as Belgium, did show homogenizing tendencies. These, however, unfolded at the local, rather than state, level.

When compared to the countries subjected to the League of Nations' minority protection system, overall, Belgium, Italy, and Spain do not stand out as having been particularly tolerant. On the contrary, they fit into a pattern of behavior that goes beyond a simplistic East-West divide. Despite not providing a systematic comparison with Eastern Europe, this chapter juxtaposes our cases with some Eastern European experiences. We show that on one end of the spectrum repressive policies were enforced in fascist Italy to a degree similar to those in Poland. On the other, more tolerant, end of the spectrum, Belgium and Republican Spain could be compared to Estonia before the 1934 putsch that turned the latter into a dictatorship.

Before examining our case studies in greater detail, we briefly describe the workings of the minority system and introduce the context of majority-minority relations in Belgium, Italy, and Spain.

The League's Minority System and Majority-Minority Relations in Belgium, Italy, and Spain

The minority treaties granted a mix of positive and negative rights to persons "belonging to racial, religious or linguistic minorities."[10] These included basic rights extended to all residents, such as the right to life and liberty, religious freedom and equality before the law as well as some minority-specific clauses relative to the establishment and control of private charitable, religious, social, and educational institutions, the right to use minority languages in court, and an adequate supply of public primary schools in the minority language.[11] The general rule with regard to minority education was that public schools (or classes) in minority languages would be established if the parents of a minimum number of pupils (usually between twenty and forty) in a municipality requested it. The League of Nations supervised the application of the treaties and accepted petitions from individual members of minorities or minority organizations, although these documents were only informative in nature.[12]

The application of these treaties was limited to fifteen countries (along with the territories of Memel and Upper-Silesia), almost exclusively in Central and Eastern Europe.[13] Although minority activists and Eastern European diplomats made several attempts to promote the extension of the system to all the members of the League, the Great Powers consistently thwarted such efforts. The only victory obtained by supporters of a generalization of minority protection was a symbolic one. It consisted of a resolution passed by the League's Assembly in 1922, and reaffirmed in 1933, that expressed the hope that the League's members not bound by the minority treaties would "observe, in the treatment of their own racial, religious or linguistic minorities, at least as high a standard of justice and toleration as is required by any of the treaties."[14] We shall assess the attitude of Western governments toward their minorities against the background of the minority treaties focusing on education in minority languages (a highly contested issue throughout the interwar period), the use of languages in court and public administration, as well as on forms of repression violating basic rights of life and liberty, religious freedom, and equality before the law.

Although majority-minority relations in Belgium, Italy, and Spain originated in specific historical and contingent contexts, they shared some common elements. In all three countries, minority questions were brought about or intensified by two factors: the annexation of new territories inhabited by people speaking a different language and democratization processes that channeled the demands of new political actors, including minority nationalist representatives. Furthermore, in all three countries, political elites voiced concerns about the state and the nation's cohesion. The presence of alternative forms of national identification in some regions, different from the identity promoted by state institutions, only made these elites more anxious about their legitimacy.[15]

Belgium, Italy, and Spain were faced with two main types of minorities. On the one hand, there were populations that lived in territories annexed by Italy and Belgium at the end of the War from the Austro-Hungarian and German Empire. These included about 200,000 German speakers in South Tyrol, 460,000 Slovenian and Croatian speakers in Venezia Giulia (both regions were annexed by Italy), and 60,000 German-speaking inhabitants in the cantons of Eupen, Malmedy, and St. Vith in Belgium. These communities could, at least in principle, count on the support of kin-states and minority organizations mostly advocated joining such states. On the other hand, in the regions of Catalonia and the Basque Country, as well as in Belgium's Flanders, endogenous processes of mobilization led to the rise of sub-state nationalism in the second half of the nineteenth century. Political leaders representing this type of minority were keener on defining their group as a nationality or minority nation, rather than a national minority. Furthermore, such minorities could not profit from the support of any kin-state and minority representatives mostly campaigned for autonomy or independence.

The Flemish population of Belgium is a peculiar case that can be considered a sociological minority despite constituting a demographic majority.[16] Belgium was founded as a francophone state led by a francophone elite, although the majority of the population spoke several Flemish dialects. Furthermore, with Flanders being the poorer region of the country, the linguistic divide between Flemings and Francophones partly coincided with a social divide. As a consequence, a strong social process of French assimilation began, causing part of the Flemish population to resist and establish a movement to promote linguistic equality between Flemish and French called the Flemish Movement.

A key factor accounting for the different evolution of majority-minority relations in Belgium, Italy, and Spain is the political regime ruling these states at any point in time. While Belgium remained democratic throughout the interwar period, Mussolini's dictatorship governed Italy from 1922 to 1943. Spain, in turn, experienced frequent regime changes. General Primo de Rivera carried out a putsch in 1923, but democracy was reestablished with the founding of the Second Republic in 1931. Yet, the democratic regime eventually collapsed at the end of the civil war, in April 1939, when General Francisco Franco took over the country.[17]

In the next section, we will take these different political regimes as our units of analysis and comparatively discuss their policies toward the respective states' minorities. We will look first at Liberal Italy (1918–22) and Restoration Spain (1918–23) before Primo de Rivera's putsch; then we will shift our focus to the dictatorships that ensued in both countries (from 1922 to 1943 in Italy and between 1923 and 1931 in Spain). Finally, we will examine the most tolerant regimes in our sample, Republican Spain (1931–9) and Democratic Belgium (throughout the interwar years). In each case, we offer some comparative reflections related to the situation in Eastern Europe that help to locate these Western European experiences in the broader continental context.

Belgium, Italy, and Spain: Assimilation, Recognition, and Homogenizing Tendencies

Even within the same state, different political regimes adopted diverging policies toward their minorities. Liberal governments tended to be more tolerant than dictatorships, but they still displayed homogenizing tendencies. In some cases, minority demands gathered stronger popular support only late in the interwar period, which suggests that national consciousness was not as strong as nationalist leaders claimed immediately after the Great War and points to the existence of nation-building projects within minorities as well. In many of the situations explored in the following sections, what was at stake for members of minority groups was the possibility to freely speak their native language and openly practice their culture. What changed from regime to regime was the degree to which central governments were willing to accommodate the minority culture and the one to which minority nationalist leaders resisted assimilationist attempts and promoted the standardization (i.e., homogenization) of the minority culture.

Liberal Italy (1918–22) and Restoration Spain (1918–23): Inaction and Resistance

In the period between the end of the Great War and Mussolini's and Primo de Rivera's coups in October 1922 and September 1923, respectively, state authorities in Italy and Spain had to address the requests for autonomy presented by different minority nationalist organizations.

For the Italian liberal regime this was an absolute novelty. When the Italian political elites were confronted with the task of integrating the "new citizens" annexed from the Habsburg Empire, they were unprepared. Opinions on what approach to take ranged from the support for a self-determination referendum proposed by some members of the Socialist Party, to an extreme assimilationist program advocated by nationalist activist Ettore Tolomei, who would later advise Mussolini on the matter.[18]

There were considerable differences between the way in which Italian authorities treated the inhabitants of South Tyrol (200,000 German speakers) and Venezia Giulia (460,000 Slovenian and Croatian speakers). While in the former military governors were more respectful of the rights of locals and schools in minority languages were left in place, in the latter several schools that taught in Slovenian and Croatian were closed.[19] With the onset of civilian rule, in mid-1919, two governors with wide-ranging powers were appointed by the central government to administer the two regions. The governor of South Tyrol, Luigi Credaro, continued the liberal policy adopted by the military authorities, although he progressively implemented more repressive measures in 1921–2. Except for a mixed language area south of Bolzano/Bozen, schools remained in German and residents were allowed to communicate with the administration in German as well.[20] Assimilationist attempts were stronger in Venezia Giulia. The region's governor, Antonio Mosconi, refused to reopen the schools in minority languages that had been closed during the military occupation and more generally tolerated, sometimes even exploited, fascist violence against minority organizations. Additionally, even though public administration in these provinces was officially bilingual until 1922, local authorities often refused to use the language of the minority.[21]

Despite repeated reassurances from several authorities that the rights of minorities would be respected, Italian liberal elites pursued an ambivalent policy. While aiming toward a middle ground between assimilation and respect for minority languages and cultures, in practice this policy often condoned, sometimes even tacitly approved of, fascist violence against minorities. This violence, especially in Venezia Giulia, became a daily occurrence causing several casualties in 1920–2. Furthermore, the hesitant attitude of Italian politicians during the negotiations for autonomy with members of the South Tyrolean minority organization *Deutscher Verband* (DV) reflects this ambivalent policy. As late as March 1922, three years after the beginning of these negotiations and despite reassurances that autonomy would be granted quickly, the Socialist MP from South Tyrol, Silvio Flor, asked the government in Parliament whether "it intended to persist with the wavering policy until then followed."[22] Prime Minister Facta's following reassurances did not turn into any concrete measures.

Contrary to Italy, Spain did not take part in the Great War and did not annex any new territory inhabited by populations speaking a different language. However, between 1917 and 1923, minority nationalist parties in the Basque Country and Catalonia submitted proposals for regional autonomy to the central government. The defense of the Basque and Catalan languages was at the core of these parties' programs.[23] Plans for regional autonomy, the Catalan one in particular, were met with strong resistance in Parliament and conflict spilled over into the streets of Barcelona in January 1919. The Spanish government repressed these protests and later used the excuse of mounting social protests in the Catalan capital as an opportunity to close Parliament and end discussions concerning autonomy. In the following four years, labor protests took center stage in Spanish politics and overshadowed demands for autonomy from minority nationalist actors until the beginning of General Primo de Rivera's dictatorship in 1923.[24]

The Basque and, even more so, Catalan languages were widely used in their respective regions, although mostly in oral form. Yet, the use of these two languages was not officially recognized in schools or in public administration. Spanish remained the official language of state education and bureaucracy, although its superior status was only made formal later under the dictatorship.[25] However, teaching in minority languages in private education, which catered to the overwhelming majority of students, was not forbidden. Hence, lack of education in minority languages was also a reflection of its low demand. Despite the strong rhetoric of Basque and Catalan nationalist parties, who promoted their languages, the local middle classes, for reasons such as improved social mobility, kept sending their children to private schools whose language of instruction was Spanish. Furthermore, the Basque and Catalan nationalist movements were only then beginning the process of homogenization of their respective languages. Hence, demands for schools in minority languages were formulated mostly from the early interwar period onward and, until the 1930s, they remained limited to a narrow elite.[26]

The immediate postwar years were also a time of experimentation. In Catalonia, the local language was taught in some professional schools promoted by the *Mancomunitat*—the union of the four Catalan provinces created in 1914—and in a few municipal schools in Barcelona.[27] In 1919, the provincial administration of Biscay (in the Basque Country) passed an ambitious project aimed at creating 100 schools, called *escuelas de barriada*, within five years. These offered education in Basque in areas where most of the population was Basque-speaking and in Spanish where the majority was Spanish-speaking. Spanish and Basque were taught as a subject in each type of school, respectively. Yet, the project was severely curtailed already in 1921 and, more decisively, with Primo de Rivera's dictatorship in 1923.[28] Attempts at introducing schooling in minority languages thus touched only a tiny fraction of the local school population in both the Basque Country and Catalonia.

Overall, during the short liberal period between the end of the Great War and the rise of dictatorial governments, education in minority languages was better protected in Italy than in Spain—although less so in Venezia Giulia than in South Tyrol. The inhabitants of the Italian "new provinces" also had some access to administration in their language. In Spain, however, the exclusion of minority languages from schools and bureaucracy was only partly due to the centralizing tendencies of the Spanish elite, as at the local level demand for teaching in minority languages remained weak. Private schools could have provided such teaching if there had been sufficient requests from parents. In both countries, calls for autonomy were approached with ambivalence, if not open hostility, on the part of central governments and Parliaments. Furthermore, state authorities tolerated, even openly exploited, violent acts committed by extreme right-wing organizations against minority nationalist leaders and organizations.

If contrasted with the policies enforced in Eastern Europe, the situation surrounding minorities within Liberal Italy and Restoration Spain can be compared to that in Czechoslovakia, one of the Eastern European countries that treated its minorities relatively liberally. In fact, on paper, Czechoslovakia offered a higher degree of protection than either of the Western European regimes, since it provided its minority groups with a wide-ranging set of rights beyond the minimum required by the minority treaties. For instance, in districts where more than 20 percent of the population spoke the minority language, the courts and civil servants had to communicate with members of minorities in their own language. Furthermore, public primary schools in minority languages had to be established whenever the parents of forty children requested it.[29] However, legislation was often poorly implemented. The state promoted land colonization in border areas inhabited by minorities to the advantage of Czechs and Slovaks and, in Moravia, Czech authorities often denied parents the right to send their children to German schools if these were considered to be of Czech descent, regardless of the fact that they often spoke German at home.[30] Czechoslovak was imposed as the official language of the state and, in 1926, 33,000 German-speaking civil servants lost their positions because they lacked proficiency in this language. Also, Czech politicians tended to exclude members of the country's minority groups (including those of Slovak origins) from positions of power in the state administration.[31] Thus, as in Liberal Italy and Restoration Spain, minorities enjoyed some protection, but this was not completely in line with the standard required by the League's minority treaties.

Fascist Italy (1922–43) and Primo de Rivera Spain (1923–31): Coercive Assimilation

In contrast with the liberal regimes just discussed, the authoritarian regimes of Benito Mussolini and Miguel Primo de Rivera set out to erase any minority nationalist movement in their respective countries and to assimilate minority populations into the majority language and culture.

In Italy, this process was more gradual than in Spain. The 1923 Gentile Law, named after the then Minister of Education and prominent philosopher Giovanni Gentile, imposed the Italian language as the only language of instruction in schools. Yet, the disappearance of minority languages from the primary school curriculum was phased out over a period of five years. Thus, by 1927–8, German and Slovenian/Croatian speakers could learn their mother tongue only as a foreign language in secondary schools. Private teaching was first impeded and then forbidden.[32] Teachers and civil servants belonging to one of these minorities were either dismissed or transferred to other Italian regions. Minority cultural associations were dissolved, while the minority's lower clergy was accused of defending minority languages and heavily harassed.[33]

Fascist assimilationist policies went beyond schooling as the regime envisaged the total Italianization of its minorities. To this effect, Mussolini tried to impose the Italianization of family names. Although officially this conversion was not compulsory, lists of "foreign" names were drafted and strong pressure was applied to transform them into "pure" Italian names.[34] Furthermore, to improve the results achieved up until that point, which they saw as disappointing, from 1933 onward the fascists scaled up the settlement of these new provinces with Italians from other regions of the country.[35] Overall, results were not satisfactory for the regime, but in the city of Bolzano/Bozen the establishment of an industrial zone settled with "pure" Italians, coming from provinces of the Kingdom without minorities, reversed the linguistic balance in the city to the advantage of Italian speakers, who by the late 1930s became a majority.[36] Although violence rarely reached extreme levels, it was institutionalized in the repressive apparatus of the regime and continuously applied to minority organizations and the wider population through policing and surveillance.

In Spain, Primo de Rivera's dictatorship repressed minority organizations and minority languages more rapidly, but less profoundly than Mussolini's. Only a few days after his coup on September 13, 1923, the Spanish leader passed a decree against separatism. This imposed Castilian as the official state language at all levels of the administration and the education system. Spreading separatist propaganda in schools was punished with prison sentences, and teachers caught speaking Basque or Catalan in class were often transferred to other Spanish regions. The regime created a system of surveillance and systematic evaluation of teachers that rewarded denunciation. The same occurred within the state administration so that officials deemed to hold nationalist sympathies were purged. As in fascist Italy, minority cultural associations were disbanded, and the minority's lower clergy accused of defending minority languages. Although family names were left untouched, the public space was Castilianized.[37]

However, Primo de Rivera did not aim at erasing Catalan and Basque completely from Spanish territory. In fact, the regime allowed the publication of newspapers in Catalan—their production in fact increased between 1923 and 1927. The regime also continued to fund studies on the Catalan language. The dictator simply strove to turn minority languages into elements of regional folklore without any connection to political identities.[38] In the Basque Country, the regime repressed the separatist *Partido Nacionalista Vasco* and all those nationalists who openly challenged the regime, but it did not dissolve the moderate *Comunión Nacionalista Vasca*, which, in turn, focused on purely cultural activities. Publications in Basque were allowed and the regime even renewed the *concierto economico*, a special agreement between the central government and the Basque provinces that guaranteed some form of fiscal autonomy for the latter.[39]

Coercive assimilation did not work in Italy or Spain. Both Mussolini and Primo de Rivera's regimes tried to force minority populations to identify with Italy and Spain, respectively, by using repression and indoctrination tactics. Yet, the nation-building efforts put forth by these two regimes only managed to increase opposition to the state and reinforced minority nationalism. In Italy, the results of the 1939 Option Agreement negotiated by Mussolini and Hitler offer the clearest evidence for this increased opposition. The Option Agreement allowed the German-speaking population of South Tyrol to choose whether they wanted to stay in Italy or move to Nazi Germany and obtain German citizenship. More than 85 percent of voters opted for moving to Germany.[40] This result was a harsh setback for the Italian regime, which had insisted for about twenty years that the inhabitants of South Tyrol could not resist assimilation to Italian majority culture. Similarly, by the late 1920s, when Primo de Rivera began losing support among the social classes that had bolstered him, the strength of minority nationalism had grown considerably. When in April 1931 the Second Republic was declared immediately after the municipal elections held throughout the country, Basque and Catalan nationalist parties came out among the biggest winners of the ballot.[41]

In a wider comparative context, both these Western European regimes showed a standard of treatment in line with, and in some respects even less tolerant than that granted to minorities in Poland—which was one of the most repressive Eastern European countries with regards to their minorities. Polish legislation was officially quite protective of minorities, and between 1926 and 1935 the József Piłsudski's dictatorship openly defended an inclusive form of civic nationalism. Yet, laws were largely disregarded and the situation degenerated after 1935, especially with the introduction of antisemitic measures.[42] The number of schools in minority languages declined dramatically throughout the interwar period and economic discrimination hit the German-speaking population in the early 1920s.[43] Large-scale violence against minorities was probably stronger in Poland than in authoritarian Italy and Spain. In the early 1930s, Piłsudski's government adopted strongly repressive policies of "pacification" under the cover of anti-terrorism activities in the areas inhabited by Ukrainian speakers,[44] while in the late 1930s Polish authorities tolerated several antisemitic pogroms.[45] Yet, violence was institutionalized in Mussolini's and Primo de Rivera's regimes as well and practiced daily through small acts of repression and surveillance.

Republican Spain (1931–39) and Democratic Belgium (1918–39): Recognition and Homogenizing Tendencies

Liberal regimes tended to integrate their minorities by recognizing cultural differences and granting a minimum degree of protection. This was especially the case in Spain during the Republican period (1931–39) and in Belgium throughout the interwar years. Yet, even in these cases one can see homogenizing tendencies in the latter and persisting conflict between minority demands and centralizing efforts in the former.

In Spain, the Second Republic originated in the combined efforts of a wide coalition of democratic republican forces in which minority nationalist parties, especially in Catalonia, played a prominent role. Catalan nationalists were among the first political leaders in Spain to proclaim the Spanish Republic on April 14, 1931. With the creation of this new democratic regime, Catalan and Basque representatives had a chance to obtain the political autonomy that had been resisted by the old Restoration elite. In Catalonia, an autonomous government called *Generalitat*, established immediately after the proclamation of the Republic, governed the territory until the end of the civil war. In the Basque Country, on the contrary, major disagreements among the drafters of the statute of autonomy delayed the creation of a regional executive until October 1936, well into the civil war.[46]

The Catalan statute affirmed the co-official nature of Catalan and Spanish in the region. Public schools remained under the control of the central executive, but the *Generalitat* was allowed to set up its own school network at its own expense. A decree signed in April 1931 ordered pupils to be taught in their mother tongue until eight years of age, thus opening up the possibility to establish Catalan as the language of instruction in public primary schools. The decree was de facto largely ignored. This however was also due to a dearth of teachers sufficiently fluent in Catalan—a reminder that the Catalan nation was still under construction. The equality of Spanish and Catalan was also extended to higher education.[47]

The Basque statute also recognized the official character of the Basque language but transferred a limited number of competences to the regional executive. The relative isolation of the Basque provinces and the weakness of the Spanish Republican government, both caused by the ongoing civil war, enabled the Basque government to exercise a much wider range of competences than those originally devolved by the central government. The Basque region was practically acting as an independent state until the conquest of this territory by Franco's troops in June 1937.[48] Even before the establishment of the Basque executive, several projects providing primary bilingual education were launched in both Biscay and Gipuzkoa, which expanded the lukewarm attempts at education in Basque of the early postwar years, although they still affected only a few thousand pupils.[49]

Republican Spain can thus be categorized as a mixed example regarding the recognition of national difference. On the one hand, it constituted an exceptional instance of devolution of powers to regional authorities in the Basque Country and Catalonia. On the other hand, it was a very brief and conflict-ridden regime. This was especially the case in Catalonia, where, in October 1934, after a few months of struggle between the *Generalitat* and the central executive over a regional agricultural law, and with the coming of a new government opposed to Catalan autonomy in Madrid, the President of the *Generalitat* Lluís Companys decided to declare a Catalan state within a Spanish Republican Federation. The new Spanish executive imposed a state of emergency on the region, closed the Catalan Parliament, and directly ruled the region until the left-wing Popular Front won new elections in February 1936 and re-instated Catalan autonomy. A few months later, the civil war began and although this was mostly an ideological conflict between the Left and the Right, Franco's rebellion was caused in part by, and aimed at uprooting, nationalist forces in the Basque Country and Catalonia.[50]

Compared to Republican Spain, Belgium did not experience the same level of minority conflict. At the end of the Great War, the Belgian political elites were confronted with two minority issues. The first concerned a population of former German subjects annexed at the end of the Great War that was living in the districts of Eupen, Malmedy, and St. Vith (the so-called Eastern cantons). The second regarded the Flemish-speaking population of Flanders, whose demands for equality between French and Flemings had grown stronger during and immediately after the conflict.

Belgian policy toward its German population in the Eastern cantons was often paternalistic, sometimes despotic. However, it generally guaranteed the protection of the language and culture of the region. Successive Belgian executives never hid their goal of assimilating the population of the Eastern cantons. Yet, they interpreted assimilation as a policy that would integrate the "new Belgians" into the administrative and social fabric of the state without necessarily implying full homogenization. For this purpose, the central government appointed General Herman Baltia as Royal High Commissioner of the region, which he ruled with wide-ranging powers from 1920 to 1925. Baltia's regime tolerated the cultural and linguistic difference of local inhabitants but was also paternalistic and authoritarian. In educational terms, the general divided the cantons into two areas: in Malmedy (where most of the population was French speaking) French was the dominant language and German the second language; in Eupen and St. Vith (where the linguistic landscape was the opposite), the situation was reversed. This generally ensured that German-speaking pupils could have most of their education in German.[51] However, similar to Italian authorities (although not to the same extent), Baltia removed German-speaking teachers from primary and secondary schools, as he believed that they were not "reliable." About one-third of the total number of these teachers left or were fired in 1920.[52] Furthermore, the regime repressed dissent, notably during the "popular consultation" on annexation imposed by the Treaty of Versailles that took place in the first half of 1920. The consultation was widely defined as a fraud, including by some Belgian politicians, and its farcical nature undermined the legitimacy of Belgian control of the area throughout the interwar years.[53]

In the immediate post-Baltia period, the Belgian central government acted inconsiderately toward the population of the Eastern cantons. For instance, it removed some elected mayors that it did not trust and leaked details of negotiations with Berlin, which occurred from 1925 to 1926, about a possible restitution of the cantons to Germany. Both occurrences convinced many locals that they were second-class citizens.[54] After 1929, Brussels started taking a more lenient approach, but the Nazi takeover in Germany complicated things further. Belgian authorities detected an intensification of covert pro-German activity in the area. Consequently, they increased surveillance and even introduced radical measures such as the implementation of a law that would denationalize citizens who were not Belgian nationals by birth if they violated "their duties as Belgian citizens."[55] At the same time, successive governments carefully avoided disaffecting the local population and creating martyrs.[56]

The fact that in 1939, 45.2 percent of the population of the cantons voted for the revisionist party *Heimattreue Front* suggests that the assimilation efforts of the Belgian authorities had worked only in part. Yet, in comparison with the situation in Fascist Italy, where more than 85 percent of the population of South Tyrol voted to move to Germany in 1939 suggests that, in relative terms, Belgium's more tolerant approach was more effective than Mussolini's attempts at forced assimilation.[57]

The second minority issue that the Belgian state had to address in the interwar period concerned the population of Flanders, which in fact was a demographic majority. We consider this population as a sociological minority on account of its lower status in a state dominated by francophone elites. However, despite this initial lower status, during the interwar years Flemish nationalism became stronger and the Flemish economy also improved, reinforcing the negotiating power of Flemish nationalist elites within the Belgian state. Thus, by the early 1930s, Flemish and francophone politicians agreed to turn Flanders and Wallonia into two homogeneous monolingual areas.

The main minority organization advocating for the rights of the Flemish people was the Flemish Movement. It had arisen in the second half of the nineteenth century to demand equality between French and Dutch in Belgium. During the Great War, the Movement divided into a radical anti-Belgian wing calling for autonomy, even independence, and a moderate faction, that rallied the Movement's large majority. This latter faction demanded the Flemishization of education (in particular secondary and higher education), the administration and the courts in Flanders, as well as equality between Francophones and Flemings in the army. At the end of the war, these requests, embodied in the "minimum program" devised by the Flemish Catholic leader Frans van Cauwelaert, met resistance from the francophone establishment, which despite the introduction of universal male suffrage in 1919 remained dominant in the executive.[58] Many francophone politicians, along with the King, were willing to provide more equality to Flemish, but not at the expense of bilingualism in Flanders, where education in Flemish was provided, but French was widely used in public administration and prevailed in higher education.[59]

At the end of the war, the use of languages in the administration and the school system was mostly regulated in accordance with the personality principle. According to this principle, every citizen should have been able to use whatever official language in his or her dealings with the state and within schools. Toward the end of the 1920s, however, support for an alternative principle, the territorial principle, grew. This postulated that the language of the majority in a specific area should have been the official language in the administration and education. Between 1930 and 1932, through the adoption of the three bills on the complete Flemishization of the University of Ghent (in 1930), the use of languages in public administration (1932) and the use of languages in primary and secondary schools (1932), most of the Belgian territory was divided into two monolingual linguistic areas. As a result, linguistic minorities in most of Flanders and Wallonia did not enjoy any protection, except for some derogations along the border between these two regions, Brussels (which remained bilingual), and the Eastern cantons—indeed the francophone Flemish elites rapidly declined after the formation of the two monolingual areas.[60]

The turn toward the territorial principle occurred as the result of a change in opinion among most Walloon MPs. In 1921, when a first reform of the use of languages in the administration that introduced a degree of territoriality was passed, politicians from Wallonia had voted overwhelmingly against the bill. MPs from Flanders, by contrast, massively supported it.[61] Eleven years later, two-thirds of MPs in both Flanders and Wallonia accepted the new bill on the use of languages in the administration that did away, almost completely, with the rights of minorities in both areas. Such change in the attitude of Walloon lawmakers occurred because of a complex set of reasons. In part, the shift reflected a generalized reaction of Belgian authorities to the election of August Borms, a Flemish radical nationalist who was in prison for collaboration with the German occupier during the First World War, at a by-election in Antwerp in 1928. The event stunned the Belgian political elites and convinced them to adopt a more lenient approach to Flemish linguistic demands. Indeed, Belgian politicians thought that an intransigent line would favor a radicalization of Flemish public opinion. However, among Walloon politicians in particular, the turnaround in favor of the creation of two monolingual regions also stemmed from fears that Flemish MPs would use their majority in Parliament to impose equality between Flemish and French in the form of bilingualism throughout Belgium. The Liberal Walloon politician François Bovesse conveyed these fears well, as well as the trade-off that many Walloon politicians were ready to accept, when he bitterly acknowledged that "it is hard, it is bitter to abandon the Francophones of Flanders. It would be certainly harder and more dangerous to sacrifice our [Walloon] linguistic unity."[62] Concerns about the linguistic integrity of Wallonia convinced most Walloon MPs to accept the Flemish MPs' proposal to divide the country into two monolingual areas. Hence, although there was no homogenization at the state level in Belgium, homogenization occurred within both Flanders and Wallonia.

Overall, with respect to our case studies, Belgium throughout the interwar period and Republican Spain from 1931 to 1936 guaranteed the best standard of protection to their minorities. Public education in minority languages was allowed (although funded by regional authorities in Spain) and the Republic even granted territorial autonomy to the Basque provinces and Catalonia. Although formal autonomy was not given to the Flemish population, the moderate nationalist leader Frans van Cauwelaert considered the implementation of his "minimum programme" (which was de facto realized in the 1930s) as a form of cultural autonomy, because it would shield the Flemish population from social dynamics favoring French assimilation.[63]

There was a comparable level of protection and recognition in the Eastern European context, namely in the Baltic Republic of Estonia until the 1934 coup d'état. There, recognition was chiefly granted through the peculiar institutional tool of non-territorial autonomy. Estonia allowed each group considered as a minority with at least 3,000 members to set up a far-reaching system of cultural (non-territorial) autonomy. These groups could establish institutions to manage their educational and cultural life. Minority organs had the authority to impose legally binding rules on their members and raise taxes (under state supervision).[64] The system was not perfect and, for instance, the German minority was heavily targeted by land redistribution measures. Nevertheless, pre-1934 Estonia still offered minorities one of the most tolerant contexts of the entire continent during the interwar period and allowed the creation of an extensive network of subsidized German and Jewish minority schools that went beyond the efforts carried out in this sector in Catalonia and the Basque Country during the Republican period.[65]

Conclusion: Locating Belgium, Italy, and Spain in the Wider European Context

Contrary to interwar assumptions that linger in historiography to this day, Western Europe experienced tense majority-minority relations between the two World Wars. Moreover, in many respects, minority treatment in Western European states and in the countries subjected to the minority treaties did not differ substantially. Hence, in the interwar years, minorities were a "problem of Europe as a whole."[66] The decision to circumscribe minority protection to Eastern Europe stemmed from power asymmetries between the European states and lingering civilizational stereotypes, rather than from realities on the ground.

This does not mean that majority-minority relations were the same in Eastern and Western Europe, but that comparable situations existed. Furthermore, both parts of the continent showed considerable variation in terms of minority treatment within their own region, sometimes even within the same country over time.

Although Western European states were not legally bound to respect the League's minority treaties, they had a moral obligation to fulfill them in light of the 1922 resolution of the Assembly of the League of Nations. We can thus evaluate their behavior against the background of these treaties. Liberal Italy and Restoration Spain provided liberal rights to their population, including minorities, but they did not fully provide minority-specific rights. Furthermore, both regimes became increasingly repressive in the early 1920s and tolerated, even publicly exploited, violent extreme-right groups attacking minority organizations, which eventually took over state institutions altogether.

Italian Fascism and Spain under General Primo de Rivera clearly disregarded most of the rights set out in these treaties. Apart from the violations of the right to liberty and equality before the law implied by their authoritarian nature (and which concerned all citizens), these two regimes consistently repressed minority organizations and imposed the majority's language as the sole language of instruction and administration. Primo de Rivera, however, left more room than Mussolini for the use of regional languages in the media and the public space as mere elements of Spanish folklore.

In contrast, Republican Spain and Democratic Belgium recognized the language and culture of their minorities. Republican Spain granted territorial autonomy to the regions of the Basque Country and Catalonia and recognized the co-official character of the languages spoken there. Although the Republic did not directly fund schools in minority language, it allowed regional executives to create their own parallel school system with their own revenues. Interwar Belgium did not concede autonomy to either the German-speaking population of the Eastern cantons or the population of Flanders, but it did establish public schools that taught in the Flemish or German language, allowed the use of these languages in court, and did not repress minority organizations. Both, however, demonstrated disadvantageous aspects with respect to their minorities as well. The Spanish Republic was short-lived and conflict-ridden, eventually leading to a civil war and a new dictatorship. Belgium's legitimacy in the Eastern cantons was undermined by the 1920 farcical plebiscite concerning annexation and by a number of other "tactless" attempts to promote French assimilation of the area (although this never meant the annihilation of German language and culture), while Flemish demands for equality between Flemish and French led to the division of the country into two linguistically homogenous areas.

Although a systematic comparison with the situation in Eastern Europe is beyond the scope of this chapter, it is possible to establish connections between Eastern and Western European cases. While Mussolini's Italy and Primo de Rivera's Spain violated minority rights to an extent and in ways similar to interwar Poland, Czechoslovakia afforded a standard of treatment in line with the mixed records of Liberal Italy and Restoration Spain. Similarly, pre-1934 Estonia granted minorities a degree of autonomy at least as extensive as interwar Belgium and Republican Spain.

Without going so far as carrying out a thorough East-West comparison, this chapter has shown that Western European countries should be located more firmly in an all-European context. It suggests that the image of a European continent split between a homogeneous, tolerant, and peaceful West and a heterogeneous, repressive, and conflict-ridden East does not hold. As a result, a more nuanced picture emerges in which policies of recognition are comparable in Republican Spain and Belgium just as in pre-1934 Estonia, while repression was a hallmark of Fascist Italy and Primo de Rivera's Spain as much as was the case in interwar Poland.

Acknowledgments

This chapter benefited from comments on earlier versions from Davide Rodogno, Eric Storm, Andre Liebich, and Kasper Swerts. We thank them very much for their insightful remarks. The research required to write this piece was generously supported by the Swiss National Science Foundation (grant n. 169568) and the European Union's Horizon 2020 research and innovation program under the Marie Skłodowska-Curie grant agreement no. 847635.

Notes

1   Eric D. Weitz, "From the Vienna to the Paris System: International Politics and the Entangled Histories of Human Rights, Forced Deportations, and Civilizing Missions," *The American Historical Review* 113, no. 5 (2008): 1314.

2   Mark Mazower, "Minorities and the League of Nations in Interwar Europe," *Daedalus* 126, no. 2 (1997): 53.
3   Matthew Frank, *Making Minorities History: Population Transfer in Twentieth-century Europe* (Oxford: Oxford University Press, 2017), 45–6. For more on this point see the introduction to this volume.
4   Jacques Fouques Duparc, *La protection des minorités, de race, de langue et de religion, étude de droit des gens* (Paris: Dalloz, 1922), 17.
5   C. A. Macartney, "Minorities: A Problem of Eastern Europe," *Foreign Affairs* 9, no. 4 (1931): 677. For a similar point see also Arnold Toynbee, *Nationality & the War* (London: Dent & Sons, 1915), 476–504.
6   See Carole Fink, *Defending the Rights of Others* (Cambridge: Cambridge University Press, 2006); Stephan M. Horak, *Eastern European National Minorities, 1919–1980: A Handbook* (Littleton: Libraries Unlimited, 1985); Raymond Pearson, *National Minorities in Eastern Europe: 1848–1945.* (New York: St. Martin's Pr., 1983); Christian Raitz von Frentz, *A Lesson Forgotten: Minority Protection under the League of Nations: The Case of the German Minority in Poland, 1920–1934* (Münster: Lit-Verlag, 1999); Martin Scheuermann, *Minderheitenschutz contra Konfliktverhütung?: die Minderheitenpolitik des Völkerbundes in den zwanziger Jahren* (Marburg: Verlag Herder-Instut, 2000); Paul Smith, *Ethnic Groups in International Relations* (Aldershot: Dartmouth, 1991). For exceptions, see Volker Prott, *The Politics of Self-Determination: Remaking Territories and National Identities in Europe, 1917–1923* (Oxford: Oxford University Press, 2016); Tara Zahra, "The 'Minority Problem' and National Classification in the French and Czechoslovak Borderlands," *Contemporary European History* 17, no. 2 (2008): 137–65.
7   For a similar focus on minority questions in Western Europe, see the chapters of Alison Carrol, Brian Hughes, Alvin Jackson, and Volker Prott in this volume.
8   For an examination of majority-minority relations through the prism of national indifference or, more broadly, nationalism from below, see the contributions of Alison Carrol, Brian Hughes, Pieter Judson, and Olga Linkiewicz in this volume. For a critical discussion of national indifference, see Omer Bartov's coda to this volume.
9   In this chapter we focus on national minorities, that is, on minority groups whose political elites claimed to represent a sovereign political community distinct from that of the state where they lived.
10 Treaty between the Principal Allied and Associated Powers and Poland, 28 June 1919, http://ungarisches-institut.de/dokumente/pdf/19190628-3.pdf (accessed June 27, 2022).
11 Carole Fink, "The Paris Peace Conference and the Question of Minority Rights," *Peace & Change* 21, no. 3 (1996): 75–76.
12 Stanislaw Sierposwski, "Minorities in the System of the League of Nations," in *Ethnic Groups in International Relations*, ed. Paul Smith (Aldershot: Dartmouth, 1991), 18–23.
13 The full list includes: Albania, Austria, Bulgaria, Czechoslovakia, Estonia, Finland, Greece, Hungary, Iraq, Latvia, Lithuania, Poland, Romania, Turkey, Yugoslavia, as well as the territory of Memel, and the region of Upper Silesia. See Pablo de Azcárate, *League of Nations and National Minorities: An Experiment* (Washington: Carnegie Endowment for International Peace, 1945), 94–5.
14 Resolutions and Recommendations Adopted on the Reports of the Sixth Committee Part IX (1922). *League of Nations Official Journal, Special Supplement*, 9: 35–8; Eighth Meeting (1933). *League of Nations Official Journal, Special Supplement* 120: 59–61.

15 Javier Tusell, "La crisis del liberalismo oligarquico en Espana. Una rivoluzione mancata a la Española," in *La transición a la política de masas*, ed. Edward Acton, Sebastian Balfour, and Ismael Saz (Valencia: Universidad de Valencia, 2001), 21–36; Andrea Di Michele, *L'italianizzazione imperfetta: l'amministrazione pubblica dell'Alto Adige tra Italia liberale e fascismo* (Alessandria: Edizioni dell'Orso, 2003), 56–153; Herman Van Goethem, *Belgium and the Monarchy from National Independence to National Disintegration* (Antwerp: University Press Antwerp, 2011), 133–9.
16 By sociological minority we mean a political stand identifying a non-dominant group as oppressed (regardless of its actual demographic size) and pursuing different emancipatory agendas to ensure equality with other groups inhabiting the state. Els Witte and Harry van Velthoven, *Languages in Contact and in Conflict: The Belgian Case* (Kapellen: Pelckmans, 2011), 15.
17 For reasons of scope, this chapter will not engage extensively with the civil war period and will mostly limit its analysis of the Spanish Republic to the period from 1931 to 1936.
18 Elio Apih, *Italia, fascismo e antifascismo nella Venezia Giulia, 1918–1943: ricerche storiche* (Bari: Laterza, 1966), 51–68.
19 Adriano Andri and Giulio Mellinato, *Scuola e confine: le istituzioni educative della Venezia Giulia 1915–1945* (Trieste: Istituto Regionale per la Storia del Movimento di Liberazione nel Friuli-Venezia Giulia, 1994), 37–8.
20 Angelo Ara, "Scuola e minoranze nazionali in Italia, 1861–1940," *Studi Trentini di Scienze Storiche* 4 (1990), 470.
21 Annamaria Vinci, *Sentinelle della Patria. Il fascismo al confine orientale, 1918–1941* (Roma: Laterza, 2011), 72–116.
22 Camera dei Deputati, Atti Parlamentari, Resoconto stenografico, 20.3.1922, 3322, https://storia.camera.it/regno/lavori/leg26/sed070.pdf (accessed December 13, 2021). See also ibid., 3337.
23 For more details on these campaigns for autonomy, see Santiago de Pablo and Ludger Mees, *El péndulo patriótico: historia del Partido Nacionalista Vasco, 1895–2005* (Barcelona: Crítica, 2005), 59–70; Javier Moreno Luzón, "De agravios, pactos y símbolos. El nacionalismo español ante la autonomía de Cataluña (1918–1919)," *Ayer*, 2006: 119–51; Borja de Riquer I Permaner, *Alfonso XIII y Cambó. La monarquía y el catalanismo político* (Barcelona: RBA, 2013), 111–42.
24 De Riquer, *Alfonso XIII*, 132.
25 Daniel Escribano, "La Introducció del concepte de 'llengua oficial' a l'ordenament jurídic espanyol (1902–1931)," *Treballs de sociolingüística catalana*, 2015: 213–29.
26 Josep González-Agàpito, *Tradició i renovació pedagògica, 1898–1939: història de l'educació : Catalunya, Illes Balears, País Valencià* (Barcelona: Publicacions de l'Abadia de Montserrat, 2002), 295–6; Maitane Ostolaza, *Entre religión y modernidad* (Bilbao: Universidad del País Vasco, 2000), 289–330.
27 Alexandre Galí, *Història de les institucions i del moviment cultural a Catalunya 1900–1936*, vol. 1 (Barcelona: Fundació Alexandre Galí, 1980), 129. Although one could argue that the *Mancomunitat* was a form of regional autonomy, the body did not receive any new competences on top of those enjoyed by the four Catalan provinces that constituted it. These competences were executive and not legislative. Furthermore, the transfer of powers (and means to exercise them) from the provinces to the *Mancomunitat* was delayed for several years and took place in 1921, only two years before the beginning of Primo de Rivera's dictatorship. Even then, the *Mancomunitat* had a lower budget and capacity to raise funds than the municipality

of Barcelona. For more details see Enric Ucelay Da Cal, "La Diputación i La Mancomunitat: 1914–1923," in *Història de La Diputació de Barcelona : 1812–2005*, ed. Borja de Riquer (Barcelona: Diputació de Barcelona, 2007), 39–211.
28 Karmele Artetxe Sánchez, "Las escuelas de barriada de Bizkaia (1920–1937): revisión y nuevos datos," *Historia y Memoria de La Educación*, no. 12 (2020): 363–94.
29 Jozef Kaldova, "National Minorities in Czechoslovakia, 1919–1980," in *Eastern European National Minorities, 1919–1980: A Handbook*, ed. Stephan M. Horak (Littleton: Libraries unlimited, 1985), 114.
30 Daniel E. Miller, "Colonizing the Hungarian and German Border Areas during the Czechoslovak Land Reform. 1918–1938," *Austrian History Yearbook* 34 (2003): 303–17; Tara Zahra, "Reclaiming Children for the Nation: Germanization, National Ascription, and Democracy in the Bohemian Lands, 1900–1945," *Central European History* 37, no. 4 (2004): 501–43.
31 Andrea Orzoff, *Battle for the Castle: The Myth of Czechoslavakia in Europe, 1914–1948* (Oxford: Oxford University Press, 2009), 140; Peter Bugge, "Czech Democracy 1918-1938—Paragon or Parody?," *Bohemia* 47, no. 1 (2007): 3–28. On the contrast between the interwar (and postwar) myth of a tolerant and democratic Czechoslovakia, the propaganda efforts of the Czech political elites to disseminate this myth, and the much more mixed reality on the ground, see Orzoff, *Battle for the Castle*.
32 Ara, "Scuola e minoranze," 479.
33 Andri and Mellinato, *Scuola e confine*, 210; Di Michele, *L'italianizzazione*, 164–77; Milica Kacin-Wohinz, *Vivere al confine: sloveni e italiani negli anni 1918–1941* (Gorizia: Goriška Mohorjeva družba, 2004), 205–12; Stefan Lechner, "*Die Eroberung der Fremdstämmigen*" *Provinzfaschismus in Südtirol 1921–1926* (Innsbruck, Wagner, 2003), 432–43.
34 Maura Hametz, "Naming Italians in the Borderland, 1926–1943," *Journal of Modern Italian Studies* 15, no. 3 (2010): 410–30; Message from the Prefect of Trieste to the Ministry of Foreign Affairs of 23.8.1931, in *Archivio di Stato di Trieste* (Trieste State Archives, Italy), Prefettura, Gabinetto, 206/68.
35 This turn coincided with a further radicalization of the authoritarian nature of the regime, which some authors qualify as totalitarian. For a short discussion of Italian fascism's totalitarian aspects, see Davide Rodogno, *Fascism's European Empire: Italian Occupation during the Second World War* (Cambridge: Cambridge University Press, 2006): 408–16.
36 Di Michele, *L'italianizzazione,* 244.
37 A. Quiroga, *Making Spaniards: Primo de Rivera and the Nationalization of the Masses, 1923-30* (Basingstoke: Palgrave Macmillan, 2007), 110–58; María del Mar Del Pozo Andrés and Jacques F. A. Braster, "The Rebirth of the 'Spanish Race': The State, Nationalism, and Education in Spain, 1875–1931," *European History Quarterly* 29, no. 1 (1999): 75–107.
38 Quiroga, *Making Spaniards*, 142.
39 De Pablo and Mees, *El pendulo*, 85–112.
40 Rolf Steininger, *Südtirol im 20. Jahrhundert: Vom Leben und Überleben einer Minderheit* (Innsbruck: StudienVerlag, 2016), 171; Roberta Pergher, *Mussolini's Nation-Empire: Sovereignty and Settlement in Italy's Borderlands, 1922–1943* (Cambridge: Cambridge University Press, 2018), 223.
41 José Luis de la Granja Sainz, Justo G. Beramendi, and Pere Anguera, *La España de los nacionalismos y las autonomías* (Madrid: Síntesis, 2001), 113.

42 Harsh antisemitic legislation was also introduced in Italy from 1938 onward. In this study we do not include the Jewish minority in Italy among our cases for two main reasons. First, the Italian Jewish community was small (about 40,000 people) and highly assimilated; hence, there was no (or at least a very weak) political stand claiming the existence of a separate Jewish national community in Italy, at least until the late 1930s. Second, although antisemitism did exist and was widespread, contrary to several other European countries, Italy lacked an overt antisemitic movement. Although the Fascist Party had an antisemitic wing and Mussolini displayed signs of unsystematic antisemitism, until the mid-1930s, it was not an antisemitic party and several Jews reached prominent positions within it. In the late 1930s, things changed radically. However, as this concerns only the last years of the timeframe considered in this chapter, including the Jewish minority in Italy in our study would create a major imbalance with the other cases. On the Jewish minority in Italy, see Michele Sarfatti, *The Jews in Mussolini's Italy: From Equality to Persecution* (Madison: The University of Wisconsin Press, 2006); Michael Livingston, *The Fascists and the Jews of Italy* (Cambridge: Cambridge University Press, 2014); Meir Michaelis, *Mussolini and the Jews; German-Italian Relations and the Jewish Question in Italy, 1922–1945*. (Oxford: Clarendon Press, 1978).

43 Stephan Horak, *Poland and Her National Minorities, 1919–1939: A Case Study* (New York: Vantage Press, 1961), 144–79. Richard Blanke, *Orphans of Versailles: The Germans in Western Poland: 1918–1939* (Lexington: University Press of Kentucky, 1993), 77–103. Raitz von Frentz, 216–26. On Polish repressive policies with regard to electoral reform, see the chapter of Marina Germane in this volume.

44 Pawel Korzec, "The Ukranian Problem in Interwar Poland," in *Ethnic Groups in International Relations*, ed. Paul Smith (Aldershot: Dartmouth, 1991), 203–4.

45 Kathryn Ciancia, *On Civilization's Edge: A Polish Borderland in the Interwar World* (New York: Oxford University Press, 2021), 219–23. Fink, *Defending*, 285.

46 Enric Ucelay Da Cal, *La Catalunya populista: imatge, cultura i política en l'etapa republicana, 1931–1939* (Barcelona: La Magrana, 1982); José Luis de la Granja Sainz, *Nacionalismo y II República en el País Vasco: estatutos de autonomía, partidos y elecciones, historia de acción nacionalista, 1930–1936* (Madrid: Centro de investigaciones sociológicas, 1986), 661–81.

47 Albert Balcells, *El nacionalismo catalán* (Madrid: Historia 16, 1999), 103–5.

48 José Luis de la Granja Sainz, *República y Guerra Civil en Euskadi: del Pacto de San Sebastián al de Santoña* (Oñati: Herri Arduralaritzaren Euskal Erakundea, 1990), 257–77.

49 Paulí Dávila Balsera, "Euskal Herria tiene forma de corazón: la escuela en la construcción de la identidad nacional vasca," *Historia de la educación: Revista interuniversitaria*, no. 27 (2008): 227–9.

50 Granja et al., *La España*, 136–9.

51 Haut Commissariat Royal d'Eupen et de Malmedy, *Rapport sur l'activité générale du Gouvernement d'Eupen et de Malmedy*, 07.1921–07.1922, *Staatsarchiv Eupen* (Eupen State Archives) (henceforth SE), Baltia Fonds, Box 193, 44–52.

52 Haut Commissariat Royal d'Eupen et de Malmedy, *Rapport sur l'activité générale du Gouvernement d'Eupen et de Malmedy*, 07.1920–07.1921, SE, Baltia Fonds, Box 192, 91–3. Baltia's measures were not unique in Belgium. Between 1918 and 1921, the country went through an administrative purge hitting civil servants who were deemed to have collaborated with the German occupier. This occurred in parallel with the criminal prosecution of high-profile collaborators. Estimates

show that about 1,600 civil servants (out of a total of around 6,200 in the central administration) were hit by a sanction. By contrast, only 300 people were sentenced in court. Although, later in the 1920s, the purge was interpreted as an anti-Flemish witch-hunt, the regional distribution of sanctions approximately reflected the relative proportion of the populations of Flanders and Wallonia. For more on this, see Stijn de Wilde, and Frederik Verleden. "'Ambtenaren in dienst van de vijand.' De bestraffing van het activisme in de Belgische rijksadministratie (1918-1921)," *BMGN—Low Countries Historical Review* 124, no. 1 (2009): 30-56. For the total number of Belgian civil servants, see Rivet, Raymond. "La Statistique Des Fonctionnaires." *Journal de La Société Française de Statistique* 74 (1933): 91-119.

53 Vincent O'Connell, *The Annexation of Eupen-Malmedy: Becoming Belgian, 1919-1929* (Basingstoke: Palgrave Macmillan, 2018), 117-45.
54 Christoph Brüll, "Eupen-Malmedy 1918-1945. Le temps des déchirures," in *Hommage à Henri Bragard (1877-1944)*, ed. Renée Boulengier-Sedyn (Liège: Société de Langue et Littérature Wallonne, 2009), 20-2.
55 Law of July 30, 1934, on deprivation of nationality, quoted in Christelle Macq, "Contours et enjeux de la déchéance de la nationalité," *Courrier hebdomadaire du CRISP*, no. 30 (2021), 18.
56 Ibid., 11-37. On the need to be very cautious and avoid creating martyrs, see the report by the Belgian ambassador in Berlin, de Kerchove, to the Ministry of Foreign Affairs of 11.1.1933, in Archives diplomatiques de Belgique, 10.777—Religious questions 1921-6, folder on the expulsion of priest Gilles.
57 Other factors influenced the decision of the inhabitants of South Tyrol to opt overwhelmingly for relocation to Germany. Yet, in many ways, the Option turned into a plebiscite against fascist Italy.
58 Niels Matheve, *Tentakels van de macht: elite en elitenetwerken in en rond de Belgische tussenoorlogse regeringen (1918-1940)* (Inni: Heule, 2016).
59 Jan Velaers, *Albert I: Koning in Tijden van Oorlog En Crisis 1909-1934* (Tielt: Lannoo, 2009), 827-50.
60 Ibid., 962-83. Witte and Van Velthoven, *Languages*, 118-20.
61 Stéphane Rillaerts, "La Frontière Linguistique, 1878-1963," *Courrier Hebdomadaire Du CRISP*, no. 24 (2010): 7-106.
62 Quoted in Astrid von Busekist, *La Belgique: politique des langues et construction de l'État, de 1780 à nos jours* (Paris: Duculot, 1998), 238. See also the comments against the personality principle, which he had previously supported, of the Socialist francophone MP Jules Destrée in Destrée, J., "Un aspect imprévu de la liberté du père de famille," *Le Soir*, February 22, 1930, in Letterenhuis Antwerp (henceforth LA), Frans Van Cauwelaert (FVC), Vlaamse Beweging (VB), Box 62.
63 Lode Wils, *Onverfranst, onverduitst? Flamenpolitik, activisme, frontbeweging* (Kalmthout: Pelckmans, 2014), 301.
64 Kari Alenius, "The Birth of Cultural Autonomy in Estonia: How, Why, and for Whom?," *Journal of Baltic Studies* 38, no. 4 (2007): 445-62; Mikko Lagerspetz, "Cultural Autonomy of National Minorities in Estonia: The Erosion of a Promise," *Journal of Baltic Studies* 45, no. 4 (2014): 457-75.
65 David J. Smith, "Estonia: A Model for Inter-war Europe?," *Ethnopolitics* 15, no. 1 (2016): 89-104.
66 In contrast with Macartney's famous article. See Macartney, "Minorities."

7

Exercising Minority Rights in New Democracies: Germans and Jews in Interwar Poland, Romania, and Latvia, 1919–33

Marina Germane

The Wilsonian doctrine "accepted nationalism, but turned it against itself," wrote a member of the American delegation to the 1919 Peace Conference in Paris.[1] In accordance with Woodrow Wilson's vision, the recognition of all new or enlarged states that had emerged from the ruins of the two great empires, the Habsburg and the Russian, was conditioned by their fair and just treatment of ethnic minorities, which in post-Versailles Central and Eastern Europe amounted to nearly 35 million people. The provisions of the minority treaties, albeit vaguely formulated, guaranteed minorities in those states not just the negative rights to equality with other citizens and the absence of discrimination, but also certain positive rights, such as the right to use one's mother tongue in court, and to control private religious, educational, and social institutions. The greatest innovation of the treaties was their internationalization through the guarantee of the League of Nations, which was charged with the oversight (but not enforcement) of their fulfilment.

The treaties were welcomed by the minorities concerned, but the new nation-states were bitterly opposed to what they saw as an intervention in their internal affairs; they had also objected to being singled out, as no "old" states were required to undertake similar guarantees. The "new" states staged a revolt against the "minority clauses" at the Peace Conference, with the head of the Romanian delegation, Ion Brătianu, taking the lead; he was closely followed by Ignacy Paderewski and Roman Dmowski of Poland.[2] But the minority clauses were firmly attached to their new sovereignty, and the Polish Minority treaty was the first one to be reluctantly signed by Dmowski and Paderewski in June 1919, with Romania following suit in December. The new Latvian government was not represented at the Peace Conference, as it was still waging a war against several enemy armies infringing on Latvian territories. Instead, Latvia would be required to sign a unilateral declaration affirming the same principles of minority protection upon its admission to the League in September 1921 and would fight it tooth and nail, citing the same reasons as the Romanians and Poles two years previously; the declaration would not be signed until July 1923.

Throughout the interwar period, the treaties' signatories would continue to repel the League's inevitably meek—in accordance with its narrow mandate—interventions on minorities' behalf, whilst other member states would resist any attempts to revise the mandate. These two factors constantly undermined the League's efforts and endlessly frustrated minorities, who took the promises of equality made at Versailles at face value, and were determined to fully realize their new rights within their new democratic homelands. Across Central and Eastern Europe, it was the Germans and the Jews who assumed the most active stance on the fulfillment of minority rights. These—in the words of Mazower—"two great minorities of 1918" spearheaded the minority rights movement in interwar Europe, often making electoral alliances on the domestic scene, as well as joining forces internationally.[3]

This alliance—or "problematic symbiosis"—between the Germans and the Jews up to the 1930s has been extensively studied, primarily from a cultural angle.[4] The two minorities' collaboration in the field of minority rights in interwar Europe, however, has attracted much less attention, leaving the full scope of this pan-European, transnational phenomenon largely unexamined.[5]

As summed up by Mendelsohn, the two groups shared remarkable similarities during the interwar period: both were extraterritorial minorities speaking their own language and professing a religion—for the Germans, often; for Jews, always—different from the majority population. Both were mainly urban minorities, whose moderate sections were keen on integrating into the life of their home countries, becoming, respectively, Hungarian Germans, or Latvian Jews. Both were internally challenged by more extreme types advocating for either German nationalism or radical Zionism. In the 1930s, the oppressive regimes at home and disappointment in the League of Nations prompted both to start looking elsewhere: Germans toward the Reich and Jews toward Palestine.[6]

And although unlike Germans, Jews had never been in a privileged position under the old imperial order, as well as not possessing a kin-state, in the eyes of their new rulers—predominantly agrarian states—they, just like Germans, wielded disproportionate economic power. They dominated the middle classes, industries, and the professions, and were overrepresented in higher education. These "structural and functional similarities" transformed the two ethnic groups into "essential others."[7] In the absence of a Jewish kin-state, international Jewish organizations such as the British Joint Foreign Committee, the French *Alliance Israélite Universelle*, the American Jewish Committee, the American Jewish Congress, and—from 1936—the World Jewish Congress advocating on behalf of East European Jews often acted as kin-state proxies.

In addition to all these similarities, there was a pre-existing cultural affinity between the two, tracing back to the German enlightenment of the seventeenth-eighteenth centuries that inspired the Jews' own enlightenment, the *Haskalah*. The Prague intellectual Max Brod aptly named this—at times uneasy—relationship as the *Distanzliebe*.[8]

Yet another link between the two minorities was the commitment of their leaders to the idea of non-territorial (cultural) autonomy as the best way of realizing minority rights. The concept of non-territorial autonomy radically divorced the notions of national self-determination and territoriality, granting autonomous decision-making to an ethnically, linguistically, or culturally defined group, irrespective of its members' places of residence. The idea has been traced to the works of several Austro-Hungarian thinkers from the mid-nineteenth century onward, receiving its most thorough treatment at the hands of the Austrian Social Democrat Karl Renner.⁹

By the end of the century, the idea of non-territorial autonomy also penetrated the neighboring Russian Empire, becoming especially popular among its sizeable Jewish population; with the Russian-Jewish historian Simon Dubnow developing his own theory of Jewish Autonomism.¹⁰ All in all, in the last decades of the multinational empires, national autonomy became—as put by Stourzh—"tantamount to a magic word,"¹¹ which seemingly held the promise of solving the problem of ethnic, linguistic, and cultural diversity in Central and Eastern Europe.¹²

This chapter looks at several instances of German–Jewish cooperation in the field of minority rights in 1920s Poland, Romania, and Latvia—a "restored," an "enlarged," and a "new" state, respectively—where both minorities were present in significant numbers. The following subchapters revisit the famous Polish Minorities' Bloc of 1922, the Romanian education reform of 1922–8, and the Latvian minorities' struggle for cultural autonomy in 1922–5. The focus is on several key individuals, whose personal backgrounds, political careers, and mutual interactions provide an insight into the origins of minorities' collaboration, its internal dynamics, and its limits in the post-Versailles world, where, to paraphrase Volker Prott, pretended national homogeneity clashed with an ambivalent situation on the ground.¹³ The main goal is "to get behind men and to grasp ideas," an endeavor that Lord Acton considered to be crucial to understanding history.

Poland

The Polish state's independence, which famously featured as one of Wilson's Fourteen Points, was celebrated by the world as a triumph of historical justice in 1919. However, as drolly observed by a British traveler in 1930, referring both to the strained international relations and the domestic struggles of the new republic, "even the Peace Conference did not bring peace to Poland."¹⁴ The relations of the newly independent country with most of its neighbors remained "unsatisfactory," from frosty relations with Czechoslovakia following an allegedly unjust border settlement, and the absence of diplomatic relations with Lithuania after the Polish acquisition of *Wilno* (Vilnius), to the threat of territorial revision from Germany and the looming menace of the Russian Bolsheviks. At home, growing inflation, a challenging agrarian reform, and a highly fragmented parliamentary system were compounded by the "critical state" of Poland's relations with its ethnic minorities.¹⁵ In the new Polish republic, ethnic minorities accounted for more than a third of the entire country's population of 30 million, the largest being Ukrainians (15 percent), Jews (8 percent), Germans (3.6 percent), and Belarussians (3.4 percent).¹⁶ As elsewhere in Central and Eastern Europe, the ethnic diversity of the population was at odds with the nationalist aspirations of the dominant ethnic group.

The Jewish community of interwar Poland was the largest in Europe both in absolute numbers and as a percentage of the general population. Making up one-third of the urban population, Jews were primarily engaged in commerce, industry, and the professions (unlike the Poles, who were predominantly employed in agriculture).[17] The Polish Jewish community was very diverse religiously and ideologically, ranging from a large Hasidic population to a militant Zionist camp, with assimilationists and acculturationists in between (the latter were not particularly successful, with the vast majority of Polish Jewry remaining unassimilated into Polish culture by 1919). Mendelsohn asserts that this very "unassimilability," coupled with the new regime's toleration of various forms of cultural and political expression, created a paradoxical situation in interwar Poland. On the one hand, Poland became "the center of autonomous Jewish cultural and political life in Europe," with an abundance of Jewish periodicals, theaters, schools, and associations. On the other, the country was consumed by "virulent and all-pervasive antisemitism."[18] The role of the international Jewish organizations in drawing the world's attention to the pogroms that broke out in the Polish territories at the close of the war, as well as their contribution to the formulation of the "humiliating" Minority Treaty provided new fuel for the centuries-old antisemitic sentiment.

The Polish German minority, at slightly over one million, was half the size of the Jewish one. Polish Germans were mainly involved in the agriculture, forestry, and food-processing industries, being urban and countryside dwellers in equal measure. Formerly privileged under the Prussian regime, Polish Germans still played a big role in the Polish economy, a source of great resentment for the Poles.[19] German minority organizations, political or not, were thriving in interwar Poland, with an extensive network of cooperatives, schools, and a lively press. Like the Jews, the Polish Germans featured prominently in the Versailles negotiations; this made it clear to the wary Poles that the German minority's welfare was a matter of international concern. In fact, during the 1920s and 1930s the Polish Germans would submit more complaints to the League of Nations than any other minority in Central and Eastern Europe.[20]

Other significant minorities, like Ukrainians and Belarusians, were concentrated in the east of Poland, in Galicia and the *Kresy*. Despite their clearly nationalist stance and aspirations for territorial autonomy, these two predominantly rural Slavic minorities were regarded, by the Polish state, as prime material for eventual assimilation; thus, they were continuously subjected to harsh Polonization policies.

The state's attitude toward the Germans and Jews was markedly different, as their assimilation was not considered possible or, indeed, desirable.[21] The memory of the Greater Poland Uprising against the Germans in 1918–19 was still fresh at the time. The Polish Jews were also not viewed as potential allies in the national cause as, for example, in Czechoslovakia and the Baltic countries in the early 1920s. The Polish state perceived them either as agents of Germanization or as Bolshevik sympathizers.[22] Besides, because of the aforementioned urban character of the Polish Jewish minority, many Poles blamed them for the existing poor conditions in cities.[23]

Having found themselves lumped together and designated as a potential "fifth column," it is perhaps no surprise that the Germans and the Jews turned to the only recourse available to them, i.e., actively pursuing the equal treatment and minority rights guaranteed to them by both the Minority Treaty and the Polish Constitution of 1921, respectively. In the 1920s, the two minorities were in the vanguard of the principled struggle for minority rights in Poland, whilst the territorially concentrated Ukrainians and Belarussians joined them on the occasions when their interest aligned with those of "extraterritorial" minorities.

The initial election to the new Constituent Assembly (1919–21) was confined to the areas under Polish control and only later extended to include the ex-Prussian province and eastern borderlands. Thus, in the absence of Belarussians and Ukrainians, and the seven Germans present understandably passive in the immediate aftermath of the war, the eleven Jewish deputies chose to represent the interests of all minorities, in the words of Joseph Rothschild, "with more valor than prudence," and to the detriment of their own relations with the majority nation.[24]

The electoral law adopted by the Assembly in 1921 for the elections to the *Sejm* and the Senate was democratic at first blush, but it favored large parties over small ones, thus immediately putting minorities at a disadvantage. Also, gerrymandering in the east made the election of Ukrainian and Belarussian deputies and senators more difficult than that of their Polish counterparts.[25]

These developments prompted two minority leaders, an estate owner from Pomerelia (*Pomorze Wschodnie*) and the head of the German parliamentary faction Erwin Hasbach (1876–1970), and a Zionist from Warsaw, the MP Yitzhak Gruenbaum (also Grünbaum; 1879–1970), to initiate a united electoral list, officially known as the Bloc of National Minorities (*Bloc Mniejczości Narodowych*), for the German, Jewish, Ukrainian, and Belarussian minorities in the elections of 1922. This idea failed to attain universal support from any of these four minorities due to their internal divisions. Notably, the main opposition to the Minorities Bloc came from within the Zionist camp, as the internal divisions among Polish Jews, besides economic and political differences, also reflected their differing experiences under their former rulers (Russians, Austrians, and Prussians). Hence the Galician Jewish leaders, in the tradition of the Habsburg Empire, favored pragmatic cooperation with the authorities over the "open insurrection" of an alliance with other minorities.

Similarly, there were regional differences between the Germans of Western Poland, who harbored profound resentment toward the new political setup, and those in the former Russian and Habsburg territories, who were quite used to their non-dominant positions among the ethnically diverse population. Moreover, as suggested by Richard Blanke, the former Russian subjects in particular had reasons to hope for better treatment by the new democratic Polish state.[26] Against this background, Erwin Hasbach cuts an intriguing figure.

His unorthodox ways may have something to do with the fact that Hasbach, the scion of a textile manufacturers' dynasty, was actually born and raised on a family estate near Białystok, which was, at the time, within the Russian Pale of Settlement, and where the majority of the population was Jewish. In addition, the cultured Hasbachs regularly mingled with Polish intelligentsia, and young Erwin took Polish lessons.[27] He studied agriculture at the universities of Halle and Berlin, before taking out a lease on an estate near Toruń in 1902. Having served in the Prussian army during the war, in 1919 he—unsuccessfully—tried to join the ranks of the Polish Army. Elected to the Constituent *Sejm* in the supplementary election of 1920, Hasbach would become the longest serving German parliamentarian of the interwar period. From the tribune of the Senate, he spoke about the "great sympathy" that the world felt toward the Polish nation, which had been deprived of statehood for 150 years. At the same time, he sought to remind Poles that the Minority Treaty "was signed with the same pen as the Treaty of Versailles" and that the Poles, who had endured the experience of being a minority in other states in the past, "should not make the same mistakes they once accused their hosts of."[28] Like Gruenbaum, Hasbach was convinced that the law on non-territorial autonomy passed by the Estonian parliament in 1925 was a "shining example" for other ethnically diverse countries to follow and ardently defended it against skeptics.[29]

As for Gruenbaum, by 1922 he had become the head of the Zionist Federation of Poland and an internationally recognized Zionist leader.[30] Gruenbaum, along with the future Revisionist leader Vladimir Jabotinsky, was the author of the famous *Gegenwartsarbeit* resolution at the Third Congress of Russian Zionists in Helsingfors (Helsinki) in 1906.[31] The resolution called for equality for all national groups in the Russian Empire, as well as for both territorial and non-territorial autonomy for minorities; many of its principles would later find their way into the Zionist Copenhagen Manifesto of 1918. Most notably, the resolution mentioned the task of identifying other exterritorial minorities "with the goal of uniting them around the platform of minority rights protection," a tenet that Gruenbaum and peers would remain faithful to.[32] Gruenbaum, a native Polish-speaker, was well versed in Polish politics and believed that Jews should participate in the municipal and parliamentary life of the new republic as equals.[33] David Vital aptly characterized Gruenbaum's stance as "*Gegenwartsarbeit* with a vengeance,"[34] as he was determined to implement the Helsingfors resolution of his youth on a full scale in Poland and elsewhere. According to Gruenbaum, the basic minority rights achieved at Versailles were just a beginning, and further struggle was necessary for their actual implementation. He believed the Polish Jews had realized this from the early days of the Constituent *Sejm*, formulating their position accordingly and aiming at joining forces with other minorities, unlike Germans, who at first put their hopes on the cooperation with the Polish right, whilst Ukrainians solicited the left.[35]

Fluent in Polish and steeped in Polish culture, Hasbach and Gruenbaum were more outspoken during the *Sejm* sessions than most minority MPs of the time, often engaging in active debates with their Polish counterparts. Overall, both were known for their assertive political stances, which were often considered too far-reaching, or provocative, by more conservative sections of their respective ethnic groups; both were, however, grudgingly respected by fellow Polish parliamentarians.[36] The two minority leaders had taken the first tentative steps toward cooperation in the last days of the Constituent *Sejm*, but their combined twenty-one votes were still not enough to gain a voice in the *Sejm*—clearly, further measures were needed.[37]

The rules of the *Sejm* set the minimum number of deputies necessary for an interpellation at ten, and Gruenbaum believed that under the new electoral law—against which he had tried, unsuccessfully, to argue in the Constituent *Sejm*—the Jews could not realistically hope to obtain more than six or seven seats on their own, thus being unable to make any tangible political input.[38] Nevertheless, they remained bitterly divided: whilst the Galician Zionists, favoring cooperation with the Poles over the

Germans, shunned the Bloc, the orthodox *Agudah Israel*, in the name of Jewish unity, lent its support to Gruenbaum. Whilst the moderate Galician *Hitahdut* also sided with Gruenbaum, the Jewish left called a possible alliance with the "bourgeois"—as well as "antisemitic"—Ukrainian and Belarussian minorities unacceptable. The Jewish *Bund* ran its own electoral list, as did the *Folkspartey*, the Zionists-Socialists, and the Right *Poalei Zion*, who formed a joint list.[39]

Numerous obstacles notwithstanding, Gruenbaum and Hasbach's initiative was a notable electoral success—the Minorities Bloc won 89 out of 444 seats in the *Sejm*, and 27 out of 111 in the Senate in total, with the Jewish share being 36 seats in the *Sejm*, and 12 in the Senate. That dramatic increase in minority representation through a joint effort was heralded by Gruenbaum and his allies as "a historic event of greatest importance."[40] The news about the Polish minorities' electoral victory reverberated throughout Central and Eastern Europe and was reflected in the majority and minority press alike. Both the Bloc itself and the media coverage it received irked the Poles.

The resulting representation, however, was still lower than the overall proportion of minorities in the country, and simply not enough to carry sufficient weight in parliament. Gruenbaum's initial hopes that internal disagreements would cease, transforming the Bloc from a purely tactical alliance into a true coalition with a common platform, never materialized.[41] One of the Bloc's rare common undertakings was the journal *Natio* (1927–8), distributed to all major embassies in Warsaw, as well as the League of Nations, in an attempt to keep the world community abreast of the minority rights situation in Poland.[42]

Many Germans and Jews initially welcomed the 1926 coup by Marshal Józef Piłsudski—largely because it brought the demise of the National Democratic Party known for its vitriolic anti-minorities rhetoric. The Jews also fondly remembered the meeting that Piłsudski had held with the Jewish community leaders at the dawn of independence in 1918 (Gruenbaum had attended). Moreover, an outline of minority-related policies adopted by the new cabinet indeed indicated desire to "mend fences": in relation to Germans, the government promised to uphold the principles of the Treaty, settling the question of citizenship, admitting minorities to civil service, and amending the School Law. Jews were promised an end to economic discrimination, modifications to the law on compulsory Sunday rest, creation of the Yiddish-language state primary schools, financial aid for Jewish private schools, and the eradication of the *numerus clausus* (not enshrined in law, but widely applied in practice).[43] Some of these promises were carried out, but overall the government-proposed measures encountered energetic resistance on the part of the civil service, and—with the *numerus clausus*—also on the part of universities. Overall, although the official state narrative became less minority-hostile, little changed on the ground and the economic downturn affected minorities disproportionally. As for civic freedoms, the aforementioned *Natio* was shut down by authorities in 1928, with Gruenbaum reportedly taking a beating.[44]

Hasbach and Gruenbaum would undertake two further attempts at uniting minorities, during the parliamentary election of 1928, and then again in 1930, after the Third *Sejm*'s dissolution. While Germans continued to perform well in elections, the Jewish seats were reduced first to thirteen, and then to six. This fiasco was largely blamed on Gruenbaum and his policies of "aggravating" the Poles and siding up with other "untrustworthy" minorities instead. In the aftermath, Gruenbaum was forced to leave Poland for a while.[45]

By the early 1930s, Poland was already in the grip of the Great Depression. In line with the German government's more assertive stance following the death of the German liberally minded Foreign Minister Stresemann in 1929, the Polish Germans were increasingly looking toward Germany for protection, rather than asserting their rights in parliamentary struggles. At the same time, the Great Depression, coupled with the news of the anti-Jewish laws adopted, in 1933, across the German border, stimulated a new growth of antisemitism among the Polish right, with the government struggling to keep it in check. These developments led to the radicalization of Jewish politics on both the left and the right, with the rise of Jabotinsky's Revisionism in the Zionist camp and the growing popularity of the *Bund* and the Communist Party. In 1934, Poland famously repudiated its Minority Treaty—this, despite being, in many ways, a *fait accompli* for the Polish Germans and Jews, was a lethal blow to the system of international minority protection as a whole.

Romania

"Roumania within her new frontiers is a great, a populous and a fertile country. Nature has omitted none of the elements upon which man can build up happiness," wrote Maynard Keynes in 1920.[46] As the biggest territorial beneficiary of Versailles, Romania gained, under the treaty, Bessarabia from Russia, Bukovina and Transylvania from Austria-Hungary, and Southern Dobrudja from Bulgaria, and was now the second biggest country in Central and Eastern Europe after Poland.

However, those illustrious gains were accompanied by the acquisition of a high share of ethnic minorities, around 30 percent (compared to the prewar eight) of the total population of 17 million. The biggest Romanian minorities were Hungarians at 9.3 percent, Jews at 5.3, Ukrainians at 4.7, and Germans at 4.3.[47] The challenge of ethnic diversity sharply contrasted with the nationalizing fervor engulfing the country. There was also the question of cultural dominance—in the newly acquired provinces, the titular Romanian culture met with tough competition from the Hungarian (Transylvania), German (Bukovina and Transylvania), and Russian (Bessarabia) ones. Adding insult to injury, Romanian Jews, present in all provinces, had been heavily acculturated into those respective cultures, to which they stubbornly clung, thus becoming, in the eyes of the Romanian majority, the agents of Magyarization, Germanization, and Russification, respectively.

Like other East European states, Romania faced, along with the recovery of wartime economic losses and an impending agrarian reform, the daunting task of integrating its newly acquired citizens culturally—something that the government under the Liberal Party started pursuing with exemplary fervor. The goal was to unite the existing four different educational systems under common standards, an understandable step in a country whose predominantly agrarian population sported Europe's highest illiteracy rate (78 percent).[48]

But the practical implementation of the education reform, dubbed the "cultural offensive," exposed underlying tensions and long-time animosities. Illiteracy, reflecting the former policies of neglect of Romanian peasants by the Russians and the Habsburgs, was more widely spread among Romanians than other ethnic groups (under the Russians, only 6 percent of Romanians knew how to read and write, whilst Hungary provided only rudimentary education for them).[49] Inevitably, other ethnic groups came to dominate both higher education and the professions—a fact that many Romanians greatly despised. Besides the general Romanization of all schools, Romanian schools were, more often than not, improved at the expense of the minority ones.[50]

In Bukovina, where different ethnic groups had enjoyed a significant degree of cultural autonomy within the latter-day Austro-Hungarian Empire as a result of the Bukovinian Compromise of 1909, minorities joined forces in trying to fend off the reform.[51] Here, it primarily targeted Ukrainians and Jews: Ukrainian schools were simply converted into Romanian ones, under the pretext of shepherding the so-called "Ruthenized Romanians" back to their true cultural identity, while Jews were deemed over-represented in secondary schools and universities.[52]

The Bukovinian Germans, being a small, territorially enclosed minority without irredentist aspirations, initially were not overly concerned with the new policies. Having pledged their allegiance to the Romanian Kingdom as early as in 1918, they negotiated the conditions of their loyalty with the provisional government. These conditions, drafted by the newly created *Volksrat* under the leadership of Alfred Kohlruss—a future Romanian parliamentarian—included citizenship with full equality, maximum autonomy in religious affairs, and the recognition of the right of the *Volksrat* to speak on behalf of Germans.[53] The Jewish National Council of Bukovina, formed around the same time under the leadership of the Zionist Mayer Ebner (1872–1955), refused to pledge allegiance to the government after it declined to recognize the Jewish autonomy project in Bukovina that had been formulated by the Council in accordance with the aforementioned Copenhagen Manifesto of 1918.[54]

By that time Ebner was a weathered Zionist, who had represented the Bukovinian Jews on the General Council of the Zionist Organization since 1897. For Ebner, the *Palästinaarbeit* and *Gegenwartsarbeit* were the two pillars on which the universality of the Zionist movement rested; he considered withdrawal from active political life "a sign of intellectual backwardness" that turns the public life of a people into a "swamp."[55] True to his word, during the interwar period he threw himself into Romanian democratic politics, becoming first an MP, and then a Senator. In Parliament, he was a fearless and persuasive speaker respected by his Romanian peers (even the nationalist Romanian politician Nicolae Iorga, a known antisemite, had allegedly professed deep respect for Ebner).[56]

Historically—just like in Poland—both Jews and Germans were over-represented in higher education and, consequently, among the educated classes and urban elite. In both countries, the *numerus clausus* was not part of the state legislation, but flourished in practice; in Romania, for the success of the education reform, the number of minority students needed to be curtailed, to give way to the masses of Romanians and the successfully Romanianized Ukrainians.[57] When the education law of 1925 declared Romanian the official language of education in private schools as well, the Jewish and

German deputies protested in unison. Kohlruss demanded, in Parliament, that the autonomy of education guaranteed in 1918 be maintained in practice, and the Jewish senator Salo Weisselberger criticized the decree in the Senate. Hoping for international intervention, but too timid to forward a petition to the League of Nations in their own name, the Romanian Jews lodged a complaint with an old friend, the *Alliance Israélite Universelle*. Neither of these efforts brought any tangible results.[58]

The reinstatement of a Baccalaureate exam in 1926 saw examiners failing minority students in great numbers, while the majority of Romanian students passed. When in the autumn of 1926, two-thirds of all examinees and 80 percent of Jewish ones failed in Bukovina, protests broke out in Czernowitz. Ebner spoke in Parliament against the "unhealthy situation" created by the exam; Ukrainian minority leaders also raised concerns. Kohlruss and Ebner organized a meeting with the regional school inspector, futilely suggesting replacing the outside examiners with local teachers. Ebner then forwarded a protest to the League, as well as publishing an article against minorities' discrimination in education in the *Ostjüdische Zeitung*. A reply followed from the Romanian League of Nations Association, stating that following Ebner's complaints, one particular professor lost their right to be an examiner—a victory, however small.[59]

During the 1920s, Ebner closely cooperated with the Saxon leader from Transylvania Rudolf Brandsch (1880–1953). Brandsch, the son of a Protestant pastor, was one of the few minority leaders in Romania with previous political experience—he was a deputy in the Hungarian Parliament from 1910 to 1918. In interwar Romania, he was first elected to Parliament, and then to the Senate. Brandsch's considerable political skills allowed him to stay on relatively good terms with majority politicians, and in 1931–2, he famously served as the Undersecretary for Minorities in Iorga's Democratic Nationalist government. Brandsch favored cooperation with the Jewish minority over the Hungarian and Ukrainian ones, believing that a union with the latter two "frontier" minorities with clearly irredentist aspirations might prove detrimental.

Similarly, Ebner believed in cooperation with Germans in Bukovina, who, having been surrounded by Romanians, Slavs, and Jews for centuries, were, in his opinion, quite different from their Prussian brethren. He did, however, think that the lack of strong political leadership among the Bukovinian Germans—as opposed to the Germans of Greater Romania, in a clear reference to Brandsch and his colleague Hans Otto Roth—hindered their participation in the common struggle for minority rights.[60]

Brandsch and Roth attempted to act as spokesmen for all Romanian minorities during the parliamentary debates on the Romanian Constitution of 1923, demanding the inclusion of minority provisions in accordance with the Trianon Treaty. However, the Jewish deputies under the leadership of Weisselberger—elected on the ticket of the ruling Romanian National Liberal Party—conducted separate negotiations with the government, eventually accepting much lesser concessions. On that occasion, Ebner sided with the German minority leaders, labeling the Jewish deputies' actions as a betrayal of the minority cause. In an editorial in the *Ostjüdische Zeitung*, he called Weisselberger's position on the matter "a little opportunistic point of view," juxtaposing him with Roth, who, in Ebner's opinion, understood "the true magnitude" of the struggle for the constitutional basis of minority rights, a struggle that had been now lost.[61]

The events of 1931, with the return of King Carol, his choice of Prime Minister Iorga, and especially the appointment of Brandsch as the Undersecretary for Minorities at first signaled hope for Romanian minorities. However, it soon became apparent that not only was his political office a mere front, but that Brandsch himself was also not the man he had once been. The transformation of Brandsch's political views was gradual, rather than sudden, reflecting the changing political situation abroad and the growing antisemitism both in the Reich and in Romania. In 1933, he publicly broke ties with the Jewish community after accusing them of only pursuing common minority interests when it suited them (a charge angrily denied by Ebner). From then on, Brandsch openly pursued the interests of Romanian Germans at the expense of other minorities.[62] After Iorga's government fell in 1932, the minorities undersecretary's post was abolished. Overall, under the authoritarian rule of Carol II and against the background of the Great Depression, Romania's policies of forceful "nationalization" of minorities were gradually replaced by policies of exclusion.

Latvia

Unlike those of Poland and Romania, the fate of Latvian state sovereignty was not decided at the Paris Peace conference by the victorious Allies. Instead, it came about as a result of the kaleidoscopic chain of tumultuous events starting with the Russian February Revolution of 1917, and ending with the optimistic proclamation of independence by the newly formed Latvian National Council on November 18, 1918, when parts of Latvia's territory were still under German control. The newly appointed Prime Minister Kārlis Ulmanis emphasized in his speech that "the rights of all ethnic groups will be guaranteed by the Latvian state."[63]

The state's independence did not change the ethnic composition of the population, as Latvian provinces had been ethnically diverse for centuries; if anything, the share of ethnic Latvians slightly increased after the war. In 1920, Latvians comprised 72.8 percent of the total population of 1.6 million with the largest minorities being Russians at 12.6 percent, Jews at 5 percent, Germans at 3.6 percent, and Poles at 3.4 percent.[64]

The centuries-long history of animosity between ethnic Latvians and their former German oppressors consistently marred their relations during the interwar period. The Agrarian Reform of the 1920s, which largely expropriated German landlords, was an imperative economic measure in a country devastated by the war; however, as in Poland and Romania, there was also a taste of "historical justice" to it.

Although in the 1920s Latvians widely perceived the Jews as their most loyal minority, who, just like themselves, stood only to gain from Latvian independence, Latvia did not escape the wave of anti-Jewish sentiment that swept across Central and Eastern Europe at the end of the First World War. Latvian Jews were charged with numerous sins, like helping the advance of the German troops, spying for the Habsburgs, and aiding the Bolsheviks. Another constant source of animosity toward the Jews—in a striking similarity to Romania—was their preference for either the German or Russian cultures over the eponymous Latvian.

In other words, neither the Germans nor the Jews in Latvia felt fully secure in their own right, making a rapprochement between the two minorities practically inevitable. The Germans, despite their cultural and economic influence, numerically were only the third largest minority in the country; the 5 percent represented by the Jews meant a welcome further reduction in the "overwhelming weight of the Latvian majority."[65] The Germans, however, were by far the best-organized ethnic group in Latvia at the time, admired and envied, especially during elections, by both Latvians and other minorities.[66]

In December 1919, the National Council passed two laws. A Law on Latvian Educational Institutions stipulated that all compulsory school studies were to be conducted in the pupil's "family language" and obliged state and municipal institutions to maintain as many schools for each ethnic group as were necessary for their children's compulsory education.[67] A Law on Minority Schools in Latvia established Minority Departments within the Ministry of Education to represent "their respective ethnic group in all cultural affairs, with the right to liaise with all departments of the Ministry of Education, as well as to participate, in an advisory capacity, in the sessions of the Cabinet of Ministers related to any aspects of the cultural life of their respective ethnic group."[68] The latter was the most liberal law on minority education in Europe at the time (the Estonian Law on Cultural Autonomy would not be passed until 1925), and the two legal acts taken together offered minorities significant control over their own education and cultural affairs.

But this "multicultural" vision of the new statehood drafted by the novice Latvian lawmakers was soon shattered by the collision with reality. Like in Poland and Romania, both domestic and international factors were at play while Latvia was getting on its feet: urgent economic and industrial reconstruction, a pressing agricultural reform, and a struggling parliamentary system were coupled with the government's determination to maintain neutrality in foreign relations at any cost (the latter left the country vulnerable and isolated).[69] The looming presence of Bolshevik Russia on the eastern border, and the gradual strengthening of Germany added to the discomfort, making Latvians constantly question their minorities' loyalty. But the real turning point in majority-minority relations came in 1921, when Latvia started protracted and unhappy negotiations with the League of Nations about the conditions of its own admission.

A Jewish MP, recollecting the joyous atmosphere at the time the education laws had been passed, observed that "the situation has changed completely, however, when the question of national minority rights was passed from the field of internal legislation to that of international security,"[70] i.e., when Latvia was required to sign a unilateral declaration affirming the principles of minority protection enshrined in the minority treaties. Prior to finally signing the declaration in 1923, the Latvian government argued, like Poland and Romania had done before, that minorities' protection was already enshrined in the country's liberal domestic legislation, that the imposition of minority treaties on selected states violated the principle of equality, whilst the internationalization of minority rights by the League endangered state sovereignty.

From that point on, majority-minority relations continued to deteriorate. Latvian politicians kept favorably comparing—arguably with some justification—the situation of their own minorities to the plight of those in other European countries, notably Poland and Romania. In parliament and in the press, it became customary to talk about "excessive democracy" and minorities as its undeserving recipients.

But those hostile innuendos only strengthened Latvian minorities' resolve to exercise their rights within the framework of the new democratic state. Minority politicians were represented in the Constitutional Assembly and in all four interwar parliaments. The German faction was invariably the biggest, holding more legislative seats than the Germans' respective share of the population would have warranted. The Jews were represented proportionally, and the Russians were underrepresented. All minorities save for the Belarussians voted for their own political parties.

In parliament, minorities formed their own bloc, under the leadership of the indefatigable Paul Schiemann (1876–1944) of the German Balt Democratic Party. The Minority Bloc dated back to the Constitutional Assembly (1920–2), where, in the absence of a clear majority, the seventeen minority votes were capable of tilting the balance, and were always sought after by both the left and the right. Minorities would trade their votes for promises to support minority-related legislation; this "bargaining" would continue until 1934.

Not just the Minority Bloc as a whole, but also its constituent parts were riddled with internal divisions that cut across ethnic, socioeconomic, and ideological lines. Even the best-organized Germans were deeply divided both socially (among craftsmen, professional classes, and the nobility) and ideologically (between conservatives and liberals). Similarly, the Germanized Jews from Courland had a higher socioeconomic status than the Yiddish-speaking Jews of Latgale; politically, the Jewish parties ranged from the Jewish *Bund* to the orthodox *Agudah Israel*, and to both socialist and religious Zionists. Those multiple divisions inevitably undermined minorities' unity, and Schiemann often walked a tightrope attempting to please both the Germans and other minorities, whilst also maintaining good working relations with the Latvian majority. His position was, perhaps, never as precarious as during the minorities' quest for national autonomy in 1922–5.

Schiemann and the Socialist Zionist MP Max Laserson (also Lazerson; 1887–1951) were the foremost proponents of non-territorial autonomy for minorities in Latvia; both extensively published on the subject in the biggest German and Russian dailies, respectively. Both spent their childhoods in Mitau (Jelgava), the capital of Courland. Schiemann, a son of a liberal Baltic German lawyer, attended a private German primary school, before continuing his education in Germany, to avoid the tightening policies of Russification. Despite studying law in Berlin, Marburg, and Bonn, Schiemann, as a foreigner (his application to be released from the Russian citizenship was unsuccessful), could not be admitted to the bar in Germany and decided to practice journalism in his native Latvia instead.[71]

The young Laserson, a scion of a wealthy tobacco merchant's family that spoke German at home, attended the famous *Realschule* in Mitau, before continuing his education at the universities of St. Petersburg, Berlin, and Heidelberg. In 1916, he became the first Jew ever appointed as a lecturer at the Law Department of St. Petersburg University. Just one year later, Laserson abandoned his post to become a deputy head of the Department for National Minorities in the short-lived Provisional Government of Alexander Kerensky. By then, Laserson had developed a profound interest in the accommodation of ethnic diversity through cultural autonomy, having recently published a book on the subject.[72]

Both Schiemann and Laserson embraced Latvia's state independence, promptly returning to their native country and immersing themselves in its new democratic politics. But they did not always see eye to eye, their first public disagreement dating back to the summer of 1922, when they assumed conflicting positions on the draft laws on minority languages. Laserson advocated for one main law, "maximally favorable for all," while Schiemann wanted each minority to propose its own.[73]

Also in 1922, to the utter dismay of Laserson, Schiemann successfully lobbied for a separate law for German autonomy at the Constitutional Assembly. Consequently, separate Baltic German, Jewish, and Russian autonomy draft laws were accepted for a review that was later postponed until the election of the First *Saeima*. In 1923, the German draft successfully made it through deliberations at the *Saeima*'s Public Law Committee, but once it was passed to the Education Committee, whose chair fervently opposed autonomy for minorities, the draft mysteriously disappeared from the agenda.[74]

This experience made Schiemann change his mind—he now put his faith in the general law on cultural autonomy, so passionately advocated by Laserson. However, this attempt at German-Jewish cooperation was thwarted by Baltic German conservatives, who described such a possibility as "detrimental to our historic position in the country."[75]

In the end, Germans, Poles, and Jews submitted separate autonomy laws—notably, Schiemann appended his signature to the Jewish draft. It was the latter that attracted the most attention and press coverage. During the deliberations at the *Saeima*, it became clear that, despite the Latvian majority's stern opposition to autonomy, there was no unity on the matter among the Jews themselves. The Zionists, the *Bund*, and the *Agudah* were unable to agree on the scope of autonomy, as well as the choice between Yiddish and Hebrew as the official Jewish language. All this disorderly confusion, which was interpreted as proof that minorities were not ready for the "gift" of cultural autonomy, added to the majority's consternation. One by one, the draft laws were dismissed from the *Saeima*'s agenda, just like the language laws earlier. Although Schiemann and Laserson were now of one mind that minorities should work together, it was also clear to both that the "honeymoon" between the Latvian majority and ethnic minorities was over.

On May 15, 1934, Kārlis Ulmanis, the same man who at the dawn of Latvia's independence gave such generous promises to its minorities, carried out a military *coup d'état*. The parliament was disbanded, political parties outlawed, and minorities' educational privileges under the aforementioned education laws of 1919 were revoked. For the remaining six years of its independence, like many other European countries during this period that became known as the "crisis of democracy," Latvia would remain an authoritarian state.

Conclusions

Having encountered increasing resistance to the implementation of minority rights in their home countries, but with their faith in the League of Nations still strong, the main protagonists of this chapter started looking for transnational solutions, joining the Congress of European Nationalities that convened for the first time in 1925 in Geneva. The organization purported to bring together all European minorities with the aim of providing them with a platform for discussing common issues and exchanging best practices, as well as optimistically hoping to inform and advise the League on minority matters. At its height, the organization claimed 200 delegates from fifteen European states representing twenty different minority groups.[76] The Germans and the Jews formed the two strongest factions at the Congress, both in numbers and in influence, and would remain the closest allies until the Jewish delegation's withdrawal, in response to their fellow members' refusal to issue an explicit condemnation of the anti-Jewish policies in Germany, at the 1933 Congress in Bern. With the Jewish faction's departure, the Congress started to lose its relevance to the international minority rights movement, eventually becoming an instrument of Nazi propaganda and ultimately dissolving in 1938.

In 1931, emboldened by the 1925 passing of minority autonomy laws in Estonia, the Congress proposed, to the League, to supplement the minority treaties with a pan-European network based on non-territorial autonomy. Upon examining the proposal, the League ruled that the Congress had failed to present a convincing case for applying non-territorial autonomy beyond Estonia, the closing argument being that a spirit of tolerance and liberalism would hardly be encouraged by institutionalizing separation between groups.[77]

However, as this chapter has demonstrated, Gruenbaum, Hasbach, Ebner, Brandsch, Schiemann, and Laserson were all deeply integrated within their respective societies; as parliamentarians, they were concerned with the overarching matters of state and specific minority interests in equal measure. In fact, they were convinced that the two formed an intrinsic whole. They were not asking for institutionalized separateness, but for the *right* to decide on the matters of their own culture, rather than being granted permission—however benevolent—to do so. In the words of Laserson, "it does not become a politician to idle, waiting for the majority to understand, spontaneously, that minority rights must be protected in the interests of the state, justice, and order. Instead of meek reminders that justice and order must be observed, we believe that a decisive language of a free citizen speaking about his legal rights is more dignified."[78]

The main protagonists of this chapter all chose to behave as "free citizens" rather than meek petitioners, often facing not just the wrath of their respective majority nations, but also consternation from more cautious minority members. Those external and internal pressures combined made them seek interethnic alliances with the "like minded" first within their own countries, and then in the international arena. It was precisely this kind of minority leadership that made Inis Claude, an astute critic of the interwar minority protection system, to argue—whilst fully acknowledging minorities' grievances—that the whole international system of minority protection under the League of Nations had potential for development that never materialized. In Claude's view, this happened "in part at least because the minorities chose to agitate for an ideal system which was unobtainable at the time, rather than to concentrate on the practical task of maximizing the usefulness of the defective system which was available to them."[79]

But even if the minority activists described in this paper "dreamed big," in practice they only exercised their rights in accordance with the treaties. The ultimate failure of their attempt at cooperation was symptomatic of a bigger failure, that of the Versailles system itself. This is, of course, hindsight wisdom, as well as a moot point. Because, as observed by a participant of those distant events, "many things looked possible to men of good will in 1919, and if their hopes were disappointed, it does not prove that the pessimists were wiser."[80]

Epilogue

In the late 1930s, both Gruenbaum and Ebner left for Palestine, where they lived until their deaths in 1970 and 1955, respectively. Hasbach joined the Nazi party in 1940; after the war, he lived in West Germany, where he died in 1970. Brandsch welcomed the idea of Greater Germany, but opposed Nazism; he died in prison in communist Romania in 1953. Roth refused to join the Waffen SS and served in the Romanian army; persecuted in communist Romania, he died in a concentration camp in 1953. Laserson left in 1934, first for Palestine and then for the United States, where he died in 1953. Schiemann, who refused to leave Latvia on Hitler's orders in 1939, passed away in 1944 in Riga, where he and his wife were sheltering a Jewish girl.

Acknowledgments

I would like to thank André Liebich, Claudia Kraft, Börries Kuzmany, Matthias Battis, Oskar Mulej, Anna Adorjáni, and Timo Aava for their very helpful comments on earlier versions of this chapter, as well as Jan Kłapa for his kind help with Polish sources. The research for this chapter was supported by funding from the European Research Council within the project "Non-Territorial Autonomy: History of a Travelling Idea," Grant Agreement No. 758015.

Notes

1 James T. Shotwell, *The Autobiography of James T Shotwell* (Indianapolis: The Bobbs Merrill Company, 1961), 84.
2 David Lloyd George, *Memoirs of the Peace Conference*, vol. 2 (New Haven: Yale University Press, 1939), 883–96.
3 Mark Mazower, "The Strange Triumph of Human Rights, 1933–1950," *The Historical Journal* 47, no. 2 (2004): 379–98.
4 See, for example, Gershom Scholem, "Jews and Germans," "The German-Jewish Dialogue," and "Once More: The German-Jewish Dialogue," in *On Jews and Judaism*

in Crisis. Selected Essays, ed. Werner J. Dannhauser (Philadelphia: Paul Dry Books, 2012); David Bronsen, ed., *Jews and Germans from 1860 to 1933: The Problematic Symbiosis* (Heidelberg: Carl Winter Universitatsverlag, 1979); and Tobias Grill, ed., *Jews and Germans in Eastern Europe. Shared and Comparative Histories* (Berlin: De Gruyter Oldenbourg, 2018).
5 Mariana Hausleitner, "Transformations in the Relationship between Jews and Germans in the Bukovina 1910–1945," in *Jews and Germans*, ed. Grill; Marina Germane, "P. Schiemann, M. Laserson and Cultural Autonomy: A Case Study from Interwar Latvia," in *The Challenge of Non-Territorial Autonomy: Theory and Case Studies*, ed. Ephraim Nimni, David J. Smith, and Alexander Osipov (Bern: Peter Lang, 2013).
6 Ezra Mendelsohn, *The Jews of East and Central Europe between the World Wars* (Bloomington: Indiana University Press, 1983).
7 See Mendelsohn, *The Jews of East and Central Europe*; Tobias Grill, "Preface," in *Jews and Germans*, ed. Grill, ix–x.
8 Max Brod, *Der Prager Kreis* (Frankfurt am Main: Suhrkamp, 1979 [1966]).
9 Karl Renner, [Synopticus] *Staat und Nation* (Wien: Verlag von Josef Dietl, 1899). *Der Kampf der österreichischen Nationen um den Staat. Das nationale Problem als Verfassungs- und Verwaltungsfrage* (Leipzig und Wien: Franz Deuticke, 1902). Karl Renner, *Das Selbstbestimmungsrecht der Nationen in besonderer Anwendung auf Österreich—Erster Teil: Nation und Staat* (Leipzig und Wien: Deuticke, 1918).
10 Simon Dubnow, *Nationalism and History. Essays on Old and New Judaism* (Cleveland and New York: Meridian Books, 1958).
11 Gerald Stourzh, "The National Compromise in Bukovina," in Gerald Stourzh, *From Vienna to Chicago and Back: Essays on Intellectual History and Political Thought in Europe and America* (Chicago and London: The University of Chicago Press, 2007), 179.
12 On the genesis and dissemination of the idea of non-territorial autonomy, see Werner J. Cahnman, "Adolf Fischhof and His Jewish Followers," in Werner J. Cahnman, *Social Issues, Geopolitics, and Judaica*, ed. Judith T. Marcus and Zoltan Tarr (Milton Park: Routledge, 2017 [2007]); Marcos Silber, "The Metamorphosis of Pre-Dubnovian Autonomism into Diaspora Jewish Nationalism," in *Homeland and Diasporas: Greeks, Jews and Their Migrations*, ed. Minna Rozen (London: I.B. Tauris, 2008); and, more recently, Börries Kuzmany, "Non-Territorial National Autonomy in Interwar European Minority Protection and Its Habsburg Legacies," in *Remaking Central Europe. The Legacies of Nations and the Former Habsburg Land*, ed. Peter Becker and Natasha Wheatley (Oxford: Oxford University Press, 2020).
13 See Volker Prott's chapter in this volume, 96.
14 E. W. Polson Newman, *Britain and the Baltic* (London: Methuen & Co., 1930), 170.
15 Antony Polonsky, *Politics in Independent Poland 1921–1939. The Crisis of Constitutional Government* (Oxford: Clarendon Press, 1972).
16 Otto Junghann, *National Minorities in Europe* (New York: Covoc, Friede Publishers, 1932), 46–7.
17 According to the 1931 census, see Ezra Mendelsohn, *The Jews of East Central Europe Between the World Wars* (Bloomington: Indiana University Press, 1983), 23.
18 Ezra Mendelsohn, "The Dilemma of Jewish Politics in Poland: Four Responses," in *Jews and Non-Jews in Eastern Europe, 1918–1945*, ed. Bela Vago and George L. Mosse (New York: John Wiley and Sons, 1974), 203.

19 See Richard Blanke, *Orphans of Versailles. The Germans in Western Poland, 1918–1939* (Lexington: The University Press of Kentucky, 2015); Winston Chu, *The German Minority in Interwar Poland* (Cambridge: Cambridge University Press, 2012).
20 Pablo de Azcárate, *League of Nations and National Minorities. An Experiment* (Washington: Carnegie Endowment for International Peace, 1945).
21 Kathryn Ciancia, in *On Civilization's Edge: A Polish Borderland in the Interwar World* (New York: Oxford University Press, 2021), describes Polish regionalists' half-hearted attempt to valorize Jewish cultural input in Volhynia in the late 1920s.
22 See Icchak Grünbaum, *Polityka Żydowska w Polsce w ostatnich dziesięcioleciach* (Warsaw, 1930); *Report by Sir Stuart Samuel on His Mission to Poland* (London: His Majesty's Stationery Office, 1920); Mendelsohn, *The Jews of East Central Europe*, 35–6.
23 See Ciancia *On Civilization's Edge*, 105.
24 Joseph Rothschild, "Ethnic Peripheries versus Ethnic Cores: Jewish Political Strategies in Interwar Poland," *Political Science Quarterly* 96, no. 4 (1981–2): 591–606, 597.
25 See Ezra Mendelsohn, *Zionism in Poland. The Formative Years, 1915–1926* (New Haven and London: Yale University Press, 1981), 213–14; Szymon Rudnicki "Politicy żydowscy wobec idei Bloku Mniejszości Narodowych w 1922 roku," in *Problemy narodowościowe Europy Środkowo-Wschodniej w XIX i XX wieku: księga pamiątkowa dla profesora Przemysława Hausera: praca zbiorowa*, ed. Antoni Czubiński, Piotr Okulewicz, and Tomasz Schramm (Poznań: Wydaw. Naukowe UAM, 2002), 321–32.
26 Blanke, *Orphans of Versailles*, 4.
27 Stefan Dyroff, "Als Deutscher unter Polen. Die Erinnerungen von Senator Erwin Hasbach," unpublished presentation given at the Workshop "Deutsche in Polen und deutsch-polnische Beziehungsgeschichte. Neue historische und kulturwissenschaftliche Forschungsansätze" Essen, October 2016. See also Elżbieta Kozłowska-Świątkowska and Józef Maroszek, *Hasbachowie. Z rodzinnego sztambucha* (Bialystok, 2011); Jacek M. Majchrowski, ed., *Kto był kim w drugiej Rzeczypospolitej* (Warszawa: Polska oficyna Wydawnicza "BGW," 1994), 514; Jarosław Maciej Zawadski, *Senatorowie losy wojenne I pozwojenne* (Warszawa: kancelaria Senatu, 2012), 399–400; and Janusz Fałowski, *Parlamentarzyści mniejszości niemieckiej w drugiej Rzeczypospolitej* (Czechostowa: Wydawnictwo Czechostowa, 2000), 26–7.
28 *Sprawozdanie stenograficzne z 100 posiedzenia Senatu Rzeczypospolitej z dn. 17 czerwca 1925 r.*, 68–9.
29 *Sprawozdanie stenograficzne z 136 posiedzenia Senatu Rzeczypospolitej z dn. 31 lipca 1926 r.*, 75.
30 David Engel, for example, describes Gruenbaum in the 1920s as "arguably the Jewish political leader with the largest following anywhere in the world." See David Engel, *The Assassination of Simon Petliura and the Trial of Sholem Schwarzbard, 1926–1927. A Selection of Documents* (Göttingen: Vandenhoeck & Ruprech, 2016), biographical note, 447.
31 *Gegenwartsarbeit* ("work for the present," also known as the *Landespolitik*, or "countries' politics," as opposed to *Palästinaarbeit*)—a concept popularized, among others, by Martin Buber ("Gegenwartsarbeit," *Die Welt*, no. 6 (1901)), and most fervently embraced by the East European Zionists.
32 "Tretii S"ezd Sionistov" [The Third Zionist Congress], *Evreiskii Narod* [Jewish People] 7, December 2, 1906, 54.

33 See Icchak Grünbaum, *Polityka żydowska w Polsce w ostatnich dziesięcioleciach* (Warszawa: Naród, 1930); Ezra Mendelsohn, *Zionism in Poland. The Formative Years, 1915–1926* (New Haven: Yale University Press, 1981); Shlomo Netzer, "Poland as the Core of the Jewish Diaspora: Jews and the March 1921 Polish Constitution," *Justice* 7, no. 28 (Summer 2001): 19–23.
34 Vital, *A People Apart*, 782.
35 Grünbaum, *Polityka żydowska,* 16–18.
36 Mendelsohn, "The Dilemma."
37 Yitzhak Gruenbaum, *Milchamot yehudei Polanyah, 1918–1940* (Jerusalem, 1941).
38 Georges Ollivier, *L'Alliance Israélite Universelle 1860–1960* (Paris: Documents et Témoignages, 1959), 147–8; Vital, *A People Apart*, footnote 34, 781. For a detailed analysis of the disadvantages that the Polish Jews encountered under the 1921 electoral law, see Rudnicki, "Politicy żydowscy."
39 Apollinary Hartglas, *Na pograniczu dwóch światów* (Warsaw, 1996); Rudnicki, "Politicy żydowscy."
40 Cited in Mendelsohn, *Zionism in Poland*, 215.
41 Gruenbaum, *Milchamot.*
42 Erwin Hasbach, "Die Lage der deutschen Volksgruppe in Polen vor dem Zweiten Weltkriege," *Zeitschrift für Ostforschung*, Bd. 1, no. 2 (1952): 262–4.
43 *Numerus clausus*, or "closed number" (Lat.)—a limitation on the number of Jews (or other ethnic minorities) admitted to universities and certain professions. On the application of this principle in interwar Poland, see Szymon Rudnicki, "From 'Numerus Clausus' to 'Numerus Nullus,'" in *From Shtetl to Socialism*, ed. Antony Polonsky (Liverpool: Liverpool University Press, 1993), 359–82.
44 See Polonsky, *Politics in Independent Poland*, 213–18; Blanke, *Orphans of Versailles*, 90–8.
45 Vital, *A People Apart.*
46 John Maynard Keynes, "Preface to the Romanian Edition," in *The Collected Writings of John Maynard Keynes. Volume II. The Economic Consequences of the Peace* (Cambridge: Cambridge University Press for the Royal Economic Society, 1972), XXIII.
47 Keith Hitchins, *Rumania 1866–1947* (Oxford: Clarendon Press, 1994), 290; Junghann *National Minorities*, 58.
48 Irina Livezeanu, *Cultural Politics in Greater Romania: Regionalism, Nation-Building, and Ethnic Struggle, 1918–1930* (Ithaca, NY: Cornell University Press, 1995), 30.
49 *Romania Ten Years After. The Report of the Commission Appointed by the American Committee on the Rights of Religious Minorities* (Boston: The Beacon Press, 1929).
50 For a detailed analysis of the reform, see Livezeanu, *Cultural Politics.*
51 Mariana Hausleitner, "Transformations in the Relationship between Jews and Germans in the Bukovina 1910–1940," in *Jews and Germans*, ed. Grill; on the Bukovinian Compromise, see Börries Kuzmany, "Habsburg Austria: Experiments in Non-Territorial Autonomy," *Ethnopolitics* 15, no. 1 (2016): 52–5.
52 Livezeanu, *Cultural Politics.*
53 See Sophie A. Weilich, "Bukovina Germans in the Interwar Period," *East European Quarterly* 14, no. 4 (1980): 423–37, 424–5.
54 Manfred Reifer, "Geschichte der Juden in der Bukowina (1919–1944)," in *Geschichte der Juden in der Bukowina*, vol. 2, ed. Hugo Gold (Tel Aviv: Lidor Press, 1962), 2.
55 Mayer Ebner, "Jüdische Realpolitik," *Die Welt*, February 22, 1901: 6–7.
56 Reifer, *Geschichte der Juden.*

57 For statistics on the overall decline of the numbers of Jewish students in higher education, and the comparative analysis of the "quasi-legal" measures behind it, see Irina Livezeanu, "Interwar Poland and Romania: The Nationalization of Elites, the Vanishing Middle, and the Problem of Intellectuals," *Harvard Ukrainian Studies* 22 (1998): 407–30. For an account of the detrimental effect of the Romanian education reform on the Bukovina Germans, see Sophie Welisch, "The Bukovina-Germans in the Interwar Period," *East European Quarterly* 15, no. 4 (1980): 423–37.
58 Gold, *Geschichte der Juden*.
59 *Roumania Ten Years After*, 87.
60 Mayer Ebner, "Deutsche und Juden," *Ostjüdische Zeitung*, January 17, 1923, cited in Hildrun Glass, *Zerbrochene Nachbarschaft. Das deutsch-jüdische Verhältnis in Rumänien (1918-1938)* (München: R. Oldenbourg Verlag, 1996), 205.
61 Mayer Ebner, "Die Juden un die Verfassung. Eine Antwort auf die Rechtsfertigung der Bukarester jüdischen Parlamentarien," *Ostjüdische Zeitung*, April 11, 1923, as cited in Glass, *Zerbrochene Nachbarschaft*, 210–11. See also Hugo Gold, *Geschicte der Juden in der Bukowina*, vol. 1 (Tel Aviv: Lidor Press, 1958–62).
62 Glass, *Zerbrochene Nachbarshaft*.
63 *Jaunākās Ziņas*, 4, November 19, 1918, 1.
64 Marģers Skujeneeks, *Latvija. Zeme un eedzīvotaji* (Rīga: A. Gulbja apgādniecība, 1927).
65 Max Laserson, "The Jews and the Latvian Parliament, 1918–1940," in *The Jews in Latvia*, ed. M. Bobe (Tel Aviv: Association of Latvian and Estonian Jews in Israel, 1971), 98–9.
66 During the elections to the Constitutional Assembly, *Segodnya* wistfully reported: "Germans close ranks at the elections. At the polling stations in the German-populated areas more than half the electors have already voted by the end of the first day. Even ill and injured people are being carried to the polling stations" ("Vybory," *Segodnya*, no. 88, April 18, 1920, 1).
67 "1919. g. 8. Decembra sehdē peenemtais Likums par Latwijas izglihtibas eestahdem," *Waldibas Wehstnesis*, December 17, 1919.
68 "1919.g. 8. decembra sehdē peenemtais Likums par mazakuma tautibu skolu eekahrtu Latwijā," *Waldibas Wehstnesis*, December 18, 1919.
69 See Andrejs Plakans, *The Latvians. A Short History* (Stanford: Hoover University Press, 1955), 138–40.
70 Laserson, "The Jews and the Latvian Parliament," 128.
71 John Hiden, *Defender of Minorities. Paul Schiemann, 1876–1944* (London: Hurst & Company, 2004).
72 Max Laserson, *Natsional'nost' i gosudarstvennyi stroi* [Nationality and the State Order] (Petrograd, 1918).
73 Max Lazerson, "Zakon o yazykah men'shinstv" [The Law on Minority Languages], *Segodnya*, June 30, 1922, 1; Paul Schiemann, "Die Sprachengesetze," *Rigasche Rundschau*, June 30, 1922.
74 Ludvigs Adamovičs, *Skolu lietas Latvijā* [School Affairs in Latvia] (Rīga: Latvju Kultūras spiestuve, 1927).
75 Hiden, *Defender of Minorities*, 104.
76 Sabine Bamberger-Stemann, *Der Europäische Nationalitäten-kongress 1925 bis 1938. Nationale Minderheiten zwischen Lobbyistentum und Grossmachtinteresses* (Marburg, 2000), 11, 118.

77 L. Krabbe, "L'Autonomie culturelle comme solution du problème des minorités." Note de M. Krabbe au date du 18 nov. 1931. League of Nations Archive, Geneva, R.2175-4-32835.
78 Max Laserson, "Otkrovennost' do kontsa" [Full Disclosure], *Segodnya*, November 19, 1925, 1.
79 Inis L. Claude, *National Minorities. An International Problem* (Cambridge: Harvard University Press, 1955), 43.
80 Maurice Samuel, *Little Did I Know. Recollections and Reflections* (New York: Alfred A. Knopf, 1963), 19–20.

8

A Double-edged Sword: The Political Use of National Heterogeneity in the Soviet Union during the Interwar Period*

Sabine Dullin

In the aftermath of two revolutions and after the civil war that shook the former Russian Empire from 1918 to 1921 and led to the Red victory, the process of reshaping the Soviet territories took the opposite direction from that of the newly independent states of Eastern Europe. The Union of Soviet Socialist Republics (USSR) foregrounded its federative status, and the ruling Bolsheviks deliberately rejected the model of homogeneous, assimilatory nation-states espoused by its neighbors to the west, preferring to embrace its own multinational status. For the Bolsheviks, multinationalism was not the opposite of national self-determination. They constructed the Union of Soviet Socialist Republics as a jigsaw of territorialized nations organized in a federal frame. In 1923, the politics of *korenizatsia*—often translated as indigenization—triggered the development of national cultures and languages in each Republic. According to Lenin, this policy of promotion of national cultures and languages would neutralize nationalist parties by preventing them from mobilizing around ethnicity. It would also compensate the harm done to non-Russian people by the Russian imperial masters. Moreover, the new external borders of the Soviet Union did not coincide with any ethnic delimitations. The same nationalities lived on each side of the border.

All these features, the multinationalism of the USSR, its blurred ethnic borders, and the state as a jigsaw of national republics did not worry Lenin. For him, it was not a source of weakness in building up the new state. Rather, he saw it as a strength. His purpose was to internationalize and expand the revolution. In parallel to the class struggle, national self-determination could fuel expansion at the edges of Soviet territory. The Bolsheviks called this the "Piedmont policy" (*pyemontnaya politika*) in reference to Italian unification, driven by the kingdom of Piedmont-Sardinia in the nineteenth century.[1] The multiple nationalities organized in the periphery of the USSR as Union Republics, autonomous republics, or national districts had to become Piedmonts to attract national minorities on the other side of the border or to become national showcases for the Sovietization of the neighboring countries.

* This chapter has been translated from French to English by Susan Pickford.

The Socialist Soviet Republic of Ukraine with Kharkiv and Kyiv was undoubtedly the main Piedmont in the 1920s. Its bold program for the development of Ukrainian language and culture showed off its ambition to become the new heartland for all Ukrainians, first and foremost those in neighboring Galicia. It reversed the situation that prevailed before the First World War. In the days of Austria-Hungary, Galicia and its capital Lviv were the Ukrainian irredentist foyer for Ukrainians living in the Russian Empire under the czarist yoke, not allowed to write or study in Ukrainian.

The Polish national district in the Zhytomyr region of Ukraine was organized on February 15–19, 1925, as a showcase for neighboring Poland. Its capital, 50 kilometers from the border, was rechristened Marchlewsk, in honor of the recently deceased Julian Marchlewski. This was a powerful symbolic gesture. Polish-born Marchlewski was one of the founders of social democracy in the kingdom of Poland and joined the Bolshevik Party in 1907. He was a leading figure in the Russo-Polish War in 1920, when Lenin and his comrades thought the Red Army could be used to Sovietize Poland, and later in the March 1921 negotiations for the Peace of Riga that enshrined the Warsaw victory and the extension of Polish territory toward the east.[2] Before his death, he was rector of the new Moscow-based Communist university of the National Minorities of the West, which trained revolutionaries for the Comintern in Central and Eastern Europe.

It might be considered odd that the new leaders in the Kremlin established Polish districts along their border. The newly independent Poland was at that point the most powerful and the most anti-revolutionary state west of Russia. Its forces led by Jozef Piłsudski had routed the Red Army. The newly formed USSR and Poland were thus sworn enemies. Yet at a time when territory, nation, and society were being recast in Eastern Europe, Polish identity was claimed not only by Polish patriots in the second Polish Republic, but also by Polish Communists living in Soviet districts that intended to show the future direction Poland must take.

Once the ex-USSR archives became available to scholars, much research focused on this new Bolshevik approach to nationality policy, leading to a deep-seated shift in how historians considered the relationship between Moscow and the Soviet nations. The USSR, seen by many Cold War historians as a prison for captive nations,[3] proved rather to be an incubator for nations in the interwar period, at least until the early 1930s.[4] The process of building a federation that territorialized nations at every level was then interpreted either as political opportunism and a temporary means of depoliticizing national sentiment prior to merging the various peoples in the new Communist society, or as evidence of the ongoing factors that made Lenin and Stalin heirs to the multinational empire and its complexities.[5]

The inherently revolutionary dimension of this policy toward non-Russian nations has similarly been revised in the new perspective of a global history of anti-imperialism. Soviet construction has been reinterpreted as both imperial and post-imperial in its policy toward its neighbors in Eurasia and its international diplomacy.[6] In this new history of transnational Communism, anti-imperialism and the support of cross-border minority identities are read as tools for promoting Bolshevism alongside class struggle. The use of national revolution as a political resource also sheds light on the way the USSR could challenge the League of Nations on the issue of the rights of peoples and the protection of minorities⁷. Eastern Galicia and Bessarabia are revealing cases in point.

Yet the Bolsheviks also had a powerful siege mentality. The image of a besieged fortress surrounded by capitalism was deeply rooted in the memory of the civil war in which white armies and nationalist forces on the periphery were able to involve foreign forces in the fight against the revolution. As a result, the Soviet leadership was obsessed with controlling its borders, capitalist infiltration, and fifth column activity.⁸ The internal and external crisis of 1927 and the period of collectivization that threw rural regions into chaos and pushed the peasantry into insurgency were a challenge for national-revolutionary optimism. For Stalin, who had been in favor of autonomy for the Soviet nations in 1923, affirming peripheral identities and the existence of diasporic ethnic minorities on the Soviet borders could no longer be considered as political resources; rather, they undermined the state and threatened its territorial integrity. This triggered a wave of repression against nations that were now seen as dangerous.⁹ Yet the USSR did not drop its irredentist, multinational project altogether, as demonstrated by the celebrations marking the "reunification" of the Ukrainians and the Belarusians when the Red Army entered eastern Poland in 1939, almost twenty years after the Peace of Riga.¹⁰

This chapter sets out to explore how the Soviets used national heterogeneity in peripheral regions of the USSR as a political tool both internally and internationally. Multinationalism at the Soviet borders proved to be a double-edged sword—a political resource available not only to the Soviets, but also to their adversaries. The back-and-forth between policies promoting and repressing national difference was inherent in Soviet *pyemontnaya politika*.

The Last Multinational State in Europe

On December 30, 1922, Lenin wrote a letter for the forthcoming twelfth party congress, stating "I was very guilty, I think, when I spoke to the Russian workers, of not using enough energy and forthrightness on the question of autonomy, known officially, if I am not mistaken, as the question of the Union of the Socialist Soviet Republics."¹¹ Lenin the *starik* (old man) had by then been forced out of politics by ill health. His last struggle,¹² conducted from his bed, involved the Georgian affair, specifically the crucial question of mutual respect between Moscow's authorities at the center—the unwilling heir of empire—and non-Russian nationalities at the periphery. Lenin's repentant tone here marked the 1920s. The Russians had to make themselves look small, but this was not easy to achieve.

After the October Revolution demolished the Russian Empire, in 1922, it was time to rebuild. Autonomous entities gradually joined Soviet Russia because of civil wars, signing agreements of friendship and protection. The first such was the Bashkir Autonomous Republic under the leadership of Akhmet-Zaki Validov.¹³ The driving force behind the process of national-territorial autonomization within Russia was Stalin. As a Gori-born Georgian, he was himself a man of the borderlands with multiple identities.¹⁴ His career as a professional revolutionary took him from the fringes of

Baku to the heart of the revolutionary empire. He had been considered an expert on the national question since his 1913 essay "Marxism and the national question," written against the backdrop of a heated debate between the Bolsheviks and the Federalist and Austro-Marxist Socialists.[15] The pamphlet drew praise from Lenin. Stalin saw the nation as a single unit consisting of one territory, one language, one history, and one culture. Centralization and modernization were ways of raising so-called "backward" peripheral nations (and here Stalin included his own native Georgia) to the level of the central regions. As the People's Commissar of Nationalities after the revolution, he negotiated the creation of eight republics and thirteen autonomous regions with the elites of the non-Russian peripheries.[16] The principle may seem counter to the working-class internationalism that sought to dismantle borders, and indeed many Bolsheviks who saw themselves as internationalists did not understand it. However, it was a purely pragmatic decision on both sides, and this principle worked very well: it hollowed out the former nationalist parties and guaranteed the crucial support of the elites, who saw the autonomy offered by the new masters of Eurasia as a means of preserving and enriching their national identity. From Lenin and Stalin's point of view, the national-territorial reorganization was a temporary concession.

The jigsaw territory of the Russian Federation was then expanded by a ring of friendly but independent Soviet Republics—Belarus, Ukraine, and the three Transcaucasian states. In 1920–1, they signed bilateral treaties with Russia, delegating the majority of their economic and military prerogatives. In the summer of 1922, a commission was hard at work on various options to integrate them. Stalin argued for autonomizing the republics within the Russian Soviet Federative Socialist Republic (RSFSR); Lenin's rival proposal for a union of European and Asian republics in which Russia would be on equal footing with the other republics was supported by Christian Rakovsky in Ukraine and Budu Mdivani in Georgia. In September, Lenin's proposal was accepted.

The picture was more complicated in Transcaucasia. In March 1922, Lenin and the other Politburo members supported the creation of a Transcaucasian Federation incorporating Armenia, Azerbaijan, and Georgia. Seen as a stepping stone to full accession to the Soviet federal state, the regional union aimed to ensure economic integration and reduce national specificities, especially in Georgia. However, the Georgian Communists refused, and their central committee resigned. They did not want to see their status reduced to such an extent and demanded the same status for Georgia as Ukraine, Belarus, and Russia within the Union. They clashed with the brutal, arrogant figure Sergo Ordzhonikidze, who led the Caucasian bureau at the Party's Central Committee and was Stalin's ally in Tbilisi. The *Critical remarks on the national question* were Lenin's furious reaction to the return of arrogant, imperialist, bureaucratic attitudes to the party ranks and to his own loss of control. The text restated the necessity of formal equality between nations, maximum transfer of government prerogatives toward the republics, and positive discrimination for formerly dominated nations.

At the twelfth party congress in April 1923, the policy of *korenizatsiya* was launched across the Union in line with Lenin's wishes. Each national territory set out to promote local languages in education and administration and recruit and train non-Russian cadres to break with imperialist Russian domination. *Korenizatsiya* promoted nationhood but led to purges for "deviant nationalism." Nations with little sense of nationalism were held up over others. Belarus, where national sentiment was underdeveloped, was considered the ideal model of a loyal republic and as such was allowed to expand its territory into the neighboring republics of Russia and Ukraine in 1924. The same was true of Uzbekistan in central Asia. Across the territorialized Communist parties throughout the USSR, *korenizatsiya* had as many detractors—particularly Russians and internationalists—as it did keen supporters, particularly among the indigenous Communist elites. Despite the argument between Lenin and Stalin over the Georgian affair, the two shared the same opinion over *korenizatsiya* and the dispute between them should not be overstated. It was a question of method rather than intent. Fundamentally, they had the same vision of the ideal state, multinational in form and socialist in nature. Lenin's federalism was driven by political opportunism. The right of secession granted to federal republics was a tactical concession. The overriding aim was to dismantle nationalism and lay the groundwork for the next step, uniting one great socialist state. With this in mind, Lenin planned the safeguards needed to keep the disparate elements together in the long term. Unity had to come from the party and from military and diplomatic institutions.

After much debate, some of it heated, the constitution adopted in January 1924 marked the birth of the Union of Soviet Socialist Republics. The new country turned its back on its Russian identity, which only featured at the lower level of the RSFSR. The newly formed USSR's federal dimension, shared by two of its constitutive republics, Russia and Transcaucasia, was embodied in the bicameral central executive committee, with a Soviet of the Union and a Soviet of Nationalities. The latter took over from the People's Commissariat for Nationalities: it had five delegates for each federal or autonomous republic and one for each autonomous region. Ukraine's demand to maintain diplomatic prerogatives failed and the commissariats for foreign affairs, military and naval affairs, foreign trade, communications, and posts and telegraphs were all wholly federalized. In the fields of economy, finance, and labor, the so-called "unified" commissariats were both federal and federative. Justice, policing, education, and culture were managed by the individual republics. The four republics constituting the USSR—Ukraine, Belarus, RSFSR, and the Transcaucasian Democratic Federative Republic—were joined in 1925 by Uzbekistan and Turkmenistan, two autonomous RSFSR republics in central Asia that rose to the rank of federative republics. Not until the constitution of 1936, however, did the three Transcaucasian states eventually achieve federal republic status alongside Tajikistan, Kazakhstan, and Kyrgyzstan.

Pyemontnaya Politika

As early as 1924, an article in *Foreign Affairs* focused on the so-called "Piedmont policy" of the USSR.[17] Ukraine was the emblematic example, aiming to attract the Ukrainians in the neighboring Polish Galicia and Czechoslovak Ruthenia, deprived of the cultural autonomy which was developing in the Soviet Republic of Ukraine. But the expression extended to all instances of national irredentism along the USSR's borders. Jean Payart, chargé d'affaires at the French embassy in Moscow, spoke out against national revolutionary expansionism along the borders with an eloquent metaphor:

> Along the edges of Soviet territory, autonomous White Russian, Moldavian, and Armenian minorities are being raised up, with the idea that they will become peripheral centers of attraction, sucking in allogenic populations from neighboring states devoid of ethnic cohesion, thus paving the way for future integrations into the Union's indefinitely extensible framework.[18]

For historian Terry Martin, the Piedmont policy was a corollary of Bolshevik ethnophilia,[19] arising from the success of *korenizatsiya* which made national experiences in border regions of the USSR attractive for cross-border minorities and diasporas. The New Economic Policy favorable to peasants did indeed create conditions in which national cultures could flourish on a territorial basis. In Belarus, all administrative documents were in four languages: Russian, Belarusian, Polish, and Yiddish. In the Republic of Ukraine, the use of Ukrainian was obligatory in the party and administration and at school, even in towns where the vast majority used Russian on a daily basis. In 1929, over 54 percent of newspapers and books were published in Ukrainian. Many members of the Ukrainian intelligentsia returned from abroad from 1924 onward, attracted by the miraculous blossoming of national culture. One such returnee was the renowned historian Mykhailo Hrushevsky, a key figure in the national Ukrainian renaissance of the early twentieth century, who had emigrated following the collapse of the independent Ukrainian National Republic. He settled in Kharkiv, where he was immediately placed under surveillance by the Joint State Political Directorate (OGPU), the Soviet secret police.[20] *Korenizatsiya* did not cancel out the October regime's mistrust of nationalism.

The principle of *korenizatsiya* was implemented all the way down to village and district level, where national groups were entitled to establish administrations and schools in their own languages. In Ukraine in 1927, 92.1 percent of Bulgarians, 85.8 percent of Greeks, and 67.8 percent of Germans lived together in national Soviets. Thirty-three national districts were established in Ukraine in the 1920s, including the above-mentioned Polish district of Marchlewsk. Jewish shtetls became national villages. Four Jewish districts and 127 Jewish villages were created in Crimea and southern Ukraine. A Jewish territory was planned for the Crimean Autonomous Soviet Socialist Republic (ASSR) in 1927 but was blocked locally by the Ukrainians and Tatars. In March 1928, the autonomous Jewish district was founded at the other end of the Soviet Union, in the Far East. In May 1934, it became the autonomous Jewish region of Birobidzhan, with Yiddish as its official language, attracting a brief flurry of impoverished Jews hoping to find a Communist alternative to Palestine.[21]

The process of grassroots territorial ethnicization was facilitated by the census of 1926.[22] Each Soviet individual was asked to define their own nationality, leading to 198 different categories. Unlike the czarist census of 1897, in which nationality was established on objective grounds based on specific criteria, the 1926 census captured each individual's understanding of their own nationality. This personal ethnic nationality became an attribute alongside Soviet citizenship. It proved impossible to drop out of the ethnic categorization and opt for a Soviet supranationality, even if the socialist and internationalist cause could make the case for it. The chosen nationality was listed in the new passports distributed to Soviet urban citizens from 1932 on. Later, in 1937, being a Soviet citizen of the Republic of Ukraine with Polish nationality could be a death sentence. In 1968, being a Soviet citizen of the RSFSR with Jewish nationality was a source of discrimination. But at this early point, nobody knew what the future held: every nation took it as a positive step, though every new Soviet or national district stirred inter-ethnic tensions at the local level.

However, the way the internal process of creating micro- and macro-territorial ethnicities was applied in border regions seems to also have arisen from an external expansion project. The USSR was created as a political structure devoid of territorial denomination and open to new republics that wished to join. This expansion project remained in place even after the Soviet Union's consolidation. The slogan of socialism in one country, building on the ebb of the revolutionary wave in Europe following the dying days of the German revolution in 1923, did not mean that the socialist state was inward-looking. At most, subversive methods were reshaped, being rooted less in the Communist International than in the territories and institutions of the USSR itself. Chekists, i.e. members of the political police, diplomats, and the military all played a part in establishing security within the country while destabilizing foreign neighbors.

The first Soviet Piedmont was doubtless Karelia on the border with Finland. In July 1920, after the Red Army's defeat in the civil war, Finnish Communists who sought refuge in Russia were supported by Lenin and Chicherin, the People's Commissar for Foreign Affairs, in organizing the Karelian Labor Commune; three years later it became the autonomous republic of Karelia. The small cross-border republic was led by Edvard Gylling, who was waiting for the opportunity to restart the Sovietization of Finland. Since the Peace of Riga had brought vast Belarusian, Ukrainian, and Jewish populations into Poland, Soviet action began to look their way, using the republics of Belarus and Ukraine as stepping stones. Two Communist parties in western Ukraine and western Belarus, regularly backed by OGPU forces from Minsk and Kyiv, were active on Polish soil. Galicia was the focus of much attention. Further south, along the Dniester, the Soviets refused to accept the Romanian army's annexation of Bessarabia following the civil war: the Bolsheviks saw the region as a local equivalent of Alsace. The establishment of the Moldavian ASSR within the Republic of Ukraine on October 11, 1924, was another clear instance of the irredentist project. The Piedmont policy was evident around the USSR: Tatar Crimea for the Tatars living in the Balkans since the Crimean war, Soviet Armenia for the entire Armenian diaspora, Azerbaijan for the Azeris of northern Persia, Kazakhstan for the Kazakhs of Xinjiang, Tajikistan for the Tajiks of Afghanistan. The creation of republics in central Asia gave rise to concerns in the British press about the irredentist leanings of such new entities toward parts of the British empire and its sphere of influence.

The irredentist aspect was fundamental to the Soviet strategy of creating autonomous entities along a border which I have elsewhere described as "thick"—a border zone rather than a border line to be used for both security and expansion.[23] Autonomous federative republics became national revolutionary showcases for their close neighbors while also acting as buffer zones between the proletarian Union and states ideologically hostile to its existence.

The USSR and Protection for Minorities

The peace conference and the implementation of the new minority treaties marked the beginning of a period in which the League of Nations sought to protect national minorities across Europe.[24] Soviet Russia, widely ostracized by those on the winning side of the conflict, was not a signatory to the peace treaties; nor was it a member of the League, which it critiqued in the Soviet press as the syndicate of imperialist great powers. The Russians presented themselves as challengers of the League's minority protection system. They defended a rival approach to the promotion of national groups' rights.

Yet Russia began the decade facing accusations of failing to respect minority rights. A complaint was made to the League of Nations over the violation of Karelian autonomy following Soviet operations to repress insurgents in some fifteen villages in eastern Karelia in November 1921. The Permanent Court of International Justice in the Hague eventually declared it could not take on the case in April 1923, since Articles 10 and 11 of the Treaty of Tartu on eastern Karelian autonomy did not include an international obligation for Russia.[25] Each side published its own argument, with a White Book from Helsinki and a Red Book from the People's Commissariat for Foreign Affairs. Russia saw the matter as a purely internal issue that was no business of the international community, dominated by the victors of Versailles.

Following the creation of the USSR, however, protecting minorities became a Soviet cause, allowing Moscow to exert soft power across Europe to its benefit. First, the policies of Ukrainianization and Belarusization in the Ukrainian and Belarusian Soviet Socialist Republics (SSR) favorably impressed foreign partisans of minority autonomy. Secondly, the appeals procedure implemented by the League of Nations on September 5, 1923, led to a flood of petitions, each of which was passed to a triumvirate for study. There was a peak in applications in 1924 from German and Jewish minorities, and to a lesser extent Ukrainian organizations, against Poland and Romania, both bound by minority treaties.[26] Accusations against Warsaw and Bucharest were echoed by the Soviets and the Germans, who had enjoyed excellent diplomatic relations since the Treaty of Rapallo, due to their shared hostility toward the Versailles treaty. At the conference marking the opening of Anglo-Soviet diplomatic relations, Soviet diplomats presented themselves as champions of national self-determination and set out to influence Europe in favor of equal rights for all peoples.[27] This was echoed in the Soviet and Communist press, who took up cause for Ireland and Alsace, argued for the federal principle in the creation of Yugoslavia, and spoke out in favor of Bulgaria's legitimate right to Dobruja. The USSR criticized the League of Nations for taking the side of states against national minority complainants and positioned itself as their protector, particularly along its own borders.

Eastern Galicia, seen by Moscow as Ukrainian territory, was at the forefront of the Soviet project to protect minorities. When the Versailles treaty was signed, eastern

Galicia was not part of Poland, whose eastern border coincided with the ethnographic line laid down by Lord Curzon. Piłsudski conquered the province in the war against the Bolsheviks; the Conference of Ambassadors of March 15, 1923, followed France in assigning the region to Poland, though it did add that given the "ethnographic conditions," an autonomous region was advisable.[28] When the diplomatic route closed down after 1923, the Ukrainian struggle in Galicia turned insurrectional against Polish authorities.[29] Ukrainians in exile, feeling betrayed by the Allies, turned to Berlin and Moscow.

The Soviets actively supported the Galician Ukrainians. They began to provide funding to Ukrainian movements; a Politburo resolution dated November 13, 1923, explicitly mentions a strategy to infiltrate the Ukrainian movement by financing nationalists and practicing entryism in a series of Ukrainian organizations active in Galicia and Subcarpathian Ruthenia, a former province of the Hungarian part of the Habsburg Empire that was now part of Czechoslovakia.[30] Yevhen Petrushevych, born in Austro-Hungarian Galicia, was a lawyer and member of parliament prior to 1914; as the president of the Western Ukrainian National Republic in exile in Vienna, he led a stirring campaign against integrating Galicia into Poland with financial support from Moscow. The famous ataman (cossack leader) Yurii Tiutiunnyk, a former brigadier general of the Ukrainian People's Army under Symon Petliura who had continued resisting the Bolsheviks on Polish soil after 1921, turned into a Soviet agent, following his arrest by the GPU in the summer of 1923.

In parallel with this clandestine action, public declarations were plentiful. Article 7 of the Peace of Riga stipulated that the Polish populations in Russia, Ukraine, and Belarus and the Russian, Ukrainian, and Belarusian populations in Poland were free to use their own languages in administration, education, and culture; the religious and teaching authorities in each community also enjoyed extensive administrative rights. The article was regularly referenced by Soviet diplomats when the Polish authorities failed to honor their undertakings.[31] On September 5, 1924, the Soviet government sent a strongly worded note to the Polish government denying that the eastern Galicia question was merely an internal matter:

> The Soviet government's renunciation under the terms of the Treaty of Riga of its rights and claims to the territory to the west of the frontiers established by the treaty does not mean that the fate of the Ukrainian people who make up over 70 percent of the entire population of eastern Galicia can be indifferent to the Ukrainian people living in the Ukrainian Soviet Socialist Republic; nor does it mean that the Soviet government acknowledges the Polish Republic's right to annex eastern Galicia, whose population has often protested in the liveliest terms against being subsumed into Poland.[32]

In December 1924, the Comintern voted for a resolution to transfer territories with a majority of Ukrainians to the Soviet Union.[33] The congress held on July 11, 1925, in Lviv to mark the foundation of the Ukrainian National Democratic Alliance—the major political force among Poland's Ukrainian minority under Dmytro Levytsky—adopted a political platform in favor of the unity and independence of the Ukrainian people. The authors of the Democratic Alliance manifesto did reject Communist principles in the debate on relations with the Ukrainian Soviet Republic, though they nonetheless saw it as an embryonic Ukrainian state. The wording changed by 1926, when Petrushevych's group, which still maintained links with Moscow, distanced itself from the Alliance by founding the Ukrainian Labor Party. The reunification of a divided Ukraine was a constant theme throughout the 1920s in Soviet and nationalist Ukrainian propaganda alike.

The challenge to Polish domination on the margins of Belarus and Ukraine also fed into international political agitation that the Soviets sought to turn to their advantage. The support of the oppressed minorities in Eastern Europe was a concern among leftist parties and defenders of the rights of the people in Western European countries, such as in France. Very often, the manifestos and petitions denouncing Polish "white terror" against minorities came from the *Ligue des droits de l'homme* (Human Rights League) and the *Ligue internationale contre le racisme et l'antisémitisme* (International League against Racism and Antisemitism). Some of these campaigns bore the mark of the emergent Soviet soft power in the 1920s through diplomacy and Comintern.

The challenge to Romanian sovereignty over Bessarabia was another common theme of propaganda after the establishment of the USSR. A convention signed on October 28, 1920, in Paris acknowledged Bucharest's sovereignty over Bessarabia. However, the Soviets refused to recognize the new border at the Dniester. In March 1924, a conference was planned in Vienna for both parties to approve the Paris convention, which had been ratified by the French government. The Soviet delegation, led by Nikolay Krestinsky, denounced the annexation, disparaging it as "Parisian business"[34] and demanding a popular vote or referendum in Bessarabia itself. In the USSR, views on Bessarabia were divided into two camps: some, like the People's Commissar for Foreign Affairs Georgy Chicherin, made a historical case for Bessarabia to be part of Ukraine, while others, such as Grigory Kotovsky, argued that the Moldavian people should be allowed self-determination. The latter argument won out over the following months. The failure of the Tatarbunary uprising in September 1924 led to the proclamation of the Moldavian Autonomous Soviet Socialist Republic within the Ukrainian Soviet Socialist Republic on October 11.[35]

Tatarbunary was a Soviet operation that sparked an international crisis. A group of thirty armed men led by Bolsheviks including local-born Andrei Kliusnikov alias Nenin fomented a popular uprising in southern Bessarabia. On September 14, a rally was held in Tatarbunary, a small town with a population of 10,000. A war council was established, and the Moldavian Soviet Republic was proclaimed. The rebels attacked the gendarmerie and town hall and raised red flags. It is difficult to evaluate how much support they had on the ground, though they did manage to attract several hundred people, including a handful of Jews, Lipovans (Russian Old Believers), fishermen settled in many local villages since the nineteenth century, and a small number of Romanian peasants. German and Bulgarian settlers, worried by the Communist threat, alerted the Romanian authorities. The army intervened and on September 17, Tatarbunary was besieged. Nenin was killed and 120 insurgents were caught by Romanian border guards as they tried to escape across the Dniester. Five hundred people were arrested. On October 11, the autonomous Moldavian Soviet

Republic was proclaimed based on the Bessarabian *vox populi*. By returning to the name of the independent republic of 1917–18, the Bolsheviks laid claim to a heritage usurped by Romania.

The Bolsheviks worked hard to bring the trial of the Tatarbunary insurgents to the attention of the international press.[36] The president of the international law bureau in Moscow sent a telegram of support to the defense lawyer Constantin Costa-Foru on June 16, 1925. The well-known author Henri Barbusse attended the trial, which inspired his novel *Les Bourreaux [The executioners]*. Barbusse's stay was funded by International Red Aid (MOPR), the section of the Communist International which defended revolutionaries facing persecution. Finding themselves in the international spotlight, the Romanians chose clemency. On December 2, 1925, the Chisinau war council convicted 287 of the accused and acquitted a further 190. The leaders of the uprising were sentenced to fifteen years of manual labor, with just one sentenced to life in prison. The Romanian authorities came out of the affair with their reputation enhanced and the Tatarbunary affair led to a clampdown by Romanian security forces at the Dniester border. However, Tatarbunary and the creation of the autonomous Moldavian republic did underline the existence of a separate Moldavian nationality, distinct from Romanian nationality, that the Soviets were able to instrumentalize. Diplomatic interventions and political support—open or tacit—for nationalist movements in Belarus, Ukraine, and Bessarabia went hand-in-hand with irredentist agitation and propaganda that combined concrete aid and actions targeting the international press, aimed both at minorities in neighboring countries and international opinion with an interest in minority affairs.

This strategy worried Poland and Romania, hostile to the minority treaties forced on them by the peace conference and, later, the League of Nations. As early as 1919, they denounced the Soviet claims to intervene in protecting what the Soviets considered to be their irredentist minorities and judged this to be as destabilizing as the Russian protection of Ottoman Empire Christians prior to 1914. Ionel Brătianu, president of the Romanian council, declared on March 3, 1919, at the peace conference that "the Russians intervened in Turkish politics in the kindliest of fashions, to protect Christians, and the result for Turkey was its dissolution."[37] The Polish delegate argued that Poland had been carved up as a result of Russia's interventions in favor of the Uniate Ruthenians and Prussia's involvement in the Tumult of Thorn in the eighteenth century.[38] In a predominantly anti-Bolshevik context, this argument hit home. The internationalization of the protection of minorities weakened states in the cordon sanitaire and no-one in Europe wanted that. At that point, many legal thinkers and politicians considered that state sovereignty over internal affairs was crucial for stability.

The Bolsheviks instrumentalized irredentism, putting them on the side of those dissatisfied with recent peace treaties, alongside Germany and Hungary. National minorities were a puny weapon against an enemy with greater military might and a source of destabilization. Unlike their German allies who fought for German minorities abroad, the Bolsheviks fought for a post-imperial panoply of nationalities. As anti-imperialists, they did not defend the Russian minorities in the neighboring countries; in any case these minorities were largely anti-Bolshevik. Rather, they defended Ukrainians and Belarusians in Eastern Poland and Moldavians in Bessarabia.

Two Challenges to Border Optimism

Two crucial events impacted Bolshevik irredentist optimism. In 1927, Soviet propaganda spread a war scare based on a renewed perception of danger at the border. In 1930, the politics of dekulakization brought insurgency and destabilization to rural border regions of the country.

In 1927, on the USSR's European border, concerns were heightened due to the threat of returning hostilities. Following Piłsudski's coup in Poland, OGPU surveillance of the Polish population in the Soviet border zone and infiltration of Ukrainian and Belarusian networks on Polish territory both increased. On June 7, the Soviet ambassador to Warsaw, Pyotr Voykov, was assassinated by a White Russian émigré for his role in executing the czar. Stalin heard the news while on vacation and sent a coded telegram to Moscow on June 8: "Received the news of Voykov's murder by a monarchist. I believe England was involved. They want to provoke a conflict with Poland. They want to repeat Sarajevo. All leading monarchists in our prisons and labor camps must immediately be considered hostages. We must execute five or ten straight away." He concluded: "Voykov's murder gives us a basis for revolutionary measures and completely dismantling groups of monarchists and white guards across the USSR. The task of fortifying our rear demands it."[39]

These events brought about a radical change in the situation of peripheral nations. The struggle to combat nationalist deviation grew. The first executions of Communists were carried out in the Crimean ASSR. The President, Veli Ibragimov, was arrested in February 1928, put on trial in Simferopol in April, and sentenced to death. As many as 3,500 Crimean Tatar cadres, many of them Communists, were arrested, executed, or forced into exile. A year later, in Ukraine, the purge reached members of the intelligentsia who had returned from abroad to help Ukrainize the republic. Forty-five alleged leaders of the Union for the Liberation of Ukraine were put on trial in Kharkiv in March 1930. A similar purge developed in Belarus, involving both the non-Communist intelligentsia and Party cadres.[40] The entire Piedmont policy was gradually called into question. Separatism within the USSR now seemed to be a greater threat than the potential positive results of the irredentism promoted by Soviet authorities in neighboring countries. Back in Moscow, the Shakhty trial took place from May 18 to July 15, 1928. Fifty-three engineers and technicians, including three Germans, based at the coal mine in Shakhty, southern Russia, stood accused of economic sabotage, spying for foreign powers, and laying the groundwork for a new military intervention against the USSR. The trial, based on charges trumped up by Stalin and the OGPU, led to the first forced confessions in the history of Soviet political justice: it brought to the foreground the bourgeois specialist as a figure of condemnation and the notion of internal and external enemies.[41]

The second moment when the Piedmont policy seemed to turn against the USSR was the period of collectivization and dekulakization. The weeks between February 20 and April 20, 1930, saw 1,716 public disturbances in the forty-one districts of the Ukrainian Republic where peasants refused to let their lands be collectivized. The

Stalinist state feared losing control and brought in targeted measures of repression. In the summer of 1932, the local authorities in Ukraine warned against maintaining very high requisition quotas in the face of a poor harvest that had seen farmers fall back on grain stocks. The Politburo responded with the "Law of Spikelets" on August 7, 1932, which punished theft of socialist property from kolkhozes with heavy sentences in camps. The main target was the peasantry in regions affected by food shortages who stole grain to survive. Stalin went further still in a letter to Kaganovich, giving his own political reading of the crisis: Ukrainian nationalism was present within the Ukrainian Communist Party, working with an external enemy, Poland. The letter is worth quoting at length:

> If we do not take immediate steps to improve the situation in Ukraine, we could lose the republic. You realize that Piłsudski is hard at work and his network in Ukraine is far more powerful than Redens and Kosior think. We must also bear in mind that within the Ukrainian party committee (which has almost 500,000 members, ha ha!) are hidden many, yes many, corrupt elements, overt or latent Petliurists and even direct agents for Piłsudski. Should the situation worsen, it would not take them long to open up an opposition front in the Party, from the inside and the outside. My objective is to make Ukraine a true fortress for the USSR, a truly exemplary republic, as soon as possible. We must not balk at the expense.[42]

The Ukrainianization policy was cut short in December 1932. Stalin established a political link between the disaster of collectivization in Ukraine, the policy of national communism, and the Piedmont policy he had himself implemented in 1923. The starving masses in Ukraine were now seen as counterrevolutionaries and abandoned to their fate. Suicide rates shot up among Ukrainian Communists. Mykola Skrypnyk, a leading Ukrainianizationist, was denounced by the new team sent from Moscow led by Pavel Postyshev; he killed himself on July 7, 1933. Food imports from other regions were limited and police cordons prevented the population from leaving the republic for neighboring regions or republics. An estimated 5 million people starved to death in Ukraine, Kuban, and north Caucasia. Since 1991, the Ukrainian independent state has called this mass starvation the Holodomor and has considered it an act of genocide against the Ukrainian population. While this view is not universally accepted, what is certain is that the war against the peasantry that shook the whole Soviet Union and was harshest in Kazakhstan and in the Ukraine aimed, in the latter, to brutally eradicate the very seeds of nationalism.[43]

Cross-border National Minorities: A New Threat

As the destabilization of rural regions progressed, Stalin, the diplomatic service, and the army turned their attention to neutralizing neighboring states. First, they began rearming along the far eastern border after the incidents with China in 1929 and the Japanese occupation of Manchuria in 1932 threatened the USSR's Asian border. Along the western borders, the threat was also met with preparations using military strategy. All of Belarus, a potential point of access for invasion from the west, was considered a military zone. In 1935, the Soviet army consisted of 930,000 men, backed up by territorial reservists.

The short-term objective was to keep the peace and neutralize the USSR's near neighbors, who were seen as a *platsdarm*—a Russified French term for military outpost—for the capitalist powers supporting them. Working the connection between relations with their neighbors and with the Great Powers was the basis of Soviet diplomacy. Non-aggression pacts were signed with Poland and France in 1932; July 1933 saw the signature of the definition of an aggressor with all the states in the cordon sanitaire, the aim being to make borders both inviolable and untouchable. The new outlook contrasted with the denunciation of peace treaties and revolutionary irredentism of the 1920s. Territorial status quo was the policy watchword of Maxim Litvinov, appointed the People's Commissar for Foreign Affairs in 1930, who argued for collective security, anti-fascism, and protecting the integrity of the small states of Eastern Europe against the threat of German colonialism.[44] This was the context in which the Soviet Union joined the League of Nations in September 1934, signing mutual assistance pacts with France and Czechoslovakia to counter the German threat. Unlike fascist Italy and Germany, the Soviet Union did not intervene directly in the Spanish Civil War which broke out in July 1936 between the democratically elected Popular Front government and Franco's putschists. Moscow had no intention of being dragged into a war that might go global, particularly as the nation found itself in a precarious situation after Germany and Japan signed an anti-Comintern pact on November 25, 1936, and could potentially be attacked on her western and eastern borders at once. The lack of Soviet military intervention in Spain did not stop volunteer fighters from joining the Communist Party international brigades or from taking action on the ground, particularly as part of police forces. Moscow's control over Spanish republicans involved repressing anarchists and Trotskyists. In fact, it was his observation of the situation in Madrid that led Stalin to use the expression "fifth column" for the traitors in his own camp.

Defending the territorial status quo went together with a Soviet narrative on the border's sacred dimension which became dominant. Since the early 1930s, border guards had been publicly honored in posters, books, and films. They stood shoulder-to-shoulder with Red Army soldiers to protect the proletarian homeland against its enemies. The border zone, which was established at the same time as the USSR, came under special surveillance by border guards overseen by the OGPU which was integrated in 1934 into the *Narodnyi Komissariat Vnutrennykh Del* (NKVD, Ministry of Internal Affairs). Their regular "border cleansing" operations mirrored Stalin's policy. The border zones were handled separately from the rest of the territory. The inhabitants there, both urban and rural, needed a special passport and anyone suspected of disloyalty could be expelled. OGPU/NKVD reports saw minority diasporas and refugees as active agents plotting against the USSR on all fronts. Equating internal and external enemies steered the policy of repression, particularly after Kirov's murder in his Leningrad fief in December 1934 that triggered fears of cross-border terrorist networks. Illegal border crossings were now viewed as espionage or treachery.

From 1935 on, the special border zone became off-limits, with restrictions on who could live and travel there. Entering the zone required a *propiska* (visa). Defense installations and no-go zones were put in place and ethnic cleansing was increasingly practiced along the border. Polish, German, Finnish, and Baltic populations on the borders were all potential enemies and formed the bulk of deportees in 1935-6. The autonomous Polish region of Marchlewsk was abolished and its population deported to Kazakhstan.[45] By late 1936, half the Polish and German population and around 30 percent of the Finnish population living in the border zone had been deported. The areas were repopulated by Communist families, civil war veterans, experienced kolkhozians, and activists, with the support of demobilized Red Army recruits. Hundreds of soldier kolkhozes were set up in the border zones. Stalin returned to Cossack border protection practices; his Red Cossacks also brought modernization, establishing schools, clubs, reading rooms, medical and veterinary facilities, and agronomic institutes. They had radios and telephones. Like border guard barracks, they relayed Stalin's civilization to the local population.

In 1937, the no-go zone system was extended to the southern and Asian borders. Between late August and late October 1937, all the Koreans in the Far East were expelled in 124 convoys of 36,442 families—a total of 171,781 individuals—to northern Kazakhstan and Uzbekistan. This was the first wholesale deportation of a national minority in the Soviet Union. The Far East border zones remained largely uninhabited: they were eventually repopulated by Slavs in the evacuation of 1941-2, when 27,000 families moved to the region. In Stalin's view, the fate of people on the ground was of little consequence and the deportations of 1935-8 were not repressions, but measures to ensure territorial security by moving categories of suspects away from the border. They were assigned to their residences as labor colony workers, not special colonists under the watch of the political police. Yet they often suffered dreadful fates, mortality rates were staggeringly high, and the conditions in which they were transported to settle in new regions were, in concrete terms, not dissimilar from the dekulakized population. Kazakhstan became a melting pot for deportees from all over the USSR's borders: German and Polish peasants rubbed shoulders with Koreans. Even so, the process of ethnic cleansing, which became mass murder in the Great Terror of 1937-8, was not similar to Hitlerian racism. Diasporic minorities were repressed because they were considered to be fifth columnists by Stalin's regime, obsessed with espionage and terrorism. Ethnic identity was liable to create bonds with enemy nations, and as such it supplanted social identity as the key criterion in identifying threats. Any extended contact with the world outside the USSR was enough to be considered a threat. This explains why ex-emigrants of all nationalities who returned to the USSR were treated almost as badly as diasporic minorities. Ethnically Russian or Ukrainian *Kharbintsy*—people from Kharbin—had been living in Manchuria working for the east Chinese railway administration long enough to become potential Japanese spies, according to the Stalinist authorities; they suffered the same fate as the Chinese and Koreans in the Far East.

In the latter half of the 1930s, the regime demonstrated a form of xenophobia rooted in both the ideology of the socialist fortress ringed by capitalist states and a feeling of vulnerability when faced with the threat of war. Anything that came from abroad was considered suspect and hostile as a matter of principle. An individual's personal nationality in their passport could become the main evidence against them. The reversal of perspective as compared to the 1920s is staggering. The Marxist-Leninist regime that once welcomed persecuted Communists now locked down its borders and the political police persecuted foreign Communist refugees. Cross-border minorities, once seen as political resources for revolution and reconquest, were now threats to be eradicated by violence, deportation, and death.

Minority Resistance: A Totalitarian Tool for Conquest

At the same time as the purges and the search for fifth columns devastated the Soviet borders, national irredentism was practiced by Piłsudskists and fascists in the opposite camp. For example, the Prometheus movement connected to Office 2 at the Polish intelligence agency actively sought to emancipate the peripheries of the USSR, forming a wide network of alliances from Japan to Finland via Caucasia.[46] German and Hungarian fascists took an interest in the Ukrainian question. The map of ethnographic Ukraine as defended by proponents of Ukrainian nationalism at the Paris conference was printed in the fascist press.[47] The newfound interest in Ukraine arose from the initial post-Munich carve-up of Czechoslovakia and contradictory demands by Hungary and Ukraine over Carpathian Ruthenia. The Vienna Arbitration of November 2, 1938, attached the Hungarian regions in southern Slovakia and western Ruthenia around Uzhhorod, Mukachevo, and Berehove to Hungary. Germany then launched a campaign in favor of a new Ukrainian Piedmont under German protection, taking Carpathian Ruthenia, eastern Galicia, and Volhynia from Poland, with the longer-term ambition of taking Soviet Ukraine. At the eighteenth Party congress on March 10, 1939, Stalin spoke ironically of the "madmen who dream of reuniting the elephant, by which I mean Ukraine, with the aphid, by which I mean Carpathian Ukraine."[48] Diplomats posted to Czechoslovakia in the immediate post-Munich period spoke out against the instrumentalization of German Bohemians, Slovaks, and Ruthenians, with the aim of organizing internal support for German demands.[49] Hungary's annexation of Ruthenia the following March closed the debate.[50] During this period, the Soviets presented themselves as protectors of the integrity and independence of small and medium Eastern European states, pointing out how the Bolsheviks had helped them form independent states in 1920–1.

The volte-face in the Molotov-Ribbentrop Pact was also a volte-face in terms of the Soviet discourse on minorities. Stalin's USSR, working to win back peripheries lost in the civil war, once again began defending oppressed Ukrainian, Belarusian, and Moldavian national minorities. The argument fed to soldiers entering Poland and spread by Soviet propaganda in the areas they occupied was that they were reuniting the Ukrainian and Belarusian "blood brothers" divided by an unjust border since the Peace of Riga. This was both revenge on Piłsudski's imperialism and the completion of national projects left to lie fallow since the end of the First World War. Similarly, when the Red Army entered Bukovina and Bessarabia, it was an opportunity to reunite peoples divided by the Dniester since the Romanian conquest and to take "ethnographic" criteria as the basis to re-draw the borders of the republics of Ukraine and Moldavia, making the latter a federative republic.

Even the outbreak of the Winter War, sparked by Finland's refusal to allow Soviet military bases on its soil and to sign a mutual assistance pact as the Baltic States, brought the opportunity for national revolutionary irredentist discourse. As early as November 13, 1939, a so-called popular government of Finland was formed by Moscow. The aim was to confront the legally elected government in Helsinki which was denounced as bourgeois and anti-Soviet. The president of this puppet government riding in the wagons of the Red Army as it attacked the Finnish army was Otto Wille Kuusinen, a Communist civil war veteran, one of the leaders of the Finnish Communist Party, and secretary of the Comintern executive committee; his ministerial team consisted of Finnish communists exiled in the USSR. The newfound "Democratic Republic of Finland" did what the Helsinki government had refused and signed the mutual assistance pact demanded by Moscow. The Kremlin's gift to communist Finland was eastern Karelia, in cruel mimicry of the reunification of the Karelian and Finnish peoples. The right of peoples armed and dragooned by the USSR fooled no-one, however: because of the Molotov-Ribbentrop pact, European support for the Soviet cause ebbed. Finland appealed to the League of Nations, whose council called the Soviet and Finnish delegates to Geneva on December 12 to explain themselves. The Soviet government declined the invitation and, on December 14, the USSR was voted out for violating all its agreements. When the Red Army finally defeated the Finnish forces in March 1940, the tiny Karelian ASSR, part of the RSFSR since 1923, became a federative republic evocatively known as the Karelo-Finnish SSR, receiving territories stripped from Finland.[51]

The conquests of 1939–40 brought the USSR new borders to make up for the defeat of 1920–1: they even expanded beyond the former Czarist empire to incorporate Galicia and Bukovina. Multi-ethnicity was once again the order of the day. Despite the anti-nationalist repression of the 1930s, irredentism as a political resource remained a tool for military conquest. At the end of the great patriotic war, the annexation of Subcarpathian Ruthenia[52] and the establishment of ephemeral republics in northern Iran and Chinese Turkestan upheld irredentist pressure in support of Soviet expansion.

Conclusion

The Soviet design of a territorialized organization of nations served as a temporary solution on the way to the great socialist melting pot of peoples. National and cultural differences were erased through the socialist reshaping of women and men and through the compensatory system of converting backward republics to modern republics. Federal institutions were intended to prevail over republican national institutions. However, this initial plan proved definitive. No Soviet nationality was ever established. Despite Stalinist repression of individual nations and despite the genocide of Jews and Romani people perpetrated by Hitler's Germany in the western territories of the Soviet Union, national diversity remained and even increased as the Soviet territory expanded. Repression, autocracy, and totalitarianism in the USSR did not prove to be incompatible with the political management of multi-ethnic diversity.

However, this ethnic diversity was domesticated within strict ethnic borders in the Soviet Union as well as in the Eastern bloc of satellite states. Marchlewski's ashes were moved in 1950 from their resting place alongside Karl Liebknecht and Rosa Luxembourg in Berlin to Warsaw, Poland, which had become a Communist satellite of the USSR. A Polish communist must be buried in communist Poland. The cosmopolitan reading of revolution using nation and class to subvert the ancient world and its borders was over.

Like his western allies, Stalin made efforts in the immediate postwar period to strengthen the homogeneity of each nation and to draw borders based on ethnic boundaries. In so doing, he pursued a territorialist understanding of nationhood that he had espoused since as early as 1913. From 1944 to 1948, peoples were moved to the "right place" to eradicate national minorities that were seen as threats to peace.[53] Within the multinational Soviet Union, the territorialized nations in the Republics came out of the war stronger, looking increasingly like nation-states in their own right. Ukraine, now expanded and led by Krushchev, presented itself as such to the United Nations, where it had a seat alongside Belarus.[54] The question of minorities then faded in both Europe and the USSR until the collapse of the Communist bloc. The wars in Yugoslavia and the Caucasus and the break-up of the Soviet empire all came as a reminder that national minorities are a non-negotiable component of so-called "homogeneous" states in Europe and Eurasia.

Notes

1 Terry Martin was the first historian to study the Piedmont policy in *The Affirmative Action Empire. Nations and Nationalism in the Soviet Union, 1923–1939* (Ithaca: Cornell University Press, 2001).
2 М. Черных М., "Ю. Марчлевкого о советской внешней политике," *Советское Славяноведение*, no. 2 (1979): 12–22 [M. Tchernykh, "On the Soviet Foreign Policy of Iulian Marchlewski," *Soviet Slavic Studies*, no. 2 (1979): 12–22]; Ю.Ю. Мархлевский, Польша и мировая революция (москва: Гос.изд-во, 1920) [Iulian Iozefovitch Marchlewski, *Poland and the World Revolution* (Moscow: Gosizdat, 1920)].
3 Richard Pipes, *The Formation of the Soviet Union. Communism and Nationalism, 1917–1923* (Cambridge, MA: Harvard University Press, 1954).
4 Jeremy Smith, *The Bolsheviks and the National Question, 1917–1923* (London: Macmillan, 1999); Martin, *The Affirmative Action Empire*; and Francine Hirsch, *Empire of Nations. Ethnographic Knowledge and the Making of the Soviet Union* (Ithaca, Cornell University Press, 2005).
5 Imperial continuity is foregrounded in Andreas Kappeler, *The Russian Empire: A Multi-ethnic History*, trans. Alfred Clayton (London: Routledge, 2001) and Juliette Cadiot, *Le laboratoire impérial: Russie-URSS, 1870–1940* (Paris: CNRS, 2007).
6 Sabine Dullin, Brigitte Studer, "Communism + Transnational: The Rediscovered Equation of Internationalism in the Comintern Years," *Twentieth Century Communism* 14, no. 4 (2018); Sabine Dullin, Naoko Shimazu, Yuexin Rachel Lin

and Etienne Peyrat, *The Russian Revolution in Asia, from Baku to Batavia* (London: Routledge, 2021).

7   Much remains to be done on this issue: see, Borzęcki Jerzy, *The Soviet-Polish Peace of 1921 and the Creation of Interwar Europe* (New Haven: Yale University Press, 2008) and my own findings presented in *La frontière épaisse. Aux origines des politiques soviétiques 1920–1940* (Paris: Éditions de l'École des hautes études en sciences sociales, 2014).

8   For a comprehensive review of the literature on this issue, see Dullin, *La frontière épaisse*.

9   Terry Martin, "The Origins of Soviet Ethnic Cleansing," *The Journal of Modern History* 70, no. 4 (1998): 813–61; Pavel Polian, *Against Their Will: The History and Geography of Forced Migrations in the USSR* (Budapest: Central European University Press, 2004).

10 The seminal work on the annexation of eastern Poland is Jan T. Gross, *Revolution from Abroad: The Soviet Conquest of Poland's Western Ukraine and Western Belorussia* (Princeton: Princeton University Press, 1988).

11 Excerpt from the notes on the national question dictated from December 23 to 31, 1922, with a supplement on January 4, 1923. The French edition of Lenin's *Œuvres* entitles them the "letter to congress" (preparations for the twelfth congress). See Vladimir Il'ich Lenin, *OEuvres* (Paris, France: Editions sociales, 1966).

12 On this topic see Moshe Lewin, *Lenin's Last Struggle* (London: Pluto Press, 1975).

13 See Smith, *The Bolsheviks*.

14 Alfred J. Rieber, "Stalin, Man of the Borderlands," *The American Historical Review* 106, no. 5 (2001): 1651–91.

15 On the debates on the national question that developed in social democracy on a transnational scale, see Georges Haupt, Michaël Löwy, and Claudie Weill, *Les marxistes et la question nationale, 1848–1914* (Paris: L'Harmattan, 1974).

16 Stephen Blank, *The Sorcerer as Apprentice—Stalin as Commissar of Nationalities, 1917–1924* (Westport: Greenwood Press, 1994).

17 Robert F. Kelley, "Soviet Policy on the European Border," *Foreign Affairs*, September 15, 1924.

18 Payart to Briand, June 20, 1931 Archives diplomatiques françaises (ADF), Paris, economic and commercial correspondence, Estonia, file 44, 117.

19 Terry Martin used this notion to underline the huge importance given to the ethnographic principle for organizing the Soviet territories and promoting non-Russians, Martin, *The Affirmative Action Empire*.

20 Alain Blum and Yuri Shapoval, *Faux coupables: surveillance, aveux et procès en Ukraine soviétique, 1924–1934* (Paris: CNRS, 2012).

21 On the brief attractivity of Birobidzhan for the Jews after a communist campaign of propaganda, see the film Искатели Счастья (Seekers of happiness) directed by Wladimir Korsch-Sablin and Iosif Shapiro, released in 1936.

22 Cadiot, *Le laboratoire impérial*.

23 Dullin, *La frontière épaisse*. For more information on the minority treaties, see Emmanuel Dalle Mulle, Davide Rodogno, and Mona Bieling's introduction to this volume, as well as Dalle Mulle and Bieling's chapter.

24 On the League of Nations stance on the protection of Ukrainian, Belarusian, and Jewish minorities in Romania and Poland, see Martin Scheuermann, *Minderheitenschutz contra Konfliktverhütung? Die Minderheitenpolitik des Völkerbundes in den zwanziger Jahren* (Marburg: Verlag Herder-Institut 2000), 112–40, 236–43, 465–8, 479.

25 On Karelia, see ADF, Paris, Russia-Europe, vols. 614–15.
26 Scheuermann, *Minderheitenschutz*, 236–43, 465–8, 479. They had to wait until 1930, when the Polish authorities established specific rules for the voivodships of Lwow, Stanislawow, and Tarnopol and numerous appeals were made to the League of Nations. See Felix Bergmann, *La Pologne et la protection des minorités,* PhD thesis (Paris: Librairie Rodstein, 1935), 164–7.
27 Документы внешней политики СССР (Documents on Foreign Policy of the Soviet Union, *DVP SSSR)*, vol. 7 (Moscow: Politizdat, 1962), 418–26.
28 *DVP SSSR*, vol. 6, 345; Bergmann, *La Pologne*, 161; Stephan Horak, *Poland and Her National Minorities, 1919–1939* (New York: Vantage Press, 1961), 58–9.
29 Pawel Korzec, "The Ukrainian Problem in Interwar Poland," in *Ethnic Groups in International Relations* ed. Paul Smith (New York: New York University Press, 1991), 187–209.
30 Proposal by the Politburo commission for international affairs, the Galician question, protocol no. 45, November 13, 1923, Российский Государственный Архив Социальной и Политикой Истории (Russian State Archive in social and political history, RGASPI), Moscow, fond 17, opis' 162, delo 1.
31 *DVP SSSR*, vols. 6 and 7, passim.
32 Note dated September 5, 1924, *DVP SSSR*, vol. 7, 444–5.
33 Quoted in Martin, *The Affirmative Action Empire*, 36–7.
34 Litvinov's declaration to press correspondents on the failure of the Soviet-Romanian conference in Vienna, April 8, 1924, *DVP SSSR*, vol. 7, 179.
35 Report on the situation in Bessarabia by de Manneville, ambassador to Bucharest, September 23, 1924, ADF, Nantes, Bucharest embassy, box 49. For further details see *Aspects des relations russo-roumaines, rétrospectives et orientations* (Paris: Minard, 1967), 115–19.
36 Numerous insurgents were put on trial in 1924–5 on both sides of the border. April 7, 1924, marked the end of a trial in Kyiv involving the "Regional action center," thought to be linked to Russian émigré organizations and French and Polish intelligence, *DVP SSSR*, vol. 7, 707.
37 Quoted in Sava Mikhaïlovitch, *La protection des minorités nationales et la souveraineté de l'État*, PhD thesis (Paris: Law faculty, University of Paris, Librairie Rodstein, 1933), 71.
38 Ibid., 89.
39 Coded telegram from Stalin to Molotov, June 8, 1927, in Владимир Н. Хаустов и др., ред., *Лубянка: Сталин и ВЧК-ГПУ-ОГПУ-НКВД, январь 1922-декабрь 1936*, документы (москва: Международный фонд "Демократия" 2003), 133 [Vladimir N. Khaustov et al., eds., *Lubianka: Stalin and the VTchK-GPU-OGPU-NKVD, January 1922–December 1936*, Documents (Moscow: International Endowment for Democracy, 2003), 133].
40 See Jeremy Smith, *Red Nations: The Nationalities Experience in and after the USSR* (Cambridge: Cambridge University Press, 2013).
41 Anna Shapovalova, *L'étranger, ressort des procès staliniens "pour l'exemple" (1928–1933). Pour une analyse de la dimension internationale de trois affaires soviétiques (Chakhty, Parti industriel, Vickers)*, PhD thesis (Paris: Institut des Etudes Politiques, 2020).
42 Олег Хлевнюк, Роберт Дэвис, и др., ред., *Сталин и Каганович: переписка 1931–1936 гг.* (Москва: РОССПЁН, 2001), 274 [Oleg V. Khlevniuk, Robert W. Davies et al., eds., *Stalin and Kaganovich: Correspondence 1931–1936* (Moscow: ROSSPEN, 2001), 274].

43 On the interpretation of starvation as genocide, see Andrea Graziosi and Frank Sysyn, eds., *Communism and Hunger: The Ukrainian, Chinese, Kazakh and Soviet Famines in Comparative Perspective* (Edmonton: Canadian Institute of Ukrainian Studies Press, 2016) and for an opposite view, Robert Davies and Stephen Wheatcroft, *The Years of Hunger: Soviet Agriculture, 1931–1933* (Basingstoke: Palgrave Macmillan, 2004). See also for an imperial/colonial perspective on the mass violence, Timothy Snyder, *Bloodlands. Europe between Hitler and Stalin* (London: Vintage Books, 2011).
44 On Litvinov's collective security diplomacy, see Sabine Dullin, *Des hommes d'influences. Les ambassadeurs de Staline en Europe* (Paris: Payot, 2001).
45 Kate Brown, *A Biography of No Place: From Ethnic Borderland to Soviet Heartland* (Cambridge: Harvard University Press, 2005).
46 Timothy Snyder, "Covert Polish Missions across the Soviet Ukrainian Border, 1928–1933," in *Confini: costruzioni, attraversamenti, rappresentazioni*, ed. Silva Salvatici (Soveria Mannelli: Rubbettino, 2005), 55–78; Marek Kornat, ed., *Ruch prometejski i walka o przebudowę Europy Wschodniej (1918–1940)* (Warsaw: Instytut Historii Polskiej Akademii Nauk, 2012).
47 See the detailed international press review on the Ukrainian issue by the International Anticommunist Entente (IAE), IAE archives (Geneva), vol. 1674.
48 Josip Stalin, Report on the Work of the Central Committee to the Eighteenth Congress of the C.P.S.U.(B.), March 10, 1939, Marxist Internet Archive, https://www.marxists.org/reference/archive/stalin/works/1939/03/10.htm (accessed June 28, 2022).
49 See George Kennan, *From Prague after Munich. Diplomatic Papers, 1938–1940* (Princeton: Princeton University Press, 1968).
50 On the history of Subcarpathian Ruthenia or Transcarpathian Ukraine, see Paul Robert Magocsi, *A History of Ukraine* (Seattle: University of Washington Press, 1996).
51 Sabine Dullin, "Où se trouve la frontière? La place de la Finlande dans la zone de sécurité de l'URSS, 1944–1956," in *L'URSS et l'Europe de 1945 à 1957*, ed. Georges-Henri Soutou and Emilia Robin Hivert (Paris: PUPS, 2008).
52 Sabine Dullin, "How the Soviet Empire Relied on Diversity. Territorial Expansion and National Borders at the End of World War Two in Ruthenia," in *Seeking Peace in the Wake of War. Europe, 1943–1947*, ed. Stefan-Ludwig Hoffmann and Peter Romijn (Amsterdam: Amsterdam University Press, 2015), 218–46.
53 Catherine Gousseff, *Echanger les peuples. Le déplacement des minorités aux confins polono-soviétiques (1944–1947)* (Paris: Fayard, 2015).
54 Sabine Dullin and Etienne Peyrat, "Flexible Sovereignties of the Revolutionary State: Soviet Republics Enter World Politics," *Journal of the History of International Law* 19, no. 2 (2017): 19, 1–22.

Part Three

Majorities and Minorities as Social Constructs: Negotiating Identity Ascription

9

Nationalism and Vernacular Cosmologies: Revisiting the Concept of National Indifference and the Limits of Nationalization in the Second Polish Republic

Olga Linkiewicz

This chapter contributes to the historical understanding of the worldview and attitudes toward politics held by Eastern European local communities during the interwar period. In the historiography of Eastern and East Central Europe this disposition has largely been reduced to the category of national indifference.[1] Although this concept is valuable for the analysis of political debates (see, for instance, Peter Judson's chapter in this volume), it does not elucidate perceptions of nationalism held among the peasantry. In other words, national indifference is a description, not an explanation. To grasp how peasants responded to the increase of nationalism in everyday life in interwar Eastern Europe, it is necessary to unravel the complexities surrounding their means of self-identification and their various worldviews.

This chapter investigates the eastern borderlands during the Second Polish Republic, where the vast majority of the population were peasants. In the 1920s and 1930s these borderlands became an arena for national mobilization and rivalry, mostly between the Poles and Ukrainians who inhabited the territories of Eastern Galicia and Volhynia (in present-day Ukraine). In Eastern Galicia, where the competition was the most intense, the peasantry comprised Greek and Roman Catholics.[2] Polish and Ukrainian elites associated the former as having a Ukrainian ethnicity, while the latter were ascribed with Polishness. Although religious identifiers overlapped with ethnic and national ones, in Eastern Galicia—unlike in Ireland described elsewhere in this volume by Brian Hughes—we cannot see a clear-cut distinction between denominations among peasantry in everyday life. This division was clear in the case of the intelligentsia. Local priests of both Churches, particularly young Greek-Catholic clergy, engaged in the national strife. Such competition occurred, for instance, during a language plebiscite setup by Polish authorities in order to choose the language of instruction in the local schools.

The first section of this chapter discusses the origins and details of this plebiscite against the backdrop of the post-Versailles order.[3] The debates around the 1919 Peace

Conference in Paris also intensified questions concerning self-determination and identification in the disputed territories within the newfound Second Polish Republic.[4] The eastern borderlands, which Poland was trying to acquire at that time, became a laboratory where, over the following years, these questions were put forth by the Polish elites, politicians, and social science experts in particular.[5] In the 1920s the debate in Poland was dominated by demographers and statisticians. Later in the 1930s, these experts were challenged by sociologists and social anthropologists whose work was seen at the time within government circles as being potentially useful for the state. In Poland and elsewhere, the political and academic elites in the post-Versailles world understood the concepts of self-determination and identification within the framework of integrating the disputed territories into the nation-states. As Alison Carrol has shown in her chapter on Alsace-Lorraine, national elites grappled with competing ideas, universalism and particularism, in their approach concerning these territories. The eastern borderlands of the Second Polish Republic were simultaneously subject to a universalist concept of national civilization and particular approaches to national and civic identities such as the Volhynia experiment, which aimed to create Ukrainians that would be loyal to the Polish state.[6]

The second section of the chapter presents the circumstances surrounding the language plebiscite, including the role of the intelligentsia in planning and implementing it, the typical conflicts that occurred as a direct consequence of the plebiscite's campaign, and the peasants' reactions to the matter. Many of these reactions could be understood as indifferent to nationalism. I show, however, that this reading is insufficient, adding little to our understanding of the events and emotions surrounding the plebiscite. By looking closely at a set of the plebiscite's scenarios, we can see that some of these responses signal attitudes typical of a borderland where certain social roles were fluid and prone to change. In the eastern borderlands these attitudes coexisted with others that indicate little agency on behalf of the peasants and, at the same time, reveal a deep distrust toward the Polish state and Polish elites, whose presence and activity caused anxiety. The Polish presence was perceived by most peasants, regardless of their religious denomination, as the continuation of a political system that upheld lordship and serfdom that had long characterized the region. For peasants this association evoked the possibility that the Poles would take away land from them. It also derived from a local, shared symbolic order in which each social group—peasants, nobility, and Jews—had its set place and fate in the world. While the precise constellation of groups within such a symbolic order would naturally vary across time and space, expanding to contain other groups, the above-mentioned triad was common to all and structured the relationships among any additional groups. Other groups might be, for instance, the petty nobility, settlers from central and western Poland or regional groups such as Hutsuls, Boykos, and Lemkos.

In the third section, I propose that two additional categories should supplement national indifference in the characterization of peasant worldviews, ideologies, and politics. These will allow us to identify the sources of phenomena that we can then recognize as national indifference. These categories are "civilization" and "vernacular cosmology." The first captures the hierarchical relationships that also contained rivalries and hostilities within local communities, such as hierarchical social divisions.

Furthermore, this often went against divisions derived from nationalism. For instance, some peasants looked down on others because of their dialect. These civilizational hierarchies, in turn, emerged from a peasant cosmology—a comprehensive set of beliefs, practices, and interpretations that formed the basis for the ways inhabitants defined their position in the world and their relationship to other people (including the above-mentioned nobility and Jews).

The categories "civilization" and "cosmology" can be seen at play in the work of interwar sociologists and social anthropologists. In Poland, a relatively large number of fieldwork studies, with differing degrees of quality and methodological approaches, were carried out in the 1920s and especially in the 1930s. Most of them focused on ethnicity, language, and other issues related to self-identification. Such expertise in the Polish context was closely connected to the political agenda and nationalism: the public debate that the studies contributed to mostly revolved around issues crucial for the nation-state, including assimilation and nationalization. These issues were then analyzed against the backdrop of political undertakings such as the censuses and plebiscites. Among other things, the interplay of expertise with a variety of expressions of local peasant populations produced a Polish version within the category of national indifference, discernible in the term *tutejsi*—the people "from here." Significantly, rather than a nationally oriented descriptor, *tutejsi* was the term created by experts to cover a wide range of peasant identifications, including religious, linguistic, and ethnic elements. It was used in Polesia (in present-day Belarus), the region which appeared to the Polish elites as the embodiment of backwardness. In what follows, I will juxtapose *tutejsi* with peasant worldviews as captured by interwar social science experts.

While the fieldwork studies of the social science experts reveal much about how the experts sought to categorize local populations, the sources are also valuable for approaching peasant conceptions that formed their worldviews and identities. Because anthropologists and sociologists recorded verbatim a great number of extended utterances by local peasants, we have access to the language and concepts many peasants used to describe their neighbors, community, and other people. With due consideration of the researchers' perspective in the creation of these sources, the studies can nonetheless help us make sense of the peasantry's beliefs and attitudes because of the rich imagery of otherness and peasant expressions of difference that they contain. As we do not otherwise have access to the words and images that interwar peasants used to describe their beliefs and attitudes, these fieldwork studies are invaluable for our attempts to reconstruct peasant worldviews.

The third section is an ethnographic demonstration of these points. Additionally, in line with social science classics such as the works of Pierre Bourdieu, John Campbell, and Sydel Silverman, I will show that certain features such as peasants' apprehensions concerning the world in which they lived appear to be universal as far as Europe is concerned. In the case of the eastern borderlands of the Second Polish Republic, despite the diversity of the population (which manifested itself in different religious denominations, ethnicities, and languages), civilizational hierarchies and vernacular cosmology appear to be a foundation of self-identification and a common lens through which communities made sense of politics.

Grabski's Plebiscite as an Exercise in Self-determination

The immediate post-Versailles world saw a number of plebiscites. They became a political experiment and, consequently, a new scientific field of study. Interwar experts, such as American political scientist Sarah Wambaugh, saw them as an instrument that gave voice to the people; they were useful politically and also just, as long as security measures and regulations were adopted to protect both plebiscite sides.[7] Although plebiscites were used to defuse national conflicts, locally they could very well increase antagonism between neighbors (even if these plebiscites were, at the same time, seen as politically successful either by those directly involved or by international observers).

Quite soon after plebiscites had been conducted under the auspices of the League of Nations, the multi-ethnic Second Polish Republic came up with its own quasi plebiscite, which took place in its eastern provinces. Why should we call it "quasi"? In essence, some of the provinces' inhabitants were given an opportunity to choose the language of instruction to be used in schools, but only if specific criteria were met. With these requirements, Poles were given an advantage over Ukrainians, Belarusians, and Lithuanians, which is unsurprising since Poland was then governed by *Endecja*— the right-wing National Democratic party.

This quasi-plebiscite was introduced with the law regulating the educational system, popularly called the *Lex Grabski*. Stanisław Grabski, an *Endecja* economist and politician, had worked twice as the Minister of Religious Affairs and Public Education—shortly at the end of 1923 and then between March 1925 and the May Coup of 1926. He was not working as minister when the new rules were passed on July 31, 1924.[8] The first article announced in the official gazette asserted that in some eastern provinces[9] the standard type of public school was to be a "joint" school, by which the authors probably meant a bilingual one. What is more, according to "the principle of uniting not dividing" and for the "harmonious coexistence of inhabitants of ethnically mixed territories," such a school would raise good citizens of the State, both Polish and non-Polish children, "to mutually respect their national features."[10] The emphasis on maintaining diversity definitely did not sound typical of *Endecja*. Since its emergence at the end of the nineteenth century, *Endecja* had evolved from the fight for Polish sovereignty to espousing illiberal views. According to National Democrats, or so-called *Endeks*, Polish national interest was superior to any other commitment. It was in Poland's best interest, they believed, for the Slavic minorities to be assimilated into a Polish nation.[11]

Although the Law was signed by Stanisław Grabski's successor, economist Bolesław Miklaszewski, the idea was attributed to Grabski. So why did an *Endek* decide to carry out a plebiscite, even if flawed by international standards? Was he inspired by the League of Nations' plebiscites? There are no straightforward answers to these questions, so we must resort to speculation. Grabski, as many other politicians at the time, was a university professor and expert economist. He did not participate in the Paris Peace Conference of 1919, as some of his fellow colleagues from the Jan Kazimierz University of Lwów did. But he certainly had a thorough understanding of the principle of self-determination. It should be noted that Grabski advocated for a plebiscite in Cieszyn

Silesia, after a confrontation between Poland and Czechoslovakia over the region. He also convinced Aristide Briand that the issue of Upper Silesia—the other disputed territory (this time between Poland and Germany)—should be resolved by the League of Nations.[12]

Yet Grabski was not the only one who worked on this law. When we look at the other actors involved and their political leanings, we can better understand both the law's relatively conciliatory tone and the presence of the concept of self-determination in its provisions. In April 1924 the government[13] established a special body to prepare administrative, legal, and educational reforms regarding the languages of the Republic's Slavic minorities. The group was called the Commission of Four. It represented a wide spectrum of political opinions. Apart from Grabski, who had a leading role in the Commission, the organization involved Stanisław Thugutt, politician of the left-wing Polish Peasant Party *Wyzwolenie* ("liberation" in Polish),[14] Eugeniusz Starczewski, landowner and politician of the conservative Polish People's Party *Piast*, and Henryk Loewenherz, who belonged to the Polish Socialist Party and was a leading expert on minorities. Both Loewenherz and Thugutt were supporters of the League of Nations and members of the Polish League of Nations Society. Additionally, Loewenherz was a delegate to the Paris Peace Conference. Despite some reservations he had toward the League, Starczewski was hoping that under its mandate Poland would assume a leading role in the East, especially regarding civilizing missions.[15] These connections to the League make it likely that the League's plebiscites provided a model for Polish experts to follow. Democracy, and direct democracy in particular, was at that time still largely an experiment, and politicians like Grabski and Thugutt might have been curious to implement it.[16] Like in the cases of Upper Silesia, Sopron, or Saar territory, the issue of self-determination lay at the core of the plebiscite in Poland's eastern provinces.[17] Despite the fact that the Polish plebiscite was not a boundary plebiscite, it took place in highly disputed territories. For Poles, claiming a popular mandate in the region would have been a desirable yet unrealistic goal.

Although the public was informed that the Commission had come into existence, the body's deliberations remained confidential. This secrecy naturally reinforced the already-existing deep distrust between the representatives of minorities in Parliament and the government. This distrust would contribute to the shaping of minorities' attitudes toward the plebiscite. After a number of formal meetings regarding education and other issues concerning language rights of minorities, the *Lex Grabski* was passed through the *Sejm*. The law, introduced in 1924, came to life at the beginning of 1925. To Thugutt's surprise, the government did not change anything in the Commission's proposal.[18] What type of plebiscite had the Commission agreed upon? In order to determine whether the plebiscite could be carried out, the legislators used data from the Republic's first census in 1921. This was an example of political maneuver on the side of the Polish state. The 1921 census included questions about religion and nationality. In Eastern Galicia a large number of Greek Catholics were registered as Poles, which was most welcomed by the Polish authorities and upset the Ukrainian elites who saw these Greek Catholics as Ukrainians. Consequently, there were far fewer Ukrainians than Greek Catholics in the census. Why this happened is not entirely clear. In some cases, religious status and nationality could have been determined by a census field-representative. In other cases, such declarations were made by the local population. Reasons behind these declarations included pragmatism and, in essence, the complex identity typical of the borderland regions. Knowing this, the authorities required that, for the plebiscite to occur, at least 25 percent of a given community (the smallest administrative unit known as *gmina*) had to have declared themselves Ukrainian in the census ("Rusyns" in the census table). If that criterion was met, and provided that forty parents of schoolchildren signed a petition for Ukrainian, Ukrainian would become the language of instruction. In other words, the plebiscite could take place only by demand. If, at the same time, twenty parents opted for Polish, the school in that *gmina* would become bilingual. Otherwise, Polish would be the language of instruction, while Ukrainian would be taught as a separate subject along with the Greek-Catholic religion. This brings us to the second reason why the Commission might have decided upon a plebiscite: the degree of national consciousness in the eastern provinces of the Republic was a hot issue disputed by statisticians, social science experts, politicians, and members of the general public. A plebiscite, and especially one which left the initiative up to the people, might have been seen as the best test concerning self-determination. From this perspective, the plebiscite was likely a suitable solution to satisfy the requirements of the minority treaty Poland had signed in June 1919. In order to protect its minorities, Poland was supposed to secure the use of minority languages for specified public purposes, including in courts and elementary schools.[19]

Petitions could be presented until the end of May 1925, and all changes were to be introduced at the beginning of the 1925–6 school year. In 1930, a presidential law stated that further changes could be made only seven years after the plebiscite had occurred. The terms of the plebiscite were met with strong opposition from Ukrainian activists, not only from deputies, who refused to participate in voting on the bill, but also from ordinary representatives of the intelligentsia. They often disputed the results of the plebiscite saying, for instance, that some Ukrainians boycotted the census and that the plebiscite was therefore invalid. In general, they opposed the plebiscite because they saw the Polish presence in the territories of Eastern Galicia and Volhynia as an occupation. The Polish authorities officially stated that the plebiscite's aim was to introduce bilingual education to the ethnically mixed territories, thereby implying that the bilingual model was preferable.[20] They also stated that citizens of the Second Republic should have a good command of Polish. To emphasize the status of the Polish language, they termed it "the state language" in the new law and related documents. Historian Andrzej Chojnowski has observed that in effect the law was more pro-state than pro-national.[21] Yet it has also been viewed as a tool for Polonization, not without a reason. Seen in this light, the *Lex Grabski* was a compromise,[22] but this compromise was an acceptable solution for opposite poles of the Polish debate yet not for the minorities. Regardless of how it was received, the reality on the ground was quite different from the ideals the law promoted. The plebiscite's consequences for local communities in territories with strong political activists such as Eastern Galicia went beyond what Grabski and his colleagues might have envisioned.

Wreaking Havoc

According to Polish statisticians who analyzed data from questionnaires gathered from teachers in the early 1930s, it was difficult to ascertain which language of instruction was used at a given school. In Eastern Galicia, despite having seemingly analogous situations, some teachers claimed it was Polish, others Ukrainian, and still others described the language as Polish-Ukrainian.[23] Regardless of the language claimed to be used in teaching, the data collected in the 1930s show that before the plebiscite, in December 1923, there were 2,576 schools with Ukrainian as a language of instruction in the three provinces that composed the region. In 1924 this number dropped to 2,391, and a year later it reduced to 2,151. In 1926 the number of bilingual schools reached 1,526. If we look at the province of Tarnopol, which was the most ethnically mixed province in Eastern Galicia, the number of bilingual schools rose sharply in the 1925–6 school year (from 7 to 304). In the following years the annual increase stabilized, reaching 504 schools in the 1929–30 school year.[24]

Whether a plebiscite took place or not largely depended on the attitude of the local intelligentsia, not the peasants. Local school inspectors had to collect all data regarding the plebiscite on site and send it to a Board of Education in Lwów (Lviv), a major city in Eastern Galicia and the capital of the province. The data included ballots, a list based on the results of the plebiscite and the 1921 census, and an inspector's application for the introduction of a language of instruction. The latter became an invitation for manipulation and fraud, as some school inspectors tried to overturn the results by claiming, for instance, that petitioners spoke in support for the Ukrainian language, which the law did not recognize (instead, Ukrainian was called the Rusyn language). After many years, Thugutt reflected that the minority deputies of the *Sejm* had been right in saying that the law would not be executed. Apparently, he had received a number of complaints from local non-Polish activists at the time of the plebiscite.[25]

By the beginning of 1925, widespread agitation arose in villages—especially in those with a significant number of Greek Catholics. Peasants were persuaded to vote for either Ukrainian or Polish. The law contained a clause requiring that inhabitants be informed when Ukrainians submitted a petition. In this way, Poles could be mobilized against the introduction of instruction in Ukrainian. The restlessness in some villages continued throughout the 1930s. Theoretically, any changes would have been possible only seven years after the plebiscite occurred, that is in the 1932–3 school year. At times the petitions would nonetheless be drawn up after May 1925 but before the seven years had passed. We shall look at a few plebiscite stories from Eastern Galicia, which will guide us through the actual course of the plebiscite and the way local inhabitants experienced it.

There were, at least, a few possible plebiscite scenarios. Although evidence compiled by the Polish administration may be misleading, it is tempting to draw a line between the cases showing more competition and conflict and those displaying an atmosphere of collaborative coexistence (these were less frequent). We shall begin with the latter. Adryanów, in Rudki county in the province of Lwów, was not considered eligible for the plebiscite. Nevertheless, a petition for Polish as the language of instruction was filed in 1934. A separate questionnaire included declarations of nationality. A few parents voting for Polish declared themselves as *Russki*. This was not an isolated case, both in terms of people who identified as *Russki* and of non-Poles voting for Polish. Why did some *Russki* in Adryanów vote for Polish at school? Did they come to see education in Polish as inevitable? Were they encouraged or pressured by the Polish majority? This we do not know. We do know, however, from other sources that *Russki* (not "Rusyn" that appeared, for instance, in the census table) was a popular term for people in villages to use for themselves and their neighbors, when they wanted to indicate a certain aspect of their identity. *Russki* was then a local term which emphasized on the one hand belonging to an East Slavic culture and on the other an identification with the peasant culture. In any case, all votes were dismissed as groundless.[26]

According to the 1921 census, in Alfredówka, in Przemyślany county in the province of Tarnopol, there were 184 Greek Catholics (out of 457 inhabitants), but only 111 declared themselves as Ukrainians ("Rusyns"). This was a little less than the necessary 25 percent for the plebiscite to occur. Still, petitions were received by school inspectors, for both Polish and Ukrainian. During the first attempt in 1925 and again in 1933, there were a few more people opting for Polish than for Ukrainian.[27] Like in numerous other cases, there were more votes than children in compulsory education. For the above-mentioned reasons the vote was deemed invalid. No fierce protest took place, however, and the one-class school kept Polish as the language of instruction.

During the plebiscite and beyond, the attitude of the Roman and Greek-Catholic priests in Eastern Galicia was mostly nationalistic and antagonistic. There were exceptions, however, especially amongst the older generation of the clergy. In Adamówka, in Radziechów county in the province of Tarnopol, the Greek-Catholic village priest Lemieszczuk, who was the head of a local school council, appealed on the behalf of the inhabitants, urging the Lwów School Board to set up a school in Adamówka. Such a school, he argued, would produce "noble and honest citizens, faithful to God and homeland."[28] It should be noted that Lemieszczuk did not opt for a school in Ukrainian. The school was opened in October 1931. Two years later it turned out that no language of instruction had been formally established. A local inspector decided that the school would become bilingual. At this point, the course of events seems ordinary. Two petitions were filed—one for Polish and one for Ukrainian. Yet there is something quite extraordinary about this attempt: a list compiled by Lemieszczuk included the names of people who voted twice—once for Polish and again for Ukrainian. Some individuals had names with two variants. For instance, Mykoła Kaszuba voted for Ukrainian; his alter ego Mikołaj Kaszuba—for Polish. Dąbrowski supported the Polish group, while as Dimbrowskij he voted in favor for Ukrainian. Miszczankiewicz/Miszczankewycz was also a double agent. Was this dual appearance Lemieszczuk's initiative only? Possibly, yet, this was a typical sign of a borderland where inhabitants used two variants of their names, sometimes in two alphabets—Latin and Cyrillic.[29] In such expressions, Adamówka was quintessentially borderland, despite being largely Greek-Catholic.[30]

Being forced to choose between Polish and Ukrainian frequently seems to have been a source of discomfort for the borderland inhabitants. The choice was often not clear. In the case of intermarriages between Greek and Roman Catholics, parents often followed a common pattern they used in other situations, such as baptism. Most often girls would follow their mother's rite and boys would follow their father's. If the mother was Roman Catholic and had daughters, she would vote in favor of Polish, while her husband, say Greek Catholic, might vote for their sons to be taught in Ukrainian. Another solution was to follow the father's rite regardless of gender. But the attitudes of inhabitants could very well change depending on the situation they found themselves in. This led to frustration on behalf of the schools' inspectors. In correspondence with the School Board in Lwów, the inspectors recounted several situations in which the inhabitants, usually influenced by "a big campaign" put forth by Ukrainian activists, at first backed a group voting for Ukrainian and then later also supported a petition for Polish. This was the case in Balicze Podgórne, in Żydaczów county in the province of Stanisławów, where inhabitants were wavering between Ukrainian and Polish. This vacillation led the inspector to apply to the Board for bilingualism. The Board counted the votes again and found that the majority chose Ukrainian which, therefore, became the language of instruction in Balicze.[31] It was not unusual for the Board to correct local inspectors to the benefit of Ukrainian activists. The latter, however, distrusted the authorities of the lower echelons and preferred to address their complaints directly to the Ministry of Religious Affairs and Public Education.

Hesitation and doubts often made the School Board launch an investigation, and this inevitably led to confrontation. Locals in a community in Bazar, in Czortków county in the province of Tarnopol, that was split on the matter, had to face an interrogation, one by one. A man named Jan Król, for instance, who was illiterate, confirmed he was present when the petition was signed. A common plebiscite occurrence was not only X-mark signatures in lieu of actual ones but also false signatures or a petition signed by someone who did not live in a village covered by the plebiscite. Król, trying to meet the needs of the investigation led by Polish authorities, declared that he would like students in the first grade to learn in Ukrainian, and starting from the second grade, for them to learn in Polish and *Russki*. Other answers were similarly equivocal: "and, then, also in Polish," "and, then, as it used to be," "the way things were," and so on. The only exception was a woman named Tatiana Tywoniak, who declared categorically: "We do not need Polish here."[32] Such investigations sometimes dragged out for months before any conclusion was reached.

In Wołoszczyzna, in Bóbrka county in the province of Lwów, a group of Ukrainian activists pursued their own investigation. "Are you Rusyns?" "Do you want to learn in *Russki*?," they allegedly asked.[33] An inspector reported to the Board of Education in Lwów that answers varied and some inhabitants refused to reply to or sign anything. In Wołoszczyzna, like in many other villages, the conflict was already initiated in 1923 by a local council, which had changed the language of instruction from Ukrainian to Polish. In response, the Ukrainian activists spread rumors that the Greek-Catholic church would be destroyed and all people would have to go to the Roman-Catholic church and "convert to Polish."[34] Actually, in the late 1930s this was not far from reality in some parts of the Second Polish Republic that were under the rule of the late *Sanacja*.[35] In 1925, however, such ideas were still far-flung. The community of Wołoszczyzna split into two camps: one which supported the local council and, therefore, education in Polish, and the other one which supported the efforts of a Greek-Catholic priest and a Ukrainian lawyer from the town of Bóbrka who wanted to make Ukrainian the language of education. The case shows how the plebiscite brought (or intensified) conflicts along national lines and increased polarization within communities.

The political agitation was widespread, especially in the vicinity of locations such as Bóbrka, Tarnopol, or Brody. Yet Ukrainian activists were deeply unhappy with the response of the Greek-Catholic peasantry to Ukrainian national mobilization. "Our society is indifferently looking at a terrible tragedy," stated one of the activists describing the course of the plebiscite in Eastern Galicia.[36] This observation explicitly raises one of the big questions in the historiography of Eastern Europe, that of national indifference and its presence in the borderlands.

National Indifference, Civilization, and Vernacular Cosmology

The concept of national indifference is not a precise one. In her well-known article, Tara Zahra has defined national indifference broadly, as an umbrella term that historically has covered phenomena such as intermarriages, regionalism, and backwardness.[37] But what, in fact, does the term mean? In essence, it is used to describe attitudes of communities or groups that, for some reason, did not embrace the ideology of nationalism. Along similar lines, Polish historian Józef Chlebowczyk, in his seminal work on national development in East Central Europe, has called such attitudes of the borderlands' inhabitants as "anational," "neutral," and "indifferent."[38] In this sense, many of the reactions coming from the protagonists discussed here with respect to the plebiscite could be considered cases of national indifference. Yet we could also describe these attitudes as being driven by hesitation, pragmatism, and reluctance to confront authority. In other words, national indifference does nothing more to explain why people had such a response to nationalism than other adjectives that we could invoke to capture a different facet of the observed behavior. Furthermore, would the reactions of these communities have been any different toward other ideologies and especially toward those associated with an outside power? In an attempt to answer this question, we need to shift the focus away from the perspective of ideologies and try to grasp a better understanding of peasant knowledge, worldview, and rationale. The point I would like to make here is that the concept of national indifference was beyond the peasant frame of reference. At the same time, it is important to see how interwar researchers understood and captured the responses of peasants to the then popular ideologies, including nationalism.

As a concept, Zahra emphasizes, national indifference evolved as a by-product of nationalism. In other words, this is "a nationalist category."[39] It is true that the subject was discussed not only by interwar politicians and researchers in Eastern Europe but also among Western specialists, such as American historian and political scientist James T. Shotwell.[40] One of the categories that branched out from the concept of national indifference was coined by Polish experts on minorities around 1919 and used then by statisticians when they created the first and the second censuses in 1921 and 1931, respectively. This was *tutejsi*—a term originating from the Polish word *tu*, or *tutaj*, which means "here." Despite national mobilization which, especially in the early 1920s, tended to reduce the meaning of censuses to national plebiscites, some Polish politicians and social science experts were in favor of the inclusion of the non-national category in the census rubric. Among them was Stanisław Thugutt, who saw this as an unavoidable stage in the process of nation-building.[41] Clearly, already in the early 1920s, census and social science experts realized that some inhabitants of the Second Republic would not adjust the expressions of their self-identification to the census' national categories. But how much did these individuals actually know about local categories concerning identification and their meanings?

Within the eastern borderlands, the region of Polesia became a focal point of discussion concerning the category of *tutejsi* soon after the founding of the Second Republic. In public debate Polesia was seen as the opposite of Eastern Galicia, which was considered a nationalist hub. Inhabitants of Polesia, according to some representatives of the Polish elites, formed a mass of thoughtless peasants whose sense of national belonging could be moved in a desirable direction. "In terms of nationalities we allowed Polish, Belarusian, Ruthenian, German and Jewish; there is also a special rubric for these people, whom we often meet in the Ruthenian-Belarusian ethnographic borderland, and who registered as *tutejsi*, *miejscowi* (local), or declared they were of *Poleski* (from Polesia) or *Russki* nationality," explained the head of the census department at the Central Statistical Office (GUS) in Warsaw, Rajmund Buławski.[42] *Tutejsi*, thus, were local people, people "from here," who did not belong to any national category. The special rubric was only included for the Polesia province despite broad agreement that some form of *tutejsi* appeared across the eastern borderlands. There were also voices to eliminate such categories from the censuses' rubrics, which, in turn, would allegedly smooth the path to nationalization.[43] The category of *tutejsi*, however, stayed in use during the second census in 1931.[44] Polesia was treated as a laboratory by both politicians and researchers to explore questions regarding nationalization, minorities, and assimilation.

Among those interested in these questions was sociologist and anthropologist Józef Obrębski, a student of the prominent Bronisław Malinowski. With his professional knowledge and having spent much time in the field applying Malinowski's methods, Obrębski had his own, in-depth view of Polesia and the attitudes of the peasantry there. First, he noted a large variety of groups that differentiated themselves from others. The relationships between these groups, insiders and outsiders, were often antagonistic. Second, he observed the existence of social inferiority among the inhabitants of Polesia. He argued that this was acquired through interactions with outsiders who showed contempt for the inhabitants' culture and values. Third, he described the peasants' responses to politics and to the Polish presence in Polesia. Obligatory school, for instance, was treated as an outside institution whose values and narratives, along with their heroes, were foreign to the peasant culture.[45] Similarly, in Eastern Galicia many peasants opposed compulsory education seeing it as competing with the needs of the peasant family. The presence of Poland, Obrębski showed, was interpreted as equivalent to the presence of lords (*pany*), who were seen as a threat to the peasant's freedom.

Tutejsi was a category constructed by census and social science experts. The people did not use the term themselves—neither as a form of self-identification nor to describe their neighbors. Depending on the region, the inhabitants of the eastern borderlands would use terms like "simple people" (*proste*), "Orthodox" (*prawosławne*), "Polish" (*Polaki, Polskie*), and *Russkie*. The creation of *tutejsi* by experts to capture elements of peasant self-identification that were outside of nationalist categories reminds us of the multifariousness of peasant culture. Moreover, it reminds us that the concept of national indifference was not native to the peasants themselves. To be able to understand their responses to nationalism, we need to develop a vocabulary that derives from peasant worldviews, not from an outsider's perspective. National indifference simply shows us what was perceived as absent, not what was present in peasants' perceptions of the world.[46] In other words, the concept of national indifference did not belong to the peasant frame of reference.

The complicated and volatile situation of the plebiscite campaign produced unintended consequences, often provoking deep antagonisms within communities. Conflicts and rivalries, however, were not uncommon beforehand in the rural areas of the eastern borderlands. On occasion, incidents regarding a church gathering, funeral, or other rite would spark a dispute between parishioners and a clergyman. Other times, one village would go against another. This is not to imply that peasant and group solidarity excluded divisions and rivalry within a given unit. Essentially, each community formed a hierarchical and divided world in which the concept of equality was foreign. This is why during the short existence of the Galician Soviet Socialist Republic, set up by the Bolsheviks in 1920, wealthier peasants did not want to join the units (*revkoms*) with the poorer peasants.[47] Wealth and descent lay at the heart of such divisions. But it is impossible to reduce these divisions to material status, class, or family background. Moreover, these attributes mingled with ethnic and regional distinctions, and later acquired a national dimension.

Concern for status and position in society manifested in frequent comparisons to others. These were socially significant behaviors that helped to maintain distinctiveness, autonomy in relation to others, and social balance within a community.[48] In order to reinforce existing differences, the inhabitants distinguished others and their otherness by language, clothing, and other signs of status—the possession of agricultural machinery or tools, ownership of farm buildings, and the performance of activities such as plowing, herding, and domestic service. The signs held in the highest regard related to modernization, urban life, and mass culture. In other words, they were signs of the aspiration to be something other than rural culture. As with any other category related to identification, the civilizational ones were situational and flexible, and the social use of them was dynamic.

How local, regional, and national factors came into play can be seen with the Hutsul, inhabitants of the Carpathian Mountains and a source of unintended symbolism for village life. For the communities in large parts of Eastern Galicia these highlanders symbolized poverty, backwardness, and inferiority. The Ukrainian intelligentsia, searching for patterns that could help in building a national symbolism, chose the Hutsuls as exemplars upholding national values. Typically, they used some elements of the regional costume to represent a Ukrainian national dress. Nearly concurrently, the Polish political elites of the *Sanacja* regime went in the opposite direction. They made conscious efforts to construct the Hutsul as regional and lacking a national component, but stressing the loyalty of the Hutsuls to the Polish state.[49] Such a tension on this figure could probably affect the way peasants perceived the Hutsuls. But such changes happened slowly. In 1936, for instance, in the region of Podilya in the province of Tarnopol "a Hutsul" was still a synonym for an ignorant or simple person, and was pictured as someone dressed in a long, loose, knee-length shirt, worn over trousers. "Such an outfit Poles would call *Russki,* and Rusyns (i.e., Ukrainians)—Hutsul," noted one of the Polish ethnographers in the field. Homespun clothes were, at the time, considered old-fashioned and treated with disdain. Only in the south of Podilya, close to the Hutsul region, where such outfits were common, did they provide no grounds for mockery.[50] Similarly, there was a difference between the north and the south of Podilya concerning peasant activities and the social status they imparted. Pasturing sheep, a common activity in the south of Podilya and in the Carpathians, was seen as degrading by northerners. During the financial crisis of the 1930s, some farmers became herders, including in the north. "It is the Hutsul thing to herd sheep," richer farmers would say with contempt.[51]

If we look at the numerous examples concerning language and the variety of dialects in the eastern borderlands, we find analogies in terms of how peasants dealt with otherness and strangeness. Outsiders, such as the Hutsuls or other highlanders—the Lemkos and Boykos—did not speak Ukrainian, according to the inhabitants of the rest of Eastern Galicia. To these other inhabitants, the highlanders' utterances were funny and difficult to comprehend, which contributed to them seeming ridiculous and unlikeable, and sometimes even as mentally disabled. "They needed to be taught culture by our people," an interlocutor from a village of Wojutycze, in Sambor county in the province of Lwów, firmly remarked.[52] Put differently, the highlanders needed to be civilized. *Civiltà* is a category used by Sydel Silverman in her study of social hierarchies among the peasants of Umbria. Silverman interprets it as "the civilized way of life," "citified," emphasizing its urban component.[53] Similar to what we see with the Galician peasants, in Umbria the concept involved behavior and qualities such as courtesy and generosity and the presence of certain patterns related to city life: a speech that is not a dialect, urban clothes, and a fashionable dwelling. Here we also detect a strong hierarchy of prestige.[54]

The concept of civilization created all-pervasive divisions. With it, two major figures that were seen in opposition to the peasant come into focus. First is the figure of the nobleman, who also may appear as "lord" or "a Pole." Again, the differentiation mostly involved language, clothing, and other visible signs of position and prestige. Cleaving to their ancestry as a means of differentiation usually meant that the nobility, even if petty, adamantly opposed marriage with peasants. They also did not stand on the same side of the church, even if it was a Greek-Catholic *cerkva* (church).[55] Petty nobles, who often did not differ from peasants in terms of their material status or educational level, stressed their alleged superiority in relation to the "boors." According to the memories of interlocutors who came from the peasantry and the nobility alike, typical features of the noble included holding oneself in high esteem, maintaining a sense of honor, and having a lordly attitude. In this same category yet farther from the world of peasants were those lords who represented the state (e.g., clerks), the Polish intelligentsia, and landlords. This difference between the world of the peasant and the outside was the most significant in comparison to the difference with the petty nobility who lived among peasants. The asymmetric relationship between peasants and noblemen was in many ways consistent across the eastern borderlands, though there were local variations with regards to this theme. The level of peasant inferiority varied, and in Eastern Galicia, for instance, peasant culture was sometimes valued positively against the culture of lords. "May a lord be praised," thus was Polish ethnographer Józef Gajek greeted, along with ironic cheers and smiles, by peasants from one village in Podilya in 1936.[56] Such presence of disrespect and disdain for the nobility helped the Ukrainian intelligentsia build a national narrative. Regardless of what peasants thought about their own culture, it always stood against the culture of nobility. Put differently, the peasantry was vehemently hostile to lordship. The village reaffirmed the importance of this opposition by annually celebrating the abolition of serfdom through the holiday called "freedom day." But *svoboda* (freedom) was more than just a celebration. It symbolized human dignity and independence endangered by the presence of the nobility. Communism, a rival ideology to nationalism, was welcomed by many peasants in the eastern borderlands as it promised that the land would be given to the people. The enthusiasm ended when rumors about the Holodomor reached Ukrainians in interwar Poland. The Second Polish Republic, to the contrary, epitomized the reign of the lords.

If there was anyone lower on the civilizational ladder than a Hutsul, it was a Jew—the second figure seen standing in opposition to the world of the peasant. A Jew was often symbolized by a goat, which had connotations associated with sin and evilness. The Jew was seen as opposed to Catholicism and, simultaneously, opposed to the laborers, with the latter binary demarcating the most significant social division. "These Jews, they opened shops; Jews lived off the people. […] They did not work the land, only the people had to," a female interlocutor from the village of Zahajpol, in Kołomyja county in the province of Stanisławów, said, with remarkable resentment toward the Jews. "They called us: these peasants, these boors!" she complained bitterly.[57] A person hired by a Jew was held in contempt. The Jew was regarded as the epitome of otherness and strangeness. A "man" (*czeławiek*) was seen as diametrically opposed to a Jew, noted one researcher concerning prevalent ideas in the village of Jasieniówka, north of the town of Brest.[58] Such otherness, anthropologist Zbigniew Benedyktowicz tells us, can be connected to the contradicting feelings of fear and fascination.[59] "They made these yellow ground clothes sometimes and they were praying and swinging; I was peeping at them. In the fall they had holiday: it was raining, they made a shed in the garden […] out of wood, leaves, and they were sitting and: oy vey, vey" the informant started laughing.[60] Compensatory laughter helped people to cope with the feelings of anxiety that accompanied contact with such otherness.[61]

Such a view of society was based on the peasant's interpretation of the Bible, according to which, peasants were the descendants of Ham, the nobles of Japheth, and the Jews of Shem.[62] According to this cosmology, each group had its faith, and the curse of Ham—also in this context—was used to explain the inferior social position of peasants. This conviction was, on the one hand, a reason for profound fatalism; on the other, it became a source of grief and resentment. In the utterances of peasants, this view accompanies stories about the three major groups. To some extent it explains to us the fatalistic attitudes that appeared during the plebiscite and that could be summed up in the common village saying "one cannot blow against the wind," a saying often used to express the powerlessness of peasants to change their position in society or to influence events.

Conclusion

The peasant worldview described above is a construct, a perspective that, in reality, differed depending on the region and local identities, proximity to towns and access to mass culture, and a person's social network. It reflected an often complex interrelation between social order and vernacular cosmology. Vernacular cosmology, as anthropologist John Campbell tells us, is a source of order that powerfully influences the shaping of everyday experience.[63] In our case, this cosmology helped to maintain balance and define the relationships between neighbors, setting a structure in which the views of the Polish administration and elites, petty nobility, Jews, and other peasants developed. The other articulation of cosmology was—to use Pierre Bourdieu's phrase—"the constant comparison of judgements about others."[64] In social interactions, such collective judgments and stereotypes made by one party went hand-in-hand with the fear of ridicule experienced by the other.

Yet cosmology and peasant worldviews, as well as investigations concerning peasants more broadly, have taken on a marginal role within historical scholarship. In the history of modern Eastern Europe, John Connelly has argued, people for whom nation was not an organizing category "were numerically insignificant."[65] Essentializing discourses are a bailiwick for historical investigations. For years there has been a widespread assumption among modern historians looking at Eastern Europe that it is sufficient to investigate the reception of nationalism through a prism of *ethnos*. Historians working within the framework of *ethnos* have mostly used materials which explicitly talk about nationalism, national activists, and institutions. Dropping the perspective of national paradigm, which Tara Zahra saw in 2010 as a major step toward a better understanding of the limits of nationalization, does not challenge the assumption that local actors behaved in accordance with Western rationality. Still, reactions and attitudes toward nationalism are studied without looking at the symbolic framework crucial for the constitution of any social relations. Western rationality, which the historiography of nationalism has aligned with, was constituted by institutional structures—here the structures of the census office, educational board, and professional institutions. This was not the same rationality shared by peasants in the eastern borderlands.

The aim of my contribution was to question the idea of understanding peasants' responses to nationalism via the term national indifference and to present an analysis that allows us to see the common ground upon which responses to nationalism were constructed. As I have shown, insiders in these communities and their outsiders were mostly seen through the idiom of civilization. Pointing out differences between people was a part of peasant culture, a celebration of superiority. Vernacular cosmology provided people with a social means of coping with strangeness and otherness. The account that I have sketched here is not, of course, comprehensive. But it helps us to examine points of contact between old and new forms of identification and association. Throughout the interwar period the roles characterized above and the superiority/inferiority calculus ascribed to them, slowly transformed into clearer and flatter, one-dimensional stereotypes labeled as Poles and Ukrainians. This process occurred through the agency of the elites. The Ukrainian intelligentsia, particularly successful in elevating some elements of peasant culture into national attributes, found direct ways to reach out to Greek-Catholic as well as some Roman-Catholic peasants. The young generation of the Roman-Catholic peasantry, in turn, came under the influence of Polish youth organizations, such as the Riflemen's Association (*Strzelec*). Similarly, the complex, multi-faceted image of the Jews (with an emphasis on the negative view) that peasants conveyed acquired features typical of modern antisemitic ideology.[66] These changes occurred across the eastern borderlands with considerable regional variations. In the process, peasant attributes were also absorbed into expert categories.

Notes

1   Classic publications on national indifference include: James E. Bjork, *Neither German nor Pole: Catholicism and National Indifference in a Central European Borderland* (Ann Arbor: University of Michigan Press, 2008); Maarten Van Ginderachter and Jon Fox, eds., *National Indifference and the History of Nationalism in Modern Europe* (London: Routledge, 2019); Peter M. Judson, *Guardians of the Nation Activists on the Language Frontiers of Imperial Austria* (Cambridge, MA: Harvard University Press, 2006); Jeremy King, *Budweisers into Czechs and Germans: A Local History of Bohemian Politics, 1848–1948* (Princeton: Princeton University Press, 2002); Gerald Stourzh, "The Ethnicizing of Politics and National Indifference in Late Imperial Austria," in *Der Umfang der österreichischen Geschichte*, 283–323 (Vienna: Böhlau Verlag, 2011); Tara Zahra, *Kidnapped Souls: National Indifference and the Battle for Children in the Bohemian Lands, 1900–1948* (Ithaca: Cornell University Press, 2008). For recent studies, see Marek Jakoubek, "National Indifference in Post-Ottoman Spaces: A Case from Northwest Bulgaria," *Nationalities Papers* 50, no. 2 (2022): 395–416; Pieter M. Judson, "Nationalism and Indifference," in *Habsburg neu Denken. Vielfalt und Ambivalenz in Zentraleuropa*, ed. Johannes Feichtinger and Heidemarie Uhl (Wien: Böhlau Verlag, 2016), 148–55; Rok Stergar, "National Indifference in the Heyday of Nationalist Mobilization? Ljubljana Military Veterans and the Language of Command," *Austrian History Yearbook* 43 (2012): 45–58. See also Pieter Judson's chapter in this volume.

2   The Greek-Catholic (Uniate) Church is an Eastern Catholic Church of the Byzantine rite, in communion with Rome since the Union of Brest in 1596. This agreement, initiated by Jesuits, united Orthodox Christians living in the Polish-Lithuanian Commonwealth with the Roman Catholic Church. As a result, part of the Orthodox clergy and believers accepted Catholic dogmas but kept Byzantine rites and legal distinctions (such as the Julian calendar). The Church was abolished in the Russian Empire in the nineteenth century and, hence, survived only in Eastern Galicia under the Austrian rule. See, for instance, Theodore R. Weeks, "The 'End' of the Uniate Church in Russia: The Vozsoedinenie of 1875," *Jahrbücher für Geschichte Osteuropas* 44, no. 1 (1996): 28–40.

3   The first section of this chapter is based on my current research project funded by the National Science Centre, Poland (project no. 2017/27/B/HS3/02572). In this chapter, I also use materials from my book; see Olga Linkiewicz, *Lokalność i nacjonalizm. Społeczności wiejskie w Galicji Wschodniej w dwudziestoleciu międzywojennym* (Kraków: Universitas, 2018).
4   On nationalism and self-determination, see John Connelly, *From Peoples into Nations: A History of Eastern Europe* (Princeton: Princeton University Press, 2020), 362–89; Bernard Yack, *Nationalism and the Moral Psychology of Community* (Chicago: University of Chicago Press, 2012), 233–52.
5   On the intersection between expertise and minority policies in interwar Poland, see Olga Linkiewicz, "Scientific Ideals and Political Engagement: Polish Ethnology and the 'Ethnic Question' between the Wars," *Acta Poloniae Historica* 114 (2016): 5–27; Stephan Stach, "The Institute for Nationality Research (1921–1939): A Think Tank for Minority Politics in Poland?," in *Religion in the Mirror of Law. Eastern European Perspectives from the Early Modern Period to 1939*, ed. Yvonne Kleinmann et al. (Frankfurt am Main: Klostermann Verlag, 2015), 1–30.
6   Kathryn Ciancia, *On Civilization's Edge: A Polish Borderland in the Interwar World* (New York: Oxford University Press, 2021); Timothy Snyder, *Sketches from a Secret War: A Polish Artist's Mission to Liberate Soviet Ukraine* (New Haven, CT: Yale University Press, 2005).
7   Sarah Wambaugh, *Plebiscites since the World War* (New York: Carnegie Endowment for International Peace, 1933).
8   The governments in the Second Republic tended to change constantly.
9   These were the provinces of Lwów, Stanisławów, Tarnopol, Volhynia, Polesia, Nowogródek, Wilno and two counties of the province of Białystok: Grodno and Wołkowysk. See "Law on Educational System of July 31, 1924," *Journal of Laws* 79 (sec. 766, item 1), 1213.
10 Ibid.
11 Paul Brykczynski, *Primed for Violence: Murder, Antisemitism, and Democratic Politics in Interwar Poland* (Madison, WI: The University of Wisconsin Press, 2016); Grzegorz Krzywiec, *Chauvinism, Polish Style. The Case of Roman Dmowski (1886–1905)*, trans. Jarosław Garliński (Frankfurt am Main and New York: Peter Lang Edition, 2016).
12 Henryk Wereszycki, "Stanisław Grabski," in *Polski słownik biograficzny: V. 8*, ed. Kazimierz Lepszy (Wrocław: Zakład Narodowy im. Ossolińskich–Wyd. PAN, 1959–1960), 522.
13 The prime minister at the time was Władysław Grabski, an economist and historian, who was famous for his currency reform. He was also Stanisław's brother.
14 Thugutt was later deputy prime minister between November 1924 and May 1926.
15 Starczewski was president of the Society of the Eastern Borderlands (*Towarzystwo Kresów Wschodnich*). See Sławomir Dębski, "Wdzięczni Wilsonowi," *Polski Przegląd Dyplomatyczny* 4 (2017): 10.
16 On democracy as an experiment in the post-Versailles world, see Connelly, *From Peoples into Nations*; Ciancia, *On Civilization's Edge*.
17 On the Upper Silesian plebiscite, see Larry Wolff, *Woodrow Wilson and the Reimagining of Eastern Europe* (Stanford: Stanford University Press, 2020), 214–27.
18 Stanisław Thugutt, *Wybór pism i autobiografia Stanisława Thugutta* (Warszawa: Wyd. Towarzystwa Kooperatystów, 1939), 105–6.

19 According to Articles 10 of the treaty, in districts inhabited by a significant number of non-Poles, the Polish government should facilitate that non-Polish children in elementary school education are taught in their own language. See Theodore S. Woolsey. "The Rights of Minorities under the Treaty with Poland," *The American Journal of International Law* 14, no. 3 (1920): 394; see also Carole Fink, "The Minorities Question at the Paris Peace Conference: The Polish Minority Treaty, June 28, 1919," in *The Treaty of Versailles: A Reassessment after 75 Years*, ed. Manfred F. Boemeke et al. (Washington, DC: German Historical Institute; Cambridge: Cambridge University Press, 1998), 249–74; Wiktor Marzec, "'One of the Oldest States in Europe Has Never Suppressed Any Nation.' The Minority Treaty, Nationalist Indignation and the Foundations of Interwar Ethnic Democracy in Poland," *Nations and Nationalism* 27, no. 4 (2021): 1080–96; Wolff, *Woodrow Wilson*, 198–207. For an overview of minority treaties, see Mark Mazower, *Governing the World. The History of an Idea* (New York: The Penguin Press, 2012), 159–62.
20 In practice that meant, for instance, that if there were two schools in one district—one with Polish as a language of instruction, the second with Ukrainian—the administration was instructed to unite them into one bilingual school "if possible."
21 Andrzej Chojnowski, "Mniejszości narodowe w polityce rządów polskich w latach 1921–1926," *Przegląd Historyczny* 67, no. 4 (1976): 609.
22 Thugutt, *Wybór pism i autobiografia*, 106; Chojnowski, "Mniejszości narodowe," 609.
23 *Szkoły Rzeczypospolitej Polskiej w roku szkolnym 1930/31*, ed. Marian Falski (Lwów, Warszawa: Państwowe Wydawnictwo Książek Szkolnych, 1933), XX–XXI.
24 See *Ridna Szkoła* 1, 5–6 (1927); *Województwo tarnopolskie* (Tarnopol: Komitet Wojewódzkiej Wystawy Rolniczej, 1931), 92.
25 Thugutt, *Wybór pism i autobiografia*, 106.
26 *Tsentralnyi derzhavnyi istorychnyi arkhiv Ukrainy* (Central Historical Archive), Lviv Branch (hereafter TSDiAL), Kuratorium Okręgu Szkolnego Lwowskiego (Lwów School Board, hereafter KOSL), f. 179, op. 2, s. 13. In Ukrainian archives, including TSDiAL in Lviv, documents are organized by a large holding called *fond*, a *fond* subjection (*opys*), and a set of files called *sprava*.
27 In 1925, there were seventeen declarations for Ukrainian ("Russki") and twenty-one for Polish ("state language"). In 1933, thirty-nine parents opted for Polish (for fifty-seven children) and twenty-five for Ukrainian (for forty-one children). TSDiAL, KOSL, f. 179, op. 2, s. 10.
28 TSDiAL, KOSL, f. 179, op. 2, s. 3.
29 See, for instance, Justyna Straczuk, *Cmentarz i stół. Pogranicze prawosławno-katolickie w Polsce i na Białorusi* (Wrocław: FNP, Wyd. Uniwersytetu Wrocławskiego, 2006).
30 TSDiAL, KOSL, f. 179, op. 2, s. 3.
31 Ibid., 41.
32 Ibid., 31.
33 Ibid., 517.
34 Ibid. See also the case of Jezierna, in Zborów county in the province of Tarnopol. TSDiAL, KOSL, f. 179, op. 2, s. 2298.
35 On the destruction of Orthodox churches in the Lublin province, see Jan Kęsik, "Udział wojska w akcji rewindykacyjno-polonizacyjnej we wschodnich i południowych powiatach województwa lubelskiego w latach 1937–1939," *Kwartalnik Historyczny* 121, no. 4 (2014): 799–831.
36 *Ridna Szkoła* 3 (September 1927), 5.

37 Tahra Zahra, "Imagined Noncommunities: National Indifference as a Category of Analysis," *Slavic Review* 69, no. 1 (2010): 98.
38 Józef Chlebowczyk, *O prawie do bytu małych i młodych narodów* (Katowice: Śląski Instytut Naukowy, Państwowe Wydawnictwo Naukowe, 1983), 361–4.
39 Zahra, "Imagined Noncommunities," 115.
40 Columbia University—Rare Book & Manuscript Library, James T. Shotwell Papers, Box 224: James T. Shotwell, Social Science Research Council, *Diary of a Research Expedition to Europe*, August 6, 1931, 42. On social scientific expertise and internationalism, see Mazower, *Governing the World*, 94–115.
41 Morgane Labbe, "National Indifference, Statistics and the Constructivist Paradigm: The Case of *Tutejsi* ('the People from Here') in Interwar Polish Censuses," *National Indifference*, ed. Fox and Van Ginderachter, 161–79. On the *tutejsi* category, see also Piotr Cichoracki, "Tak zwani 'tutejsi' na Polesiu jako zagadnienie polityczne w Polsce w latach 1921–1939," *Sprawy narodowościowe* 42 (2013): 101–13.
42 *Skorowidz miejscowości Rzeczypospolitej Polskiej opracowany na podstawie wyników pierwszego powszechnego spisu ludności z dn. 30 września 1921 r. i innych źródeł urzędowych. Województwo poleskie*, VI.
43 One of the proponents for eliminating the *tutejsi* category was Leon Wasilewski, an activist in the Polish Socialist Party and the head of the Institute for Nationality Research. See Leon Wasilewski, *Sprawy narodowościowe w teorii i życiu* (Warszawa: Wyd. J. Mortkowicza, 1929), 104.
44 The number of such declarations for Polesia—this time as a language category—was much higher than in 1921.
45 Józef Obrębski, *Polesie*, ed. Anna Engelking (Warszawa: Oficyna Naukowa, 2007).
46 I would like to thank my colleague Joanna Wawrzyniak for this simple and brilliant observation.
47 Stanisław Klimecki, *Galicyjska Socjalistyczna Republika Rad: okupacja Małopolski (Galicji) Wschodniej przez Armię Czerwoną w 1920 roku* (Toruń: Wyd. UMK, 2006).
48 Pierre Bourdieu, *The Bachelor's Ball. The Crisis of Peasant Society in Béarn*, trans. Richard Nice (Chicago: The University of Chicago Press, 2008), 64–80.
49 See Patrice Dabrowski, "Borderland Encounters in the Carpathian Mountains and their Impact on Identity Formation," in *Shatterzones of Empires: Coexistence and Violence in the German, Habsburg, Russian, and Ottoman Borderlands*, ed. Omer Bartov and Eric D. Weitz (Bloomington: Indiana University Press, 2013), 193–208.
50 Józef Gajek, "Zarys etnograficzny zachodniej części Podola," *Acta Universitatis Mariae Curie-Skłodowska* II.1, Section F (1947): 103.
51 *Archiwum Naukowe Polskiego Towarzystwa Ludoznawczego we Wrocławiu* (Scientific Archive of the Polish Ethnological Society in Wrocław), Folder 478: Józef Gajek, *Podole*.
52 Interview with a woman born in 1924 in the village Wojutycze, in Sambor county in the region of Lwów, conducted in the Lower Silesia in 2005.
53 Sydel F. Silverman, "Patronage and Community-Nation Relationships in Central Italy," *Ethnology* 4, no. 2 (1965): 175.
54 Sydel F. Silverman, "An Ethnographic Approach to Social Stratification: Prestige in an Italian Community," *American Anthropologist* 68, no. 4 (1966): 899–921.
55 Interview with a man born in 1920 in the village Wysocko Wyżne, in Turka county in the region of Lwów, conducted in the Lowers Silesia in 2005.
56 Józef Gajek, *Problemy etniczne i narodowościowe na Podolu* (Tarnopol: Związek Okręgowy Kół TSL, 1937), 19.

57 Interview with a woman born in 1916 in the village Zahajpol, in Kołomyja county in the region of Stanisławów, conducted in the Lower Silesia in 2005.
58 Wincenty Krzysztofik, *Jasieniówka, wieś powiatu sokólskiego. Monografia ze szczególnym uwzględnieniem zmian wywołanych komasacją gruntów* (Poznań: Uniwersytet Poznański, 1933).
59 Zbigniew Benedyktowicz, *Portrety "obcego." Od stereotypu do symbolu* (Kraków: Anthropos, 2000), 185–6.
60 Interview with a woman born in 1924 in the village Wojutycze, in Sambor county in the region of Lwów, conducted in the Lower Silesia in 2005.
61 Benedyktowicz, *Portrety "obcego,"* 182.
62 See, for instance, Anna Engelking, *Kołchoźnicy. Antropologiczne studium tożsamości wsi białoruskiej przełomu XX i XXI wieku* (Toruń: FNP, Wyd. Naukowe UMK, 2012), 583–717; Magdalena Zowczak, *Biblia ludowa. Interpretacje wątków biblijnych w kulturze ludowej* (Toruń: FNP, Wyd. Naukowe UMK, 2013), 155–66.
63 John Campbell, *Honour, Family and Patronage: A Study of Institutions and Moral Values in a Greek Mountain Community* (London: Clarendon Press, 1964).
64 Bourdieu, *The Bachelor's Ball*, 12.
65 Connelly, *From Peoples into Nations*, 20.
66 On premodern antisemitism in villages, see Alina Cała, *Wizerunek Żyda w polskiej kulturze ludowej* (Warszawa: Wyd. UW, 1992); Rosa Lehmann, *Symbiosis and Ambivalence: Poles and Jews in a Small Galician Town* (New York and Oxford: Berghahn Books: 2001); Joanna Tokarska-Bakir *Rzeczy mgliste. Eseje i studia* (Sejny: Pogranicze, 2004), 49–72.

10

Survival and Assimilation: Loyalism in the Interwar Irish Free State

Brian Hughes

In 1997, historian R. B. McDowell suggested that when "compared to the thorough methods for dealing with unpopular minorities ... in eastern and central Europe and elsewhere, the harassment of the Southern [Irish] loyalists was not notably severe" in Southern Ireland.[1] When measured in lethal violence (a crude and sometimes unreliable metric), there is much truth in this. Between 1919 and 1921, during an Irish War of Independence which was followed by a short, sharp civil war and part of a longer "Irish Revolution," just over 2,300 people were killed in ways that can be directly linked to the conflict. The separatist Irish Republican Army (IRA) killed 184 alleged civilian "spies" and informers, out of a total of just under 1,000 civilian casualties.[2] Elsewhere, the "Posen Uprising" claimed twice as many lives in seven weeks as the Irish War of Independence did in three years.[3] There were over 36,000 fatalities in less than five months during the Finnish Civil War, 3,000 or so in a few days in Bulgaria in September 1918, and another 1,500–3,000 over five days in September 1923. The shorter Estonian and Latvian Wars of Independence saw 11,750 and 13,246 fatalities, respectively.[4] And as Charles Townshend has written, the significant reduction of the non-Catholic minority in Southern Ireland between 1911 and 1926 "may appear trivial in comparison with the massive dislocation of peoples in Europe, starting with the Greek-Turkish conflict in the early 1920s."[5]

Anne Dolan has recently pointed to the limits of such comparisons, noting that violence in Ireland gained its reputation from "its nature not because of its extent," and warns against any simple assumptions that they might bring.[6] Perhaps because of the perceived scale of the Irish Revolution, and Ireland's position on the western periphery of Europe, Southern Irish loyalists have yet to be integrated into major studies of minorities in interwar Europe (though some fruitful comparisons have been made between Ireland and Poland).[7] If "trivial" by some standards, Irish loyalists arriving into Britain in early 1922 were widely described as refugees but have yet to be considered by scholars of interwar refugee crises.[8] Irish historians have often been guilty of insularity in return (if increasingly less so). The Irish loyalist experience, however, was not unique. Forced to accept the dismantling of the century-old Act of Union between Ireland and Britain and abandoned by their Northern (or "Ulster") brethren, by 1922 the Southern Irish loyalists—like other European minorities—found themselves on the "wrong" side of a new border drawn as a response to nationalist insurgency.[9]

Southern Irish loyalists do, however, stand apart in some respects. They were, for instance, part of a union with Britain but separated from their heartland by the sea. And, as Alvin Jackson points out in his chapter in this volume, there was no permanent royal residence in Ireland (unlike in Scotland). This allowed nationalists to take a permanent, unalterable island border for granted and meant that loyalists were "conscious that they both dwelt in the empire's heartland" and "were stationed on the imperial *limes*."[10] The Southern Irish case is one of the few in this volume where a religious divide took precedence over linguistic differences. While loyalists' perceived betrayal of the nation was, rhetorically at least, based on their allegiances and behavior rather than denomination or ethnicity, religion was the most durable means of differentiating between the majority and the minority (notwithstanding the existence of Catholic loyalists).[11] Southern Ireland was also a territory seceded from a victorious power after the Great War and has maintained a stable democracy since. Where the drawing of a new border in Ireland was an exception in Western Europe, the map of Eastern Europe looked radically different after 1919. Pieter Judson has suggested that the 1916 Easter Rising in Dublin—in "a peripheral crownland capital of one of Europe's empires"—should be "of special concern to historians who study the character of Central Europe's empires."[12] The "everyday" experiences of the "imagined noncommunity" in Southern Ireland can similarly contribute to an understanding of the quest for homogeneity in interwar Europe and its limits.[13]

The behavior of civilians in Ireland during the revolution was often similar to that observed by Stathis Kalyvas in his seminal *Logic of Violence in Civil Wars*. Kalyvas found that civilians tend to offer incomplete collaboration or neutrality toward any side in areas where no armed actor exerts full control. This "hedging" or "fence-sitting" is variable and aligned with the nature of the conflict, the party in control, and how much power they exercise. Essentially, it involves a pragmatic approach that prioritizes personal safety and economic well-being over political preferences.[14] Civilians with nationalist or republican sympathies could, for instance, resist IRA taxes and levies and disobey republican edicts when they felt they were unfair (and that they could get away with doing so), or refuse to comply with boycotts where the financial benefits of serving the police or military outweighed the potential cost of non-compliance. Loyalists, meanwhile, contributed to republican collections under duress or to avoid trouble (though others claimed resistance as evidence of their allegiances).[15] Southern Irish loyalists first had to withstand efforts to enforce nationalist/republican hegemony in their communities and then negotiate a passage in a nationalist and Catholic-dominated state. In defining the concept of "national indifference," Tara Zahra has written that it can "apply to many different kinds of behaviour and people."[16] But as Olga Linkiewicz points out elsewhere in this volume, national indifference essentially refers to behaviors and peoples that did not embrace nationalism. In assessing the experiences of the loyalist minority in post-independence

Ireland, this is how "national indifference" will be understood in this chapter. It will also acknowledge, however, as Linkiewicz does, "hesitation, pragmatism, and reluctance to confront authority."[17]

The Southern Loyalist Minority

Who were the Southern Irish loyalists? Unionism can be defined as support for an unreformed union with Britain and the maintenance of the constitutional settlement of 1801, with loyalism a potentially broader category (though with some overlap and use of both terms interchangeably). Loyalism is understood here as an allegiance to, or service to, Britain, the Crown, or the Empire. This essentially encompasses two groups. The first are those who were ideologically committed to the continued connection with Britain. The second is trickier to define and encompasses soldiers, civil servants, policemen, and others who served or acted in the interests of Britain, both in Ireland and abroad. Though an identity closely associated with Protestants and Protestantism,[18] both groups—and particularly the second—included a minority of Catholics. These are found among the landed gentry who advocated for the status quo before 1922, but even more commonly among the police (the Royal Irish Constabulary or RIC) and the British army where Catholics made up the majority of rank and file Irish recruits.[19] These policemen and soldiers did not always consider themselves "loyalists" but were regularly labeled that way by others. While there was no conscription in Ireland, service in the Crown forces or in imperial administration created a similar "common experience" of popular engagement with Britain and the Empire—with similar material benefits—for men and their families as Pieter Judson has identified in the Habsburg case (but with English as a common language).[20]

Though an official border only existed on the island from 1920, this chapter will focus on loyalists in "Southern" Ireland—the twenty-six Irish counties granted dominion status in 1922 as the Irish Free State. Distinct from their majority Ulster brethren in many respects, Southern loyalists were a relatively small and scattered minority. In 1911 there were just over 311,000 Protestants in the twenty-six county area that became the Irish Free State (10 percent of the total population), compared to 2.8 million Catholics. In the remaining six counties, there were 768,000 Protestants and 430,000 Catholics. If the small but influential sets of Protestant nationalists and republicans might be very roughly offset by cohorts of Catholic loyalists, this gives some sense of the size of the loyalist minority. By 1926, Catholics made up 2.7 million of a total Free State population of 2.9 million, while the Protestant population had dropped to 207,000 (7 percent of the total).[21] Southern unionist and loyalist culture had been diverse and impressively organized in Dublin, comprising a small but strong working-class Protestant community; clerks, shopkeepers, and professionals concentrated in suburban townships; and a "haute bourgeoisie." Elsewhere outside of Ulster, unionism was usually—but not exclusively—concentrated around the big landed estates and "networks of aristocrats and squireens who dominated rural

Protestant society in the south and west," or in small urban clusters.[22] Unlike in East Central Europe, where high illiteracy has been identified as a contributor to postwar instability, the Southern Irish minority was widely literate and often well-educated.[23]

Survival

In July 1921 a truce was agreed between republicans and the British government to end the Irish War of Independence, followed by an Anglo-Irish Treaty signed in December 1921. As a split in the republican movement over the terms of the treaty descended into a short but bitter civil war (June 1922–May 1923), a provisional government oversaw the formal creation of a partitioned state with dominion status in December 1922. With the union between Great Britain and Ireland thus "gone beyond recall," considering oneself a unionist or loyalist in Southern Ireland after 1922 was, as R. B. McDowell described it, "an attitude of mind rather than membership of a political party."[24] In reality, the process of accepting and adapting to the prospect of a new dispensation had begun much earlier.

There were very genuine fears among loyalists for their safety in the new order. This was prompted by a decade of unionist political rhetoric about the consequences of a Dublin parliament, by low-level incidents of sectarian violence—including the burning of churches and raids on Protestant homes—and by the shooting of Protestants as alleged spies between 1919 and 1923. Such fears were confirmed for those who wished to see it that way by a series of murders in West Cork in April 1922 (during a period of supposed "peace" between the July 1921 truce and the outbreak of civil war in June 1922). Seemingly sparked by the shooting of an IRA member who had entered a known Protestant/loyalist home late at night, thirteen Protestant men were killed over three nights in the Bandon Valley area. In the 1990s, Peter Hart concluded that "in the end, the fact of the victims' religion is inescapable. These men were shot because they were Protestant."[25] Hart further suggested that this was not an "isolated event," but an eruption of latent distrust and paranoia.[26] This, and Hart's broader conclusions about the nature of republican violence, has since been robustly challenged (and defended) and remains a source of debate.[27]

Some of Hart's critics have gone too far in removing sectarianism as a motivation for violence against the minority, while Marie Coleman has recently pointed to the need for a broader understanding of sectarianism than has often been the case. This, Coleman argues, should include attitudes, beliefs, and practices containing a religious element that may not necessarily extend to bigotry or prejudice, and account for the consequences as well as the motivations for violent actions.[28] While religion was not necessarily the primary explanation for violence, it did not have to be and remained an important label and identifier within communities.[29] As R. B. McDowell suggested, "there was no declared hostility to protestants on religious grounds. But the protestant was often a unionist where a unionist was a *rara avis*."[30] Moreover, even if there is little evidence of a systematic national campaign of violence, arson, or intimidation aimed at removing Protestants from their communities, it was possible for some Protestants to believe—

even incorrectly—that there was.³¹ The Bandon Valley killings were widely denounced, and the provisional government offered a Church of Ireland deputation assurances that it "would protect its citizens," but one Protestant bishop described the violence as "a grim reminder of our helplessness" and another noted a "week of v.great [sic] anxiety as to the church's future."³² The *Cork Examiner* reported an "exodus" from the Bandon area, though framed it as a "temporary" withdrawal until peaceful conditions had resumed.³³ While most "either resisted the pressure to leave home or subsequently returned," including the wife of one of the victims, the communal impact of violence should not be underestimated.³⁴ For some, survival meant temporary or permanent exile.

As noted above, between the 1911 census of Ireland and the first Irish Free State census in 1926 the Protestant population fell by about one-third.³⁵ Explaining this decline has proven challenging, particularly the part played by "forced" migration. Scholars have accounted for the impact of Protestant fatalities of the Great War and the withdrawal of British forces in 1922, and debated the extent to which the remainder was the result of longer-term natural decline or abnormal emigration prompted by violence and threats.³⁶ Most provocative was Hart's tentative use of the term "ethnic cleansing." While downplaying comparisons with other ethnic conflicts elsewhere in the same chapter, Hart also argued that it was ultimately the shock of the violence of 1920–3 that precipitated the "Protestant exodus."³⁷

In a more recent study of West Cork Methodists, David Fitzpatrick (Hart's doctoral supervisor) concluded that the impact of violence was "fairly minor" and "the inexorable decline of southern Protestantism was mainly self-inflicted."³⁸ Andy Bielenberg's wider study of Protestant demographics suggested that only between 2,000 and 16,000 Protestants could have left Ireland owing to revolutionary terror from a total decline of over 100,000.³⁹ Donald Wood's 2020 analysis, however, leaves a much larger estimate of 40,000 potential Protestant emigrants.⁴⁰ Some perspective might be provided by the contemporaneous exodus of German speakers from Western Poland. Though the precise figures are similarly contested, the number of Germans who left Pomorze and Poznania after 1918 was much more significant—perhaps around 800,000 with some estimates as high as 1 million; by 1926 the German population there had declined by 85 percent. The language barrier was a notable reason to leave that did not apply in Ireland, but Irish Protestants and loyalists also shared many of the same concerns for employment, prosperity, and treatment under the new majority government (including those that ultimately proved unfounded or exaggerated) identified by Richard Blanke in his study of the German exodus (exacerbated in both cases by a new conflict: the Russo-Polish War and a civil war in Ireland). There are also many of the same—unresolved—debates about the extent to which this migration was voluntary or involuntary.⁴¹

The exact scale and timing of the Irish loyalist "exodus" remains difficult to discern. The 1926 census of Northern Ireland suggested that about 10,000 people had moved from the Irish Free State area to Northern Ireland between 1911 and 1926.⁴² Others crossed to Britain, with a notable peak beginning in spring 1922. In May 1922, the British government was sufficiently concerned by an influx of Southern Irish loyalist "refugees" to establish an Irish Distress Committee for "persons ordinarily resident in Ireland who, for reasons of personal safety, have come to Great Britain and are represented to be in urgent need of assistance." As of March 1923—by which time it had become known as the Irish Grants Committee and had its remit expanded—7,500 applications for loans or grants had been received, including 5,600 for immediate assistance of which 4,330 were approved. A "large proportion" of applicants were married men with wives and children and, while not all of those who arrived in Britain sought or needed relief, when dependents of those who did are included there are potentially several thousand southern loyalist "refugees." Nor were they all Protestant: it was recorded that 598 grants were awarded to Protestants and 1,063 to Catholics between May and October 1922—most, but not all, from the Free State.[43] These included "ex-service men, members of the Royal Irish Constabulary, ex-civil servants in our service in Ireland … who cannot return to Ireland."[44]

The private, voluntary Southern Irish Loyalists Relief Association (SILRA) was founded in summer 1922 "for the relief of distress amongst the Southern Irish Loyalists."[45] Around the same time, the Ulster Unionist Council formed a "Refugee Committee" for those crossing the border into Northern Ireland.[46] SILRA's membership was drawn almost exclusively from the diehard wing of the Conservative party, with a scattering from elsewhere on the British right.[47] The creation of the Irish Free State was, as Paul Stocker has suggested, a "moment of profound trauma" for SILRA members and their political circles, representative of "the growing trend of subversion which was spreading like a virus around the world."[48] SILRA's chairman from 1924 until his death in 1930 was the Duke of Northumberland, a reactionary diehard and fiery orator and propagandist. Though it survived until the early 1960s, the association was at its most active and provocative under Northumberland and held public meetings, produced propaganda pamphlets, ran fund-raising balls, bazaars, and open houses, and organized clothing drives across Britain.[49] Like some commentators in Germany in reference to the exodus from western Poland, SILRA and its circle defined Irish loyalist migration as involuntary, enforced by "impoverishment and misery" (though tended to place the blame on the British surrender and withdrawal).[50]

By the mid-1920s, the diehards' persistent lobbying convinced the British government that Southern Irish loyalists had not been adequately compensated for losses suffered after the July 1921 truce. A second Treasury-funded Irish Grants Committee (IGC) duly met for the first time in October 1926. Eventually, it would deal with over 4,000 applications and recommend 900 awards. Given the nature of the scheme and its purpose, surviving application files must be treated with some caution but are an invaluable source of near first-hand testimony of Southern loyalist experiences of the revolution in Ireland and its aftermath.[51]

Some applicants had left Ireland between 1920 and 1923 and had either returned from a period of exile or remained in Britain in the late 1920s. Their depictions of flight from Ireland frequently involved periods of separation from loved ones, shattered mental health, property stolen, damaged, or sold at a loss, and struggles to find suitable work and accommodation. Leaving Ireland was also equated with the disappearance of good prospects, comfortable standards of living, or an inability to make a living in one's own country. Jonathan Darby, for instance, noted that he and his wife had "lost all the comfort and amenities of the home they had built up during a period of over 40 years."⁵² Abraham Good was doing a "good practice" as a vet in Bantry before he fled for South Wales where his new practice was "heavily in debt" and made only "the bare expense of living."⁵³ These Irish loyalists were in the unusual position of appearing in front of sympathetic British audiences as both "refugees" and "British citizens."⁵⁴ Indeed, while the narratives that appear in sources like the IGC make clear that integration was less than seamless, this was often not categorized as migration at all.⁵⁵

SILRA, in turn, drew on these narratives in its propaganda. A typical pamphlet entitled "Victims of the suspension of the law in southern Ireland" highlighted the case of "a young man" with a "good and rapidly expanding business" in Cork. "When the massacre of Protestants took place there he managed to escape, but had to abandon his house, shop, general store and goods, valued at a large amount. He was for a long time in a state of absolute penury, and has to start all over again, having lost all his capital."⁵⁶ In another case, an ex-soldier in a small country town had been "boycotted and threatened, and finally had to give up his shop and come to England, leaving his wife and children behind." With SILRA's assistance, this "destitute" ex-soldier was able to "send for his wife and start a small shop in one of the suburbs in London."⁵⁷ This is what SILRA suggested revolution in Ireland had meant for loyalists; respectable, successful members of their communities whose lives and livelihoods had been destroyed through no fault of their own. As Mo Moulton has pointed out, the rhetorical value of this tale is also clear: with a small financial grant, a ruined loyalist refugee in England was put in a position to make an honest living and provide for his family while contributing to the metropolitan core.⁵⁸

The Irish Free State administration was naturally concerned about its reputation and external perceptions about the safety and security of its minority. In May 1922, one Irish official complained to a British counterpart about an "organized movement … in both countries which has for its purpose and political objective the discrediting of the Provisional Government in Ireland and of His Majesty's Government in Great Britain."⁵⁹ It was "common knowledge," he suggested, that "a considerable number [of refugees] have left on a plea of compulsion without any justification whatever for that plea."⁶⁰ By 1931, a British Home Office memorandum on RIC pensioners agreed that "many men who alleged that their lives would be endangered if they ever returned to Ireland have now taken the risk and no grievous harm has come to them."⁶¹ Other exiles remained unconvinced. Fifteen months after Travers Blackley fled Ireland after shooting raiders at his home, the Free State government stopped paying his under-sheriff's salary arguing that it was by then safe for him to return to his work. "Mr. Blackley naturally took a different view of the situation"; he remained in London earning a "precarious living by selling on Comm[ission]."⁶² Not all migration, however, was "forced," and personal and economic emigration continued even in the most violent period of 1920–3.⁶³ While of little consolation to the many individuals who endured traumatic experiences of flight and exile, the worst fears of Southern Irish loyalists or their advocates did not ultimately come to pass.

Assimilation

However difficult the experiences of the exiles, more southern Protestants and loyalists ultimately remained in the Irish Free State than left. An editorial in the unionist *Irish Times* proclaimed that in accepting the Anglo-Irish Treaty the Southern loyalists

> have watched the passage, in mournful procession, of the host of laws, institutions, traditions, and ideals that bound them to Great Britain. They have embarked—not gladly, yet not afraid—on uncharted seas. They are entrusting themselves to the good-will of a majority from which, politically, they have suffered much, and with which in the past they have had little in common save love of Ireland. The Southern loyalists accept the Treaty because the country accepts it and invites their aid in making it a success.[64]

The main Protestant denomination's *Church of Ireland Gazette* expressed concern for the safety of its communities but also a similar commitment "to recognise the legitimacy of the new administration."[65] This was made easier by a comparatively swift restoration of order from late 1923, and, indeed, the continued publication of newspapers representing minority interests throughout the interwar period and beyond.

Assimilation could, however, be challenging in a state that wished to set itself apart from its former rulers, and to define itself as Gaelic and Catholic. A way of thinking and acting in conformity with a Catholic worldview permeated society, and over the first half century of independence the Catholic hierarchy and state leaders shared, as Daithí Ó Corráin has put it, "a desire to develop the country according to a philosophy of Catholic nationalism."[66] Catholic moral code on issues like sexuality and family relations was enshrined in law and, while conservatism was cross-denominational and the Protestant churches broadly welcomed strict censorship legislation and the constitutional ban on divorce (1937), the most vocal opponents tended to be Protestant.[67]

Even as violence subsided in Ireland after 1923, complaints remained about discrimination against the loyalist minority in the Irish Free State. As they became a less pressing or visible concern, SILRA turned its attention from Southern Irish loyalists in Britain to those who remained in the Free State. From the mid-1920s, the association repeatedly highlighted cases of poverty and destitution among loyalists in the Free State and continued to blame the coalition government who had made the settlement and abandoned the Southern loyalists in the first place.[68] In February 1928, for instance, SILRA's London relief secretary publicly insisted that he was not "criticising the Free State Government in any form … It is the British Government that have let these poor people down."[69] Calls for the reconquest of Ireland were rare on the British right, "suggesting that while Irish independence from Britain was a tragedy, it was accepted and its reversal was not seen as realistic."[70] The "plight" of the Southern Irish loyalists instead served as a reminder of past treachery and a warning of continued threats to the Empire. SILRA's public rhetoric, propagandistic by its nature, drew some justifiable complaints. This included one correspondent to the local Irish press who noted that a SILRA notice published in an American travel magazine would give potential tourists the unfortunate impression of a country blighted with poverty, want, and consumption.[71] At the same time, the IGC often vividly demonstrates the long-term personal and financial consequences of revolution not only for Southern Irish loyalist exiles, but also for a portion of those who remained at home.[72]

A more recent study by Robin Bury is much more willing to blame successive administrations in the Irish Free State for a rather bleak picture of minority life. At its worst Bury found "cultural and constitutional discrimination"—a state that was "institutionally and emotionally anti-Protestant" and practicing a form of "social and cultural apartheid."[73] For some Protestants in some places, and perhaps especially at specific times of crisis, it may have felt that way. But other work has convincingly highlighted a "self-assurance" among the minority "in the practice of its religion and place in Irish society."[74] Protestant isolation was also often self-imposed rather than enforced, and could be liberating in a society where a domineering Catholic Church held significant control over individuals' daily lives.[75] Catholics and Protestants were quite content to be schooled and to socialize separately. The Catholic Church dominated education and welfare provision, but rather than actively enticing Protestant children into Catholic schools, the state facilitated small Protestant schools and focused on concessions rather than changes of policy. From the 1930s, a subsidized transport scheme allowed Protestant children to attend a school of their denomination.[76]

If they so wished, Protestants who had formerly been aligned with unionist politics could seek and even secure election in the Irish Free State on a range of different political platforms.[77] A prominent figure in Dublin Unionism before 1922, Major Bryan Ricco Cooper sat as an independent Teachta Dála (TD, member of parliament) for Dublin South from 1923 until his death in 1930. Former Unionist MP for Rathmines J. P. Good was returned as a Businessmen's Party TD in the same constituency from 1923 to 1937.[78] By the early 1930s, the integration of former unionists into Cumann na nGaedheal, the majority governing party in the Free State for the first decade of its existence, was obvious enough to be regularly pilloried by the cartoonist in the (then opposition) Fianna Fáil's *Irish Press* newspaper.[79] It is hard to judge the impact of more sinister accusations about ex-unionists and freemasons that appeared in local Fianna Fáil campaigning, but their presence at all suggests that—in spite of much successful integration—an underlying suspicion could remain. In that sense, Southern Irish Protestants and "ex-unionists" offer a useful cohort in which to emphasize the fluidity of national indifference and majority-minority relations in a Western European context. Even if they felt themselves at times an isolated or persecuted minority, they continued to demonstrate their "Britishness" where it suited. A term like "ex-loyalist," thus, seems less useful than Ian d'Alton's "cultural royalism."[80]

These "royalist" remnants can be easily found in places with traditionally strong unionist and loyalist communities. The Church of Ireland congregation in Dublin, for instance, continued to maintain what Martin Maguire has described as "an emotional link to the crown and empire," seen in the cancellation in 1928 of all parish entertainments in Clontarf "on account of the dreadful gloom everywhere felt on the death of His Majesty King George V."[81] Journalist Brian Inglis recalled that in Malahide, "in everyday matters, the fact than an Irish Free State did exist was hardly noticeable."[82] It was still possible to spend time with "like-minded people," and to "ignore repugnant elements of the new regime."[83] Leaving the theater before the national anthem was played, listening to British radio stations, eschewing Gaelic football and hurling in favor of "English" games like soccer, rugby, or cricket, or insisting that Dún Laoghaire was still Kingstown, Portlaoise was still Maryborough, and Cobh was still Queenstown were more subtle forms of resistance.[84] Associations, clubs, and professional bodies continued to carry the "Royal" prefix, Dublin had more streets named after Queen Victoria than London, and, though literally painted over in green, the post-boxes still contained the royal cipher.[85] Nationalists had in fact been winning and losing battles for the streetscapes and place names of Dublin since the early twentieth century. The shamrock was a common motif on the street furniture in the city, for instance, but not in the unionist Rathmines township.[86] Nationalist councillors had succeeded in renaming Great Britain Street as Parnell Street and Carlisle Bridge as O'Connell Bridge, but not Sackville Street, which was colloquially rather than officially known as O'Connell Street until 1924. Statues to nineteenth-century constitutional nationalists Daniel O'Connell and Charles Stewart Parnell stood at either end of that street, which was dissected by a forty-foot column for Admiral Horatio Nelson.[87]

Displays of loyalism were not the preserve of Protestants. Service and sacrifice in the Great War provided a particularly powerful, if complex, motivation for remembering the British connection. In 1924, 20,000 veterans were joined by an estimated crowd of 50,000 in observing the two-minute silence at College Green in Dublin. These included large numbers of Catholic ex-servicemen and their families. Reasons for attending were as personal as political but "God Save the King" was sung and the Union flag was flown while a Celtic cross was unveiled in honor of the 10th (Irish) Division.[88] That same year, the bitter divides of civil war meant the first official state commemoration of the 1916 Easter Rising was a small, sombre affair.[89] Over 250,000 poppies were sold in Dublin in 1925 alone and high sales continued into the 1930s.[90] While the size of the crowds diminished over the years, and they were moved further away from the city centre, the Union flag was seen and "God Save the King" heard at armistice ceremonies in Dublin into the 1950s. None of this happened, of course, without occasionally violent protests against what some saw as undesirable displays of "imperialism." While not overtly hostile, and sometimes accommodating, the government tended to stay at arm's length.[91]

Lionel Fleming suggested that the majority of his Protestant co-religionists "remained unconverted to the new way of life" and "did not regard the Irish nation as having anything to do with them":

> It had to be accepted, of course, as a system to which one must now pay one's income tax, but never, until the end of their lives, would they speak of the government as 'our government.' In spite of the supposed treachery of Britain, their flag remained the Union Jack and their anthem 'God Save the King.'[92]

There was no newfound devotion to nationalist Ireland, but nor was there a challenge to its authority. Loyalty to Britain, moreover, did not necessarily have to mean a rejection of the Irish Free State. Trinity College, traditionally associated with Protestant ascendancy, flew the tricolor *and* the Union flag in the 1930s. As Nora Robertson put it in 1960, "in respecting new loyalties it had not seemed incumbent upon us to throw our old ones overboard."[93] Irish men and women from the twenty-six counties continued to seek service in the Empire throughout the interwar years: in the British Colonial Service and as soldiers and NCOs in the British army.[94]

Tara Zahra's understanding of "national indifference" includes intermarriage and bilingualism, and this is where the behavior of the Southern Irish minority presents some complications. Whereas Czech and German speakers regularly married in the Bohemian Lands, mixed marriage in Ireland remained relatively uncommon until the 1950s. Even then, it was contentious within both communities and often split families.[95] Indeed, Marie Coleman has found that in County Longford it was not a dilution of religious identity through mixed marriage that accounts for a disproportionate decline among Presbyterian and Methodist women between 1911 and 1926, but a willingness to move to find a marriage partner of the same denomination (less challenging for the larger Church of Ireland congregation).[96] The Catholic *Ne Temere* decree—effectively insisting that children of a mixed marriage be raised as Catholic—was particularly contentious among Protestant congregations concerned about the survival of their flock.[97]

There were Protestants who spoke Irish and they initially dominated the Gaelic League, a cultural nationalist movement founded in 1893 to promote Irish as a living language. The movement also inspired some Protestants (mostly in Dublin) to engage in nationalist activism or republican militancy. In the early twentieth century, however, the League expanded, became more obviously Catholic and increasingly politicized, and Protestant membership declined.[98] Unionists had long despised the idea of compulsory Irish teaching in primary schools or as a requirement in public appointments. When the Free State Minister for Education prioritized Irish in the primary school curriculum from 1922, compulsory Irish was opposed by Protestant stakeholders in education. It was, though, compulsion rather than the language itself that was most divisive, and some individual Protestants even embraced it.[99] As there were very few monolingual Irish speakers, and English remained the dominant language of communication, this was a rather different situation than in the Second Polish Republic as described by Olga Linkiewicz elsewhere in this volume (nor were there any plebiscites carried out in Ireland in this period). For its part, the Department of Education allowed Irish language policy to be diluted in practice in Protestant schools and "was prepared to make significant practical concessions toward the convictions of the religious minority."[100] The department was similarly willing to concede to requests (if only on an ad hoc basis) regarding school textbooks, many of which were deemed by Protestants to "unquestioningly equate Irish nationality, language revival and Catholicism" or rely exclusively on "the Catholic-nationalist perspective of Irish history."[101] For those who could afford it, sending children to school in Britain or Northern Ireland was another means of avoiding the perceived impositions of a Catholic/nationalist educational environment.[102]

Catholic Loyalists

As a distinct minority (or a minority within a minority) the Catholic (English-speaking) loyalist occupied a unique space. Like Protestants, Catholic unionists and loyalists had mixed experiences during the struggle for independence. The "occasional Catholic," for instance, had been included among the burnings of big houses and mansions between 1920 and 1923.[103] At first glance it might appear that Catholic unionists and loyalists endured a less turbulent transition to the new order. When he died in 1941, the *Irish Times* described how the Earl of Kenmare, a Catholic former member of the Irish Unionist Alliance, had lived "a quiet, retired life in Killarney for many years, where he was well known in the countryside."[104] Kenmare had continued a long family tradition of promoting "not only their tenants, but the whole community" in development, sporting, and cultural pursuits.[105] This, however, was likely as important as Kenmare's religion. The Protestant owners of nearby Muckross House believed that their own family home was spared burning on account of their standing in the community and treatment of employees.[106]

In some cases, politics and allegiances shifted over generations. William Monsell, 1st Baron Emly (d. 1894), had been a liberal unionist and firm opponent of home rule. His son and heir Gaston was a "strong Conservative" in his youth before showing "much sympathy with the more popular Nationalist movement" in later years.[107] Nor was a former career in Crown service necessarily a barrier to integration into the institutions of the state. In 1934, a compensation hearing was held in County Cavan relating to the burning of a RIC barracks on a night in September 1920. Two of those who gave evidence (including the claimant) were men who had defended the barracks that night. The other was a member of the IRA who had attacked it. All three were serving in the Irish Free State's police force, An Garda Síochána. The two former RIC had resigned from the force in 1920.[108] Remaining out of trouble during the War of Independence offered no guarantees, but could make integration easier afterward.[109] Others suffered as a result of their past careers. One RIC pensioner felt safe enough to return to Castletownbere in West Cork in 1924, but by 1930 complained that "Ex R.I.C. men wont [sic] get any employment on account of remaining in the force until disbandment."[110] In 1936 a local Fianna Fáil councillor "strongly objected to, and protested against" a town clerkship being given to "a man who served in the RIC during the troubles."[111] A month later, in another part of the country, "ill-feeling" surrounding the appointment of a teacher ended with the burning of the school and was attributed to her father's service as a sergeant in the RIC.[112] SILRA believed it was "still necessary to help the widows and children of men who had served in the Royal Irish Constabulary" in 1935.[113] Catholic loyalists were also excluded from what Ian d'Alton has described as a convivial "Protestant Free State."[114]

Former servants of the Crown had developed bonds and communal experiences during war and revolution but did not share a homogeneous political identity. Their experiences of life in the Free State were thus mixed. Many Catholic ex-servicemen endured hardship and poverty (for a myriad of reasons), but the Irish government did not interfere with British efforts to meet legal obligations to its veterans. There were persistent complaints from Irish ex-servicemen, but they were ultimately often better off than their British counterparts (who, in turn, received less state assistance than veterans in France and Germany).[115]

Conclusion

The nature of the division between the majority and the minority impacted the levels of violence in Ireland. In Ulster this was mostly inter-communal and based on religious grounds rather than between the IRA and the Crown forces. The conflict between the Ulster Special Constabulary (recruited locally but only organized in six counties of Ulster) and the IRA, for instance, was essentially a conflict between two rival communities.[116] This was explicitly sectarian in a way rarely seen outside of the northeast. The IRA in Ulster also viewed the conflict (and their enemies) in these terms and shot proportionally fewer Catholics than IRA units elsewhere.[117] As T. K. Wilson has put it, "victims were chosen as representatives of their communities, not as individuals."[118] In southern counties, meanwhile, victims of republican violence and intimidation were primarily, if not exclusively, selected based on individual behavior.

The dynamics of violence were also markedly different in the six counties. At least 90 percent of the fatalities between 1920 and 1922 occurred in Belfast and the overwhelming majority of those were civilian victims of inter-communal rioting and sniping.[119] The conflict in Belfast was "a communal war and sectarian war, fought on the basis of ethnic mobilisation."[120] Moreover, more people were killed in Belfast in the five months after the July 1921 truce than during the previous seven months, while the opposite was the case in the twenty-six counties.[121]

The basis of the cleavage in Ireland—religious rather than linguistic—also helped to define the nature of the conflict. Wilson found that Ulster was more deeply divided than Upper Silesia, for instance, but clearer lines of demarcation between communities served to lessen the severity of the violence there.[122] In Southern Ireland, the size of the minority also mattered. It was large enough to survive but not to mount any serious challenge to separatist hegemony either during the revolution or afterward (though this was not inevitable and assumptions that a small German minority in western Poland would lead to better relations with the Polish Republic do not seem to have been borne out in practice).[123] Whereas the large minority Catholic community claimed to be victims of a "pogrom" in Belfast between 1920 and 1922, Protestant minorities in Cavan, Monaghan, and Donegal (three northern counties that became part of the Irish Free State) found that "any contest was practically over before it had begun in earnest."[124] This was also the case elsewhere, as the loyalists who suffered most severely from threat and violence (real or perceived) were those in smaller and more isolated communities.[125] There was no single experience of revolution and secession for Southern Irish loyalists. Some suffered loss, exile, or isolation where others did not, and in that sense one of the challenges encountered in analyses of national indifference is mirrored in the Irish case.[126]

J. J. Lee's suggestion that the Irish Free State was "subjectively virtually 100 percent homogenous, and that was all that politically mattered" has much truth in it.[127] But it also underestimates the resilience of the minority and the ways in which they subtly challenged nationalist and Catholic orthodoxies. Wilson has written that the comparably "mild" experiences of the Irish minority were "largely due to the totality of their defeat and the resulting inevitability of their surrender."[128] While the assimilation that followed that surrender was incomplete and sometimes stubbornly begrudging, the unionist and loyalist community in Southern Ireland had suffered a long decline rather than a sudden implosion. Unlike in Poland, where the "final defeat for the German communities" came in 1945, Southern Irish loyalists had been abandoned early—"something of blessing in disguise," as Wilson has put it.[129] Once the inevitable occurred, flexibility and adaptability were key to efforts to unobtrusively carry on with their own allegiances under the new dispensation, helped by a state that may not always have been friendly but was not, by wider European standards, especially hostile either.

Notes

1. R. B. McDowell, *Crisis and Decline: The Fate of the Southern Unionists* (Dublin: Lilliput Press, 1997), 135.
2. Eunan O'Halpin and Daithí Ó Corráin, *The Dead of the Irish Revolution* (Yale: Yale University Press, 2020), 1–22, 544. Some scholars question or reject the suitability of the term "revolution" for the series of interlinked and overlapping conflicts that took place from *c.*1912 to 1923.
3. Tim Wilson, "Ghost Provinces, Mislaid Minorities: The Experience of Southern Ireland and Prussian Poland Compared," *Irish Studies in International Affairs* 13 (2002): 69.
4. Anne Dolan, "Killing in 'the Good Old Irish Fashion?' Irish Revolutionary Violence in Context," *Irish Historical Studies* 44, no. 165 (2020): 13.
5. Charles Townshend, *The Republic: The Fight for Irish Independence* (London: Allen Lane, 2013), 452.
6. Dolan, "Irish Revolutionary Violence," 13–14.
7. Maarten von Ginderachter and Jon Fox, eds., *National Indifference and the History of Nationalism in Modern Europe* (Abingdon: Routledge, 2019) broadens the traditional focus on East Central Europe to include Belgium and France, and territories in Central and Southern Europe, but not Britain or Ireland. For comparisons of Ireland and Poland, see T. K. Wilson, *Frontiers of Violence: Conflict and identity in Ulster and Upper Silesia, 1918–1922* (Oxford: Oxford University Press, 2010) and Julia Eichenberg, "The Dark Side of Independence: Paramilitary Violence in Ireland and Poland after the First World War," *Contemporary Irish History* 19, no. 3 (2010): 231–48.
8. Michael R. Marrus, *The Unwanted: European Refugees in the Twentieth Century* (Philadelphia: Temple University Press, 2002); Panikos Panayi and Pippa Verdi, eds., *Refugees and the End of Empire: Imperial Collapse and Forced Migration in the Twentieth Century* (Basingstoke: Palgrave, 2011); Peter Gatrell, *The Making of the Modern Refugee* (Oxford: Oxford University Press, 2013); and Matthew Frank and Jessica Reinisch, eds., *Refugees in Twentieth-Century Europe: A Forty Years' Crisis?*

(London: Bloomsbury, 2017) for instance, make no mention of the movement of Southern Irish loyalists from 1920.

9   The territory that became the Irish Free State in 1922 comprises twenty-six Irish counties. The six remaining counties, in the north-east of the island where there was a Protestant/unionist majority, became a separate jurisdiction that remained part of the United Kingdom but with its own parliament. Though the historic province of Ulster is made up of nine counties, three of which were excluded from Northern Ireland, unionists and loyalists in the six counties regularly referred to it as Ulster and are usually described as Ulster unionists.
10 Wilson, "Mislaid Minorities," 71–3.
11 Wilson, *Frontiers of Violence*, 136; Wilson, "Mislaid Minorities," 64; Eichenberg, "Dark Side of Independence," 233, no. 6, 243.
12 Pieter M. Judson, "'Where Our Commonality Is Necessary … ': Rethinking the End of the Habsburg Monarchy," *Austrian History Yearbook* 48 (2017): 1–17. See also Judson's chapter in this volume.
13 Tara Zahra, "Imagined Noncommunities: National Indifference as a Category of Analysis," *Slavic Review* 69, no. 1 (2010): 93–119.
14 Stathis Kalyvas, *The Logic of Violence in Civil Wars* (Cambridge: Cambridge University Press, 2006), 104, 226–9.
15 For more on this see Brian Hughes, *Defying the IRA? Intimidation, Coercion, and Communities during the Irish Revolution* (Liverpool: Liverpool University Press, 2016).
16 Zahra, "Imagined Noncommunities," 98.
17 See Olga Linkiewicz's chapter in this volume, 180.
18 See Alvin Jackson's chapter in this volume. In an Irish context this primarily means three main denominations, the Church of Ireland (by far the largest in Southern Ireland), Presbyterian, and Methodist. While treating these denominations as a homogeneous whole has its problems, it has been done here for convenience unless a specific denomination is mentioned.
19 Elizabeth Malcolm, *The Irish Policeman, 1822–1922: A Life* (Dublin: Irish Academic Press, 2006), 58–67; Peter Karsten, "Irish Soldiers in the British Army, 1792–1922: Suborned or Subordinate," *Journal of Social History* 17, no. 1 (1983): 31–64.
20 Pieter M. Judson, *The Habsburg Empire: A New History* (Cambridge: Harvard University Press, 2016), 363–70. For Irish involvement in colonial service, see David Fitzpatrick, "Ireland and the Empire," in *The Oxford History of the British Empire, Vol. III: The Nineteenth Century*, ed. Andrew Porter (Oxford: Oxford University Press, 1999), 509–15; Seán William Gannon, "Southern Irish Loyalists and Imperial Service," in *Southern Irish Loyalism, 1912–1949*, ed. Brian Hughes and Conor Morrissey (Liverpool: Liverpool University Press, 2020), 155–72.
21 *Saorstát Éireann. Census of Population, 1926*, vol. 3 (1929), Table 1A; *Census of Population of Northern Ireland, 1926. General Report*, 15 & 16 Geo. V, c. 83 [N.I.] (1929), Table XXVIII, 1i. There were also tiny numbers of Jews, Baptists, and others, accounting for about 13,400 people.
22 Alvin Jackson, "Irish Unionism, 1870–1992," in *Defenders of the Union: A Survey of British and Irish Unionism since 1801*, ed. D. George Boyce and Alan O'Day (Abingdon: Routledge, 2001), 121–3.
23 Sabrina P. Ramet, "Interwar East Central Europe, 1918–1941: The Failure of Democracy-building, the Fate of Minorities—an Introduction," in *Interwar East Central Europe, 1918–1941: The Failure of Democracy-Building, The Fate of Minorities*, ed. Sabrina P. Ramet (Abingdon: Routledge, 2020), 7–8.

24 McDowell, *Crisis and Decline*, 163.
25 Peter Hart, *The I.R.A. and Its Enemies: Violence and Community in County Cork, 1916-1923* (Oxford: Oxford University Press, 1998), 288-92, quote at 288.
26 Ibid., 292.
27 See Brian P. Murphy and Niall Meehan, *Troubled History: A 10th Anniversary Critique of Peter Hart's "The I.R.A. and Its Enemies"* (Aubane: Aubane Historical Society, 2008); John M. Regan, "The 'Bandon Valley Massacre' as an Historiographical Problem," *History* 97 (2012): 70-98. For a defense of Hart, see David Fitzpatrick, "Ethnic Cleansing, Ethical Smearing and Irish Historians," *History* 98 (2013): 135-44 and for a more recent evaluation of the "Peter Hart affair" see Ian McBride, "The Peter Hart Affair in Perspective: History, Ideology, and the Irish Revolution," *The Historical Journal* 61, no. 1 (2018): 249-71.
28 Marie Coleman, "Protestant Depopulation in County Longford during the Irish Revolution, 1911-1926," *English Historical Review* 135, no. 575 (2020): 934.
29 Hughes, *Defying the IRA?*, 129-36, 181-2.
30 R. B. McDowell, *The Church of Ireland, 1869-1969* (London: Routledge, 1975), 109.
31 Jack White, *Minority Report: The Anatomy of the Southern Irish Protestant* (Dublin: Gill & Macmillan, 1975), 84.
32 Brian M. Walker, "Southern Protestant Voices During the Irish War of Independence and Civil War: Reports from the Church of Ireland Synods," in *Southern Irish Loyalism*, ed. Hughes and Morrissey, 79-80.
33 *Cork Examiner*, May 1, 1922.
34 David Fitzpatrick, *Descendancy: Irish Protestant Histories since 1795* (Cambridge: Cambridge University Press, 2014), 240.
35 *Saorstát Éireann, Census of Population, 1926*, vol. 3 (1929), Table 1A.
36 See Robert E. Kennedy, *The Irish: Emigration, Marriage, and Fertility* (Berkeley and Los Angeles, CA: University of California Press, 1973), 119, 138; Kurt Bowen, *Protestants in a Catholic State: Ireland's Privileged Minority* (Kingston and Montreal: McGill-Queen's University Press, 1983), 21-5; Enda Delaney, *Demography, State and Society: Irish Migration to Britain, 1921-1971* (Liverpool: Liverpool University Press, 2000), 69-83.
37 Peter Hart, *The I.R.A. at War, 1916-1923* (Oxford: Oxford University Press, 2002), 225-8, 239.
38 Fitzpatrick, *Descendancy*, 159-80.
39 Andy Bielenberg, "Exodus: The Emigration of Southern Irish Protestants during the Irish War of Independence and the Civil War," *Past & Present* 218, no. 1 (2013): 199-233. See also Barry Keane, "Ethnic Cleansing? Protestant Decline in West Cork between 1911 and 1926," *History Ireland* 20, no. 2 (2012): 35-8.
40 Donald Wood, "Protestant Population Decline in Southern Ireland, 1911-1926," in *Southern Irish Loyalism*, ed. Hughes and Morrissey, 27-47. Another recent study of one county reinforces the prevalence of long-term natural decline and emigration: Coleman, "Longford," 931-7.
41 Richard Blanke, *Orphans of Versailles: The Germans in Western Poland, 1918-1939* (Lexington, KY: University Press of Kentucky, 1993), 32-53.
42 *Census of Population of Northern Ireland, 1926. General Report*, 15 & 16 Geo. V, c. 83 [N.I.] (1929), xxv.
43 *First Interim Report of the Irish Distress Committee* (London, 1922); Irish Grants Committee second interim report [Cmd. 2032], HC, 1924.
44 Hansard 5 (Commons), vol. 154, col. 2160 (May 31, 1922).

45 Minutes of meeting of SILRA provisional committee, June 13, 1922 (Public Record Office of Northern Ireland [PRONI], D989/B/1/3).
46 Minutes of Ulster Unionist Council (UUC) "Refugee Committee," June 6, 1922 (PRONI, D1327/15/6); Minutes of UUC "Refugee Committee," June 12, 1922 (PRONI, D1327/15/6). See also *Belfast News-letter*, March 3, 1923. The meeting was told of refugees who had come "from out-lying parts of the Six Counties, and even from the South and West of Ireland."
47 McDowell, *Crisis and Decline*, 132.
48 Paul Stocker, *Lost Imperium: Far Right Visions of the British Empire, c. 1920–1980* (Abingdon: Routledge, 2021), 61.
49 See, for example, *Manchester Guardian*, July 23, 1923 [open house]; Pamphlet announcing a ball to be held in Hyde Park Hotel in aid of SILRA, June 12, 1930 (PRONI, D989/5/2); *Aberdeen Press and Journal*, January 3, 1923 [clothing drive].
50 Blanke, *Orphans of Versailles*, 40. For similar SILRA rhetoric, see speech by Northumberland reported in *Daily Mail*, May 16, 1923.
51 IGC application files, The National Archives, Kew (TNA), CO 763/3–202.
52 Jonathan C. Darby claim, TNA, CO 762/11/1.
53 Abraham Good claim, TNA, CO 762/66/9. He owed £250 to his brother.
54 "The Plight of Irish Loyalists. Our Obligations. Terrible Cases of Victims. Terrible Suffering," 1923, London School of Economics Archives (LSE), COLL MS 0028; *Belfast News-letter*, May 12, 1922; *Yorkshire Post*, September 27, 1922.
55 Mo Moulton, *Ireland and the Irish in Interwar England* (Cambridge: Cambridge University Press, 2014), 216–17.
56 "Victims of the Suspension of the Law in Southern Ireland," SILRA, n.d., LSE, COLL MS 0028.
57 "Victims of the Suspension of the Law," c.1923, National Library of Ireland (NLI): ILB 300 p3 [Item 112].
58 Moulton, *Ireland the Irish in Interwar England*, 209–10.
59 O'Hegarty to Curtis, May 18, 1922, in *First Interim Report of the Irish Distress Committee*, H.C. 1922.
60 Ibid.
61 Memorandum on "Question of Furnishing Addresses and Supplying Information concerning Former Members of the Royal Irish Constabulary," April 17, 1931, TNA, HO 144/22600. I am grateful to Dr. Seán William Gannon for alerting me to this file.
62 Travers Robert Blackley claim, TNA, CO 762/37/6.
63 Coleman, "Longford," 963–6.
64 *Irish Times*, December 10, 1921.
65 *CoIG*, January 13, 1922. See also *Irish Times*, January 16, 1922; McDowell, *Crisis and Decline*, 177–96; White, *Minority Report*, 86–8.
66 Daithí Ó Corráin, "Catholicism in Ireland, 1880–2015: Rise, Ascendancy and Retreat," in *The Cambridge History of Ireland, Vol. IV, 1880 to the Present*, ed. Thomas Bartlett (Cambridge: Cambridge University Press, 2018), 733–4.
67 Ibid.; Senia Pašeta, "Censorship and Its Critics in the Irish Free State, 1922–1932," *Past & Present* 181 (2002): 193–218.
68 See, for example, SILRA pamphlets available in the Public Record Office of Northern Ireland (D989), the LSE, COLL MS 0028, and in the NLI, ILB 300 p3.
69 *Irish Independent*, February 10, 1928.
70 Stocker, *Lost Imperium*, 61.
71 *The Liberator (Tralee)*, May 1, 1928.

72 Applicants were required to give details of their present financial situation when applying. See Irish Grants Committee claim files, 1926–30, TNA, CO 726/3–202.

73 Robin Bury, *Buried Lives: the Protestants of Southern Ireland* (Dublin: The History Press, 2017). For alternative interpretations see reviews of the book by Ian d'Alton, *Irish Times*, March 4, 2017, and Kim Bielenberg, *Irish Independent*, March 19, 2017.

74 See, for example, Heather Crawford, *Outside the Glow: Protestants and Irishness in Independent Ireland* (Dublin: University College Dublin Press, 2010). Also, Marianne Elliot, *When God Took Sides: Religion and Identity in Irish History, Unfinished History* (Oxford: Oxford University Press, 2009), 216–35; Daithí Ó Corráin, *Rendering to God and Caesar: The Churches and the Two States in Ireland, 1949–73* (Manchester: Manchester University Press, 2008), 70–105; Ian d'Alton and Ida Milne, eds., *Protestant and Irish: The Minority's Search for Place in Independent Ireland* (Cork: Cork University Press, 2019). See also Caleb Richardson, *Smyllie's Ireland: Protestants, Independence, and the Man Who Ran the Irish Times* (Indiana: Indiana University Press, 2019).

75 There is an extensive literature on Catholic influence on life in the Irish Free State. For a succinct summary, see Ó Corráin, "Catholicism in Ireland, 1880–2015," 729–39.

76 Zahra, "Imagined Noncommunities," 100–1; Martina Relihan, "The Church of Ireland, the State and Education in Irish Language and Irish History, 1920s–1950s," in *Educating Ireland: Schooling and Social Change, 1700–2000*, ed. Karin Fisher and Deirdre Raftery (Kildare: Irish Academic Press, 2014), 154–6.

77 Bowen, *Protestants in a Catholic State*, 48–65; McDowell, *Crisis and Decline*, 55; David Fitzpatrick, *The Two Irelands, 1912–1939* (Oxford: Oxford University Press, 1998), 203.

78 Martin Maguire, "'Our People': The Church of Ireland and the Culture of Community in Dublin since Disestablishment," in *The Laity and the Church of Ireland, 1000–2000: All Sorts*, ed. Raymond Gillespie and W. G. Neely (Dublin: Four Courts Press, 2002).

79 *Irish Press*, December 5, 1931; December 12, 1931; December 25, 1931; January 2, 1932; January 7, 1932; January 14, 1932; January 27, 1932; February 6, 1932; February 15, 1932. Fianna Fáil was founded in 1926 after a split within the anti-Anglo-Irish Treaty Sinn Féin party. It entered the parliament, Dáil Éireann, for the first time in 1927. Fianna Fáil first came to power in 1932 and was electorally dominant for much of the remainder of the century.

80 Ian d'Alton, "Protestant 'Belongings' in Independent Ireland, 1922–49," in *Protestant and Irish*, ed. d'Alton and Milne, 28.

81 Maguire, "Our People."

82 Brian Inglis, *West Briton* (London: Faber & Faber, 1962), 15.

83 McDowell, *Crisis and Decline*, 167.

84 Ibid.; d'Alton, "Protestant 'Belongings,'" 29; Elliot, *When God Took Sides*, 225–6.

85 Ian d'Alton, "'A Vestigial Population?' Perspectives on Southern Irish Protestants," *Éire-Ireland* 44, no. 3&4 (2009): 39.

86 Ciarán Wallace, "Fighting for Unionist Home Rule: Competing Identities in Dublin 1800–1929," *Journal of Urban History* 38, no. 5 (2012): 941.

87 Yvonne Whelan, "The Construction and Destruction of a Colonial Landscape: Monuments to British Monarchs in Dublin before and after Independence," *Journal of Historical Geography* 28, no. 4 (2002): 508–33. The Nelson pillar survived until 1966.

88 Jane Leonard, "The Twinge of Memory: Armistice Day and Remembrance Sunday in Dublin Since 1919," in *Unionism in Modern Ireland: New Perspectives on Politics*

and Culture, ed. Richard English and Graham Walker (Basingstoke: Palgrave, 1996), 102; Mandy Link, *Remembrance of the Great War in the Irish Free State, 1914-1937* (Cham: Palgrave, 2019), 135-46.
89   *Irish Times*, May 5, 1924.
90   Paul Taylor, *Heroes or Traitors? Experiences of Southern Irish Soldiers Returning from the Great War* (Liverpool: Liverpool University Press, 2015), 213.
91   Leonard, "Twinge of Memory," 102-5; Taylor, *Heroes or Traitors?*, 241; Link, *Remembrance*, 148-57.
92   Lionel Fleming, *Head or Harp* (London: Barrie and Rockliff, 1965), 93.
93   d'Alton, "Protestant 'Belongings,'" 31.
94   Gannon, "Imperial Service," 155-72; Keith Jeffery, "Ireland and the British Army since 1922," in *A Military History of Ireland*, ed. Thomas Bartlett and Keith Jeffery (Cambridge: Cambridge University Press, 1996), 431-58; Steven O'Connor, *Irish Officers in the British Forces, 1922-45* (Basingstoke: Palgrave, 2014), 16-22.
95   Zahra, "Imagined Noncommunities," 103; Michael Viney, "The Five Per Cent—4: The Mixed Marriage," *Irish Times*, March 25, 1965.
96   Coleman, "Longford," 947-52, 974.
97   Eoin de Bhaldraithe, "Mixed Marriages and Irish Politics: The Effect of 'Ne Temere,'" *Studies: An Irish Quarterly Review* 77, no. 307 (1988): 284-99.
98   Conor Morrissey, *Protestant Nationalists in Ireland, 1900-1923* (Cambridge: Cambridge University Press, 2019), 32-44.
99   Relihan, "Church of Ireland," 147. See *Church of Ireland Gazette*, March 10, 1922, for criticism of the policy and a letter to the editor, March 17, 1922, for individual Protestants embracing the language.
100 Relihan, "Church of Ireland," 157.
101 Ibid., 159-61.
102 McDowell, *Crisis and Decline*, 167, 180.
103 James S. Donnelly, Jr., "Big House Burnings in County Cork during the Irish Revolution, 1920-21," *Éire-Ireland* 47, no. 3 & 4 (2012): 141, 179, note 166.
104 *Irish Times*, November 22, 1941.
105 Ibid.
106 Notes on an interview between Eunan O'Halpin and Billy Vincent, Monaco, March 16/17, 2012. I am grateful to Professor O'Halpin for sharing these notes.
107 "Monsell, William" by Matthew Potter, *Dictionary of Irish Biography*; *Irish Times*, November 26, 1932.
108 *Irish Times*, November 17, 1934.
109 Hughes, *Defying the IRA?*, 197.
110 Michael Flynn to RIC Pensions Committee, August 1, 1930, TNA, HO 144/22575.
111 *Irish Times*, January 4, 1936.
112 *Irish Times*, July 11, 1936.
113 *The Times (London)*, July 17, 1935.
114 See d'Alton, "Protestant 'Belongings.'"
115 Taylor, *Heroes or Traitors?*, 91-136.
116 Wilson, *Frontiers of Violence*, 17.
117 Ibid., 155. Peter Hart found that even in Cork, where he argued that IRA sectarianism was widespread, 36 percent of civilian victims of the IRA were Protestant. While this was far out of proportion with their percentage among the civilian population, it still amounts to a substantial number of Catholic victims: Hart, *The I.R.A. at War*, 234.

118 Wilson, *Frontiers of Violence*, 196.
119 Ibid., 175–6; Hart, *The I.R.A. at War*, 247–8.
120 Hart, *The I.R.A. at War*, 249.
121 Robert Lynch, *The Northern IRA and the Early Years of Partition, 1920–1922* (Dublin: Irish Academic Press, 2006), 2.
122 Ibid., 5–6.
123 Blanke, *Orphans of Versailles*, 52–3.
124 Wilson, *Frontiers of Violence*, 198.
125 Hughes, *Defying the IRA?*, 186–7; Wilson, "Mislaid Minorities," 66–7; Coleman, "Longford," 936.
126 Zahra, "Imagined Noncommunities," 106.
127 J. J. Lee, *Ireland 1912–85: Politics and Society* (Cambridge: Cambridge University Press, 1989), 77.
128 Wilson, "Mislaid Minorities," 86.
129 Ibid.

11

Navigations of National Belonging: Legal Reintegration after the Return of Alsace to France, 1918–39

Alison Carrol

As the First World War neared its end in the autumn of 1918, the territory of Alsace-Lorraine was gripped by rumors that Germany's defeat would mean return to France.[1] The region had been under German rule since the 1871 settlement that ended the Franco-Prussian War, and return became the primary French war aim after the outbreak of conflict in 1914. During the war, both France and Germany had taken efforts to secure the support of the population, but when French troops marched into the region in November 1918, they were greeted by a sea of blue, white, and red. Upon their arrival in Strasbourg on November 8, the city was "en fête": tricolor banners and flags covered the cathedral, town hall, and former imperial palace, as well as shop windows, houses, and buttonholes.[2] These scenes were captured in the national French press, which heralded the return of the "lost provinces" after almost half a century of patiently awaiting their liberation by France. For French President Raymond Poincaré, the crowds that had turned out to welcome the troops offered ample evidence of a widespread desire to return to France.[3]

When the victorious powers arrived in Paris to discuss the parameters of the peace two months later, Alsace-Lorraine was not an issue on the agenda. France's claims to the region had been recognized as part of the armistice, and while Volker Prott has shown that transferring Alsace-Lorraine without consultation provoked a widespread sense of unease, such anxieties did not challenge the region's return to French rule.[4] Instead, discussion focused upon the other territories and populations of the imperial states which had dominated Central and Eastern Europe, and on this question, the notion of national self-determination became an underpinning principle of the negotiations. The Paris discussions, along with the peacemakers' efforts to build a new international order and the subsequent state-building initiatives of the successor nation-states have recently become the subject of renewed scholarly attention.[5] The focus of much of this work has been upon Central and Eastern Europe, where research has cast new light on the efforts of the post-imperial states to deal with heterogeneous national populations, and equally upon the implications of the conferences for international relations.[6]

Alsace began the war as part of central Europe; yet, its end triggered its return to the major Western European continental power. Its history in the following two decades is revealing of the ways in which heterogeneous populations and contested visions of sovereignty were not restricted to the "shatter zone" of the former imperial states. On the contrary, Alsace's return to France underlines that states *across* Europe grappled with the challenges posed by territorial shifts, the presence of minority populations, and a myriad of claims to sovereignty.[7]

A Clash of Expectations: The Recovery of the "Lost Provinces"

After Alsace's return to France, Alsatian politicians and representatives of civil society articulated their visions of the region's place within the French nation. These views were varied, and the extent of the differences came as a surprise to many in both Paris and the so-called lost provinces who had expected Alsace's return to be relatively straightforward. French authorities found that contrary to their expectations the Alsatian population did not resemble the caricatures of the *images d'Epinal*, frozen in time by the cult of Alsace which had presented them as patiently waiting for their liberation by France during the years of annexation.[8] Equally, large sections of the Alsatian population rapidly became disappointed with the return to France when the universalist and centralizing initiatives of the Third Republic appeared to leave little space for alternative visions of national belonging. At the heart of the resulting clash was the question of how to deal with difference, as return revealed a wide spectrum of understandings of belonging in both Alsace and the French interior.[9]

This was not the first time that France had been confronted with such questions. Upon its foundation in 1871, the Third Republic had faced populations who spoke regional languages and dialects, had varied cultural mores, and deep attachment to their localities.[10] In response, the Republic embarked upon policies including the dissemination of the French language, the construction of railways linking far-flung parts of French territory, and the introduction of compulsory schooling, national markets, and military service. According to Eugen Weber, these processes had the cumulative effect of spreading a sense of national belonging amongst France's regional populations, or to borrow Weber's phrase, of turning "peasants into Frenchmen."[11] Research since Weber has underlined that difference persisted in a variety of ways long after 1914, and important work by Caroline Ford, Peter Sahlins, and others has stressed the role that local populations played in forging their own place within the French nation, not least by filtering national values through local understandings.[12] In this view, the construction of the French nation-state was not completed from Paris outward, but rather through interaction between center and periphery.

The focus of much of this research on the creation of a sense of belonging in France has been on the period prior to the First World War, and research on the interwar period has paid greater attention to the challenge of maintaining an integral conception of law while preserving difference in Algeria and across France's colonies.[13] Yet the Alsatian case underlines that there was still work to be done in integrating minority populations within France's borders after 1918, as Alsace-Lorraine returned to a regime that had changed in fundamental ways from the Second French Empire that it had left in 1871. Crucially, whereas the Second Empire had allowed space for regional particularity, the Third Republic had been built upon the principle of uniformity. The return of Alsace-Lorraine thus casts an alternative light on the tensions between particularity and universalism in twentieth-century France by revealing their dynamics *within* the boundaries of the French hexagon.

The world after the First World War was very different to the high point of nation-building at the end of the nineteenth century. The conflict had seen a growth of the state across Europe, as well as a hardening of national categories which frequently clashed with the ways in which people living across Europe saw themselves, as the chapters in this volume underline. The challenge for the French authorities was: which (if any) regional particularities could remain intact as French institutions and systems were introduced? The answers did not prove to be straightforward, and Alsatian and Lorrain political and cultural elites laid claim to visions of national belonging which challenged the universalist model of the French Third Republic. In turn, their articulations were challenged, nuanced, or in some cases, supported by politicians and civil servants in Paris. As a result, return became a protracted and multi-cornered struggle that provoked a renegotiation of what it meant to be French in the late Third Republic.

This chapter uses the case of Alsace's return to France to rethink the navigation of national belonging which resulted there and traces the reciprocal influence which Paris and periphery exercised upon one another. Its focus is upon Alsace, rather than on "Alsace-Lorraine." While Alsace-Lorraine was united in its experience of German rule, the paths of the two regions diverged after their return to France, and annexed Lorraine (which returned to France as the department of the Moselle) had a distinct experience of reintegration which demands a separate history.[14] In common with people across Central and Eastern Europe, the population of Alsace lived through the transfer from empire to nation-state. But their experience was nonetheless particular, as they transitioned from empire to an established (and celebrated) nation-state, or in terms of the First World War, from loser to winner. The Alsatian experience of transition was thus one of regime change and transfer of sovereignty. But it was also one of disappointment, and frustrated expectations on both sides. These frustrations were compounded as Alsatian difference was frequently viewed by civil servants and political elites in Paris not as "regional," but as "foreign." While the Alsatian population was deeply attached to its local dialect and cultural traditions, to the eyes and ears of civil servants and politicians from the French interior, these mores appeared to be suspiciously German. To make matters worse in terms of the resulting tensions, many of the French authorities assumed that such connections to Germany through language, culture, or family ties meant that the population of Alsace had an alternative nation, which threatened the very coherence of France as a nation-state.

Although French officials fretted about Alsatian ambivalence to the nation in their private correspondence, there was no official recognition of the population of Alsace as a minority on either the national or international stage. In one exchange at the League of Nations, the French representative Henry de Jouvenel batted off the proposal that the League's minority rights protections and standards should be applied to all member states with the retort that France "has no minorities."[15] In the absence of this official acknowledgment, the process of navigating the position of the Alsatian population within France could not follow parallel processes in Central and Eastern Europe, where the League emerged as a space for discussion of questions of sovereignty and successor states experimented with the meaning of post-imperial statehood in concert.[16] While Alsatian elites made international and colonial comparisons and appeals for support, the process of reworking the boundaries of sovereignty in French Alsace was focused upon negotiations within France. What is more, outside the flash points of high tension provoked by the emergence of an autonomist movement, the problems of reintegrating Alsace remained outside the consciousness of much of the rest of the French population.[17] As a result, most of these negotiations took place within institutions and structures in Alsace. These discussions, as they took shape concerning the laws that framed the Alsatian population's place within France, are the focus of this chapter. As representatives of different sectors of Alsatian society responded to the introduction of the Third Republic's laws, the process is revealing of both their myriad of visions of national belonging, and the French state's efforts to deal with the difference that it confronted following the return of Alsace after the First World War.

The Challenges of Reintegrating the "Lost Province" of Alsace

When French troops entered the towns and villages of Alsace in November 1918, the cheering crowds that greeted them were famously described by French President Raymond Poincaré as evidence of the widespread desire to return to France. In reference to Ernest Renan's description of nationhood as a "daily plebiscite," he stated that the enthusiastic reception demonstrated that "the plebiscite [was] complete."[18] Scholarship on 1918 has revealed that the reality was more complex: Laird Boswell has argued that the reception of the French troops was more muted amongst Protestants and residents of the villages in the northeast part of the region bordering Germany, while Sebastian Döderlein's analysis of the postal control has revealed that much of the Alsatian population's dominant concern had to do with their material conditions rather than national status.[19] And, before the war was over, British Foreign Secretary Arthur Balfour had already noted "that there was unlikely to be a clear majority" in the region which would vote in favor of returning to France.[20] Similar doubts were raised at the Berne conference of international Socialist parties held after the war in February 1919, when the Alsatian socialist Salomon Grumbach argued that the answer to the Alsatian situation was a plebiscite. This, he suggested, would settle the "Alsace-Lorraine question" once and for all.[21]

These debates took place within the landscape of broader discussions and plans for international political reorganization after the war. Like the proposals for Alsace's future, conversations over the nature of the peace had started before the war ended. Following the Revolution of 1917, Soviet Russia had announced that "every nation, large and small, should be given the right to determine the form of its state life."[22] In January 1918, British Prime Minister David Lloyd George had proclaimed that Britain and its Allies were fighting for a peace which was only possible if a "territorial settlement ... be secured, based on the right of self-determination."[23] And US President Woodrow Wilson's Fourteen Points of January 1918 centered the principle of national self-determination as the basis of the new international order. In this way, the Paris Peace Conferences imbued an older set of ideas about national self-determination with "new energy and legitimacy," centering them in the new world order.[24]

Such references to self-determination were not applied to Alsace, however. In the October 1918 document which had noted the unlikeliness of a majority of Alsatians voting to return to France, Balfour rejected a plebiscite for that very reason.[25] During the negotiations at Paris, lively discussions followed French Premier Georges Clemenceau's proposal for the creation of a neutral buffer state in the German Rhineland, but the question of Alsace's future status received limited attention.[26] The French government presented support for Alsace's return as unanimous in order to justify the return to its international allies, while offering some recompense for France's wartime sacrifices to the French population. Yet from the moment the French troops crossed the Vosges mountain range into Alsace, it became clear that they were not in the region of the pre-1918 French national imagination. While the nineteenth-century cult of Alsace-Lorraine had presented the population as the epitome of Frenchness and awaiting their liberation from the German yoke, the troops found that most Alsatians did not speak French, and were linked to Germany through culture and family ties.[27] What is more, almost fifty years of annexation into German institutions and systems had left their mark on the region: its laws, administrative institutions, education system, railway network, cityscapes, and cultural traditions all stood apart from their French equivalents. This posed important questions about how to complete this return: how should the extrication from German institutions and systems take place, and what was necessary to make the region an integral part of the French nation-state?

Before the return was ratified at Versailles, France began work on making the region French. Many of these early measures were based on the proposals of the wartime Conférence d'Alsace-Lorraine when the Francophile Catholic priest Abbé Emile Wetterlé had recommended the removal of German influence as the best means of reintegrating Alsace. This proposal was seized by the French authorities to remove the German mark and replace it with the French franc, to sequester German companies, such as the potash mines, and to classify the population into A-D category citizens with identity cards issued based upon place of birth and parentage, and to expel German nationals.[28] During the period between the armistice of November 1918 and the ratification of the Peace Treaty in June 1919, Alsace and annexed Lorraine were provisionally placed under military occupation with overall control by the Premier and Minister of War.[29]

Before the return was ratified, the French authorities restricted themselves to policies deemed to be "essential" in order to avoid further change rendered necessary by the discussions at Versailles.[30] The word "essential" was of course highly subjective, and for France such so-called essential measures included the introduction of the French currency and removal of those who had been born in the German lands on the east of the Rhine (or whose place of birth was Alsace, but whose parents had been born in the territories that now constituted Weimar Germany), as well as those who had demonstrated suspect national loyalty to France.[31]

The French language was introduced, and the authorities made efforts to ensure that French replaced Alsatian dialect as the dominant language in Alsace. Schoolteachers were instructed to teach French through immersion, orders were published in French, street signs were translated, and cinemas began to show French films.[32] But, as problems emerged the authorities increasingly recognized the need for bilingualism. This included providing a translator for the *Cours d'Assise* and *Cabinets d'Instruction* to translate witness testimonies if necessary, and introducing an *arrêté* which allowed trials to be stopped and conducted in German or Alsatian if the parties were having trouble following the arguments.[33] All important documents, notably the *Bulletin officiel*, official correspondence and electoral posters were bilingual, and administrators generally conducted all of their correspondence with the local population in German.[34]

Initial French policy also included the creation of a temporary administrative structure, the General Commission of the Republic, in order to oversee reintegration and to replace the German regional administrator, the *Statthalter*. The Commission was headed by a General Commissioner, answerable first to the Minister of War and then to the Premier, who maintained close links with Paris through daily reports. Alsace-Lorraine was broken up into the three *départements* of the Bas-Rhin, the Haut-Rhin, and the Moselle, and each department received a Prefect who worked under the Commissioner.[35] From September 1920, a Consultative Council for Alsace and Lorraine, with councilors constituted of members of the departmental councils and Alsatian and Mosellan members of the National Assembly also tackled the reintegration problems. These administrative institutions set to work on the question of how to integrate Alsace, with its distinctive administrative structures, laws, and education system into France. But they were not alone in their efforts to shape reintegration. Further views were advanced by the region's political, cultural, and economic elites, as well as by their counterparts from elsewhere in France. These negotiations did not prove to be straightforward, and at their heart was the question of whether difference was permitted, and, if so, how would it be maintained? A principal area for discussion was law, which administrated daily life, framed the place of the Alsatian population within the French Republic, and created the spaces within which representatives of the Alsatian population attempted to navigate national belonging.

Defining and Redefining Alsatian Law after the Return to France

Upon its return to France in 1918, Alsace had a legislative patchwork composed of laws introduced by national French or local authorities before 1871, and by the German Imperial Government or its Alsatian administrators between 1871 and 1918. In the first weeks and months of French rule, an additional layer of this legal framework was added by *arrêtés* issued by the Civil Authorities for urgent issues such as the introduction of the franc, which could not wait until the conclusion of the discussions at Versailles. Once return had been ratified, further delays followed the introduction of French laws as local officials hurried to accustom themselves to France's legal code.[36]

This layering of the law posed an important question for the new authorities in Alsace. The French Third Republic had been created upon the principle of universalism and uniformity, but Alsace was subject to laws that did not cover the rest of France. Was it possible for a region of France to have distinctive laws? What would be the implications of such a concession to particularity for the region and its population, and for the French nation? For many in Alsace, the key to understanding Alsatian laws lay in the region's historic ties to France. Having been a French region in the years between the Revolution of 1789 and its annexation into Germany in 1871, Alsatian elites argued that many of the laws in place after 1918 had their roots in Alsace's French past. In this view, such a shared history offered a means to reconcile difference after the region's return in 1918.

Many of these conversations took place in concert with discussions over the region's administrative institutions. Although the General Commission had been established in March 1919 as a temporary solution to reintegration, it staggered on throughout the 1920s.[37] In July 1924 Premier Raymond Poincaré announced plans to dissolve the Commission, but regional representatives and the General Commissioner made the case that some form of transitional body was necessary as multiple questions remained over the region's legislative framework. As a result, Poincaré's plans were shelved, but picked up again by his successor Edouard Herriot.

Herriot led the Centre-Left coalition which won power in 1924, and he charged newly elected Strasbourg Socialist Deputy Georges Weill with working on the region's reintegration. Weill authored a 1924 law which dissolved the General Commission and stipulated that regional administrative sections that had not been transferred to their respective ministries by 1925 were to be passed to a General Directorate, based in Paris. In the event, a number of important policies maintained their Strasbourg base, including those dealing with churches and education. The Directorate became a replacement for the Commission, and like the Commission, it was intended to be a temporary solution. But despite a brief suppression in 1935–6, the Directorate remained in place in 1939 when the Second World War broke out.[38] With the gradual trickling of administrative structures to Paris, Alsatian elites attempted to maintain authority over regional affairs and to redefine sovereignty as stemming from ever-evolving practices of legislation.

The French authorities had assumed that legal reintegration would parallel processes adopted concerning citizenship or currency, and that the introduction of French laws and systems would be accompanied with the removal of their German equivalents. This worked in some areas, and the French penal code was introduced without major opposition in November 1919.[39] But in other areas of law, this approach was met with immediate resistance from the population in Alsace, and it soon became clear that a straightforward replacement of one legal system with another would not be possible. There were two main reasons for this. First, some German laws had no equivalent in the French legal system. This was the case for the legislation covering the postal service or pharmacists, where the laws in place in Alsace were more expansive and covered areas neglected by the French laws.[40] In this case, should the French law be introduced even though it left legal gaps over areas which had previously been subject to legislation? In such situations keeping the German laws in place served the pragmatic purpose of allowing for continuity of legislation. Second, and more controversially, there were elements of German legislation which appeared to be more advantageous to the population than the equivalent French law.[41] This was the case, local politicians argued, for social security, company law, property rights, and municipal laws.[42]

In an effort to bring some form of legislative order, when the Conservative Bloc National won power in 1919, it established commissions to examine penal, civil, commercial law, and civil procedure. These commissions made the decision to retain those laws which had no equivalent in the French statute, in addition to maintaining those which were likely to become part of French law anyway. Their decision to permit the retention of laws without equivalent posed further questions: if German law was allowed to stay in situations where it had no French equivalent, such as those regarding the post office or pharmacists, did that create a precedent for the retention of other regional laws? And if these laws were permitted to stay in force in Alsace, should they be restricted to the recovered region or applied to the rest of France? Further discussions were needed, and the government set a ten-year limit for the introduction of all French laws and legal instruments into Alsace.

In those cases where local law was deemed to be preferable to French law, supporters of its retention were faced with the question of how to present this situation to the French interior. While Alsatian supporters of retaining law described existing legislation as "local," many of these laws had been introduced by the German Empire and were consequently viewed with suspicion as "foreign" by the French authorities. This foreignness was rendered even more suspect through their connection to Germany, and when combined with fears over Alsatian ambivalence to the French nation, such attachment to what appeared to be "German" law served to create concerns, which were compounded by French fears about the threat that Germany posed to national security.[43]

Proponents of the retention of Alsatian laws attempted to assuage such fears by arguing that legislation in Alsace was Alsatian, not German, or in other words not foreign but *French*.[44] By these means, they attempted to remove it from national suspicion and treat it as compatible with French systems. In order to present existing legislation as Alsatian rather than German, supporters of retaining local laws went to great efforts to stress their laws' French roots by demonstrating that they dated from earlier periods of French rule over Alsace. For example, politicians from across Alsace came together to demand the retention of the municipal law of 1895, which legislated for the power and autonomy granted to communes and communal government. The mayors of Alsace's three largest towns, Strasbourg, Colmar, and Mulhouse, stressed its advantages over the equivalent French legislation, most notably in granting communes far greater autonomy, particularly over their finances.[45] They argued that it offered a range of advantages, including allowing the Prefect more authority over communal budgets, and according communes the opportunity to participate in the local economy by creating and running municipal companies, which presented the chance to generate extra income. Such initiatives would be impossible if French law was introduced, they stressed.[46] The mayors succeeded in articulating the advantages of Alsatian communal law to their counterparts across France and were able to secure the support of a number of mayors and municipal officials from the French interior in their efforts to retain their municipal legislation and to see it introduced across France.[47]

In this campaign, as he made arguments for the retention of Alsatian municipal law, Socialist Mayor of Strasbourg Jacques Peirotes argued that the local law in Alsace in 1918 had been introduced when the region opted to become French in the immediate aftermath of the Revolution of 1789. He explained that it was then reversed by Napoleon, but reintroduced "on the initiative of the local population" after 1871.[48] That it shared inspiration with French municipal law could be seen in the similarities between the two, while, Peirotes pointed out, it was entirely different to the equivalent legislation in the other states of Germany.[49] Similar arguments (albeit from a different historical link) were developed by the departmental council of the Bas-Rhin, which stressed that Alsatian local law was based "on French communal administration and the law of ... 1837," rather than on any German initiative.[50]

In her study of Fiume after 1918, Dominique Reill has argued that while Fiumans may have desired an Italian future, they did not simply reject all Hungarian law in order to embrace it. Instead, they studied their options and selected the best of both to create a piecemeal marriage of the two, and, in so doing they cemented a culture of local self-determination.[51] In a similar fashion, Alsatians attempted to retain elements of existing law, and many of these efforts were not incompatible with a future within France. On the contrary, the fact that the law dated from the period of German rule was less important than its earlier origins in French history. This relabeling served the purpose of attempting to preserve these laws within a political context that was reluctant to allow the integration of any German systems and instruments. In this way, Alsatian elites offered a vision of sovereignty rooted in the region's past as a province of France as a means of accommodating difference after its return in 1918.

Competing Visions of Law and Sovereignty

The next point of contention regarding the reintegration of Alsatian legal systems into France was that of which laws should be introduced, which replaced and which, if any, should be allowed to remain. Of course, the answers to these questions depended on one's political standpoint. Making his case in 1922, Socialist Georges Weill argued that "the recovered provinces must not be deprived of the moral and political advantages of the fundamental laws of the Republic, in particular the secular laws, which clearly characterize the regime." But, he continued, in those areas which were not central to Frenchness, such as social insurance or municipal law, it should be possible to maintain local law until they could be extended to the rest of France.[52] For Weill the secular laws were fundamental to French identity because of the separation of church and state across France in 1905. This law was one of the most important elements of legislation introduced by the early Third Republic. Its introduction followed years of debate and controversies surrounding the role of the Catholic Church within France and set the tone for the subsequent years of the regime.[53] It was also part of the negotiation of the accommodation between regional and national identities; in her study of the department of the Finistère, for example, Caroline Ford showed how the local Catholic Party played an important role in the creation of a sense of French identity which was filtered through local values and understandings.

Weill's wish for the extension of separation appeared to be granted in 1924 when the center-left coalition led by Edouard Herriot won power. New Premier Herriot announced his government's intention to introduce "the whole of the republican legislation into Alsace and Lorraine" and specified that this would include the secular laws.[54] This declaration provoked spontaneous protests and demonstrations across the three departments. In the summer of 1924, 50,000 people participated in a demonstration over the issue in Strasbourg.[55] In Parliament, Mosellan deputy Robert Schumann stated:

> In the name of 21 of the 24 Alsatian and Lorrain deputies ... we were painfully shocked by the government's declaration, in that it proposes the introduction of the whole of the religious and educational legislation into the recovered departments. The governments which have taken power since 1918 have all reaffirmed the promises made during the War in the name of the French nation. We cannot watch the government outline a program that is in total contradiction with the programs on which seven eighths of the deputies of the affected departments were elected. Carrying out such a program would not only be contrary to ... democratic principles ..., but would also create serious problems in our region, for which we would take no responsibility.[56]

Schumann's opposition was echoed by departmental and municipal councils across the recovered departments, and by representatives of the region's Catholic and Protestant communities.[57] When Herriot announced that the abrogation of the Concordat would also mean the end of religious education, Catholic politicians, the clergy, and the population responded with a protest petition which collected 375,000 signatures, and protest resolutions were issued by the Catholic *Union Populaire Républicaine* and by municipal councils and Catholic Associations across Alsace.[58] At stake in these protests was the question of Alsatian traditions and culture, which, the protestors argued, would be lost if secularity was introduced.

Others adopted a different stance and offered an alternative vision of Alsatian culture which was compatible with the introduction of the secular legislation.[59] The 1924 General Assembly of the Protestant Federation of France offered proposals for how separation might be introduced into the three recovered departments.[60] Socialist Mayor of Strasbourg Jacques Peirotes sought to stress the existence of non-Catholic political cultures by arguing that Alsatian tradition, customs, and beliefs were not dependent on the Concordat, and that separation would not have a negative effect on regional culture.[61] It thus got to the heart of how to define what was quintessentially French on the one hand, and the space for Alsatian particularities within such a definition on the other. Both sides staked their claims for belonging based upon sharply contrasting views of what constituted France's essential cultures.

The supporters of separation were drowned out by the region's Catholic clergy, press, and politicians. Faced with continuing opposition Herriot announced that the

Concordat would remain in place. He resigned four months later in April 1925, and his successors proved reluctant to carry through the plans. The introduction of the secular laws was simply not a priority for the governments of the interwar years, which were more preoccupied with the introduction of the French language, and with maintaining popular opinion within the region. As a result, the Concordat remained in place in Alsace and the Moselle, within a universalist Republic which had separated Church and State in 1905.

In this sense, the case of Alsace stands apart from other examples covered in this volume where religion became a marker of nationality.[62] In the case of Alsace, the issue of religious denomination was not the central issue. Rather it was the question of secularity that proved contentious, as the political became national. France's official version of citizenship was based on the idea of "civic" belonging. According to this model, over and above ethnic criteria, participation in the national community was rooted in the desire to be French. This meant that how Frenchness was to be fashioned, through laws and other legal instruments which regulated belonging, appeared to be up for debate and Alsatians seized upon the question of secularity as one that was fundamental to the shaping of their place within the French national community. As a result, it proved to be especially controversial. For the government in Paris, the range of views in Alsace made decision-making challenging. Ultimately, the scale of the protests left them unprepared to risk further escalation of the movement which might provide an example to other regions seeking greater autonomy and could eventually undermine the coherence of the French nation-state.

In leaving the Concordat in place in Alsace and the Moselle, the French authorities avoided an escalation of Alsatian protest and ensured that such protest did not spread to other regions. But the failure to introduce separation created a sense of persistent difference, one which was compounded by distinct linguistic and cultural traditions. Laird Boswell's study of the reception of the Alsatian and Mosellans evacuated to the Limousin in anticipation of a German invasion in September 1939 highlights both the hosts' confusion at hearing the refugees speak a Germanic dialect and the animosity at the creation of schools which offered religious instruction.[63] Part of the problem was that such difference came as a surprise to the population of the Limousin. The loss of Alsace had formed part of a nationalist cult, and return had been presented as justification for the sacrifices of the First World War. As a result, it was difficult for the authorities to admit to either the extent of Alsatian difference, or the problems that they had encountered in reintegrating the recovered departments after 1918. Consequently, such problems (and the resulting difference) remained beyond the consciousness of much of the population of the French interior.

Throughout the interwar years, those local elites engaged in discussions over law accepted the return to France but staked their own visions of Alsace within it. Not everyone had the same view on this issue; for some, such as Robert Schumann, there needed to be space within French law for Alsatian distinctiveness, while for others Alsace would be the trigger for widespread change at the center. At the root of their arguments were distinct ideas of belonging, shaped by historical experience, regional attachment, and political worldviews. Meanwhile, the French authorities attempted the difficult balancing act of integrating the Alsatian population into the French national community, whilst avoiding any major upset that could destabilize popular opinion in the region. As demands for Alsatian *Heimatrechte* (homeland rights) proliferated in the 1920s, the government feared that the forced imposition of laws may lead to overt expressions of desire for autonomy from France, or even return to Germany. And they were keen to avoid such demands at all costs.

Unitary Law and the Third Republic

As the controversies over the Concordat suggested, a major issue was the question of *how* local law could be retained. Was it possible to be French and have distinct laws? Arguments for the retention of any regional particularities within the universalist French Republic were met with resistance because the Republic had been founded on the principle of universalism, which left little (if any) space for regional particularities. While much of this resistance came from Parisian academics, lawyers, and politicians, it also came from Alsatians.[64] For Strasbourg Socialist Deputy Georges Weill, it was not possible to maintain a separate legislature in Alsace, as this countered the "principle of unity, which, for centuries, had been the basis of [French] politics."[65] The result of doing so was that it left the population of Alsace languishing "on the edge of French life … in isolation."[66]

What is more, opponents of local law argued that granting concessions to the retention of local law in Alsace risked becoming a precedent, and they were keen to ensure the introduction of the French legal system and avoid the risk of another region demanding separate legislation. In response to such concerns, supporters of a counterproposal put forth the idea not only to keep local law intact in Alsace, but to introduce Alsatian law across France. This argument that the return of Alsace presented an opportunity for widespread national legislative reform was one that was taken up at various moments throughout the years after the region's return. For the Mulhousian politician, Jean Martin, Alsace's border position left the population particularly well placed to make comparisons with neighboring states, and they should be at the forefront of the wholesale reform that the return of Alsace needed to trigger.[67]

This was the position of Strasbourg Socialist Georges Well, whose 1924 proposed law on the reintegration of Alsace stated that in cases where German legislation was superior to its French equivalent, the government should modify the French legislation, as it would be "senseless to sacrifice progress already realized on a local level, and which will soon be acquired by France as a whole."[68] And, just as the inclusion of Alsace within the Republic's universalist legal framework had been proposed at both center and periphery, so too did the idea that there were cases where Alsatian law was superior. The view that Alsace represented a potential model for the rest of France was set out by Alexandre Millerand, the first *Commissaire Général* of the region and subsequent President of the Republic, who took a particular interest in the region's welfare laws.[69] With his support, the Bismarckian social insurance system which remained in Alsace after 1918 influenced parliamentary discussions over the extension of the system of medical and old-age insurance from the recovered departments to the rest of France.[70] And, in 1928 French legislators approved a German-style obligatory social insurance law over the objections of employers, who opposed any sort of state-mandated social welfare. In other areas, such as family support, it was the French system that was introduced into the recovered departments with the 1939 *Code de la Famille*. This swept away the former employer-led payments in Alsace and the Moselle and replaced them with a state scheme which rewarded large families at the expense of their smaller counterparts in a reflection of fears about depopulation and the growing pro-natalist movement.[71]

As had been the case with the laws of separation, no firm decision was reached over the wider introduction of Alsatian laws across France. The debates and discussions that the issue provoked were brought to a rapid and abrupt end by the outbreak of War in 1939. The following year, the invasion of France led to Alsace's de facto annexation into the Third Reich, and the introduction of an entire new set of laws and legal instruments as part of the Nazi regime. At the end of the War, Alsace returned to France and the dominant regional narrative was one of victimhood, as Alsatian representatives described the population as having been abandoned by France.[72] That Alsatians were victims of their circumstances was summed up in the label "*malgré nous*" (in spite of ourselves), used to describe those Alsatians who were forcibly conscripted into the German armed forces.

The Alsatian population's presentation of its victimhood clashed with the experiences of citizens from elsewhere in France who had been victims of Nazi violence and persecution in different ways. This triggered the ignition of tensions between Alsace and regions in the French interior, most notably when Alsatians had been participants in Nazi violence, albeit in many cases after coercion to join the German army or Waffen SS.[73] In an effort to avoid any threat to national coherence, the French authorities focused upon the issue of language and ensuring that French replaced Alsatian dialect as the dominant language in the region. The introduction of the laws of separation was quietly abandoned, and, in 1951 it was decided that local law would remain in place in Alsace without a time limit.[74] As a result, Alsace was left with its own separate legal instruments, many of which remain in place today.

Navigations of National Belonging

Today, the persistence of legal recognition of difference in Alsace remains. Good Friday, a bank holiday introduced under the German Empire, is celebrated throughout the region but not in the rest of France. It is possible to study theology at Alsatian universities, and to display religious insignia in the departments' classrooms, while the French Interior Ministry pays salaries to priests, pastors, and rabbis as civil servants. Such particularities are not, however, the result of a conscious decision to permit difference. Instead, they followed indecision and protests in response to proposals to introduce French law across the years after Alsace's 1918 return to France, and the interwar context left the French authorities unable to risk destabilizing national coherence by pushing through with reform. In light of these difficulties, the first interwar government set a limit of ten years for the introduction of all French laws into Alsace and the Moselle. But, by 1934, this goal was still far from reach and a subsequent law was passed in December 1934 prolonging the period of integration to 1945. In 1939, the Second World War intervened, and in the aftermath of Alsace's second annexation into Germany and return to France, regional legislative particularities were permitted to avoid the risk of destabilizing national cohesion as France attempted to rebuild and reshape French national identity after the conflict.

While this chapter has focused upon process rather than outcome, this situation is nonetheless revealing of the effects of the multiple visions of law which were staked in Alsace after the First World War, and of the ways in which Alsatians attempted to anchor sovereignty in their legal distinctiveness. Alsatians had long negotiated a multi-legal system—a world of "layered sovereignty" as scholars of international relations have described it.[75] As they attempted to pick and choose from the patchwork of laws that remained in 1918, they cited historical roots and visions of what they viewed as fundamentally French, as well as fundamentally Alsatian. And, as they engaged with the question of whether it was possible for a region of universalist Republican France to maintain a separate legislative structure, or whether the return of Alsace represented an opportunity for widespread national reform, Alsatian elites challenged dominant ideas about heterogeneity and sovereignty in France.

The process of the renegotiation of laws and legal instruments after the return of Alsace thus shows that France was prepared to listen to appeals for minority status if the failure to grant them threatened national cohesion. However, the lack of a final decision on many issues is indicative of just how challenging these questions were. After all, they remain in place today only because the Second World War interrupted the process of negotiation, not because the French authorities decided to make permanent exceptions. What is more, such tolerance of difference was not extended to other peripheral or marginalized communities within France. Therefore, while the case of Alsace's attempts to navigate national belonging after its return to France in 1918 reveals that there was space for particularism in French universalism, it equally demonstrates that this space was both limited and context specific.

Notes

1   Schoolteacher Philippe Husser, who lived in the southern Alsatian city of Mulhouse, noted in the summer of 1918 that the price of wine had gone up, leading to increased speculation that return to France was imminent. See Philippe Husser, *Un Instituteur Alsacien. Entre France et Allemagne: Le Journal de Philippe Hussuer, 1914–1951* (Strasbourg: La Nueé Bleue/Paris: Hachette, 1989), 115.
2   *L'Excelsior*, November 27, 1918; *Le Petit Parisien*, November 27, 1918.
3   *Le Temps*, December 10, 1918. On return more broadly, see Alison Carrol, *The Return of Alsace to France, 1918–1939* (Oxford: Oxford University Press, 2018).
4   See Volker Prott's chapter in this volume, and also Volker Prott, *The Politics of Self-determination: Remaking Territories and National Identities in Europe, 1917–1923* (Oxford: Oxford University Press, 2016), 69–72.
5   Peter Becker and Natasha Wheatley, eds., *Remaking Central Europe. The League of Nations and the Former Habsburg Lands* (Oxford: Oxford University Press, 2019); Marcus M. Payk and Roberta Pergher, eds., *Beyond Versailles: Sovereignty,*

Legitimacy, and the Formation of New Polities After the Great War (Bloomington, IN: Indiana University Press, 2019); Eric Weitz, "From the Vienna to the Paris System: International Politics and the Entangled Histories. of Human Rights, Forced Deportations, and Civilizing Missions," *The American Historical Review* 113, no. 5 (2019): 1313–43; Natasha Wheatley, "Central Europe as Ground Zero of the New International Order," *Slavic Review* 78, no. 4 (2019): 900–11; Norman Ingram and Carl Bouchard, eds., *Beyond the Great War. Making Peace in a Disordered World* (Toronto: University of Toronto Press, 2022); Robert Gerwarth, "The Sky beyond Versailles: The Paris Peace Treaties in Recent Historiography," *Journal of Modern History* 93, no. 4 (2021): 896–930; Paul Miller and Claire Morelon, eds., *Embers of Empire: Continuity and Rupture in the Habsburg Successor States after 1918* (New York: Berghahn, 2019).

6   Dominique Kirchner Reill, *The Fiume Crisis. Life in the Wake of the Habsburg Empire* (Cambridge, MA: Belknap Press of Harvard University Press, 2020). See also the Nepostrans project led by Gabor Egry, https://1918local.eu/ (accessed June 28, 2022).

7   For an alternative experience in Western Europe, see Brian Hughes' chapter in this volume, which traces the experience of loyalists in Southern Ireland and the strategies by which they maintained their existing loyalties while adapting to life in the Republic.

8   On the cult of Alsace see Laurence Turetti, *Quand la France pleurait Alsace-Lorraine. Les "provinces perdues" aux sources du patriotisme républicain* (Strasbourg: La Nueé Bleue, 2008) and Karine Varley's chapter, "The Lost Provinces," in Varley, *Under the Shadow of Defeat. The French War of 1870–71 in French Memory* (Basingstoke: Palgrave Macmillan, 2008).

9   Carrol, *Return of Alsace*.

10 Eugen Weber, *Peasants into Frenchmen. The Modernization of Rural France 1870–1914* (Stanford, CA: Stanford University Press, 1976).

11 Weber, *Peasants into Frenchmen*.

12 Caroline Ford, *Creating the Nation in Provincial France: Religion and Political Identity in Brittany* (Princeton, NJ: Princeton University Press, 1993); Peter Sahlins, *Boundaries. The Making of France and Spain in the Pyrenees* (Berkeley, CA: University of California Press, 1989); Sharif Gemie, *Brittany 1750–1950: The Invisible Nation* (Cardiff: University of Wales Press, 2007).

13 Judith Surkis, *Sex, Law and Sovereignty in French Algeria, 1830–1930* (Ithaca, NY: Cornell University Press, 2019); Gary Wilder, *The French Imperial Nation State: Negritude and Colonial Humanism between the Wars* (Chicago, IL: University of Chicago Press, 2005).

14 For the divergent history of annexed Lorraine, see Carolyn Grohmann, "Problems of Reintegrating Annexed Lorraine into France, 1918–1925" (PhD thesis, University of Stirling, 2000); Louisa Zanoun, "Interwar Politics in a French Border Region: The Moselle in the Period of the Popular Front, 1934–1938" (PhD thesis, The London School of Economics and Political Science (LSE), 2009).

15 C. A. Macartney, *National States and National Minorities* (Oxford: Oxford University Press, 1934), 482.

16 Leonard V. Smith, *Sovereignty at the Paris Peace Conference of 1919* (Oxford: Oxford University Press, 2018); Payk and Pergher, *Beyond Versailles*.

17 Philip Charles Farwell Bankwitz, *Alsatian Autonomist Leaders, 1919–47* (Lawrence: Regents Press of Kansas, 1978); Samuel Huston Goodfellow, *Between the Swastika and the Cross of Lorraine: Fascisms in Interwar Alsace* (De Kalb: Northern Illinois University Press, 1999).

18 David Stevenson, "French War Aims and the American Challenge, 1914–1918," *The Historical Journal* 22, no. 4 (1979): 877–94, 884.
19 Laird Boswell, "From Liberation to Purge Trials in the 'Mythic Provinces': Recasting French Identities in Alsace and Lorraine, 1918–1920," *French Historical Studies* 23, no. 1 (2000): 129–62; Sebastian Döderlein, "Not so Republican After All? The Ambiguous End of the Great War in Alsace-Lorraine, 1918–1919," in *Beyond the Great War*, ed. Ingram and Bouchard.
20 The National Archives (hereafter TNA) CAB/24/70 Note by Arthur Balfour, October 18, 1918.
21 "Berne Conferees Vote for Alsace Plebiscite," *The New York Times*, February 9, 1919. On proposals for neutrality, see Archives Departémentales du Bas-Rhin (hereafter ADBR) 121AL 207, Commissaire Générale de la République to Garde des Sceaux, Strasbourg, January 1923. See also Christian Baechler, "La question de la neutralité de l'Alsace-Lorraine à la fin de la Première Guerre Mondiale et pendant le Congres de Paix (1917–1929)," *Revue d'Alsace* 114 (1988): 185–208; François G. Dreyfus, *La vie politique en Alsace, 1919–1936* (Paris: Les Presses de Sciences Po, 1969), 32.
22 Vladimir Lenin, "Decree on Peace, 26 October 1917," in *The Bolshevik Revolution 1917–1918: Documents and Materials*, ed. James Bunyan and Harold Henry (Stanford, CA: Stanford University Press, 1961).
23 David Lloyd George, "British War Aims, 5 January 1918," in *English Historical Documents, 1906–1939*, ed. J. H. Bettey (London: Routledge and Kegan Paul, 1967).
24 Marcus M. Payk and Roberta Pergher, "Introduction," in *Beyond Versailles*, ed. Payk and Pergher, 1.
25 TNA, CAB/24/70 Note by Arthur Balfour, October 18, 1918.
26 Prott, *Politics of Self-Determination*, 69–72.
27 Just 6.1 percent of the Haut-Rhin population and only 3.8 percent of Bas-Rhiners spoke French as their first language. Christopher J. Fischer, *Alsace to the Alsatians? Visions and Divisions of Alsatian Regionalism, 1870–1939* (New York and Oxford: Berghahn Books, 2010), 135. On the other hand, 93 percent of the Haut-Rhin and 95.8 percent of the Bas-Rhin population were able to speak dialect in 1910. The number of Bas-Rhiners that spoke only French increased from 26,365 to 60,465 (or 3.9 percent to 9.9 percent) and in the Haut-Rhin the total increased from 31,760 to 53,351 (or 6.3 percent to 11.6 percent) by 1931, and the number that spoke French as their habitual language increased in the Bas-Rhin from 4.1 percent to 20.2 percent and in the Haut-Rhin from 6.5 percent to 22.5 percent. According to the 1910 census, 93 percent of the Haut-Rhin and 95.8 percent of the Bas-Rhin population spoke dialect as their first language. See Marcel Koch, "Les Mouvements de la Population," in *L'Alsace depuis son retour à la France, 3 Vols*, vol. 1, ed. Comité alsacien d'études et d'informations (Strasbourg: Comité alsacien d'études et d'informations, 1932), 345–6. French use varied by generation, gender, class, religion, and locality. On the use of French amongst different sections of the population, see Carrol, *Return of Alsace* (especially Chapter 5). On the gendered dimensions of language, see Elizabeth Vlossak, *Marianne or Germania? The Nationalisation of Women in Alsace 1870–1946* (Oxford: Oxford University Press, 2010).
28 A cards were issued to those born in Alsace to French or Alsatian parents, B cards to those born in Alsace-Lorraine with only one French or Alsatian parent, C cards were issued to foreign subjects of non-enemy states such as Italy, and D cards were given to all those who were born in enemy countries, or to two parents from enemy countries. As these "enemy countries" included Germany alongside Austria, Hungary, Turkey,

and Bulgaria, a large proportion of the population of Alsace received them. As many as 513,800 D cards were issued, alongside 1,082,650 A cards, 183,500 B cards and 55,050 C cards. This process is covered in Volker Prott's chapter in this volume, in addition to David Allen Harvey "Lost Children or Enemy Aliens? Classifying the Population of Alsace after the First World War," *Journal of Contemporary History* 34, no. 4 (1999): 552–84; Carolyn Grohmann, "From Lothringen to Lorraine: Expulsion and Voluntary Repatriation," *Diplomacy and Statecraft* 16, no. 3 (2005): 571–87, 576; Irmgard Grünewald, *Die Elsass-Lothringer im Reich, 1918–1933* (Frankfurt am Main: Peter Lang, 1984), 29; Tara Zahra, "The 'Minority Problem' and National Classification in the French and Czechoslovak Borderlands," *Contemporary European History* 17, no. 2 (2008): 141–4.

29 ADBR, 121AL 204, Projet de loi relatif au régime transitoire de l'Alsace et de la Lorraine. Exposé des motifs, 1919.
30 ADBR, 121AL 204, Commissaire Général de la République to Président du Conseil, Strasbourg, April 7, 1919.
31 For more details on these expulsions, see Volker Prott's chapter in this volume.
32 See Carrol, *The Return of Alsace*, 144–59.
33 ADBR 286D 46. Président du Tribunal de Première Instance (Carré de Malberg) et le Procurer de la République (Corbière) près les Tribunal de Première Instance to Préfet de Bas Rhin, Strasbourg, November 3, 1930.
34 ADBR 286D 46. Sous-préfet de Sélestat (Bastier) to Préfet du Bas Rhin, October 29, 1925; Sous-préfet de Saverne (Peyromaure-Debord) to Préfet du Bas Rhin, October 30, 1925; Sous-préfet d'Erstein (Hoerter) to Préfet du Bas Rhin, October 27, 1925; Sous-préfet Chathonet of Wissembourg to Préfet du Bas Rhin, October 23, 1925; President du Conseil (Poincaré) to Préfet du Bas Rhin, July 16, 1927; Sous-préfet of Haguenau (Le Hoc) to Préfet du Bas Rhin, October 29, 1925; President du Conseil (Poincaré) to Préfet du Bas Rhin, July 16, 1927.
35 ADBR, 121AL 205, Questionnaire No. 2 de M. le Président de la Commission d'Alsace et Lorraine du Sénat.
36 ADBR 286D 44, Mayor of Schiltigheim to Préfet du Bas-Rhin, March 30, 1922.
37 *Archives Municipales de la Ville et Communauté Urbaine de Strasbourg* (hereafter AMVCUS) 113Z 29, Jean Kuntzingen to abbé Muller, Strasbourg, June 6, 1921.
38 When it was reconstituted in 1936, Alsatian deputies proposed that it be based in Strasbourg. This was refused by the government, and by the Mosellan senator Stuhl, who stated that the Moselle did not wish to return to the days of dependency upon Strasbourg. Gustave Mary, "L'évolution politique depuis 1932," in *L'Alsace depuis son retour à la France. Premier supplément: Vie politique administrative et sociale; Vie intellectuelle; artistique et spirituelle; Vie économique*, ed. Comité alsacien d'études et d'informations (Strasbourg: Comité alsacien d'études et d'informations, 1937), 28.
39 F. Pfersdorff, "Le Droit Penal et l'Organisation Penitentiaire," in *L'Alsace depuis son retour à la France*, vol. 1, ed. Comité alsacien d'études et d'informations, 117.
40 ADBR 121AL 207, Directeur Régional des Postes et des Télégraphes to Commissaire Général de la République, Strasbourg, November 29, 1922; *Journal Officiel*, Séance du May 25, 1925, 2331.
41 ADBR 121AL 207, Note to the Secrétaire Général, Strasbourg, September 27, 1922.
42 AMVCUS 125Z 52, Discours de Jacques Peirotes; ADBR 121AL 207, Commissaire Général de la République to Garde des Sceaux, Strasbourg, January 1923.
43 Conan Fischer, *A Vision of Europe: Franco-German Relations during the Great Depression, 1929–1932* (Oxford: Oxford University Press, 2017); Peter Jackson,

Beyond the Balance of Power. France and the Politics of National Security in the Era of the First World War (Cambridge: Cambridge University Press, 2013); Michael E. Nolan, *The Inverted Mirror. Mythologizing the Enemy in France and Germany, 1898–1914* (New York and Oxford: Berghahn, 2005). On perceived Alsatian ambivalence to France, see Alison Carrol, "Paths to Frenchness. National Indifference and the Return of Alsace to France, 1919–1939," in *National Indifference and the History of Nationalism in Modern Europe*, ed. Maarten van Ginderachter and Jon Fox (London: Routledge, 2019).

44 *Archives Nationales* (hereafter AN) 470AP/44, Journal officiel du 2 octobre 1919. Chambre des députés 1ère séance du 1 October 1919.
45 AMVCUS 204MW 16, Jacques Peirotes to Mayors of Alsace and Lorraine, Strasbourg, November 20, 1922; ADBR 121AL 740, Resolution of Mayors of large communes of Alsace and Lorraine, Strasbourg, July 21, 1923.
46 AMVCUS 125Z 38 (nd) Exposé: "La Loi Municipale d'Alsace-Lorraine du 6 June 1895."
47 In 1920, the Eleventh Congress of Mayors of France adopted a resolution demanding that the departments of Alsace and the Moselle should retain their law, and that the French law should be modified to bring it closer to the Alsatian Law. See AMVCUS, 204 MW 16, Strasbourg, November 23, 1922, Speech by Jacques Peirotes to assembled mayors of Alsace-Lorraine.
48 AMVCUS 125Z 32, Discours de Jacques Peirotes, nd; AMVCUS 125Z 38 (nd) Exposé: "La Loi Municipale d'Alsace-Lorraine du 6.6. 1895" historique, grandes et petites communes- composition et fonctionnement des conseils municipaux, la municipalité, les employés municipaux, l'autonomie communale, le budget communal, l'activité économique des communes, conclusion.
49 AMVCUS 125Z 38 (nd) Exposé: "La Loi Municipale d'Alsace-Lorraine du 6 June. 1895."
50 ADBR 121AL 740, Conseil Général du Bas-Rhin, Session de Septembre 1921. Extrait du procès verbal des délibérations, Séance du 23 septembre 1921.
51 Reill, *The Fiume Crisis*, 126.
52 AN AJ30 173 Session of the Conseil Consultatif of October 2, 1922.
53 Othon Guerlac, "The Separation of Church and State in France," *Political Science Quarterly* 23, no. 2 (1908): 259–96.
54 *Le Temps*, June 22, 1924.
55 Christian Baechler, "Espoirs et désillusions," in *Histoire de Strasbourg*, ed. Georges Livet and Francis Rapp (Toulouse and Strasbourg: Les Dernières Nouvelles d'Alsace, 1987), 411. The Commissaire Générale wrote that agitation was livelier and more widespread in Alsace than in the Moselle: AN AJ30 207, Commissaire Général de la République to the Président du Conseil, Strasbourg, July 11, 1924.
56 Cited in Pierre Zind, *Elsass-Lothringen Alsace Lorraine, une nation interdite, 1870–1940* (Paris: Copernic, 1979), 224.
57 The *Elsässer Kurier* of June 19 and the *Elsässer* of June 20 demanded a referendum on the educational question in Alsace.
58 ADBR 98AL 661, Resolution of the Ligue Catholique de Thann, Thann March 24, 1926; 1927 Ligue des Catholiques d'Alsace pamphlet entitled "Pour Dieu et pour la France." According to the *Elsässer*, by September 1924, 509 of 946 communes in Alsace had protested against the proposed introduction of separation. *Elsässer*, September 27, 1924; Jean-François Kovar, "Religion et Éducation: De la concorde à

la discorde," in *Chroniques d'Alsace au Champs, à l'Usine, au Messti 1918–1939*, ed. Bernard Vogler (Strasbourg: Editeur G4j, 2004), 46–9, 51.

59 AMVCUS 125Z 18, Rapport fait au nom de la commission chargée d'examiner le projet de loi portent réorganisation du régime administratif des départements 68, 67, et 57 par Georges Weill; ADBR, 121AL 856, Commissaire Spéciale. Rapport, Strasbourg, January 13, 1923. Report on a meeting of Ligue des Droits de l'Homme held at Strasbourg, January 12, 1923; AN AJ30 173, Session of the Conseil Consultatif of October 2, 1922; ADBR, 286D 328 *Die Freie Presse,* July 5, 1924.

60 ADBR 121AL 95, Commissaire Spécial to Préfet du Bas-Rhin, October 27, 1924; *Le Journal d'Alsace et de Lorraine,* October 24, 1924; for the government's response see AN AJ30 207 Commissaire Général de la République to Président du Conseil, Strasbourg July 11, 1924.

61 AMVCUS 125Z 37, A14. May 20, 1927, Proposition de loi.

62 See in particular Brian Hughes', Olga Linkiewicz's and Volker Prott's chapters in this volume.

63 Laird Boswell, "Franco-Alsatian Conflict and the Crisis of National Sentiment during the Phoney War," *The Journal of Modern History* 71, no. 3 (1999): 552–84.

64 ADBR 121AL 207, Introduction des Lois Françaises en France. Conférence faite le 1er mai 1922 par M. Albert Chéron; Marcel Nast, *Le Malaise Alsacien-Lorrain* (Paris: G. Crès, 1920), 49.

65 ADBR 121AL 204, Projet de Loi par Georges Weill. Rapport fait au nom de la Commission d'Alsace-Lorraine, chargée d'examiner le projet de loi portant réorganisation du régime administratif des départements du Haut Rhin, du Bas Rhin et de la Moselle par M. Georges Weill. No. 965, annexe au procès verbal de la 2e séance du 26 décembre 1924.

66 ADBR 286D 336. Programme for the legislative elections of May 11, 1924, SFIO, Fédération of Bas Rhin.

67 Archives Municipales de Mulhouse (hereafter AMM) Fonds Jean Martin 40TT 8, *La Revue d'Alsace et de Lorraine,* no. 33, September 1921.

68 AMVCUS Fonds Jacques Peirotes 125Z 18, Rapport fait au nom de la commission chargée d'examiner le projet de loi portent réorganisation du régime administratif des départements 68, 67, et 57 par Georges Weill.

69 AN 470AP/44, Fonds Millerand, Discours prononcé à la Première Assemblée de l'Office général des assurances sociales, le 5 mai 1919; Alexandre Millerand, *Le retour de l'Alsace-Lorraine à la France* (Paris: Bibliotheque Charpentier, 1923), 70.

70 Paul V. Dutton, *Origins of the French Welfare State. The Struggle for Social Reform in France, 1914–1947* (Cambridge: Cambridge University Press, 2002).

71 Paul V. Dutton, "French versus German approaches to Family Welfare in Lorraine, 1918–1940," *French History* 13, no. 4 (1999): 439–63.

72 Thomas Williams, "Remaking the Franco-German Borderlands: Historical Claims and Commemorative Practices in the Upper Rhine, 1940–49" (Unpublished DPhil. dissertation, University of Oxford, 2010).

73 This clash of ideas of victimhood was most evident in the 1953 Bordeaux Trial of the perpetrators of the massacre at Oradour-sur-Glane. Of the twenty-one men brought to trial, fourteen were from Alsace and the Moselle, and thirteen of this number had been conscripted by force into the Waffen SS. The guilty verdicts delivered to the men were followed by an amnesty in the name of national reconciliation. See Sarah Farmer, *Martyred Village. Commemorating the 1944 Massacre at Oradour-sur-Glane* (Berkeley, CA: University of California Press, 2000); Frédéric Mégret, "The Bordeaux

Trial," in *The Hidden Histories of War Crimes Trials*, ed. Kevin Heller and Gerry Simpson (Oxford: Oxford University Press, 2013).
74 H. Patrick Glenn, "The Local Law of Alsace-Lorraine: A Half Century of Survival," *The International and Comparative Law Quarterly* 2, no. 4 (1974): 769–90.
75 Lauren A. Benton, *A Search for Sovereignty: Law and Geography in European Empires, 1400–1900* (Cambridge: Cambridge University Press, 2010).

Part Four

Minority Mobilization beyond the Nation-state

12

Internationalist Patriots? Minority Nationalists, Ethnic Minorities, and the Global Interwar Stage, 1918–39

Xosé M. Núñez Seixas and David J. Smith

In the aftermath of the First World War state borders in Central and Eastern Europe were redrawn at the Paris Peace Conference. Large numbers of the region's inhabitants were thereby consigned to minority status within new, putatively national states, while the armed conflicts that subsequently broke out between various successor states, along with the progression of the Russian Civil War, also forced hundreds of ethno-nationalist and minority activists into exile. Many of those belonging to national and ethnic minorities could easily find refuge in their respective kin-states, from Weimar Germany to post-Trianon Hungary. They set up networks of political and cultural associations that served as the bases for stirring up irredentism, with official state support and often also with the collaboration of large portions of the homeland's revisionist and nationalist parties.

These activists were joined by many other ethno-nationalists with no motherland, who took refuge in former imperial centers such as Vienna and Berlin, as well as Paris, London, and Geneva. The latter acquired new visibility when the League of Nations was established there in 1920. All these cities became centers of agitation for ethno-nationalist émigrés, who tried to influence neutral public opinion in favor of their respective causes. Paradoxically, imperial capitals such as Paris or London, as well as former imperial cities like Vienna and Berlin, became "anti-imperial metropoles," where anti-imperialist and anti-colonial agitation was triggered. Anti-colonialist students from the imperial peripheries had the chance to exchange views with Eastern European nationalist exiles, White Russians, social revolutionaries from Latin America, and irredentist activists.[1]

As the preceding example illustrates, ethno-nationalist and minority activists did not only look to kin-states and their own diaspora networks when seeking to promote their cause internationally. They also came together within a variety of transnational alliances and organizations. The most notable among these was the Congress of European Nationalities (CEN), which provides the focus for the second part of this chapter. Established in Geneva in 1925, the Congress continued to meet annually until 1938, bringing together around 300 spokespersons for twenty national minority groups from fifteen European states during the course of its existence. The prominent place of German minorities within the CEN meant that from 1933, the organization increasingly came under the sway of external influence from Nazi Germany. As such, it was understandably portrayed in highly negative terms after 1945, within a literature that generally cast ethno-nationalist leaders and émigrés more broadly as professional troublemakers and—willingly or unwillingly—fellow travelers of the Fascist powers.

The picture is, however, more complex and nuanced than previous accounts often suggest. As will be shown in this chapter, ethno-nationalist activists and exiles in fact identified with a wide range of different political creeds. Some certainly came under the influence of integralist visions of the nation and were subsequently seduced by the fascist worldview. In their eyes, fascist Italy and/or Nazi Germany incarnated the best of values such as the cult of the nation, while upholding a strong anti-communist stance. Indeed, early fascists such as Gabriele D'Annunzio identified sub-state nationalists and/ or ethnic activists as possible allies for challenging the Versailles settlement.[2] In other cases, activists' allegiance to the ethnic and cultural concept of the nation led them to take strategic risks, or simply seal pragmatic alliances with Nazis and Fascists. Yet, the activist movement was also home to anti-fascists during the 1930s, while another strand found inspiration in the Marxist-Leninist approach to national liberation and was fascinated by the nationalities policy of the Soviet Union. In fact, Moscow became at times a pole of attraction for non-communist nationalist émigrés seeking external support, and until 1934 communist parties embraced the Bolshevik doctrine of self-determination following the Peoples' Conference of Baku (1920) and the first Soviet Constitution issued in 1924. To them, support for anti-colonial aspirations and national minority claims was highly instrumental in destabilizing and destroying the capitalist states.[3]

New groups of ethno-nationalist exiles also appeared in the 1920s and 1930s. These included Catalan, Basque, Galician, Sardinian, South Tyrolean, and Slovenian exiles from Spain and Italy, alongside Irish political exiles in the early 1920s (particularly *Sinn Féin* activists and later on Irish Republican Army members). These were accompanied by nationalist activists from the distant peripheries of the British, French, and Dutch empires (India, Vietnam, Indonesia), who frequently interacted with European ethno-nationalists.[4] This latter group generally remained committed to democracy, while some leaned toward communism, and were much less susceptible to the "lure" of fascism than their Eastern European counterparts. Finally, the leaders of Jewish minorities in Central and Eastern Europe constituted another faction.

While activists from different parts of Europe could all be broadly labeled as "ethnic entrepreneurs," they often interacted and merged with liberal activists, academics, and intellectuals in Paris, London, Vienna, or Geneva, who intended to represent broader segments of European public opinion concerned with the pursuit of peace and the freedom of peoples, nations, and races. This interaction can be understood as a facet of the new internationalism that took shape after 1918.[5] It was enhanced by the existence of the League of Nations, as well as by the implementation within the

League of a system of protection of minorities that, despite its limitations, established for the first time a transnational framework of principles and rules that attempted to prevent ethnic minorities from forceful assimilation by the ethnic majorities of their nation-states.

The first part of this chapter maps out these varied orientations within the activist movement, as well as its interactions with broader transnational networks concerned with finding solutions to the "minority problem" in interwar Europe. The chapter then proceeds to explore further the dynamics at work during this period through an analysis of the Congress of European Nationalities. It seeks to demonstrate that while the CEN certainly encompassed a broad spectrum of different orientations from the very outset, it was initially conceived and nested within the new international legal framework of minority protection embodied by the League of Nations. As such, leading CEN activists such as Paul Schiemann participated actively in European discussions of what minority rights were, what national, ethnic, and religious/racial minorities were, and how to reconcile the principle of state sovereignty with the accommodation of ethnic and national diversity. This in turn gave rise to a transnational discussion on nationality theory that paralleled the first steps of nationalism studies in the United Kingdom, Germany, France, and the United States, and that of the protection of human rights. To a certain extent, the transnational debate on minority protection picked up where the previous debate on the nationality principle during the conflict had left off.[6] As the chapter will show however, the Congress—like other attempts to forge transnational alliances at the time—was hampered and ultimately undermined by the internal heterogeneity of its membership. It proved to be extremely difficult to reconcile the diverse demands stemming from divergent national claims, such as those of autonomist factions versus irredentist or pro-independence groups, or those of national minorities seeking reintegration into their motherland as opposed to groups seeking independent recognition of their nationalities.[7]

Mapping Transnational Activist Networks for Minority Rights in Interwar Europe

Nationalist émigrés and transnational activists had existed throughout the nineteenth century, from the Italian Giuseppe Garibaldi and his fellow leaders of *Risorgimento* nationalism to Romanian and Bulgarian exiles in London and Paris, Irish nationalists in the United States, and Polish émigrés in Paris. Until the end of the nineteenth century, they were overwhelmingly liberal or republican oriented.[8] From the beginning of the twentieth century until the eve of the First World War, in great European capitals such as London and Paris new alliances emerged between nationalist émigrés and the British, Swiss, and French liberal left. Some republicans and radical liberals, many of them professional opinion makers, journalists, and academics, advocated the right to self-determination for European (and occasionally even non-European) nationalities, as a means to better achieve peace and freedom for all citizens of Europe. They criticized the purported oppression of national minorities and stateless nations within multinational empires, particularly within the Ottoman and Austro-Hungarian (and sometimes Russian) domains, and established close links between the full democratization of Europe, the pursuit of peace, and the satisfaction of national demands all over Europe. Certainly, this was not deprived of some degree of national chauvinism. Macedonian, Armenian, Lithuanian, and other émigrés managed to establish some connections with broader segments of French and British public opinion through liberal associations such as anti-slavery societies. These and other associations had positioned themselves at the origins of organizations such as the *Ligue des Droits de l'Homme* (Human Rights League), the Fabian Society, and several peace associations that attempted to establish a transnational network. British "champions of nationalities" were eager to accept self-determination for Slovakia and Croatia, but not for Ireland. Their French counterparts firmly believed that France was ethnically homogeneous; therefore, as a full-fledged democratic nation-state it was entitled to raise the banner of self-determination.[9]

Alongside the defense of worldwide peace, tolerance, international cooperation, and human equality, Western European intellectuals and politicians became firm defenders of the rights of "oppressed nationalities," though generally limiting self-determination to "civilized" peoples. Minority leaders did not always share this political agenda and were far more interested in attaining external support for their national freedom. In this respect, a contradiction emerged. The "champions of nationalities" were motivated by liberalism, the rejection of "backward" empires, and the search for a new international order based on the peaceful coexistence of nations. However, ethno-nationalists searched for strategic allies among those who embraced their cause, regardless of their political orientation.

This pragmatic strategy was fully developed during the First World War and became the norm among nationalist exiles after 1918. Being heard in the emerging sphere of international public opinion also became a parallel objective for political and intellectual representatives of "oppressed" nationalities. This strategy had led earlier to the emergence of international platforms such as the *Union des Nationalités* (1912), an initiative founded in Paris by some exiled Lithuanians, Jewish Zionists, and other nationalist émigrés from Eastern Europe, shortly after they had met one year earlier at the Universal Race Congress held in London. At the Congress, the founder of the initiative, the Lithuanian exile Jean Gabrys, had also met the French journalist, René Pélissier, who was committed to the cause of oppressed peoples and who would work later for the French information services. Gabrys and Pélissier also attracted some Irish and Catalan nationalists and enjoyed the support of British writers and journalists, along with prominent French intellectuals such as the historian Charles Seignobos.[10]

Political contradictions between nationalist activists and international pacifists became evident during the Great War. Both sides, but especially the Entente, presented the conflict as a war to liberate the small nations oppressed by the enemy. This strategy opened certain doors in the foreign ministries in London, Paris, and Washington for ethno-nationalist émigrés from the Austro-Hungarian and Ottoman Empires, although ethno-nationalist exiles from the Caucasus and the Baltic countries first attempted to win German support for their cause. They founded committees to carry out propaganda activities in Paris and London but preferred neutral soil, particularly in Switzerland. They first prioritized finding allies among the public opinion makers of the countries whose support they sought. They additionally looked for sympathizers with their cause who could "lobby" the staffs of the ministries of foreign affairs of those states. Good examples of this were the Czech nationalist leaders Tomás Masaryk and Edvard Benes. Their contact with the British Foreign Office was facilitated by influential mediators who endorsed their cause, such as the historians Robert W. Seton-Watson and Edward H. Carr.[11] The US President Woodrow Wilson enhanced the new legitimacy of nationality claims in his speech on war aims in January 1918. The presentation of his "Fourteen Points" program gave some groups of ethno-nationalist émigrés new opportunities for proto-diplomatic agitation, which was now rhetorically reinforced by their appeal to Wilsonian principles: the term "Wilsonianism" was almost equated to national self-determination.[12]

The final break-up of European multi-ethnic empires was not only achieved by the direct influence of ethno-nationalist émigrés. The latter certainly benefited from exceptional geopolitical circumstances. Ethno-nationalist exiles and activists could rely on a robust propaganda network abroad and on mediators in the diplomatic staffs of the Entente powers. The academic advisors of the main delegations, who drew the new map of Europe at the Paris Peace Conference, were influenced to some extent by émigrés. The representatives of the Jewish minorities in Paris, such as the British journalist Lucien Wolf, also played a crucial role behind the scenes. First imposed on Poland, in part as a result of Jewish lobbying activities and of the impact on European public opinion of notorious antisemitic pogroms in late 1918 and early 1919, the minority treaties soon extended to all minorities "of race, language and religion" in the successor states of Central and Eastern Europe and the Middle East, as well as in some states already in existence before the war (Greece, Bulgaria, and Romania). This established the framework for an international system of minorities protection under the umbrella of the League of Nations.[13]

The elites of nationalist movements in Europe saw proto-diplomatic agitation in times of global turmoil as an important element for more effectively attaining their objectives.[14] However, not all émigrés enjoyed similar opportunities. Irish and Indian nationalists sent delegations to Paris but were not allowed to present their claims at the Peace Conference because during the Great War they had opposed the eventual winners. Something similar happened with several political groupings from Catalonia to Brittany. They all attempted to send memorandums to the various delegations at the Peace Conference.[15] Even so, the example of ethno-nationalists who succeeded in achieving their objectives after 1918 influenced the strategies of those who sought to follow in their footsteps. They learned the compulsory nature of setting up propaganda bureaus in the greatest European capitals; they presented their claims in multilingual brochures and journals to influence international public opinion. They sought to gain the support of intellectuals, journalists, and influential elites in London, Vienna, Paris, Berlin, or Geneva, and they established what amounted to a permanent siege of the fledgling League of Nations.

Nationalist, but Anti-fascist Émigrés

As the Catalan leader Joan Estelrich wrote to a fellow Catalanist in November 1927, "Europe is full of desperate people like us," i.e., nationalist exiles in search of external support for their homelands. This was the reason why "our presence in international organizations" was the best way to "add value to our task."[16] In fact, many of them were sheer political opportunists able to seal an alliance with any great power ready to promise them national freedom. The "Promethean" networks promoted by Polish intelligence, and directly inspired by Marshal Pilsudski's policy of contention of Soviet expansion, attempted to gather Ukrainian, Crimean Tartars, Caucasian, and Central Asian nationalists opposed to Moscow's rule. "Prometheans" sustained the activities of the latter groups, as well as the publication of several journals and anti-Soviet propaganda, in Paris, Warsaw, and Istanbul, among other cities. Moreover, the research conducted by the Polish Institute of Oriental Studies (*Instytut Wschodni*) also served the objectives of the Prometheans. However, from the mid-1920s onward, two varieties of ethno-nationalist émigrés and activists consciously raised the banner of anti-fascism and attempted to combine an agenda of national liberation (or at least of gaining political recognition of collective rights for their territories) with opposition to fascist and authoritarian regimes.[17]

The first was a group that emerged from ethnic parties in Italy after the rise of fascism. It included some leaders of the Sardinian home-rule movement that had emerged in 1918, as well as representatives of the Slovenians from the Gorizia region. One example was Josip Vilfan, a lawyer from Trieste and former deputy in the Italian parliament in Rome. Until his exile to Vienna in 1928, he was a moderate who, along with the other Slovenian deputies from Gorizia-Trieste, aimed at a fruitful collaboration with the Italian majority.[18] Unlike Sardinians, who opted for joining Italian anti-fascist platforms, exiled Slovenian and South Tyrolean leaders gave priority to defending their respective motherlands within the framework of European alliances. This strategy found resonance in German revisionism, which sponsored committees of fellow countrymen established in Germany and Austria, with the objective of agitating for the "recovery" of South Tyrol.[19]

Catalan, Basque, and Galician ethno-nationalist exiles constituted the second group. They were forced to leave Spain during the Primo de Rivera dictatorship (1923–30) and again after the rebel victory in the Spanish Civil War (1936–9). During the second half of the 1920s, Catalan émigrés were especially active in France, Belgium, and Latin America. However, they were politically very fragmented and followed divergent strategies. Conservative and moderate Catalanists in exile attempted to present Catalonia as a "national minority" not covered by the minority treaties. They denounced the oppression of the Catalan language by the dictatorship as a violation of the rights granted by the treaties, hoping to force the League of Nations to intervene. Catalanist moderate exiles established some links with French liberals and regionalists in the *Fédération Régionaliste Française* (French Regionalist Federation).[20] For their part, Catalan left-wing and radical nationalists found support among Catalan immigrants in France and the Americas, as well as among some groups of Italian anti-fascists in exile. Other relevant allies among the nationalist émigrés and representatives in Paris included the Irish Bureau, the Committee of Jewish Delegations (*Comité des Délégations Juives*), and certain German representatives of the later Congress of European Nationalities founded in 1925 (see below). The *Estat Català* (Catalan State) group, led by Francesc Macià, represented the separatist faction of Catalan émigrés. They were the first to propose the creation of a League of Oppressed Nations that would bring together Irish, Galicians, Basques, and anti-colonial nationalists.[21]

Liberal and Pacifist Networks: A Platform for Minority Rights Advocacy

The emergence of an international system for protection of minorities under the legal umbrella of the League of Nations added to the newly acquired legitimacy of the nationality principle among broad sectors of organized public opinion in Britain and France.[22] Liberal and pacifist associations such as the Human Rights League and the League of Nations Union helped shape a transnational space that gave a platform to the claims of representatives of national minorities. At least four partially overlapping international networks articulated that space.

The first was the international League of Nations movement, supported by left-wing and liberal associations in the most important European and American states. Their social impact was uneven in the various parts of Europe. In some countries, notably Britain, the League of Nations Unions enjoyed widespread social support. In other states, such as Germany, they were mostly supported by the government and amalgamated naïve pacifists, radical democrats, and liberals along with representatives of Protestant churches, all of whom sought to establish a new international order.[23] Before the consolidation of the minority protection system at the League of Nations, there were attempts at founding international committees for the defense of "peoples' rights." For example, the *Bureau International pour la Défense du Droit des Peuples* (International Bureau for the Defense of the Rights of Peoples) was active in Geneva between 1920 and 1922. Though presumably sponsored by the Polish government, it was directed by Swiss journalist René Claparède, who had been engaged in the pacifist movement. In theory, the Bureau sought to uphold the cause of national minorities within the framework of human rights and participated in the first meetings of the international League of Nations movement.[24]

Minority activists soon discovered that founding League of Nations associations to represent their ethnic groups provided a good instrument for participating in the international conferences of the movement (renamed as the *Union Internationale des Associations pour la Société des Nations*, International Federation of League of Nations' Societies, UIA), which annually hosted representatives from all over the world. The first president of the organization, French Law Professor Théodore Ruyssen, was himself a defender of minority interests. He advocated a liberal concept of the nation based on the will of the people. Some British and continental champions of minorities had a prominent role in the UIA as well. Liberal MP Lord Willoughby Dickinson and the Dutch feminist Christina Bakker van Bosse paved the way for the active commitment of the UIA to improving and expanding minorities treaties.[25] This turned the organization into an interesting platform for representatives of nationalities and national minorities, who saw the Union as an appropriate place for gaining visibility and respectability alike. The UIA set up an advisory body on national minorities alongside similar organs—often with the same protagonists—established by the Interparliamentary Union, the World Alliance for the International Friendship through the Churches and the International Law Association. These attempted to play an avant-garde role in the emerging field of minority law. They also served as informal advisors to certain governments, although they were usually met with indifference by the League of Nations.[26]

Central and Eastern European émigrés and minority leaders played the card of cultivating the friendship of liberal internationalists. Thus, some British Labour and Liberal MPs committed themselves to defending the claims of Ukrainian minorities from Poland, or Hungarians from Romania.[27] French liberal and humanitarian internationalists also embraced the claims of European national minorities during the 1920s. Platforms could be found with links to the political factions of the French liberal left, such as the journal *Le Cri des Peuples*, edited by Bernard Lecache, a Jewish lawyer of communist leanings who was committed to defending the rights of the Jewish minorities.

A mixture of aesthetic avant-garde, revolutionary rhetoric, and petty-bourgeois non-conformism, the mouthpiece *Le Cri des Peuples* was first published as a weekly and later as a monthly journal between May 1928 and April 1929. From the very first issue, the journal proclaimed its aim of providing a "platform of solidarity" for "national, philosophic and religious minorities" around the globe. *Le Cri des Peuples'* commitment to national minorities reflected its liberal humanist stance. It held that weak individuals, groups, and minorities should be protected from states and gave priority to freedom of conscience and speech over all other matters. This did not mean that the journal embraced the nationality principle.[28] Furthermore, the journal also took an interest in the evolution of the minority question at the international level, first of all its management by the League of Nations. The journal addressed liberal internationalists, French Socialist and Radical-Socialist Party factions, anti-fascist, and nationalist exile committees, from Catalans to Egyptians. During the second half of 1928, *Le Cri des Peuples* increasingly reflected the claims and strategic demands put forward by the CEN.[29] However, in April 1929 *Le Cri des Peuples* ceased to exist. Though no evidence of German financial support has been found, the disappearance of the journal coincided with chancellor Gustav Stresemann's diplomatic offensive in Geneva. But the Comintern also seems to have endorsed the publication.

Transnational Organizations of Ethnic Activists

There also were specifically transnational platforms that were set up to represent the interests of specific ethnic groups, nationalities, and/or national minorities at the international level, with the purpose of developing a paradiplomacy of their own. A first platform was composed of the propaganda network of British, French, and Eastern

European Zionists acting through the Committee of Jewish Delegations (*Comité des Délégations Juives*), which was established in Paris in 1919 as an umbrella office for coordinating démarches to favor the interests of Jewish minorities on the international scene. The Committee also followed up on Jewish minorities' petitions to the League of Nations and established regular contacts with political and cultural representatives of other ethnic minorities covered by the treaties, in part thanks to the activity of its representative, the Ukrainian-born Zionist exile Leo Motzkin.[30]

A second network involved transnational organizations representing German national minorities from various Central and Eastern European states. The most representative was undoubtedly the Union of German Minorities in Europe (*Verband der Deutschen Minderheiten in Europa*, VDM), which was founded in Vienna in October 1922 and directly supported by the government in Berlin. It incorporated delegates from most moderate and pragmatic German minority parties in Central and Eastern Europe, and at its forefront were some Baltic German leaders who were in favor of achieving an enduring agreement with ethnic majorities in the states in which they lived, based on the mutual recognition of cultural autonomy for minorities and loyalty to the state.[31] With discreet support from the governments of their respective motherlands, representatives of Hungarian and Polish minorities took similar initiatives, usually by means of the establishment of a delegation in Switzerland.

In fact, a dense network of institutes, associations, and journals seeking to defend the rights of "Germans abroad" (*Auslandsdeutsche*) supported a mid-range revision of the borders that had been drawn at Versailles. They set the German appeal in the context of a larger claim for European minorities' self-determination. Most German minority leaders were increasingly drawn to radical nationalist ideas. Yet they also wanted to enlarge the League of Nations' minority treaties to include all member states, as a step toward the revision of European borders according to the nationality principle. They also pressed the League of Nations to expand the rights granted to ethnic groups by the treaties. During the 1920s frequent calls to generalize the minority treaties to all member states of the League, and to make them more functional for the interests of the protected minorities, became common slogans for most ethno-nationalist and minority émigrés in Europe.

Short- and medium-term strategies of some ethno-nationalist émigrés and revisionist states could overlap at times. The German *völkisch* groups and their mouthpieces, as well as certain revisionist authors who were fiercely committed to defending the rights of Germans abroad, embraced the concept of Wilsonian self-determination, or at least pretended to advocate it. They mostly ignored its most radical democratic side and soon realized that promoting the ethnic deconstruction of Europe went hand in glove with their national interests.[32] Some *völkisch* journals that championed the cause of German minorities abroad also devoted articles to the home rule demands of the Scots, the Bretons, and the Flemish. Furthermore, some radical *völkisch* nationalists attempted to found committees representing oppressed nations, where German minority leaders would supposedly cooperate with the exiles of Western European nationalities and even anti-colonialist leaders from Africa and Asia.[33]

There also was a variety of modest bureaus established by ethno-nationalist movements without a kin-state, such as the Irish Bureaus in Paris and other capitals at the beginning of the 1920s. They also established some contacts with substate nationalists from France and Spain, particularly Catalans and Basques.[34] Other examples include the Macedonian nationalist clubs in Vienna, the Ukrainian exiles in Paris, the Caucasian offices in Istanbul, and the Armenian associations in France and other countries.[35] Many of these relied on the support of their migrant diasporas as they attempted to access the ministries of foreign affairs in their host countries and gain the attention of international public opinion regarding the fate of their respective homelands.

The interwar ethno-nationalist émigrés included party leaders, elected deputies and senators, and representatives of cultural associations and institutions from national minorities scattered all over Europe. After 1919, they attempted to join some of the pre-existing international networks set up by liberal internationalists, the peace movement, and the emerging League of Nations movement. Certainly, not all of them were anti-fascists, and even fewer were fully convinced democrats. In fact, most Central and Eastern European émigrés were full-fledged anti-communists. Many shared antisemitic attitudes and sentiments with radical *völkisch* nationalists in Germany and found it convenient to look for support from Mussolini's Italy after 1925. A good example of this was Gustave de Köver, a former deputy of the Hungarian Party in Romania, who founded a *Bureau Central des Minorités* in Geneva, which set up delegations in Paris and in London (from 1938 on) with the cooperation of some exiled Ukrainians. It sought to mediate in Central European minority petitions to the League of Nations while seeking international visibility for the cause of Transylvanian Magyars.[36]

The Congress of European Nationalities (1925–38): A Reassessment

The best example of joint cooperation between the political representatives of the German, Jewish, Magyar, and Slavic minorities covered by the minority treaties, along with Catalan nationalists and other groups, was the Congress of European Nationalities. The Congress was founded in 1925 on the initiative of the Estonian-German Ewald Ammende (its General Secretary until his death in 1936) and other VDM activists, and German representatives constituted by far the largest and most influential group within it. The strong German imprint meant that later historiography frequently characterized the CEN as never anything more than a Trojan Horse for revisionist German nationalism. Nevertheless, in the course of its existence this transnational umbrella organization brought together around 300 spokespersons for no less than twenty national minority groups from fifteen European states, and sought to consolidate itself as the main mediator between European minorities, the League of Nations, and state diplomatic corps.

The Congress of European Nationalities was a broad organization and included ethno-political activists embodying all of the currents described in the first part of this chapter. As discussed below, later behavior by Ammende and the aforementioned Josip

Vilfan[37] supports the hypothesis that minority activists often exhibited a high degree of opportunism in their interactions, allying themselves with anyone who would advance their cause internationally, irrespective of political orientation. Other founding CEN members such as Werner Hasselblatt, also an Estonian-German, would later show themselves to be integral *völkisch* nationalists who plainly viewed the organization as a means to the particularist end of German revisionism. The founding statutes of the Congress, however, explicitly rejected any change to the territorial borders drawn by the peace settlements of 1919–23. Participating minority organizations were required to pledge loyalty to their states of residence and commit to working positively within them. Accordingly, attacks on the policies of individual governments were forbidden—discussions were to focus on general principles that would improve the lot of all European minorities.[38] These requirements suggest that in its initial incarnation the CEN was motivated by a genuine liberal universalism that championed the rights of all nationalities and was committed to working with the League of Nations to improve the machinery of international minority rights protection.[39]

That this was the case owes much to the leading role within the Congress of key Baltic German activists that had previously been instrumental in shaping VDM during 1922–5. Chief amongst these was Paul Schiemann—an implacably anti-fascist lawyer, parliamentarian, and newspaper editor from Latvia—whom Vilfan described as the "Thinker of the European Minorities Movement."[40] Schiemann merits particular attention due to his central role in developing an alternative approach to addressing interwar nationality issues, which stimulated extensive debates at the international level during the late 1920s and early 1930s. Whereas Schiemann's more conservative and *völkisch* Baltic German contemporaries dismissed the status of "*Minderheit*" (minority) as "*minderwertig*" (inferior), he accepted the changed realities arising from imperial collapse and advocated rapprochement and cooperation with national majorities within the newly created successor states of Central and Eastern Europe.[41] His guiding philosophy can be summed up in his statement that "politics entails work for the good of the place one inhabits. Any diversion to other ends is suicide."[42] In common with other CEN activists, Schiemann was concerned to preserve the distinct cultural identities of ethnic minority communities, arguing that this required guarantees of collective as opposed to simply individual rights. Yet, as the emphasis on place within the preceding quote implies, satisfying particular minority claims was seen as a means to the ultimate end of forging overarching pluralistic state communities as a foundation for durable European peace and prosperity.

Non-territorial Autonomy as a Guiding Principle within the CEN

Schiemann's prescription for reconciling state and nation was heavily influenced by the concept of national cultural (non-territorial) autonomy inherited from early-twentieth-century Austrian Social Democracy as well as from corporatist, self-governing traditions of Jewish and German communities within the former empires.

Uniquely in interwar Central and Eastern Europe, this concept was carried over into the newly constituted Baltic States, shaping Estonia's 1925 Law on National Minorities as well as a system of autonomous schooling for national minorities in Latvia.[43] A marked contrast to the narrowly nationalizing practices adopted by other new states in the region, this Baltic approach inspired Schiemann to propound the alternative of an *anational* state, defined as a territorial space shared by a number of autonomously organized ethnic groups. In line with this understanding, an early meeting of the CEN adopted the following resolution:

> In European states containing other national groups, each national group must be authorized to preserve and develop its national individuality in organizations at public law constituted—according to circumstances—either territorially or on the basis of the personal principle. In the opinion of the delegates, the said right to autonomy offers a path to ensuring that the loyal cooperation of all—minorities and majorities—within the aforementioned states can take place without conflicts and that relations between the peoples of Europe are improved.[44]

The model that Schiemann devised and propagated through the Congress therefore sought to break the conceptual link between ethnicity and exclusive ownership of territory, which lay at the root of continued nationality disputes in postwar Europe. Significantly, though, the 1925 founding declarations of the CEN underlined that minorities had both the right and the obligation to learn the dominant language of the state in which they lived, so as to enable their full participation in political life.[45] In this respect, Schiemann's conception of nationality rights was not—as some of his critics contend—entirely "state-free": when he spoke of an "anational state," he was essentially talking about a state that had an overarching civic identity but was as culturally pluralistic as it could possibly be.[46] It is notable also that, when advocating the creation of collective minority "organizations at public law," the Congress followed the "personal principle" enshrined in Estonia's 1925 autonomy law—namely, such organizations were to be constituted on the basis of individual citizens freely choosing their ethnic affiliation and voluntarily enrolling on a national electoral register. While not all founding members subscribed to this principle, it nevertheless remained a key tenet of the CEN's program during the initial phase of the organization's existence. This can be seen in Josip Vilfan's speech at the 1932 Congress, where he declared that "the right to assimilate, although we oppose this idea, we grant to anyone who wishes to assimilate: the obligation to assimilation we reject."[47]

In Schiemann's words, then, the Congress was "striving basically for the inclusion of minorities in normal state life." Moreover,

> a minority that is more concerned with its own interests than with the general good acts against public interest and violates the fundamental idea of our Nationalities Congress, which seeks not to set minorities apart from the state but to engage them in its life. We want to show the world that granting rights to minorities does not threaten the state but strengthens it. We can only win this trust by taking an honourable line in all matters concerning the generality.[48]

In looking at the CEN's founding declarations, it becomes clear that its primary goal was to create institutional mechanisms for majority-minority negotiation *within* states, so as to render external intervention by the League of Nations unnecessary.[49] At the same time, there can be no doubt that the organization arose out of the post-1918 internationalization of minority issues, framing its activity with strong reference to international law. In this regard, CEN leaders welcomed the League's engagement to address minority issues, declaring a "firm will to contribute as far as possible to [the achievement of this goal]."[50] As Ammende and Vilfan would later reiterate, even in the far less propitious international context of 1933, "the Congress does not envisage sweeping away the foundations in place, but rather seeks to increase the sturdiness of the existing edifice on a platform that is much bigger, better cemented and designed to satisfy everyone."[51] The Congress was thus not conceived as "a type of competing organization to the dissatisfying League of Nations"[52]; rather, it aspired to amend and improve League structures and procedures which—it insisted—did little to counteract the de facto assimilation or exclusion of minorities. The League Council was thus called upon firstly to replace the existing petitions system with a permanent Minorities Commission, and, secondly, to institute a generalized pan-European guarantee of minority rights applicable to all states, in place of a treaty system confined to Central and Eastern Europe. As was observed at CEN gatherings and elsewhere, this system elicited inevitable accusations of double standards which undermined the credibility of the League's claim to defend minorities.[53]

The CEN, Minorities, and State Sovereignty

The Congress of European Nationalities' founding program also reflected its close coordination (and interpenetration) with the broader-based non-minority organizations mentioned earlier in this chapter—the International Federation of League of Nations Societies, Interparliamentary Union, and the International Law Association. Indeed, it was within these broader organizations that proposals for a standing minorities commission and generalized pan-European guarantees of minority rights first originated.[54] In this respect, the CEN emerged out of a broader international civil society network that aspired to work with and through the League of Nations. This would provide the necessary framework for moving beyond the status quo of minority protection toward a system that would *empower* minorities as active subjects in their own right, rather than leaving them as simply objects of international law.[55]

As part of this assertion of political subjectivity, the Congress maintained already in the late 1920s that ethnic minorities could legitimately claim belonging not only to the state community (*Staatsgemeinschaft*) of their home state but also to a suprastate national community (*überstaatliche Volksgemeinschaft*).[56] This claim invites close scrutiny, given the instrumentalization of cross-border ethnic ties by states like Germany and Hungary during the interwar period and (especially) the connotations arising from the Nazis' use of the *Volksgemeinschaft* term. Yet, consistent with Schiemann's maxim that politics must be for the good of the place in which one resides, the CEN of the 1920s insisted that trans-border relationships between minorities and external "kin"-states should be solely cultural and economic and most emphatically *not* political in nature.[57] In this sense, it was the state of residence that was assigned primary responsibility for ensuring that minorities enjoyed equal rights and possibilities for sustainable cultural reproduction: subsidies from the kin-state were envisaged as a means of supplementing the resources of autonomous minority communities committed to developing their own distinct cultural identities linked to the place they inhabited. External political interference, the CEN argued, was more likely to occur in cases where the state of residence did not discharge its responsibilities with regard to minorities, thus inflaming nationalist feeling in the "parent" state.[58] As well as anticipating contemporary post-Cold War debates around minorities in inter-state relations,[59] the Congress' deliberations in this area call to mind the 1921 report on Eastern Europe that Sir Willoughby Dickinson submitted to the League Council, in which he observed:

> It is noticeable that nearly all these states are concerned with minorities in a duplicate capacity:
>
> (1) As being responsible for the protection of minorities of foreign race within their own borders and
> (2) As being interested in minorities of their own race in foreign territories.
>
> This is important because it shows that the question of the minorities is one of common concern, and, therefore every government should be anxious to reach a settlement as soon as possible.[60]

This notion of "common concern" was central to the approach to nationality issues which Schiemann developed through the Congress. Arguing that a preoccupation with state sovereignty and narrow national interest lay at the root of the problem, Schiemann and other CEN activists (such as Estonian Russian Vice Chairman Mikhail Kurchinskii) nested their pursuit of minority autonomy within a commitment to building a future "United States of Europe." According to Schiemann, national minorities were "good Europeans because of their fate."[61]

Fractures within the CEN

A review of materials from the Minorities Section of the League of Nations Secretariat suggests that the initial CEN agenda found sympathy among officials working there. For instance, in 1932, Ludvig de Krabbe, a Danish official at the Secretariat who attended Congress' meetings as an observer, wrote:

> One cannot fail to be impressed by this meeting of … minorities experiencing a political, economic and cultural situation which in too many cases is painful and unworthy of modern civilisation … one could note in the speeches a spirit of respect for the law, human solidarity and high ideals to which the highest

respect is due ... Provided this spirit predominates within the Congress, it could create a place and an authority among the organizations working to develop international society.⁶²

At the same time, this emerging dialogue with League officials also sheds light on multiple fractures within the CEN that undermined its effectiveness and claim to represent the 40 million Europeans who belonged to national minorities with a single voice. At its meetings in 1930 and 1931, the Congress had devoted much attention to positive developments in Estonia following the introduction of its 1925 minority law. In light of this experience, it was argued, the League of Nations should consider the case for a Europe-wide application of national cultural autonomy.⁶³ Responding to this call, Krabbe acknowledged that the national cultural autonomy model merited serious scrutiny as a possible means of reducing frictions between majorities and minorities. He nevertheless concluded that the Congress leaders had failed to make a convincing case, for their arguments had not looked beyond the specific experience of Estonia's small and territorially dispersed German and Jewish minorities.⁶⁴ Krabbe's assessment seems entirely justified given the diverse range of minorities arrayed within the CEN. Advocating non-territorial autonomy as a panacea may have fitted with the circumstances (and guiding philosophy) of liberally minded activists from the Baltic States, but was a far less obvious option for larger, more territorially compact minority communities. Also, the accommodationist minority politics advocated by *Auslandsdeutsche* such as Schiemann did not resonate to the same extent with *grenzlanddeutsch* (border German) communities in Poland and Czechoslovakia that had been separated from or denied adhesion to the German Reich following the peace settlements and which would go on to attain much greater prominence within the CEN during the 1930s.⁶⁵ Moreover, as Krabbe also remarked in his report, far from all minority activists were sold on the desirability of institutionalized collective autonomy (as opposed to a more liberal conception of individual rights). In this respect, he cited the example of German minority representatives from Denmark (Northern Schleswig) and Hungary, who feared that enrollment on a national register might lead to minorities being viewed as a "caste apart," while simultaneously undermining minority identity by introducing an element of legal differentiation and dissension within the group.⁶⁶

Krabbe's 1931 report therefore usefully highlights the difficulties inherent in any attempt to mobilize disparate minorities transnationally around a common agenda, especially when inter-state disputes frequently spilled over into relations between particular groups. The latter dimension became apparent as early as 1927, when Germany's large Polish as well as other minorities formally left the Congress. Such episodes gave League officials and others who observed CEN proceedings cause to question the representativeness and legitimacy of the organization, as well as the democracy of its internal procedures.⁶⁷ The lack of real debate noted by observers, as well as the automatic adoption of resolutions at the behest of the leadership, may well have reflected the rule prohibiting attacks on specific governments. While this rule was adopted with the best of intentions, limiting the deliberations of the Congress to matters of general concern for all minorities appeared less and less credible as more and more examples of egregious nationalizing practices began to appear.

More importantly, the CEN leadership could not evade the growing rift between pro-democratic, anti-fascist factions and pro-authoritarian nationalists that became ever-more palpable from the start of the 1930s. As the VDM (headed by Werner Hasselblatt from 1931 onward) came under the sway of more *völkisch*-minded German activists, the latter began to make their influence felt within the wider Congress, where Germans constituted the preponderant group. With the VDM dependent on subsidies from the *Reich*, the German state was able to exert indirect control over the CEN, whose credibility and integrity were fatally compromised after the Nazis came to power. The decisive turn came at the Ninth Congress meeting in 1933, when Jewish minority representatives—finally breaking with the CEN's precedent of not singling out individual states—tried and failed to obtain support for a resolution condemning the antisemitic policies of Germany's Nazi government. Decisive in the rejection of this initiative was the position of German delegates at the Congress, who argued that the CEN's opposition to assimilation necessarily precluded it from condemning "dissimilation." At this point, Jewish activists—hitherto the second largest contingent of delegates—broke definitively with the Congress. Thereafter, the organization was obviously understood by its core German contingent as an instrument for Nazi German Foreign Policy, especially after the National Socialist Sudeten German Konrad Henlein assumed the leadership of VDM in 1935.

Among other things, the Ninth CEN meeting revealed the essentially opportunistic character of Ewald Ammende and Josip Vilfan. While both may have been sincere in their initial commitment to promoting the rights and interests of all minorities rather than simply their own ethno-national communities, neither proved willing to prejudice the main source of funding for the Congress by taking a decisive stand against the VDM in 1933. Following the meeting, Vilfan did at least try to persuade the Jewish delegates to remain within the Congress, the better to counter Nazi German influence. However, his argument that German Jews should redefine themselves as a national minority and seek guarantees of protection from the League understandably received short shrift. In this regard, Jewish representatives reminded Vilfan of his words at the Eighth Congress in 1932, when (consistent with the "personal principle") he had stated that the CEN supported the right to assimilation provided this was undertaken freely. They also pointed out that Jews in Hitler's Germany were not simply being ascribed a distinct ethnic identity but were being denied basic civil and human rights and suffering violent attacks on this basis. Ammende for his part did not appear inclined to pursue things any further with the Jewish representatives after the 1933 Congress.[68] As for Paul Schiemann, the 1933 meeting led him to break with both the CEN and the *Verband*. Three years later, Schiemann would go on to found his own alternative anti-Nazi *Deutscher Verband zur nationalen Befriedigung Europas*.

In light of these events, there has been an understandable tendency for historians to begin from the 1930s and work backward, arguing that, from its very inception, the CEN was nothing more than a vehicle for a *völkisch* nationalist VDM backed by a revisionist Germany.[69] On further inspection, however, a more nuanced picture seems to be in order. At its inception in 1925, the Congress of European Nationalities had the character of a genuinely transnational movement, with German-Jewish cooperation at its core. While hindsight shows that it encompassed all of the orientations found within the broader field of interwar minority activism, the organization bore a strong liberal universalist imprint during the 1920s, bringing forth interesting alternatives to the then prevailing nation-state idea. In this respect, it is worth recalling Ludvig de Krabbe's 1931 report for the League of Nations, in which he declared that "the 'complete' solution to the minorities problem remains the development in countries of mixed population of a spirit of national tolerance and liberalism, a development ... which will become all the more difficult if a system of separatism in certain branches of the state becomes generalized."[70]

With this comment, Krabbe rejects collective autonomy for minorities in favor of the liberal unitary nation-state model upheld by the treaties and the League of Nations. However, as Krabbe would himself admit the following year, CEN leaders were becoming increasingly frustrated with the League's minority protection system by the early 1930s.[71] Though Krabbe was fully aware of the mounting problems arising from "nationalizing" state practices in Europe, he was left curiously unmoved when Paul Schiemann warned the 1931 Congress of the dangers posed by "irrational states" basing their policies on the "fictions" of economic autarchy and the idea that each could function as the bearer of a single national culture applicable to all residents. In reality, Schiemann argued, "thousands, millions have their own culture and if these are forced to bow to alien beliefs then the state will be threatened; hatred will be born precluding peaceful coexistence within it."[72] Krabbe insouciantly dismissed Schiemann's speech as "purely theoretical and philosophical"[73]; yet, it arguably encapsulated interwar Europe's drift toward the "new nationalist wave" of the 1930s.[74]

Conclusion

As Rogers Brubaker has observed, the redrawing of territorial borders in Central and Eastern Europe through the Paris Peace Conference did not "solve" the region's national question, but simply "recast it in a new form."[75] The First World War had given impetus to the principle of nationality and the idea of national self-determination—the concept of states as being of and for particular nations, which meant that each nation had to possess a state of its own. However, the fact that the new successor states were not only poly-ethnic but multinational in character meant that they essentially recreated the problems of the old empires in miniature. Efforts to replicate what, in Western Europe, was called "nation-building" were experienced in practice as narrowly ethnic, "nationalizing" state policies, since they took place belatedly, and were not accompanied by upward social mobility for minority members and the establishment of citizenship as a main criterion for building nationality, as had (in theory) happened in Western Europe. Solutions designed for the Bretons or the Welsh did not work in the same manner for the Ukrainians in Poland or the Magyars in Transylvania. For defeated powers, most notably Germany and Hungary, the redrawing of borders also entailed the "loss" of large co-national populations, creating fertile ground for irredentist nationalism committed to overturning the terms of the peace settlement. Caught between two competing forms of state nationalism, newly created minority populations in the region became the focus of what was immediately dubbed the "minority problem"—though, as the discussion of Catalan and other Western nationality claims within this chapter makes clear, this "problem" was by no means confined to Central and Eastern Europe during the interwar period.

The foundation of the League of Nations, supported by liberal public opinion and activism across Europe, nevertheless gave hope that a new internationalism might prevail and that minorities might obtain legal protection of their collective rights within a prevailing spirit of democracy. This chapter has examined how ethnonational minority activists navigated this nexus of relationships linking their home states, "kin"-states, international organizations, and wider international civil society within the postwar European order. To some extent, transnational activists for the cause of minority rights followed the path opened during the Great War by nationalist exiles, and benefited from the new international audibility that now was granted for private, i.e., "non-governmental" international organizations that gravitated around the League of Nations, though not being formally part of the new international system created by the Versailles Treaties. By bringing to light the wide range of different political orientations and particular agendas that motivated this activism, the chapter has shown that the commitment of many groups to internationalism (and, indeed, democracy) was questionable at best. At the same time, the analysis demonstrates that these activists cannot be uniformly painted as nothing more than "professional troublemakers."[76] Certain individuals among them displayed a genuine commitment to transnationalism and the development of universal principles of minority rights alongside the defense of individual rights and the pursuit of peace that merits renewed scrutiny today. It was this commitment that drove the CEN—Europe's largest transnational umbrella organization of minorities—during the 1920s, when Paul Schiemann's influence plotted a course based on democratic accommodation within existing states, and leading members of the Congress of European Nationalities simultaneously participated in the wider structures of international civil society represented by organizations such as the Inter-Parliamentary Union (IPU) and the International Law Association (ILA). Ultimately, however, the differences within the CEN (and the transnational minority camp more broadly) inevitably undermined its capacity for effective transnational mobilization around common principles. Equally if not more detrimental to its cause was the unstable European environment of the day, which, by the 1930s, shifted the balance away from minority activism and liberal nationalism toward exclusivist ethnonationalism, under the shadow of the emerging Third Reich and other Fascist and para-fascist states.

Notes

1   See Michael Goebel, *Anti-imperial Metropolis: Interwar Paris and the Seeds of Third World Nationalism* (Cambridge: Cambridge University Press, 2015).
2   D'Annunzio had already planned to set up a league of "oppressed peoples" on the occasion of the occupation of Fiume in 1919–20. He regarded the inhabitants of all Italian irredenta as potential members of a new coalition of European, Asian, and African peoples, which also included Irish, Flemish, Egyptians, and Macedonians.

However, these plans were never realized. See Enric Ucelay-Da Cal, "Cómo surgieron las internacionales de nacionalistas. La coincidencia de iniciativas sociales muy diversas, 1864–1914," in *Patrias diversas, ¿misma lucha? Alianzas transnacionalistas en el mundo de entreguerras (1912–1939)*, ed. Enric Ucelay-Da Cal, Xosé M. Núñez Seixas, and Arnau Gonzàlez Vilalta (Barcelona: Bellaterra, 2020), 25–66.

3   This was the case with the League against Imperialism and Colonial Oppression, founded in Brussels in 1927 by thirty-four anti-colonialist and communist groupings and parties from Europe, America, Africa, and Asia, among them the Indian National Congress, Indonesian nationalists, the French communist intellectual Henri Barbusse, and the Senegalese leader L. Senghor. Yet, this alliance was short-lived and hardly operative: following its Frankfurt Conference (1929), the political agreement between Communists and "bourgeois" anti-colonial activists entered into crisis. See Martin Mevius, ed., *The Communist Quest for National Legitimacy in Europe, 1918–1989* (London: Routledge, 2011), as well as Klaas Stutje, *Campaigning in Europe for a Free Indonesia: Indonesian Nationalists and the Worldwide Anticolonial Movement, 1917–1931* (Copenhagen: NIAS Press, 2019).

4   Erez Manela, *The Wilsonian Moment: Self-determination and the Origins of Anticolonial Nationalism* (Oxford: Oxford University Press, 2007).

5   See Glenda Sluga, *Internationalism in the Age of Nationalism* (Philadelphia: University of Pennsylvania Press, 2015). See also Glenda Sluga and Patricia Clavin, eds., *Internationalisms. A Twentieth-century History* (Oxford: Oxford University Press, 2017).

6   See Stefan Dyroff, "From Nationalities to Minorities? The Transnational Debate on the Minority Protection System of the League of Nations, and Its Predecessors," in *The First World War and the Nationality Question in Europe: Global Impact and Local Dynamics*, ed. Xosé M. Núñez Seixas (Leiden and Boston: Brill, 2020), 245–65.

7   For a general overview, see Heiner Timmermann, ed., *Nationalismus und Nationalbewegung in Europa, 1914–1945* (Berlin: Duncker & Humblot, 1999); Ugo Corsini and Davide Zaffi, eds., *Die Minderheiten zwischen den beiden Weltkriegen* (Berlin: Duncker & Humblot, 1997); Xosé M. Núñez Seixas, *Entre Ginebra y Berlín. La cuestión de las minorías nacionales y la política internacional en Europa, 1914–1939* (Madrid: Akal, 2001); Mathias Beer and Stefan Dyroff, eds., *Politische Strategien nationaler Minderheiten in der Zwischenkriegszeit* (Munich: Oldenbourg, 2014).

8   Joop Leerssen, *National Thought in Europe: A Cultural History* (Amsterdam: Amsterdam University Press, 2006).

9   Jean-Michel Guieu, *Le rameau et le glaive. Les militants français pour la SDN* (Paris: Presses de Sciences Po, 2008); Thomas Davies, *NGOs: A New History of Transnational Civil Society* (Oxford: Oxford University Press, 2014).

10 See Charles Seignobos, *Les aspirations autonomistes en Europe* (Paris: Felix Alcan, 1913); Jean Gabrys (E. Demm, ed.), *Auf Wache für die Nation—Erinnerungen* (Frankfurt am Main: PL Academic Research, 2013); Georges-Henri Soutou, "Jean Pélissier et l'Office Central des Nationalités, 1911–1918: Un agent du gouvernement français auprés des nationalités," in *Recherches sur la France et le problème des nationalités pendant la premiére guerre mondiale (Pologne, Ukraine, Lithuanie)*, ed. Georges-Henri Soutou (Paris: Presses de l'Université de Paris-Sorbonne, 1995), 13–38.

11 Hugh Seton-Watson and Christopher Seton-Watson, *The Making of a New Europe: R. W. Seton-Watson and the Last Days of Austria-Hungary* (London: Methuen,

1981); Frank Hadler, ed., *Weg von Österreich! Das Weltkriegsexil von Masaryk und Benes im Spiegel ihrer Briefe und Aufzeichnungen aus den Jahren 1914–1918. Eine Quellensammlung* (Berlin: Akademie Verlag, 1995).

12 See Derek Heater, *National Self-determination: Woodrow Wilson and His Legacy* (New York: St. Martin's Press, 1994).

13 For a reappraisal of the Peace Conference, see Margaret Macmillan, *Peacemakers: The Paris Conference of 1919 and Its Attempt to End War* (London: Murray, 2003). For the role of Jewish organizations, see Carole Fink, *Defending the Rights of Others. The Great Powers, the Jews, and International Minority Protection, 1878–1938* (Cambridge: Cambridge University Press, 2004), and Simon Rabinovitch, *Jewish Rights, National Rites: Nationalism and Autonomy in Late Imperial and Revolutionary Russia* (Stanford, CA: Stanford University Press, 2014), 258–71.

14 See, e.g., the reflection by the Catalanist leader Antoni Rovira I Virgili, "Necessitat de que tot nacionalisme tingui una política internacional," *Revista Anyal*, 1915, reproduced in *El catalanisme i la Gran Guerra. Antologia*, ed. David Martínez Fiol (Barcelona: La Magrana/Diputació de Barcelona, 1988), 79–85.

15 Stephen Bonsal, *Suitors and Suppliants. The Little Nations at Versailles* (Port Washington: Kemikat Press, 1969); Xosé M. Núñez Seixas, "Wilson's Unexpected Friends: The Transnational Impact of the First World War on Western European Nationalist Movements," in *The First World War and the Nationality Question*, ed. Núñez Seixas, 37–64.

16 Letter of Joan Estelrich to Hipòlit Nadal i Mallol, n. p., November 10, 1927 (Joan Estelrich Papers, National Library of Catalonia, Barcelona).

17 See Zaur Gasimov and José M. Faraldo, "Las alianzas desde arriba: los nacionalismos antirrusos y antisoviéticos (1914–1939)," in *Patrias diversas*, ed. Ucelay-Da Cal, Núñez Seixas and Gonzàlez Vilalta, 173–95; Xosé M. Núñez Seixas, "Unholy Alliances? Nationalist Exiles, Minorities and Antifascism in interwar Europe," *Contemporary European History* 25, no. 4 (2016): 597–617.

18 Joze Pirjevec, "Die politische Theorie und Tätigkeit Josef Wilfans," in *Die Minderheiten*, ed. Corsini and Zaffi, 167–74.

19 See some references in Claus Gatterer, *Im Kampf gegen Rom. Bürger, Minderheiten und Autonomien in Italien* (Vienna: Europa-Verlag, 1968), as well as Sandro Fontana, ed., *Il fascismo e le autonomie locali* (Bologna: Il Mulino, 1973).

20 See Xosé M. Núñez Seixas, *Internacionalitzant el nacionalisme. El catalanisme polític i la qüestió de les minories nacionals a Europa (1914–1936)* (Valencia: Afers/PUV, 2010), 115–21.

21 G. Cattini, *Nel nome di Garibaldi. I rivoluzionari catalani, i nipoti del Generale e la polizia di Mussolini (1923–1926)* (Pisa: BFS Edizioni, 2010).

22 As a whole, the League of Nations has recently been reappraised from a more positive perspective, and seen not only as a failure. See, for instance, Peter Hilpold, "The League of Nations and the Protection of Minorities—Rediscovering a Great Experiment," *Max Planck Yearbook of United Nations Law*, 17 (2013): 87–112.

23 Marta Petricioli and Donatella Cherubini, eds., *Pour la paix en Europe. Institutions et société civile dans l'entre-deux-guerres* (Berne: Peter Lang, 2007).

24 René Claparède, *L' Organisation de la Lutte pour la Liberté des Peuples* (Geneva: Publications du Bureau International pour la Défense des Droits des Peuples, 1921).

25 See Théodore Ruyssen, *Les minorités nationales d'Europe et la guerre mondiale* (Paris: Presses Universitaires de France, 1924); Willoughby H. Dickinson, *Minorities*

(London: League of Nations Union, 1928). See also René Fabre, "Un exemple de pacifisme juridique. Thédore Ruyssen et le mouvement 'La Paix par le Droit' (1884–1950)," *Vingtième Siècle* 39 (1993): 38–54.

26 See Daniel Gorman, "Ecumenical Internationalism: Willoughby Dickinson, the League of Nations and the World Alliance for Promoting International Friendship through the Churches," *Journal of Contemporary History* 45 (2010): 51–73, and Stefan Dyroff, "Avant-garde or Supplement? Advisory Bodies of Transnational Associations as Alternatives to the League's Minority Protection System, 1919–1939," *Diplomacy & Statecraft* 24 (2013): 192–208.

27 Stefan Dyroff, "Minority Rights and Humanitarianism. The International Campaign for the Ukrainians in Poland, 1930–31," *Journal of Modern European History* 12 (2014): 216–30.

28 G. Renard, "Pourquoi et dans quelle mesure nous défendrons les minorités," *Le Cri des Peuples*, May 30, 1928.

29 Bernard Lecache, "En suivant les travaux du IVe. Congrés des Nationalités," *Le Cri des Peuples*, September 5, 1929.

30 Fran Nesemann, "Minderheitendiplomatie. Leo Motzkin zwischen Imperien und Nationen," in *Synchrone Welten. Zeiträume jüdischer Geschichte*, ed. Dan Diner (Göttingen: Vandenhoeck & Ruprecht, 2005), 147–74.

31 See John Hiden, "Der Verband der Deutschen Minderheiten in Europa 1922–1936: Von der Verteidigung der deutschen Minderheiten zum Werkzeug des Nationalsozialismus," in *Politische Strategien*, ed. Baar and Dyroff, 297–308. See also Marina Germane's chapter in this volume.

32 Bastiaan Schot, *Nation oder Staat? Deutschland und der Minderheitenschutz. Zur Völkerbundpolitik in der Stresemann-Ära* (Marburg a. Lahn: Herder Institut, 1988).

33 A good example were the various "committees of violated [sic] peoples" supported by the Hungarian government during the early 1920s. Projects were also put forward by the Viennese Law Professor Viktor Otte, who in 1925 attempted to hold in Berlin a conference of oppressed peoples ranging from German minorities in Romania to Armenians. Around the same date, some *völkisch* activists in Berlin sponsored the secretive "Committee of Oppressed Peoples" and invited exiled Catalanists to join them. See, e.g., Viktor Otte, *Die unterdrückten Völker der Welt: Gegen Lüge und Gewalt* (Vienna: Ostmarken-Verlag, 1926).

34 See Dermoth Keogh, "The Origins of the Irish Foreign Service in Europe (1919–1922)," *Études Irlandaises* 7 (1982): 145–64. On the links between the Irish nationalists and Catalan, Basque, and Galician nationalists, see Xosé M. Núñez Seixas, *Patriotas transnacionales. Ensayos sobre nacionalismos y transferencias culturales en la Europa del siglo XX* (Madrid: Cátedra, 2019), 121–53.

35 Stefan Troebst, "Wien als Zentrum der mazedonischen Emigration in den Zwanziger Jahren," *Mitteilungen des bulgarischen Forschungsinstituts in Österreich* 2, no. 2 (1979): 68–86; Jean-Bernard Dupont-Melnyczenko, *Les Ukrainiens en France. Mémoires éparpillées* (Paris: Autrement, 2007), 44–64; and Michael Esch, *Parallele Gesellschaften und soziale Räume. Osteuropäische Einwanderer in Paris, 1880–1940* (Frankfurt and New York: Campus, 2012), 411–27.

36 Gustave de Köver, *Histoire d'une trahison: le calvaire des minorités nationales et la Société des Nations* (Geneva: Éditions du Bureau central des minorités, 1939).

37 Vilfan served as CEN President from 1925 to 1938.

38 John Hiden, *Defender of Minorities. Paul Schiemann, 1876–1944* (London: Hurst, 2004), 127.

39 On the different orientations within transnational discussions of the "minority problem," see Núñez Seixas, "Unholy Alliances," 597–600.
40 Hiden, *Defender of Minorities*, 127.
41 Michael Garleff, "Nationalitätenpolitik zwischen liberalem und völkischem Anspruch. Gleichklang und Spannungbei Paul Schiemann und Werner Hasselblatt," in *Reval und die Baltischen Länder. Festschrift für Hellmuth Weiss zum 80. Geburtstag*, ed. Jürgen von Hehn and Csaba-Janos Kenez (Marburg: Herder Institute, 1980), 113–32. In this regard, it is notable that the German Association formed in 1922 was initially entitled *Verband der deutschen Minderheiten*, before being renamed the *Verband der deutschen Volksgruppen* in 1928.
42 Paul Schiemann, *Ein europäisches Problem. Unabhängige Betrachtungen zur Minderheitenfrage* (Vienna and Leipzig: Reinhod-Verlag, 1937), 31.
43 David J. Smith and John Hiden, *Ethnic Diversity and the Nation State* (London and New York: Routledge, 2012).
44 "Résolutions adoptées par les Congrès des Nationalités Européennes," League of Nations Archives, Geneva (LONA), R1686-R1687/41/30181.
45 "Resolutions of the European Nationalities Congress," Российский государственный военный архив [Russian State Military Archive], Moscow, F.1502, O.1, D.113, 34–35.
46 Hiden, *Defender of Minorities*, 143. For a critique of Schiemann's "anational state" concept, and a response to this, see Ivars Ījabs, "Strange Baltic Liberalism: Paul Schiemann's Political Thought Revisited," *Journal of Baltic Studies* 40, no. 4 (2009): 495–515, and David J. Smith, "Why Remember Paul Schiemann?," in *Latvia—A Work in Progress? One Hundred Years of State- and Nation-building*, ed. David J. Smith (Stuttgart: Ibidem-Verlag, 2017), 71–90.
47 Sabine Bamberger-Stemann, *Der europäische Nationalitätenkongress 1925 bis 1938* (Marburg: Herder Institut, 2000), 176–7.
48 From Paul Schiemann's editorial "Minderheitenziele," *Rigascher Rundschau*, April 23, 1927. Cited in Hiden, *Defender of Minorities*, 139.
49 "Résolutions adoptées par les Congrès des Nationalités Européennes," LONA R1686-R1687/41/30181.
50 Ibid.
51 Letter from Josip Vilfan and Ewald Ammende to Pablo de Azcárate, August 29, 1933, LONA 4/6731/6638. On the reaction of Azcárate and other members of the League's Secretariat to this letter, see Núñez Seixas, *Entre Ginebra y Berlín*, 385–6.
52 Volker Prott, *The Politics of Self-determination. Remaking Territories and National Identities in Europe, 1917–1923* (Oxford: Oxford University Press, 2016), 288.
53 "Zur Gründung einer permanenten Minderheitenkommission beim Völkerbund, n. d. (1929)," Bundesarchiv Koblenz, Vilfan Papers.
54 On the proposals made by the CEN and other non-governmental organizations to improve the system of protection of minorities, see Núñez Seixas, *Entre Ginebra y Berlín*, 353–7.
55 Dietrich Loeber, "Die Minderheitenschutzverträge. Entstehung, Inhalt und Wirkung" in *Ostmitteleuropa zwischen den beiden Weltkriegen, 1918–1939*, ed. Hans Lemberg (Marburg: Herder Institut, 1997), 189–200.
56 "Résolutions adoptées par le 4-ème Congrès des Nationalités Européennes, Genève, août 1928," LONA R1686-R1687/41/30181; L. Krabbe, "Le Congrès des Nationalités Européennes à Vienne, 29 Juin-1 Juillet 1932," LONA R2161/4/37541/3817; Krabbe to Pablo de Azcárate, August 5, 1932. LONA R2176/4/38372/38372.

57 "Relations culturelle entre les minorités et leurs peuples d'origine, en savoir l'ensemble de leurs nations," LONA R2176/4/6738/3817; "Le VIIe Congrès des Nationalités Européennes," Elemér Radisics, Section d'Information, le 5.IX.1931. LONA R2161/4/31096/3817. Schiemann would himself later lament how the concept of *überstaatliche Volksgemeinschaft* was poisoned by the totalizing conception that the Nazis attached to it. See Núñez Seixas, "Unholy Alliances," 615.

58 See, for instance, Ammende's report on "the unsolved minority problem and the peace of Europe," presented at the Seventh Congress meeting, August 1931. LONA R2161/4/31096/3817.

59 See: Andreea Udrea and David J. Smith, "Minority Protection and Kin-State Engagement: *Karta Polaka* in Comparative Perspective," *Ethnopolitics* 20, no. 1 (2021): 67–82; Myra A. Waterbury, "Divided Nationhood and Multiple Membership: A Framework for Assessing Kin-State Policies and Their Impact," *Ethnopolitics* 20, no. 1 (2021): 39–52.

60 Sir Willoughby Dickinson, note to the President of the Council of the League of Nations "on the position of the minorities in Eastern Europe under the recent minorities treaties," November 14, 1921, LONA 41/17505/7729, 3.

61 Hiden, *Defender of Minorities*, 225. On Kurchinskii, see David J. Smith, "Retracing Estonia's Russians: Mikhail Kurchinskii and Inter-war Cultural Autonomy," *Nationalities Papers* 27, no. 3 (1999): 455–74; Martyn Housden and David J. Smith, "A Matter of Uniqueness? Paul Schiemann, Ewald Ammende and Mikhail Kurchinskii Compared," in *Forgotten Pages in Baltic History: Diversity and Inclusion*, ed. Martyn Housden and David J. Smith (Amsterdam and New York: Rodopi, 2011), 161–86.

62 L. Krabbe, "Le Congrès des Nationalités Européennes à Vienne, 29 Juin-1 Juillet 1932," LONA R2161/4/37541/3817.

63 "Le VIIe Congrès des Nationalités Européennes," Elemér Radisics, Section d'Information, le 5.IX.1931. LONA R2161/4/31096/3817. "Deuxième jour de séance. Séance de l'après-midi," LONA R2161/4/31096/3817.

64 L. Krabbe, "L'Autonomie culturelle comme solution du problème des minorités," Note de M. Krabbe, November 18, 1931, LONA, R.2175-4-32835.

65 David J. Smith, Marina Germane and Martyn Housden, "'Forgotten Europeans': Transnational Minority Activism in the Age of European Integration," *Nations and Nationalism* 25, no. 2 (2019): 523–43, here 529.

66 Krabbe, "L'Autonomie Culturelle."

67 "Le VIIe Congrès des Nationalités Européennes," Elemér Radisics, Section d'Information, le 5.IX.1931. LONA R2161/4/31096/3817; L. Krabbe, "Le Congrès des Nationalités Européennes à Vienne, 29 Juin-1 Juillet 1932," LONA R2161/4/37541/3817.

68 Smith and Hiden 2012, 88–9. On Ammende's difficulties in reconciling the particular interests of his own national group with the general interests of minorities, and in navigating the relationship with Germany through VDM, see Martyn Housden, *On Their Own Behalf. Ewald Ammende, Europe's National Minorities and the Campaign for Cultural Autonomy, 1920–1936* (Leiden and Boston: Brill, 2014).

69 This view is expressed most graphically by Samuel Salzborn, *Ethnisierung der Politik. Theorie und Geschichte des Volksgruppenrechts in Europa* (Frankfurt and New York: Campus, 2005); however, see also Bamberger-Stemann, *Der Europäische Nationalitätenkongreß*.

70 Krabbe, "L'Autonomie Culturelle."

71 Krabbe, "Le Congrès des Nationalités Européennes à Vienne, 29 Juin-1 Juillet 1932."

72 Discours du délégué, M. Le Dr. Schiemann. LONA R2161/4/31096/3817.
73 Krabbe, "L'Autonomie Culturelle." See also Núñez Seixas, *Entre Ginebra y Berlín*, 485–9.
74 "The New Nationalist Wave" was the title of the final speech Schiemann delivered to the VDM on June 26, 1932. Paul Schiemann, "Die neue nationalistische Welle. Rede gelegentlich der Jahrestagung des Verbandes der deutschen Volksgruppen, Baden bei Wien, 26 Juni 1932," *Nation und Staat*, 12 (September 1932): 1–13.
75 Rogers Brubaker, *Nationalism Reframed. Nationhood and the National Question in the New Europe* (Cambridge: Cambridge University Press, 1996), 3–4.
76 CEN's activity during the 1920s, for instance, should qualify the initial negative assessment of the organization by League of Nations Secretary General Sir Eric Drummond, who, on hearing of the first congress, remarked that "a meeting of this kind shows that the Minorities who come to it do not appreciate their obligations of loyalty towards their new countries." Drummond to Colban, October 5, 1925. LONA R1686-R1687/41/30181.

13

Transnational Collaborations among Women's Organizations and Questions of Minorities and Macedonia, 1925–30

Jane K. Cowan

Rogers Brubaker's tripartite schema of nationalizing state, national minority, and external national homeland, understood as a dynamic set of relations, has been very useful for analyzing transformations in Europe in the interwar period.[1] In particular, by conceptualizing these three "elements" not as entities or groups but as political fields within which a range of "stances" are taken, he has invited attention to the internal complexities and contestations within them. Yet, as we argue in this volume, even this tripartite structure does not account for all the actors and institutions involved in national and minority projects. For actors within the "new states" bound by minority protection agreements,[2] "the international" bore directly on the dynamics of domestic politics concerning minorities in three relevant ways: as a hierarchically structured political context in which great and small powers maneuvered, as an imagined community institutionally manifested through the League of Nations (LoN) with obligations of oversight of new states' treatment of their newly designated "minorities," and as a realm of "world opinion" and of explicitly internationalist social and political movements and transnational civic organizational activity to which national activists could appeal and seek alliance.

It was while reading in the LoN Secretariat archives—specifically, those files classified under the Secretariat's rubrics of "Bulgarian minorities" (*"les minorités bulgares"*) and "the situation in Macedonia" (*"la situation en Macédoine"*)—in early spring 1998 that I chanced upon a bureaucratic file that revealed the socially thick, politically layered, and ideologically messy character of interactions around minority claims. That file, to which I will return later in the chapter, alerted me to the involvement of several international women's organizations in petitions concerning Macedonia. One of these organizations, the Women's International League for Peace and Freedom (WILPF), was a product of the 1915 International Congress of Women at the Hague, a defiant expression of women's international solidarity for peace in time of war by women who had worked together in common struggles for women's suffrage and rights to education.[3] WILPF's aim, both ambitious and idealistic, was to bring women together to form a single international organization, pursuing a shared project of peace, justice, and social transformation, starting with local problems.[4] From their Geneva headquarters, *La Maison Internationale*, WILPF was prominent within a lively network of private associations that operated energetically at the edges and interstices of the LoN, assuming roles of expert, advisor, and critic, while also advocating for specific groups and causes. Discovering the bureaucratic file mentioned above inspired me to investigate the complex relationships between WILPF, particularly its international secretary, executive committee, and a few key activists, and the leaders of several women's organizations in Bulgaria.

In this chapter, I examine WILPF's involvement in the question of "minorities" at a critical moment: when the minority treaties were beginning to consolidate what had been a vague and inconsistently deployed descriptive term into a more substantial—yet still controversial—legal-political category within the architecture of the post-Great War "New Europe" of nation-states.[5] For WILPF, minorities were one issue of concern within a broad political agenda. For women's organizations in the Baltic, Balkan, and Eastern European nation-states that had been created, wholly or partially, out of the Ottoman, Habsburg, Hohenzollern, or Romanov empires, minorities were a central, even overriding, concern. The chapter considers WILPF's engagement with three women's organizations in Bulgaria whose activities were framed by Bulgarian revisionism with respect to communities that all three organizations considered—but in different ways—co-nationals living beyond Bulgarian borders, in lands under Greek or Serb, Croat, and Slovene Kingdom sovereignty. It addresses a minority question that was exceptionally complex: the nationality of what the LoN Secretariat, in its pragmatic shorthand, called "Bulgarian minorities" (*les minorités bulgares*), which was highly contested not only from the outside but also from within.[6] Equally contested were claims regarding the political status of Macedonia, the territory which those minorities inhabited and whose division between Bulgaria, Greece and the Serb, Croat, and Slovene Kingdom was finalized and definitively sanctioned by the Paris peace treaties.

Examining communications among women's organizations on the vexed questions of these minorities' plight, and of a "just" future for Macedonia, allows us to trace differing stances within a field that Brubaker calls civil society homeland nationalism, but also to connect it to international practices.[7] The international guarantee of minority treaty rights and protections, operationalized through the LoN's minority petition procedure, opened new space for claims and counter-claims regarding minorities and Macedonia, along with appeals for justice. Although the LoN's decision to treat petitions as "information only" meant that petitioners were not only excluded from formal deliberation processes but were also kept "in the dark" about a petition's progress, the procedure generated hope: devised to supervise states,[8] it inspired mobilization and contestation from all parties. To investigate these intertwined processes, I consider the triadic—yet asymmetrical and not fully reciprocal—relation between three categories of actor. These include, first, the WILPF international leadership, comprising the international secretary, executive committee members,[9] and close associates. The second category of actor is women in leadership roles of three Bulgaria-based organizations: the Bulgarian Women's Union (BWU), an "apolitical" national umbrella organization, the Macedonian Women's Union (MWU), an association of Macedonian refugees created by the Macedonian Revolutionary Organization, and WILPF's Bulgarian Section. The third is international civil servants, known as "officials," in the LoN Secretariat's Administrative Commissions and Minorities Questions Section—generally called the Minorities Section—all of them male.

I look, first, at WILPF's broad approach to addressing conflict arising from different national loyalties between and within nation-states within this transnational feminist, pacifist, and internationalist organization. Guided by principles of feminist pragmatism, their approach involved recognition of nationality, ritualized gestures of solidarity between women of enemy nations, and the nurturing of dialogue across national differences. I then explore two major forms of WILPF's engagement on minority matters evident in this case: first, support, advice, and mediation in relation to minority petitioning, and second, periodic visits by WILPF activists to female colleagues in the Balkans that combined information-gathering for political analysis, peace work, recruitment, encouragement of cross-national collaborations, and moral support. A focus on petitioning and visiting allows us to see how individuals from these three categories of actor connected or refused connection, how they shared—or did not share—information, how they understood and misunderstood each other. As the historical materials reveal, WILPF women in international leadership roles acted as cultural translators, political advocates, and mediators between LoN officials and Bulgarian and Macedonian female activists; yet, the disparate objectives of these various actors could not be reconciled.

WILPF's Approach to Justice for Minorities

The most radical of the international women's organizations of the time, distinctive for its anti-imperialist stance, WILPF was composed of women whose political views ranged from progressive to socialist. Inspired, variously, by feminist, pacifist, socialist, religious, or secular humanist principles, yet generally committed to liberal internationalism, its members were "united by the belief that warfare should be eliminated and that economic and social justice was part and parcel of a system of peace."[10] Contrary to the postwar focus of most international women's organizations, which primarily involved humanitarian relief, WILPF's leadership, especially its first international secretary, the American economist and sociologist Emily Greene Balch, insisted that WILPF's purpose was to contribute to remove the causes of war, not allay the suffering it brought.[11] Efforts toward peace, and later, disarmament, became increasingly central to WILPF activities over the course of the interwar period.

Minorities were a significant concern for WILPF from the start. "Respect for nationality," including the right to democratic self-government and "no transference of territory without the consent of the men and women residing therein," was the first of five Principals for a Permanent Peace they declared at the 1915 Hague International Congress of Women.[12] However, what was meant by this crucial yet ill-defined term, and how respect for nationality might be implemented in territories with many nationalities, were left unspecified. By the time the LoN began to function, WILPF were calling on LoN statesmen to address the terror and violence minorities were facing at the hands of agents of the "new"—most of them vigorously nationalizing—states.[13] Through memoranda that WILPF members circulated at this first assembly, the organization also recommended that the LoN appoint a commission to investigate reports of minorities' ill treatment and to make a state's good behavior toward minorities a condition of LoN membership.[14] WILPF denounced violence and unjust treatment of minorities as abhorrent in themselves. Like officials in the LoN Secretariat's Minorities Section,[15] WILPF activists also recognized the threat that oppressed minorities posed to peace.

WILPF's involvement in minority issues was thus a matter of principle; yet, it was also a lived experience, an element of the organization's continuous, often fraught, efforts to manage the competing demands of internationalism and nationalism for its members. International women's organizations generally—and perhaps WILPF, most of all—labored to "forge an international 'we'" that comprised women globally, while acknowledging women's loyalties to their nation.[16] Their approach was pragmatic, rather than theoretical. International women's organizations advocated respect for national autonomy and incorporated this into their organizational practices, but then had to face the issue of national differences within a polity. As minority issues across Europe intensified through the 1920s, WILPF grappled with conflicts within their membership between Belgians and Germans, Poles and Ukrainians, and Hungarians and Serbs, among others; animosities between Czech, German, and Jewish women in Czechoslovakia, despite having created separate national sections, became so intense that they threatened WILPF's very survival and in 1929 led to changes in WILPF's constitution.[17]

Although WILPF became familiar with these kinds of conflicts, they rarely encountered a "separate nationality" that was as contested in terms of its national character as the one being addressed in this chapter. LoN bureaucrats labeled these people "Bulgarian minorities," but this implied, on the grounds of language, a nationality that some parties disputed. The people referred to were speakers of various South Slavic dialects;[18] to distinguish the speakers from the various claims about their nationality, I follow widespread scholarly practice and call them Slavic-speakers. They constituted the majority of the Christian Orthodox inhabitants of this Ottoman hinterland until most of the Macedonian territories were finally acquired by Greece and the Serb, Croat, and Slovene Kingdom through the 1913 Treaty of Bucharest after the 1912–13 Balkan Wars.

In the pre-national Ottoman context, the relevant terms—Turk, Moslem, Greek, Rum, Bulgarian, Serbian, Albanian—had evolving, contextually specific religious, occupational, educational, cultural, and social status, as well as linguistic, connotations.[19] Moreover, they were not mutually exclusive: Ottoman subjects could be "Greek when they traded, Albanian when they married, and conceivably Muslim when they prayed."[20] With nationalism came a narrowing and hardening of these terms. As the largest component of the Orthodox Christian community, Slavic-speakers were especially targeted by intensive nationalist campaigning by Greece and Bulgaria (and after 1903, Serbia), initially using propaganda, schools and churches, and later armed bands. From 1893, many Slavic-speakers were enlisted into the secretive Macedonian Revolutionary

Organization, carrying out anti-imperial insurgency and building a movement of "Macedonia for Macedonians" that sought Macedonian autonomy.[21] Armed violence ranging from individual assassination to full-scale war, along with deportations and population displacement, continued through the new century's first two decades. By the time the LoN Assembly held its opening ceremony in Geneva in November 1920, the majority of Macedonian Slavic-speakers were, in Liisa Malkki's sense, people "out of place."[22] They were anomalous citizens—newly classified as "minorities"—in someone else's nation-state, or refugees displaced far from their homes.[23]

The governments concerned with these people in their capacity as minorities described them in quite different ways. The Serb, Croat, and Slovene Kingdom government representatives claimed that those Slavic-speakers living in their recently acquired southern districts were not Bulgarian: they were South Serbs who spoke a dialect of Serbian, and thus, did not constitute a minority at all. Bulgarian government representatives, citing language and "race," argued that all members of this population were self-evidently Bulgarian.

Greek government representatives were more equivocal, and their arguments and terminology shifted across the decade in response to political contingencies as well as longer-term nationalizing processes. Until 1925, the Greek government spoke of this population as Bulgarians or Bulgarian speakers but differentiated them according to what they called "national sentiment." They acknowledged that many in this population supported the Bulgarian Exarchate, but they pointed to the significant portion who remained loyal to the Ecumenical Patriarchate (by then, under Greek hegemony), and who supported Greek learning and the civilizational ideal of Hellenism, insisting that they should be counted as Greeks. They argued that national sentiment or consciousness, expressed in attachment to faith and Greek national traditions, were less subject to outside pressure than language and thus a more reliable indicator of nationality.[24] Greek officials also admitted that many Slavic-speaking peasants were indifferent to nationality, and just wanted to be left alone to make a living in peace.[25]

Responding to processes of refugee resettlement and expulsion of minorities in both countries in 1923–4, representatives of Greece and Bulgaria negotiated and signed the Geneva Protocol for the Protection of Minorities (also known as the Politis-Kalfoff protocol) in September 1924. Within this agreement, the Slavic-speaking minority was explicitly identified as Bulgarian, a fact that angered Greece's ally, Yugoslavia, as well as many Greeks.[26] After the Greek Parliament refused to ratify the protocol in early spring 1925 and was eventually released by the LoN from its protocol obligations, the Greek government abandoned the term "Bulgarian minority." In response to LoN pressure, it agreed to uphold its prior commitment to develop teaching materials for its "Slav-speaking population,"[27] henceforth treating it as a linguistic—and not national—minority.

While the three governments' positions regarding "the Bulgarian minorities" ranged from absolutist to situationally adaptable, among the individuals who constituted the category there was considerable complexity concerning affiliation. With respect to those who had inhabited Ottoman territories that became Greece's "New Lands" in 1912, many who supported the Bulgarian church or the Bulgarian army, and feared reprisal, had already crossed the border into Bulgaria at some point since 1912. Joining fellow Macedonians who had taken refuge in Bulgaria at various moments since the 1870s, these more recent arrivals were now living in refugee camps in southern Bulgaria or in impoverished quarters of cities and towns like Sofia and Plovdiv. Other refugees had been driven out of their homes by violence or its threat. Greece's military invasion of Turkey's western ("Asia Minor") coast in 1919 in a vain effort to recuperate its "lost homelands" provoked fierce retaliation by Turkish forces against Orthodox civilians and Greek military alike, culminating ultimately in a compulsory population exchange between Turkey and Greece agreed by diplomats in Lausanne in January 1923. Already in late 1922, Orthodox Christian refugees from Turkey were arriving to Greece; the Greek government began resettling several hundred thousand of these refugees in the "New Lands" of Macedonia and Thrace, housing them in the "exchanged" Muslims' former properties, and then, when these houses and fields were insufficient, billeting them with Slavic-speaking families, thus Hellenizing the territories at the same time.[28] In the turbulent years of 1923–4, desperate Asia Minor refugees often simply took matters into their own hands, driving the Slavic-speakers from their houses. While many Slavic-speakers who had fled to Bulgaria under duress later regretted their decision and demanded to be allowed to return to their homes in Greece, others agreed to renounce Greek citizenship and accept Bulgarian nationality under the auspices of the Greco-Bulgarian Voluntary and Reciprocal Emigration scheme, the consequence of a bi-lateral protocol agreed at Neuilly in 1919 and operating from 1920 to 1932, supervised by the LoN.[29]

Of the Slavic-speakers who remained in Greece after the Balkan Wars, there were many permutations. A few were "fanatically Greek," while many others supported the Greek side as a political or socioeconomic choice, by virtue of religious affiliation to the Ecumenical Patriarchate, or in hopes of being left alone to get on with their lives.[30] Some continued to feel Bulgarian or Macedonian but kept quiet about it, in order to keep their homes and fields and because they faced pressure to remain in place from the Macedonian Revolutionary Organization.

Of those who arrived in Bulgaria as refugees from Greece or the Serb, Croat, and Slovene Kingdom, most would have understood themselves as Bulgarian. Many emphasized their distinctiveness as Macedonian Bulgarians (Macedonian being a regional qualifier; the term Macedo-Bulgarian was often used) or simply as Macedonians and wished Macedonia to be returned to Bulgaria. Other Macedonians, some through the bitter experience of refugeehood, favored international recognition of Macedonia, reunited with its territories now "under occupation," as an autonomous or fully independent political entity, separate from Bulgaria.

Few WILPF activists were aware of these complexities concerning affiliation and loyalty, whether among Macedonian refugees in Bulgaria, or among those who remained in their natal lands and experienced the assimilationist policies of Greece or the Serb, Croat, and Slovene Kingdom. What they heard from their contacts in Belgrade, Sofia, and Athens tended to reiterate the nationalist positions of their governments. But being aware more broadly of heightened sensitivities around national loyalty among their members, WILPF developed approaches to minorities, as well as to national rivalries, that were grounded in the organization's foundational principle: feminist pragmatism. These approaches emphasized democracy, education, non-violence, working through conflicts by means of discussion to find common ground, and the commitment to respect, and learn from, lived experience.[31] WILPF established a Minority Commission in July 1925 "to study and give publicity to the Minority Problem."[32] Commission members met, corresponded with, and sought to influence national diplomats and LoN delegates as well as LoN bureaucrats (particularly the Minorities Section); they also communicated with government officials and minority representatives and intellectuals in the countries concerned. They shared information with other non-governmental organizations and consulted with their own WILPF members with direct knowledge of local conditions. They published analyses and opinion pieces in major newspapers, organized fact-finding visits to Eastern Europe and the Balkans, and spoke on the topic at WILPF meetings, congresses, summer schools, and occasional public discussions.

WILPF's work on minorities emphasized sharing of information, discussion, and active development of empathy across national—indeed, across enemy—lines. The organization tried to get its members to see beyond the preoccupations of their own country, to acknowledge the difficulties of women in neighboring (even hostile) countries and to make small, concrete gestures of solidarity. In 1928, WILPF international secretary Mary Sheepshanks responded to a letter from Calliope Parren, President of WILPF's (rather inactive) Greek Section, commiserating with her people's suffering after an earthquake, then urging her to consider the effects of this same earthquake for Bulgaria, the devastation of which made payment of war reparations even more punishing. Sheepshanks suggested that the Greek Section approach its own government, asking it to relieve Bulgaria of its obligations of making reparations payments, permanently or at least temporarily: a practical gesture that "would be a real work of peace and conciliation and would arouse a spirit of gratitude and friendliness in Bulgaria."[33] Sheepshanks sent a similar request to a contact among the women starting to form themselves into a WILPF group in Belgrade.[34]

Finally, the WILPF international secretary maintained active communications with national sections facing minority issues. With respect to the Balkans, she corresponded with local contacts in major cities like Athens, Bucharest, Belgrade, Ljubljana, Zagreb, Tirana, Sofia, and Bourgas, as well as with British, French, Swiss, and American women who had settled in those countries. These contacts were renewed when the women met in person at WILPF's—or other international women's organizations'—international events. These many interactions, conducted through letters as well as face-to-face, provided the foundations of collaboration. They enabled relations of solidarity, as well as a number of personal friendships, to develop.

If recent feminist scholarship has rightly called attention to an implicit civilizing mission within Western-dominated international women's organizations, *within* Europe this played out in complex ways. WILPF's leadership was, indeed, composed predominantly of relatively privileged, white, middle class, highly educated European and North American women. In terms of class, education and cultural capital, they actually shared much with their counterparts in Bulgaria, who had a similar profile. Yet Bulgaria's defeat, humiliation, and impoverishment framed these transnational encounters. Moreover, usually left unspoken was the fact that women on either side of the divide saw their political projects differently. WILPF's leadership and long-term activists viewed their engagement in practical approaches to minority problems as part of a mentoring role; they saw themselves as guiding their Bulgarian and Macedonian (and other Balkan and East European) counterparts beyond nationalism, toward a "higher" mission of internationalism and the work of peace. For their part, the Bulgarian and Macedonian women embraced the values of peace and internationalism, to some degree. Yet primarily, they sought to mobilize the help of WILPF women in righting national wrongs.

Speaking Alongside rather than Speaking For: Women's Collaborations and Encounters around Petitions

In December 1924, Julia Malinoff and Dr. Z. Dragnewa, president and secretary, respectively, of the Bulgarian Women's Union (*Bulgarski Zhenski Suyuz*, hereafter BWU), sent a letter to the President of WILPF in Geneva, asking the organization to intercede for them.[35] Women leading women's organizations in the Balkans regularly wrote to WILPF headquarters in Geneva recounting their own national troubles, often actively enlisting the WILPF international leadership to present their appeals for justice and calls for action to the international community. Within Bulgaria, the BWU was particularly active in launching such appeals.[36] Founded in 1901, the BWU was intended to be an umbrella organization representing all of Bulgaria's women's organizations established since 1878, most of which were oriented toward charity and education with a few working for women's political, suffrage, and labor rights.[37] Early on, its leadership built ties with women internationally: in 1908 it joined both the International Council of Women and the International Women's Suffrage Alliance.

The BWU saw a myriad of splits and divisions during its first decade between "moderates" and "radicals" over how to address the question of women's suffrage, as well as efforts by its socialist members to align the union's activities with the class struggle. After the socialist women departed in 1914, the BWU put itself forward as "above party" and "above class," adopting a gradualist approach to the achievement of women's civil and political equality.[38] From 1912 onward, however, the women were diverted by more pressing issues of war and its consequences: first, by the outcome of the Second Balkan War (June–July 1913), the first "national catastrophe," in which Bulgaria lost significant territory including most of Macedonia, and then, by Bulgaria's defeat in the Great War and the crushing terms of the 1919 Treaty of Neuilly (for Bulgarians, "the second national catastrophe"), which brought "continued misery, ongoing food shortages and repeated outbreaks of political violence, which only began to subside in the mid-1920s."[39]

It was within this context of continuing turmoil and material privation within Bulgaria that Malinoff and Dragnewa drafted their December 1924 letter. Describing the terrible conditions facing the refugees crossing the border from Greece into Bulgaria, they begged WILPF "to intercede with the League of Nations and elsewhere, wherever possible" to ensure that the influx of refugees into Bulgaria be stopped, the minority treaties "be applied in a precise way," the latest agreement between the Greek and Bulgarian governments be implemented,[40] and the unfortunate Bulgarian émigrés be guaranteed safe return to, and a calm life in, their natal country (that is, Greece):

> We remember that you have not been indifferent toward the innumerable refugees in Russia, Poland, Armenia and other countries; and we hope that you will take the case of the Bulgarian émigrés to heart, as well, and through your organs influence public opinion, which could put an end to such iniquity. This is not a political question that we put before you. As women we address ourselves to our sisters throughout the world, who have always been the first to respond to the call of the unfortunate and oppressed, from whatever corner of the world they arise.[41]

Vilma Glucklich, WILPF's international secretary and a Hungarian national, promptly responded to this request. Glucklich attached the BWU letter to a cover letter she had drafted addressed to Minorities Section Director Erik Colban. The Bulgarian women's letter, she insisted, "expresses so precisely the facts … and speaks in such a calm and impartial manner, that it may perhaps help you to find the remedy to the misery of 250,000 persons forced to leave their home."[42] Two weeks later, having received an acknowledgment of this initial missive, she wrote again, enclosing this time a typewritten report from an H.M. Wallis of the "Friends Centre in Macedonia."[43] As Glucklich explained, "[this] correspondence published in *The Friend*[44] … confirms their complaint by the experience of a reliable witness. Perhaps the complaints from both sides will make it easier for your section to bring about an agreement for just and fair mutual treatment."[45]

Indicative of the networks of cooperation among the wider community of internationalist women, an additional communication from a second international women's organization is found in this same Minorities Section file, as well. On February 10, 1925, the Geneva headquarters of the International Woman Suffrage Alliance (IWSA) submitted to the Minorities Section a copy of the very same letter from the BWU, one of its affiliate members. The Alliance "agrees with the desire expressed by the society of Bulgarian women," the prominent Swiss feminist and IWSA Secretary Emilie Gourd wrote in her cover letter, "but must remain neutral."[46]

If we consider the content of these three communications together, the first thing we notice is how the BWU has solicited and mobilized the aid of two international women's organizations, a strategy well-honed by 1925. Bulgaria's largest and most broad-based women's organization, the BWU was engaged in civil society homeland nationalism, but carved out here a careful position. Malinoff and Dragnewa's letter acknowledges WILPF's concerns with refugees throughout the world, placing the Bulgarian émigrés within this frame. It adopts a maternal stance, expressing scrupulously moral and explicitly "non-political" concern for the plight of the "unfortunate" Bulgarian émigrés. Rather than challenging Serbian or Greek sovereignty, it asks for international agreements to be honored and the minority treaties to be strictly applied. Its tone is strikingly moderate, rather than militant.

Interestingly, this measured quality is what Glucklich has emphasized, in explicit terms, in her cover letter (it "expresses so precisely the facts … and speaks in such a calm and impartial manner"). She has, moreover, confirmed its objectivity by means of the Friends' report that she has attached. Similarly, in the third letter Gourd emphasized her organization's own commitment to political "neutrality," despite their agreement with the Bulgarian women's claims. We can read the affirmations in Glucklich's and Gourd's accompanying letters in light of two dynamics in which WILPF, IWSA, and the LoN were all implicated, albeit to varying degrees. The first dynamic was animated by an underlying discourse of Orientalism[47] (or in this case, Balkanism[48]) that was ever alert to signs of a potential lack of reason—an irrationality or unreasonableness—on the part of non-Western subjects and their demands. The second was a related, but institutionally specific, insistence in the LoN, particularly with respect to minority petitions, on moderate, as opposed to passionate or "violent," language.[49] Sensitive to these dynamics, Glucklich and Gourd have reassured the League bureaucrats of the reasonableness, thus legitimacy, of Bulgarian women's claims.

The collaborative quality of the two international women's organizations' missives is also remarkable. Each transmitted Malinoff and Dragewa's letter, accompanying it with a cover letter of its own. As we shall see, this mode of "speaking alongside" (rather than "speaking for") came to characterize WILPF's active mediation between female petitioners and the Minorities Section officials over the course of the following years.

Two Petitions from the Macedonian Women's Organization and LoN Minorities Section Responses

In communications to female allies and LoN officials in Geneva, Bulgarian women's organizations emphasized the continuing injustice of the peace treaties and its material effects: onerous reparations, impoverishment and poor health of the population, chronic political violence and state repression. Macedonia and the future of the Macedonian refugees (also called "Bulgarian émigrés") were, however, pre-eminent concerns, uniting Bulgarian women across a wide political spectrum. Hence, the BWU was not the only women's group to seek a hearing on Macedonia through the LoN minority petition procedure. Among others, the LoN archives contains two communications from the Macedonian Women's Union (MWU), Sofia, submitted on behalf of their first Congress from May 30 to June 1, 1926: each contains a cover letter together with the relevant resolutions voted on by the membership.

The MWU was created in 1926 by the Union of Macedonian Emigrants Associations (*Union des associations des émigrés macédoniens en Bulgarie*) to gather together female émigrés and refugees that were attached to a multitude of separate Macedonian refugee and emigrant associations. Its creation is attributed to Ivan Mihailov who, after taking control of the Macedonian Revolutionary Organization in late 1924, focused on organization-building of this transnational revolutionary movement, promoting associational and communication networks among Macedonian émigrés and refugees in North America as well as Europe.[50] By this time, the Macedonian Revolutionary Organization was operating, with the Bulgarian government's uneasy tolerance, as a "state within a state" in Bulgaria's southwest Pirin region. It worked to levy taxes, carry out assassinations, and sponsor hit-and-run attacks across the border into Greece and the Serb, Croat, and Slovene Kingdom, keeping alive pressure for an autonomous Macedonia. The Macedonians in Bulgaria were a powerful constituency who exercised influence through civic and political institutions but also, at times, opposed the state: the relationship between Macedonians and the Bulgarian government was volatile. By early 1927, Catherine Karavéloff,[51] the president of WILPF's Bulgarian Section as well as a co-founder of the BWU, had drawn some members of the MWU into WILPF's Bulgarian Section. Although "fully alive to the dangers of Macedonian irredentism," British WILPF activist Mosa Anderson observed, "she believes she can exercise a moderating and pacifying influence on their turbulent feelings."[52]

The MWU's first communication to the LoN minority petition procedure conveyed the founding congress' views on the present situation in "the part of Macedonian territories annexed to Greece."[53] It provoked a stern response. The resolution in the LoN archives file shows various phrases underlined in blue pencil, presumably by the Minorities Section (as I have reproduced below):

> The Congress of 30–31 May 1926 … asserts with bitterness … that our brothers and sisters in the Macedonian region annexed to Greece are <u>treated as slaves</u> and suffer endlessly at the hands of the Hellenic forces. … They use the emigration convention to cover the eyes of the world to their <u>atrocities</u> as they chase out a population resident in Macedonia for centuries. … We beg the League for justice, <u>to suppress this medieval regime</u>. … The liberty of <u>Macedonia</u> corresponds to the most noble aspirations of its people for peace and well-being.[54]

When asked to review the petition for receivability, Minorities Section official William O'Sullivan Molony insisted that

> the violence of the language of the resolution communicated to us by the petitioners … is such that its communication to the Greek government for observations could not be envisaged. I have therefore concluded that the petition does not meet the fourth condition of receivability. Under these circumstances, I do not consider it necessary to apply the other conditions of receivability to the petition, although, at first sight, it would seem apparent that the petition also fails to meet the second condition. I beg to submit herewith, for your approval, a simple acknowledgment of receipt in the third person.[55]

The MWU submitted a second petition at the same time, including a similar resolution, but this time concerning the part of Macedonia "annexed to Serbia."[56] When evaluating the petition for receivability, Minorities Section official A.M. Céspedes reasoned that "given the violence of its language," the document seemed incompatible with the (fourth) condition of receivability:

> The State concerned here is, in effect, accused of placing a part of its population under 'an unbearable regime' of 'terror,' of attacking 'family morals and women's

and girls' chastity,' of 'permitting atrocities' of which the said signatories of the document are 'terrified and disgusted' and of 'excesses committed on the part of persons responsible, or irresponsible, in a country deprived of the most elementary rights.'[57]

Céspedes concluded that, "under these conditions, I think the petition can be dismissed, without it being necessary even to examine the non-receivability that could result, equally, from the fact that Macedonia is here considered as <u>a nation</u> placed under foreign 'domination' and that no allusion is made to the minority treaties."[58]

Like the BWU, the MWU was engaged in civil society homeland nationalism, but their stances overlapped only partially. The MWU petition denies Greece's sovereignty in Macedonia, as well as that of the Serb, Croat, and Slovene Kingdom; it refuses the category "minority" in favor of "nation"; and the homeland on whose behalf it speaks is Macedonia, whose connection to Bulgaria is unclear. While the petitions of the two organizations differ in content, the defiant tone of the Macedonian women is more consequential. Both Minorities Section officials evaluating the petitions have reiterated the same point: that violent language makes a petition non-receivable and non-transmissible. Moreover, once violent language had been identified, it was not even necessary to examine whether other conditions have been fulfilled. These evaluations reveal that a petition's avoidance of "violent language" was, in fact, the pre-eminent condition for receivability in the eyes of Minorities Section officials.

Referring to language that was either passionate or critical, or both, "violent language" was a kind of "unruly" linguistic behavior that transgressed codes of diplomacy, but also codes of class and race hierarchy cultivated within the League of Nations' institutional space.[59] Significantly, governments of treaty-bound or "minority states" were particularly prickly about such language. Already facing the humiliating challenge to their sovereign authority in having to submit to minority treaty supervision in the first place, they repeatedly insisted that they would not tolerate what they perceived as provocative and insulting challenges to their rule from their own subjects.[60] Anticipating how minority states would respond to such petitions (which experience often confirmed), Minorities Section officials were preoccupied with such language. As we saw in the cases just examined, they sometimes preemptively refused petitions they felt had no chance of being considered.[61]

Transmitting petitions at the request of Bulgarian women to LoN officials, WILPF leadership became increasingly aware of the sensitivity surrounding violent language. As part of her general efforts to strengthen WILPF's influence at the LoN,[62] Sheepshanks, who became WILPF international secretary in the summer of 1927, was a particularly energetic mediator. In response to a request from Catherine Karavéloff on November 20, 1927, to transmit a petition, Sheepshanks met and discussed the Bulgarian women's grievances with Director Erik Colban and his officials in the Minorities Section.[63] Those discussions prompted Sheepshanks to remind Karavéloff of the procedures for evaluating petitions and to offer help with composing them. Consistently with the practice of speaking *alongside*, rather than *for* Bulgarian organizations, Sheepshanks warned Karaveloff that

> one can best render service to the minorities if one pays attention to conforming to these rules [of receivability]. If you do not, it is impossible for the Minority Section [sic] to consider [the petitions]. It is necessary first of all to avoid all violent expressions, however justified they seem. … We could perhaps help the Macedonian women to compose their complaints in an acceptable form.[64]

Sheepshanks shared her insight into the Minorities Section's bureaucratic process with Karaveloff, knowing of her influential position among women's groups in Bulgaria. She stressed the need to be strategic in the ways claims were phrased: indeed, she advised that the Macedonian women should "appear to accept" the status of loyal minority within the newly anointed nation-states as the necessary price for their complaints to be heard and addressed.[65] I have seen no evidence that Sheepshanks' offer to assist the Macedonian women in composing their petitions was ever taken up. The fact that similarly worded petitions continued to be sent by these and other Macedonian organizations until the mid-1930s indicates the petitioners' awareness of the performative character of their claims of Macedonian nationhood, and their reluctance to abandon them. They persisted in their demands for recognition of their nation, describing Greece and "Serbia" as violent and illegitimate occupying powers.[66]

WILPF Missions to the Balkans

Although international travel, which fostered interactions and exchanges among women, was a core practice of international women's organizations in general,[67] WILPF was particularly active in sending its own leaders, as well as encouraging individual WILPF members, to undertake visits to their contacts and national sections in Eastern Europe and the Balkans. WILPF saw these missions as opportunities to speak about pacifism, gather information, recruit new members, encourage friendship and collaboration among women of hostile states, and persuade their local contacts already involved in women's organizations to establish a WILPF national section in countries where it did not exist. Yet the pressure for missions was not unidirectional. Women based in Balkan and East European towns often clamored for visits so that their predicaments could be better known, as well as to enlist the Geneva office's support.

In late November 1927, around the time that Sheepshanks was mediating between Karaveloff and the Minorities Section regarding petitions, Dr. Hilda Clark—obstetrician, Quaker activist and organizer of large-scale relief operations, member of WILPF's three-person Minority Commission and a longstanding friend—wrote to Sheepshanks. She advised her that she had secured the help of Mosa Anderson, the British Labour MP Charles Roden Buxton's private secretary, "a member of this

Section [who] often does work for us" and a Quaker, for two months' work in the Balkans, with her expenses to be covered by WILPF's British Section. "I have had the importance of this work in the Balkans very strongly in my mind for a long time," Clark confessed. She recommended Anderson as extremely well-qualified with "her thorough-going pacifist views, excellent training in political matters" and fluency in Russian, French, and German.[68]

Between December 16, 1927, and February 6, 1928, Anderson visited Yugoslavia and Bulgaria. The objectives of her visit were to move forward on setting up a Yugoslav Section, visit the Bulgarian Section, investigate "certain aspects" of the political and economic situation of both countries, and accompany a fellow Quaker, Christine Ellis, to Stanimaka, near Philippopolis [Plovdiv] to open a Health Centre for Mothers and Children.[69] Her 16-page single-spaced typed summary of her visit, comprised of seven distinct smaller reports, is vivid, detailed, and analytically sharp. She writes that "it was ... mainly by what I saw and heard in Bulgaria that I became convinced of the great urgency and reality of the Macedonian Problem."[70]

Anderson was impressed by the Macedonians' persuasiveness: "The Macedonians are determined; they are ruthless, but they are also extraordinarily charming and clever and attractive. I attended many tea parties where people told me, in matter-of-fact tones, heart-rending stories of their sufferings."[71] Far from being trapped in an introverted Balkan reality, she found them sophisticated observers of the wider field of national struggles. They claimed inspiration, she observed, from the Irish anti-colonial resistance. Any time she argued for the need to use peaceful methods, "the Macedonians continually pointed to Ireland as an instance of the success awaiting methods of force."[72] Anderson also emphasized the international framework in terms of which the Macedonians understood the ongoing violence: notably, the failure of the governments acting through the LoN to place limits on state violence. "They feel that the outside world has not done its duty by them, and that it is not they, but we, who are responsible for the era of violence in Yugo-Slav Macedonia."[73]

During her travels in Yugoslavia, she found Slovenes and Croats who sympathized with the Macedonians, as all had suffered from Serb hegemony within the state apparatus. She thought decentralization of the state administration, which many were demanding, could be a first step toward a federation of autonomous states or provinces, and eventually lead toward a Balkan Slav Federation, "the only solution of the Macedonian question which is likely to be satisfactory in a land of such mixed population."[74] She recognized that this would not happen quickly. Acknowledging the varying aspirations among Macedonians, she argued for conscientious application of the minority treaties in the meantime: "I believe the great mass of the Macedonians, including the most influential leaders in Bulgaria, would be satisfied with conditions which secured them the opportunities of free life and development within the frontiers of Yugo-Slavia."[75]

Anderson's interlocutors in Geneva, both at WILPF headquarters and at the LoN Secretariat, were keen for her to share her observations from her visit. She reported having long talks upon her return with Miss Sheepshanks and useful conversations with Molony and Céspedes; the latter, she noted, asked for a copy of her report and promised to "annotate [it] and send it up to the gentlemen (of the League of Nations Council?) who are dealing with these questions."[76]

Mosa Anderson had made an excellent impression on WILPF's Bulgarian Section and their pacifist circles as someone extremely intelligent and knowledgeable about Near Eastern issues, and they were hopeful she would be able to "clarify public opinion" regarding their sufferings and claims.[77] A few months before, Hilda Clark also visited Bulgaria, but the outcome of that visit turned out to be turbulent. Clark had spoken to public audiences on pacifism and the question of minorities but recognized that the Macedonian refugees were "not at all pleased" with what she said. However, it was an article in the Manchester Guardian reporting on Clark's lecture to the Manchester WILPF regarding her spring 1927 Balkan tour that caused the most serious ruckus. On June 10, Karavéloff described to Madeleine Doty (Sheepshanks' predecessor as international secretary) the dismay surrounding the Bulgarian press' transmission of the contents of the Manchester Guardian article: "I want to believe the translation is wrong, I'm waiting for the English version to arrive to see for myself."[78] Ten days later, enclosing with her letter an excerpt from the Manchester Guardian piece, Karavéloff reported the trouble it had caused, the potentially "unfortunate consequences for our section," and the outraged irritation of the Macedonian women.[79] The passage that offended most deeply read:

> In the Balkans, Dr. Clark proceeded, ... the clauses which provided that the racial or linguistic minority should have the right to use the mother tongue in schools and churches were difficult to apply and perhaps not so much needed, because there was not any real culture or love of the language behind these patois languages. She agreed with the Greeks that they were not worth saving.[80]

Clark's relief work with Quaker organizations in Europe since 1915, and her work-related travels in Greece, Turkey, Serbia, and Bulgaria, familiarized her with other perspectives on the Macedonian situation, and enabled her to develop a certain distance from the Bulgarian women's absolutist claims of a homogeneous minority. Her reported reference to "patois languages" indicates an awareness that local inhabitants were speaking a range of Slavic dialects; her assessment that "there was not any real culture or love of the language," if an accurate attribution, suggests she was persuaded by the Greek government's claims that many Slavic-speakers were indifferent to nationality and willing to assimilate. Clark recognized, in any case, that among the Slavic-speakers in Greek Macedonia who had remained in their villages and towns, after so much turmoil, were those who were willing—for a variety of reasons—to live under Greek rule. She also knew that by 1927, the Greek government's resettlement of Orthodox Christian refugees from Turkey in the region, a resettlement that had forced out tens of thousands of Slavic-speakers as well as Muslims since 1922, had Hellenized this part of Macedonia, creating new "facts on the ground" that could only be undone through more violence. As she confessed to Doty,

> I wish we could do more to help them forget the past and build up a new life in Bulgaria. For the peasants this is not so difficult and [were it not for] the

propaganda the peasants will settle and stay. It is the educated refugees in the town who keep up the propaganda and hatred, and I rather regret that they win a good deal of support from foreigners. Great sympathy they should have, but it really is absolutely impracticable for them to return to Greece or to keep a foot-hold there and their propaganda, if it is successful, could only result in war.[81]

Notwithstanding her misgivings with the MWU's political strategies as well as her disagreement with their representation of the Macedonians as a homogeneous entity, Clark transmitted an appeal from the organization—now affiliated with WILPF's Bulgarian Section—addressed to WILPF's branches throughout the world, to be considered at the WILPF's international executive committee meeting in September. It was duly scrutinized by WILPF president Jane Addams and former international secretary Emily Greene Balch. The Macedonian women had asked WILPF to mobilize its international network to "arouse public opinion in favor of justice," but Addams and Balch advised against emotional appeals: "we think the solution lies in trying to allay nationalistic feeling and to do what is possible to minimize suspicion and resentment while working for a rectification of injustices."[82]

In the years that followed, the Bulgarian Section repeatedly urged the WILPF international executive committee to put pressure on the LoN as well as specific states regarding "the Bulgarian minorities": they reported the intensification of Yugoslav nationalizing measures, warned that "the purely Bulgarian" population of Yugoslavia was being "reduced to slavery," and in 1929 enlisted the WILPF executive committee to call for an enquiry into "constant assassinations" of Bulgarians by Yugoslav authorities in villages divided by the Serbian-Bulgarian border.[83] Yet a desire for cooperation among Balkan women also existed within the Section, coinciding with the longstanding WILPF goal. Dragnewa—co-author of the December 1924 BWU letter, now writing to Sheepshanks at Karavéloff's request as one of the Bulgarian Section's designated delegates for WILPF's upcoming Prague conference, to be held in late August 1929—praised the efforts of WILPF activist Camille Drevet[84] in facilitating the setting up of new WILPF sections in Yugoslavia and Romania.[85] She emphasized that, as a trusted person among the various groups, Drevet would be able to arrange private meetings in Prague where the delegates, for the first time, could freely exchange ideas and discuss their projects: "We are very much counting on Madame Drevet to reunite [WILPF] representatives of the Balkan countries and inspire them for a common task."[86] News of a plan dreamed up by the Bulgarian women, along with Drevet, for a peripatetic multi-national Balkan women's delegation in April 1930, starting in Bucharest, moving on to Belgrade and then Sofia, was received "with sympathy and animation" by members of the Yugoslav Section.[87] However, despite the Yugoslav women's invitation for the Bulgarian women to visit Belgrade and much planning, facilitated by Drevet and Sheepshanks, the illness of both Sections' presidents, but more importantly, political disagreements over Macedonia and minorities between the two women's groups, meant that the post-Prague reunions fell through.

These conflicts, along with the obsessive focus on the Macedonian issue, frustrated Sheepshanks, who in February 1930 felt compelled to inquire directly whether her

Bulgarian colleagues were, in fact, committed to the organization's broader work and its pacifist objectives:

> I serve the Committee and it's not my place to judge whether a national section's activities are useful. However, I've noticed many times that the only news we receive of the Bulgarian Section is nationalist by nature. … We have not received from you news of any pacifist work at all. So, I have asked myself many times, "Is our Bulgarian Section working in the WILPF spirit?"[88]

Possibly without realizing it, Sheepshanks had put her finger on the difficulty faced by WILPF's Bulgarian Section. Along with the other women's organizations in Bulgaria, it operated within the field of civil society homeland nationalism, adopting its discourse of loss and injustice while rarely questioning the Bulgarian government's policies. At the same time, WILPF's Bulgarian Section also promoted non-violent approaches to conflict resolution and tried to cultivate a desire for peace and international cooperation even though they often stressed, especially in relation to Macedonia and minorities, WILPF's own principle, "no peace without justice."

The Bulgarian Section's ambiguous position and constrained field of action must have been exhausting for its leaders. During her 1927 visit to Sofia, Clark recognized Karavéloff's herculean efforts "to find peaceful methods of righting wrongs" within an extraordinarily difficult and complicated situation; she praised Karavéloff's grasp of pacifism and appreciated the challenges of advocating for it given Bulgaria's postwar conditions and continuing regional unrest. It was in recognition of these circumstances that she insisted that "one has to regard things in the Balkans as being at a different stage from anything we are accustomed to in our own countries."[89] Sheepshanks, who worked closely and energetically through letters with Karavéloff as well as with the Bulgarian Section's secretary, Lydia Chichmanova, but rarely saw them in person, may have found it more difficult to appreciate the Bulgarian women's sense of isolation, their vulnerability to accusations of disloyalty, and their reliance on allies. What she felt was the burden of their hopes, and she wanted to bring some realism into their expectations. While reiterating WILPF's commitment to work for peace, she also pointed out to them that "it is too much to expect that we have such influence with political men to be able to remedy these ills. All we can do is to attempt to inform public opinion and to link women from all countries in a common work for peace and justice."[90]

By the end of the 1920s, then, volatile, often tense yet enduring collaborations had been established between the leaders of three women's organizations in Bulgaria, and the mostly British and French international leadership of WILPF, in which minorities and Macedonia loomed large as issues requiring attention. As the WILPF Yugoslav group began to coalesce in 1928–29 and the question of cooperation between women of the two countries (as well as Greece and Romania) became more tangible and immediate, their radically incompatible understandings of these issues undermined a still incipient entente. The efforts of Bulgarian and Yugoslav women to convince WILPF's executive committee to recognize their pursuit of both pacifist and national aims as legitimate continued into the next decade, as conditions for minorities and for democracy worsened.

Conclusion

Like "nation," "minority" is a category of practice: of asserting, defining, contesting, and denying, as well as making real (or undermining its reality) through material and social actions. In this chapter, focusing on the period 1925–30, I have offered a glimpse of the complexities surrounding alliance among a range of female activists collaborating transnationally on questions of minorities and Macedonia, and their encounters with the LoN's international regime of minority treaty supervision. Taking as my point of departure Brubaker's conceptualization of the minority phenomenon as arising from plural and dynamic relations between a nationalizing state, national minority, and external national homeland, I have emphasized the complexities *within* these fields.

If, in relation to this minority question, there were two self-evidently nationalizing states (Greece and the Serb, Croat, and Slovene Kingdom/Yugoslavia), the second category—national minority—was a field of multiple and often shifting stances. For over half a century, the Slavic-speaking population responded to the evolving claims and counter-claims of four nations (three recognized, one unrecognized) regarding their nationality, and their status—or not—as minorities. In this chapter, I addressed the intricacies within these categories by pointing out the diverging, yet partially overlapping, stances of three women's organizations based in Bulgaria operating within the field of civil society homeland nationalism. Making things even more complicated, one of these organizations, the MWU, straddled different categories: being composed of refugees from two nationalizing states and now inhabiting the ostensible homeland (Bulgaria), they may have counted as (members of) the national minority, yet the female activists repudiated this designation. They saw themselves, in fact, as members of an unrecognized nation: Macedonia.

Acknowledging this intra-categorical contestation and inter-categorical ambiguity, I have looked at the three Bulgaria-based women's organizations not in isolation, nor (primarily) in relation to each other, but through their interactions with two other categories of "external" actor: activists within an internationalist, feminist, pacifist organization (WILPF) and international civil servants within the LoN Secretariat's Minorities Section, both with headquarters in Geneva (formulating, thus, a second tripartite relation). Surprisingly, these categories of actor, both characterized as international though in different ways, remain outside of Brubaker's model, yet the minority phenomenon in the interwar period, especially, can hardly be understood without taking them into account.

My approach to analyzing the three women's organizations based in Bulgaria was not only a theoretical approach, informed by Brubaker's framework. It followed my empirical observation of their habitual modus vivendi: that they tended to initiate "from below" unabashedly hierarchical, clientelistic relationships. They approached women they perceived to have more power and better connections and elicited their help, especially in transmitting, vouching for, and disseminating international appeals. Their demands for help were, nonetheless, articulated through a discourse of sisterly solidarity and shared commitment as women to specific claims for justice. Although the activism of all three Bulgaria-based women's organizations was framed by Bulgaria's revisionist claims toward recently "lost" Macedonian territories and their suffering co-nationals—whether regarded as Bulgarians or Macedonians, as minorities or members of a nation—their female leaders shared some elements in common with WILPF's purpose and leadership. Because of this, Bulgarian and Macedonian women enlisted the WILPF leadership's assistance for support in public appeals on those matters, as well as mediation in relation to petitions with LoN officials. WILPF international activists, in turn, sought to recruit the Bulgarian and Macedonian women into their wider project for peace and progressive social transformation.

Importantly, the claims of the various Bulgaria-based women's organizations concerning Macedonian minorities—or would-be nationals—asserted homogeneity as much as any nationalizing state. The quest for homogeneity was a shared quest. It was at moments when WILPF activists pointed out heterogeneity within the category, as did Clark in spring 1927, that relations became fraught.

Acknowledgments

I am grateful to Keith Brown, Francesca Piana, Vessi Ratcheva, and the volume's three editors for stimulating feedback on this chapter. An earlier version was presented at the conference "Versailles and Rights: A Centenary Appraisal" in Helsinki in June 2019. I warmly acknowledge the penetrating engagement of fellow conference participants, as well as the unwavering support of the Helsinki Collegium for Advanced Studies during my tenure as the Jane and Aatos Erkko Visiting Professor in Studies on Contemporary Society in 2018–19.

Notes

1 Rogers Brubaker, *Nationalism Reframed: Nationhood and the National Question in the New Europe* (Cambridge: Cambridge University Press, 1996).
2 For further detail on the formation of these states and the minority treaties, see Emmanuel Dalle Mulle, Davide Rodogno and Mona Bieling's introduction to this volume.
3 On the Hague Congress, see Jane Addams, Emily G. Balch, and Alice Hamilton, *Women at the Hague: The International Peace Congress of 1915* (Amherst, NY: Humanity Books, 2003); Gertrude Bussey and Margaret Tims, *Women's International League for Peace and Freedom, 1915–1965: A Record of Fifty Years' Work* (London: George Allen and Unwin, 1965), 17–33; Lela B. Costin, "Feminism, Pacifism, Internationalism and the 1915 International Congress of Women," *Women's Studies International Forum* 5, no. 3/4 (1982): 301–15.
4 On the history of WILPF see Gertrude Bussey and Margaret Tims, *Women's International League*; Leila Rupp, *Worlds of Women: The Making of the International Women's Movement* (Princeton: Princeton University Press, 1997); Jo Vellacott, "A Place for Pacifism and Transnationalism in Feminist Theory: The Early Work of the Women's International League for Peace and Freedom," *Women's History Review* 2, no. 1 (1993); Sybil Oldfield's, *Spinsters of this Parish: The Life and Times*

of F.M. Mayor and Mary Sheepshanks (London: Virago, 1984). More broadly on feminism and internationalism in the interwar period, see Glenda Sluga, "Women, Feminisms and Twentieth Century Internationalisms," in *Internationalisms: A Twentieth Century History*, ed. Glenda Sluga and Patricia Clavin (Cambridge: Cambridge University Press, 2017), 61–84.

5   Jane K. Cowan, "Fixing National Subjects in the 1920s Southern Balkans: Also an International Practice," *American Ethnologist* 35, no. 2 (2008): 338–56; Mark Mazower, "Minorities and the League of Nations in Interwar Europe," *Daedalus* 126, no. 2 (1997): 47–63.

6   A few examples from a vast literature include D. M. Brancoff, *La Macédoine et sa population chretienne* (Paris: Librairie Plon, 1905); Keith Brown, *The Past in Question: Modern Macedonia and the Uncertainties of Nation* (Princeton, New Jersey: Princeton University Press, 2003); Keith Brown, *Loyal unto Death: Trust and Terror in Revolutionary Macedonia* (Bloomington: Indiana University Press, 2013); Iakovos D. Michailidis, "The War of Statistics: Traditional Recipes for the Preparations for the Macedonian Salad," *East European Quarterly* 32, no. 1 (1998): 9–21; H. R. Wilkinson, *Maps and Politics: A Review of the Ethnographic Cartography of Macedonia* (Liverpool: University of Liverpool Press, 1951).

7   Brubaker, *Nationalism Reframed,* 120–3.

8   Jane K. Cowan, "The Supervised State," *Identities: Global Studies in Culture and Power* 14, no. 5 (2007): 545–78.

9   The executive committee always had a mixed—though, in this era, exclusively European and North American—composition, as members were elected on an individual, not national, basis. In 1929, it was comprised of two members each from United States, Britain, and France, and one member each from Germany, Switzerland, Austria, Canada, Netherlands, Czechoslovakia, and Sweden. Bussey and Tims, *Women's International League*, 78. The international secretary, the primary point of connection with national sections, had immense influence but no voting rights.

10 Catia C. Confortini, *Intelligent Compassion: The Women's International League for Peace and Freedom and Feminist Peace* (Oxford: Oxford University Press, 2012), 12.

11 Confortini, *Intelligent Compassion,* 11; Bussey and Tims, *Women's International League,* 34–5.

12 "Resolutions Adopted by the International Congress of Women at the Hague, May 1, 1915," in Jane Addams et al., *Women at the Hague*, 125.

13 WILPF Executive Committee to Representative of Members of the League of Nations on the Council and Assembly, December 15, 1920. WILPF Archives, Reel 102.

14 Bussey and Tims, *Women's International League,* 36.

15 Pablo de Azcárate, *League of Nations and National Minorities: An Experiment* (New York: Columbia University Press, 1945).

16 Rupp, *Worlds of Women,* 107.

17 Ibid., 113–14.

18 In eighteenth- and nineteenth-century geographical Macedonia "the term 'Bulgarian' was used to refer to speakers of South Slavic dialects from the Black Sea to the Adriatic," but by the late nineteenth century there were efforts to gain recognition for a separate Macedonian language; it was eventually codified in 1944. Victor Friedman, "The Modern Macedonian Standard Language and Its Relation to Modern Macedonian Identity," in *The Macedonian Question: Culture, Historiography, Politics*, ed. Victor Roudometof (Boulder: East European Monographs, 2000), 176–7.

19 Traian Stoianovich, "The Conquering Balkan Orthodox Merchant," *Journal of Economic History* 20, no. 2 (1960): 234–313.
20 Piero Vereni, "Boundaries, Frontiers, Persons, Individuals: Questioning Identity at National Borders," *Europea* 2, no. 1 (1996): 4.
21 Brown, *Loyal Unto Death*, 4.
22 Liisa Malkki, "National Geographic: The Rooting of Peoples and the Territorialization of National Identity among Scholars and Refugees," *Cultural Anthropology* 7, no. 1 (1992): 22–44.
23 For more detailed historical summaries see Brown, *Loyal unto Death,* Misha Glenny, *The Balkans 1804-1999: Nationalism, War and the Great Powers* (London: Granta, 1999); Mark Mazower, *The Balkans* (London: Weidenfeld and Nicolson, 2000).
24 John S. Koliopoulos, *Plundered Loyalties: World War II and Civil War in Greek West Macedonia* (New York: New York University Press, 1999), 17.
25 See Anastasia Karakasidou, "Transforming Identity, Constructing Consciousness: Coercion and Homogeny in Northwestern Greece," in *The Macedonian Question*, ed. Roudometof, 64.
26 Αρετή Τούντα-Φεργάδη, *Ελληνο-βουλγαρικές Μειονότητες. Πρωτόκολλο Πολίτη-Καλφώφ 1924-25* (Θεσσαλονίκη: Ι.Μ.Χ.Α, 1986) [Aretí Toúnda-Fergádi, *Greek-Bulgarian Minorities: The Politis-Kalfoff Protocol 1924-25* (Thessaloniki: Institute for Balkan Studies, 1986)]; Patrick Finney, "Greece, the Great Powers and the Politis-Kalfoff Minorities Protocol of 1924," *Diplomacy and Statecraft* 8, no. 1 (2007): 20–48; Iakovos D. Michailidis, "Minority Rights and Educational Problems in Greek Interwar Macedonia: The Case of the Primer 'Abecedar,'" *Journal of Modern Greek Studies* 14, no. 2 (1996): 329–43.
27 In early 1925, the LoN Secretariat Legal and Minorities Sections compiled research on these dialects to determine "whether a strict legal interpretation of the text of the Greek Minorities Treaty makes it possible to admit the Slav dialects of Macedonia as a basis for primary instruction of the minorities' children: or whether Bulgarian should be used." "The Macedonian Question: Notes on the dialects in use in Greek Macedonia," League of Nations (LoN) Archives Box R1660, 41/42722/11974, January 6–26, 1925. The Greek Ministry of Education prepared a primer using the Latin alphabet but, facing local opposition in the Florina region, it was never used. See Michailidis, "Minority Rights and Educational Problems."
28 Renée Hirschon, ed., *Crossing the Aegean: An Appraisal of the 1923 Compulsory Population Exchange between Greece and Turkey* (Oxford: Berghahn, 2003); Elisabeth Kontogiorgi, *Population Exchange in Greek Macedonia: The Rural Settlement of Refugees, 1922-1930* (Oxford: Oxford University Press, 2006).
29 Cowan, "Fixing National Subjects"; Theodora Dragostinova, *Between Two Motherlands: Nationality and Emigration among the Greeks of Bulgaria, 1900-1949* (Ithaca, NY: Cornell University Press, 2011); Kontogiorgi, *Population Exchange;* Stephen Ladas, *The Exchange of Minorities: Bulgaria, Greece and Turkey* (New York: Macmillan, 1932); Finney, "Greece, the Great Powers," 22.
30 Such Bulgarian-speaking but Greek-identified individuals were pejoratively labelled "grkoman" ("Greek lovers" or "pretending to be Greek") by those identifying as Bulgarian or Macedonian.
31 Deegan, "Introduction: Women and World Peace," in *Women at the Hague,* ed. Addams, Balch and Hamilton; Judy Whipps and Danielle Lake, "Pragmatist Feminism," in *The Stanford Encyclopedia of Philosophy*, ed. Edward N. Zalta, 2020,

https://plato.stanford.edu/archives/win2020/entries/femapproach-pragmatism/ (accessed June 28, 2022).

32. Its members were Yella Hertzka (Austria), Dr. Hilda Clark (England) and Mrs. Cederfield (Denmark). Yella Hertzka, "Italian Fascism in the South Tyrol," *Pax International* 1, no. 4 (1926).
33. Mary Sheepshanks to Calliope Parren [undated typescript], WILPF Archives, Reel 74.
34. Mary Sheepshanks to Marcelle Vorokassovitch, June 25, 1928, WILPF Archives, Reel 97.
35. Julia Malinoff and Z. Dragnewa to President of the Women's International League for Peace and Freedom [undated], WILPF Archives, Reel 57. Vilma Glucklich immediately replied to Malinoff, confirming receipt and promising to transmit the letter to the Minorities Section. Glucklich to Malinoff, January 2, 1925, WILPF Archives, Reel 57. I first discovered the evidence of this correspondence in a large LoN file, initiated when Glucklich transmitted to Colban on January 2, 1925, the undated letter "that we have just received" from Malinoff and Dragnewa, an indication that it was probably composed in December 1924. Vilma Glucklich to Erik Colban, "Communiqué from Women's International League for Peace and Freedom, International Office, Geneva, to the League of Nations." LoN Archives, Box R1660, 41/41548/11974.
36. Ingrid Sharp, Judit Acsády, and Nikolai Vukov, "Internationalism, Pacifism, Transnationalism: Women's Movements and the Building of a Sustainable Peace in the Post-War World," in *Women Activists between War and Peace: Europe, 1918–1923*, ed. Ingrid Sharp and Matthew Stibbe (London: Bloomsbury Academic, 2017), 87.
37. Sharp et al., "Internationalism, Pacifism, Transnationalism," 84–90.
38. Nikolai Vukov, "The Aftermaths of Defeat: The Fallen, the Catastrophe and the Public Response of Women to the End of the First World War in Bulgaria," in *Aftermaths of War: Women's Movements and Feminist Activists, 1918–1923*, ed. Ingrid Sharp and Matthew Stibbe (Leiden: Brill, 2011), 32–3.
39. Vukov, "The Aftermaths of Defeat," 19.
40. They are referring to the Politis-Kalfoff Protocol, discussed earlier.
41. Malinoff and Dragnewa to WILPF President [undated], "Communiqué." See note 35 for full reference. Henceforth this document will be referred to simply as "Communiqué."
42. Glucklich to Colban, January 2, 1925, "Communiqué."
43. Glucklich to Colban, January 16, 1925, "Communiqué."
44. A Quaker weekly magazine published in London since 1843.
45. Glucklich to Colban, January 16, 1925, "Communiqué."
46. Emilie Gourd to Erik Colban, February 10, 1925, "Communiqué."
47. Edward Said, *Orientalism: Western Conceptions of the Orient* (London: Pantheon Books, 1978).
48. Maria Todorova, *Imagining the Balkans* (Oxford and New York: Oxford University Press, 1997).
49. Jane K. Cowan, "Who's Afraid of Violent Language? Honour, Sovereignty and Claims-making in the League of Nations," Special Issue on Violence and Language, *Anthropological Theory* 3, no. 3 (2003): 271–91.
50. Александър Гребенаров, *Легални и тайни организации на македонските бежанци в България, 1918–1947* (София: Македонски научен институт, 2006), 199 [Alexander Grebenarov, *Legal and Secret Organizations of the Macedonian Refugees in Bulgaria, 1918–1947* (Sofia: Macedonian Studies Institute, 2006), 199].

51 Although in WILPF correspondence she usually signed her name as Catherine P. Karavéloff, in other WILPF papers she sometimes appears as Catherine Karavelov; elsewhere, she appears under the Bulgarian form of her name, Katerina Karavelova.
52 Mosa Anderson, "Bulgarian Problems and the Bulgarian Section of the W.I.L.," 1, WILPF Archives, Reel 99.
53 "Resolution votée par le Congrès de l'Union des Femmes de Macédoine à la Societé des Nations," LoN Archives, R1660, 41/52483/11974.
54 Ibid.
55 Ibid.
56 "Resolution votée par le Congrès de l'Union des Femmes de Macédoine à la Societé des Nations," LoN Archives, R1660, 41/52504/11974.
57 Ibid.
58 Ibid.
59 Cowan, "Who's Afraid of Violent Language?."
60 Cowan, "The Supervised State."
61 Interestingly, the League's other petition procedure—overseen by the Permanent Mandates Commission—operated differently. Relishing the opportunity to scrutinize the British and French governments on their mandatory rule, the Italian chairman of the Commission adopted a much more lenient approach. See Susan Pedersen, *The Guardians: The League of Nations and the Crisis of Empire* (Oxford and New York: Oxford University Press, 2015), 85, 446.
62 Oldfield, *Spinsters of This Parish*, 262.
63 Mary Sheepshanks to Kathleen Courtney, November 25, 1927, WILPF Archives, Reel 43.
64 Mary Sheepshanks to Catherine Karavéloff, November 28, 1927, WILPF Archives, Reel 57.
65 Ibid.
66 On why petitioners continued to submit petitions that they expected to fail, see Jane K. Cowan, "The Success of Failure? Minority Supervision at the League of Nations," in *Paths to International Justice: Social and Legal Perspectives*, ed. Marie-Bénédicte Dembour and Tobias Kelly (Cambridge: Cambridge University Press, 2007), 29–56.
67 Marie Sandell, *The Rise of Women's Transnational Activism: Identity and Sisterhood Between the World Wars* (London: I.B. Tauris, 2015), chapter 6.
68 Hilda Clark to Mary Sheepshanks, November 22, 1927, WILPF Archives, Reel 43.
69 Mosa Anderson, "Report of Visit to Yugo-Slavia and Bulgaria, December 16, 1927–February 6, 1928," WILPF Archives, Reel 99.
70 Mosa Anderson, "The Macedonian Problem," February 1, 1928. WILPF Archives, Reel 99.
71 Anderson, "The Macedonian Problem," 2.
72 Ibid.
73 Ibid.
74 Mosa Anderson, "The Macedonian Minority Question in Yugoslavia. The Ultimate Solution: Balkan Slav Federation," February 1, 1928. WILPF Archives, Reel 99.
75 Anderson, "The Macedonian Problem," 4.
76 Mosa Anderson, "Report of Visit to Yugo-Slavia and Bulgaria, December 16, 1927–February 6, 1928," 3. WILPF Archives, Reel 99. The question mark appears in the original and indicates Anderson's uncertainty.
77 Lydia Chichmanova to Mary Sheepshanks, February 12, 1928, WILPF Archives, Reel 57.

78 Catherine Karavéloff to Madeleine Doty, June 10, 1927, WILPF Archives, Reel 57.
79 Catherine Karavéloff to Madeleine Doty, June 21, 1927, WILPF Archives, Reel 57.
80 "Obstacles to Peace in the Balkans: Habit of Threatening War. Woman Doctor's Report on Her Tour," *Manchester Guardian,* May 31, 1927.
81 Hilda Clark to Madeleine Doty, June 9, 1927, WILPF Archives, Reel 56.
82 Emily Greene Balch to Madeleine Doty, "Reply to Macedonian Appeal" [undated], WILPF Archives, Reel 56.
83 "Rapport de la Section Bulgare de la Ligue des Femmes pour la Paix et la Liberté" for the Vienna Congress, March 20, 1929, WILPF Archives, Reel 57; Bulgarian Section to Mary Sheepshanks, May 4, 1929, WILPF Archives, Reel 57.
84 Camille Drevet, a French journalist, peace and anti-imperialist activist and a war widow, travelled extensively in the Balkan and Baltic countries for WILPF. She replaced Sheepshanks as WILPF international secretary in December 1930.
85 The Yugoslav Section was founded on July 8, 1929, but in April 1930 the executive committee declined to recognize them as a section, finding them "not yet ready." Rupp, *Worlds of Women,* 117; Clara Ragaz to Milena Petrovich, April 29, 1931, WILPF Archives, Reel 97.
86 Z. Dragnewa to Mary Sheepshanks, June 10, 1929, WILPF Archives, Reel 57.
87 Milena Petrovich to Mary Sheepshanks, October 26, 1929, WILPF Archives, Reel 97.
88 Mary Sheepshanks to Lydia Chichmanova, February 28, 1930, WILPF Archives, Reel 57.
89 Hilda Clark to Madeleine Doty, June 9, 1927, 2.
90 Sheepshanks to Chichmanova, February 28, 1930.

Coda

14

The Difference Nationalism Makes: Jews and Others in the Twentieth Century

Omer Bartov

Since it was introduced in the first decade of the present century, the term "national indifference" has presented scholars of modern Europe and beyond with a particularly vexing conundrum. On the one hand, this concept was meant to remind us that we should not be taken in by a host of "nationalizers," who labored to convince both their own publics and future generations that the nation had always existed and merely needed to be "awakened from its slumber" and perceive itself as what it had always been since time immemorial; that it had unique, eternal, and precious traits rooted in ancient, pre-historic times; that its history, culture, language, physical features, mentality, and soul were singular, if not, indeed, superior to those of all other nations; and, that it could look forward to an ever brighter future, to a destiny that distinguished it as a chosen member of humankind. Along with earlier critiques of nationalism, which pointed out that nations were constructed over a longer or shorter time span and a continuous or uneven process, and that they only subsequently invented their past existence and traditions, the term "national indifference" was meant to indicate that this entire massive undertaking over many decades across the European continent and beyond its borders left many of those subjected to it entirely or partially indifferent to its exhilarating rhetoric. As discussed for instance by Pieter Judson in this volume, people, especially the vast rural masses of Europe, as well as its numerous linguistic, religious, and what came to be seen as ethnic groups, never perceived themselves as merely members of a single nation, were often far too preoccupied with more immediate and mundane concerns, switched relatively easily from one language, identity, and set of relationships to another, and consequently remained a source of immense frustration to the nationalizers and what emerged especially after the First World War as the nationalizing nation-state.[1]

On the other hand, anyone remotely familiar with the history of twentieth-century Europe cannot possibly ignore the power that nationalism has had on individuals, groups, and organizations during much of that century. In view of the successful mobilization of national sentiments, most evident in the wars waged by states and substate organizations, which entailed extreme violence, ethnic cleansing, and genocide of groups designated as enemy nations, races, or classes, by other groups, organizations, and nations motivated by national ideologies, as well as considering the creation of more or less distinct cultures with which large segments of Europe's population began to identify, any reference to personal or group indifference seems out of sync with the vehemence, sacrifice, and bloody-mindedness that have characterized much of the twentieth century. In other words, what is the relationship between the concept of national indifference and the horrors, as well as the intense loyalties, that nationalism has engendered in the twentieth century? How could an ideology, a worldview, and a sentiment mobilize millions of people to perpetrate extreme violence upon each other if large sectors of these same populations were "nationally indifferent"? What difference, then, did nationalism make, how did it do it, by whom, and to whom? Were the masses, which nationalism claimed to have awoken from their slumber, actually still asleep while all this was happening, were they forcibly engaged in an undertaking they did not understand and did not wish to participate in, or did they eventually buy into this pernicious and intoxicating idea of nationalism?

For the last few decades, we have seen a growing trend, especially among Western intellectuals and academics, of dismissing the power of nationalism; increasingly, we have been told that nationalism was an anachronism, if, indeed, it ever existed as anything more than a phantom, a bad dream, or a nightmare, in the first place. In a famous 2003 article in the *New York Review of Books*, the late Tony Judt wrote:

> At the dawn of the twentieth century, in the twilight of the continental empires, Europe's subject peoples dreamed of forming "nation-states," territorial homelands where Poles, Czechs, Serbs, Armenians, and others might live free, masters of their own fate. When the Habsburg and Romanov empires collapsed after World War I, their leaders seized the opportunity. A flurry of new states emerged; and the first thing they did was set about privileging their national, "ethnic" majority—defined by language, or religion, or antiquity, or all three—at the expense of inconvenient local minorities, who were consigned to second-class status: permanently resident strangers in their own home.

Among those national movements was also Zionism. Yet Zionism, as Judt noted,

> was frustrated in its ambitions. The dream of an appropriately sited Jewish national home in the middle of the defunct Turkish Empire had to wait upon the retreat of imperial Britain. ... And thus it was only in 1948 that a Jewish nation-state was established in formerly Ottoman Palestine. But the founders of the Jewish state had been influenced by the same concepts and categories as their fin-de-siècle contemporaries back in Warsaw, or Odessa, or Bucharest; not surprisingly, Israel's ethno-religious self-definition, and its discrimination against internal "foreigners," has always had more in common with, say, the practices of post-Habsburg Romania than either party might care to acknowledge.

Consequently, as Judt saw it, "the problem with Israel" was

> that it arrived too late. It has imported a characteristically late-nineteenth-century separatist project into a world that has moved on, a world of individual rights, open frontiers, and international law. ... In a world where nations and peoples increasingly intermingle and intermarry at will; where cultural and national impediments to communication have all but collapsed; where more and more of us have multiple elective identities and would feel falsely constrained if we had to answer to just one of them; in such a world Israel is truly an anachronism. And not just an anachronism but a dysfunctional one. In today's "clash of cultures" between open, pluralist democracies and belligerently intolerant, faith-driven ethno-states, Israel actually risks falling into the wrong camp.[2]

Since these words were written, but in fact also in previous decades, as indicated, for instance, by the wars in the former Yugoslavia of the 1990s, we have seen a growing surge of nationalism, not least ethno-nationalism, along with authoritarianism, racism, xenophobia, and democratic erosion in many parts of Europe, not least in Poland and Hungary, but also in such Western countries as France and Britain, as well as in the United States. That is not to say that the values and beliefs extolled by Judt as characterizing the West have disappeared, but rather that they are being contested and appear to be under threat, with varying degrees of intensity. The progress toward ever-more "open, pluralist democracies" and their anticipated victory in this "clash of cultures" against "belligerently intolerant, faith-driven ethno-states" does not seem to have trended in the right direction. Looking back from where we stand today, I am reminded of what some people said in Israel after the attacks on the United States on September 11, 2001, namely, that following a period in which they had believed that Israel would become increasingly more like the United States, it now appeared that the United States was becoming more like Israel. Two decades later, the January 6, 2021, assault on the Congress and everything it represented for American society and politics ought to raise the alarm for all those who still believe that violent and racist nationalism is an anachronism in the West.

Similarly, the illegal and brutal Russian invasion of Ukraine in February 2022 must make us rethink our optimistic analyses of the decline of ethno-nationalism, as well as the extraordinary power of patriotism. Russia and Ukraine have competing national historical narratives. For the current Russian leadership, as well as apparently a significant share of the population, Little Russia, that is, Ukraine, is an inherent part of a historical Russian entity that includes Great Russia, White Russia (Belarus), and Little Russia (Ukraine).[3] According to Ukrainian national leaders, and over the last few years an increasing share of the population, Ukrainians have been struggling to create an independent Ukrainian state since at least the seventeenth century. Moreover, whereas Russia believes that its own beginning can be traced to medieval Kievan Rus, Ukrainian nationalism sees it as the birthplace of the Ukrainian nation, annexed into the emerging Russian Empire only in the seventeenth and eighteenth centuries.[4] With the fall of the Soviet Union and the creation of independent Ukraine in 1991, it appeared that this harkening back to separate historical narratives was over, or at least no longer politically relevant. Instead, Vladimir Putin's power politics have resulted in bringing history back with a bang. And what is just as extraordinary, while Ukrainian society and politics experienced a great deal of tension between a Russian and a Western orientation (associated but not entirely consistent with Russian- and Ukrainian-speaking citizens), it gradually developed a self-image, partially consistent with reality, of being a multi-ethnic and pluralistic society, to the extent that it elected a president of Jewish origin in a landslide election with little reference to his ethnicity, which only came up after Russia's preposterous justification of its invasion as a denazification operation.

And yet, reactions around Europe and in the United States have been overwhelmingly supportive of Ukraine and have expressed widespread admiration for Ukrainian patriotism and sacrifice. Nowhere do we hear any talk of indifference. There are those who call for more support for Ukraine, and those who call for caution. But the general sentiment in those presumably post-national societies of Eastern, Central, and Western Europe, as well as the United States, verges on veneration of the Ukrainian struggle to preserve national independence against an invading power. One may debate who precisely is Ukrainian; but the Ukrainian flag, national anthem, the symbol of the trident, such greetings as "Slava Ukraini" (Glory to Ukraine)—whose less than savory origins no one wishes to recall, not least its widespread use by the violently anti-Polish and antisemitic followers of Stepan Bandera, the leader of the radical faction of the Organization of Ukrainian Nationalists before and during the Second World War—are now everywhere in the Western media. Is nationalism back, or is this just one more fad, a momentary media event that will soon recede into general indifference?

The notion that nationalism was a spent force has a much longer history than the concept of national indifference. During the Yom Kippur War of 1973, in which the Israeli army took an unexpected battering by the Egyptian and Syrian military, "educational officers" and mobilized intellectuals and academics were sent to bolster the morale of Israeli troops at the front. In one such morale-boosting lecture, a certain academic who had read various studies on "why soldiers fight" lectured to a group of reserve soldiers in the Sinai Peninsula. Combat troops, he explained to them, don't fight for any ideological or political ideas; they fight primarily for each other. This was known as the "primary group" theory of motivation, popularized by the American sociologists Edward Shils and Morris Janowitz in the wake of the Second World War. The Israeli reservists, who had already seen combat at the front, were taken aback. Of course we fight for each other, one of them said. But we are here to defend the state, the country, the Jewish people. The reservist had clearly not read the relevant scholarly literature.[5]

The heavy losses and trauma of that war also occasioned a large number of cases of what we now refer to as post-traumatic stress disorder (PTSD). As one psychoanalyst who diagnosed Israeli troops suffering from PTSD (previously known as battle fatigue or shell shock) later argued, the Holocaust played a strangely prominent role in some of the soldiers' mental disintegration, either as an experience they had personally undergone as children, or as a transmitted experience in their families or cultural and social surroundings. Hence the war was perceived as another potential genocide, that is, an attempt to destroy the people, or nation. Loyalty to one's comrades was merely one part of this much larger picture within the soldiers' minds and their willingness to fight for what they perceived as national survival.[6]

Emancipation and Homogeneity

As Tony Judt wrote in 2003, Zionism arose in response to the ethno-nationalism that emerged in the lands where the vast majority of European Jewry resided, not least in the Austro-Hungarian province of Galicia, which saw also the emergence of Polish and Ukrainian nationalism. These ethno-nationalisms were deeply territorial, and the struggle between Polish and Ukrainian nationalism was over the territory of Galicia, which Poles saw as part of the legacy of the Polish-Lithuanian commonwealth—partitioned in the late eighteenth century—and Ukrainians saw as their native land colonized by Polish estate owners and their Jewish lackeys. Zionism borrowed many of its symbols and much of its phraseology from Polish and Ukrainian nationalists (themselves influenced by German nationalism), not least their essentialist ethnic assertions. But as for territory, it sought it elsewhere, in what Jews referred to as Eretz Israel, where the same kind of struggle soon ensued between Jewish colonizers claiming to be returning to their ancestral land, and Palestinian Arabs claiming to be the indigenous population colonized by European settlers.[7]

Were all those Poles, Ukrainians, and Jews truly nationalized, or was this all a tale told by nationalist and nationalizing leaders, intellectuals, priests, popular writers of historical novels and journalists, as well as, of course, historians? Did Polish and Ukrainian peasants and Jewish workers and artisans buy into this new nationalist rhetoric? And if they eventually did, when and under what circumstances did that happen? Before there was nationalism, I would argue, there was emancipation.[8] This was not only the case in Eastern Europe of course. As Tony Judt might have noted, East European nationalism itself was in a certain sense an anachronism, coming to the rural populations of the region decades or more after it had become a major project in Central and Western Europe, although not as belatedly as all that. Before the peasants of Third Republic France could be made into Frenchmen, there first had to be a republic; and a republic could not come into being without emancipating the peasants in the French Revolution, since the vast majority of the nation were, in fact, peasants.[9] It was that revolution that also brought about the emancipation of the Jews, on the assumption that all citizens of the republic had equal rights. The ideas of nationalism came to the German lands on the bayonets of Napoleon's soldiers, as did the emancipation of the peasants; Prussia abolished serfdom in 1807 and was followed by other German states in 1815. These were essential preconditions for German unification, as was the need to remove the economic constraints on the multiple German-speaking states and principalities, leading to the creation of a confederation enjoying a customs union. Once the empire was established, the Jews, now deemed sufficiently assimilated, could also be emancipated on the same principle of individual equal rights before the law.

Reeling from the 1848 revolutions, the Austrian Empire was similarly constrained to fully emancipate the peasants, as well as the Jews, although final full emancipation of the empire's Jews had to wait another two decades.[10]

Without emancipation, there would have been no nationalism. Emancipation was a crucial feature of the Enlightenment, and at the root of creating the modern state, one of whose most central components was those peasants turned into nationals. Jewish emancipation could not but logically follow. The status of Jews in European society was as medieval as was serfdom, and contrary to all Enlightenment principles. But without the emancipation of the Jews, modern antisemitism would have been unthinkable; and without modern antisemitism, itself an outgrowth of ethno-nationalism, there would have been no Zionism, which eventually perpetuated the ongoing conflict with the Palestinians, who have largely come to define themselves under the rubric of ethno-territorial nationalism.[11]

When did the peasants of the French Republic become French? Arguably, the process began in 1870 through a public education system and universal conscription culminated in the First World War under the slogan of protecting France from a German invasion. And while France boasted a civic nationalism rather than an ethnic one, it was in France that a powerful ethno-national or integral nationalist movement was born in the wake of the Dreyfus trial and the establishment of the *Action Française*. When Maurice Barrès published his novel *Les Déracinés* in 1897, true France was imagined as the nation of those rooted in the land, the now emancipated peasants; the rest, the fickle urbanites and the Jews were the opposite of everything that France stood for. The struggle over the meaning of true France, which persisted throughout the interwar period and Vichy, presented a polar image of the rooted peasant and the rootless Jew. The nation, homogeneous in all its regional diversity, was in the village, the land, rooted in a thousand years of civilization. Its natural opposite was the Jew, transformed from a theological to a sociological role in this imaginary of true versus false.[12]

The birth of the term antisemitism in 1879 followed swiftly in the wake of German unification. Unification was a political act, born, in Bismarck's depiction, of blood and iron. But the notion of a German nation preceded unification by decades, and at the same time had to be implanted into people's minds over many decades thereafter. When did Bavarians and Prussians begin thinking of themselves as Germans?[13] Here too, as in France, the First World War arguably played a major role, as socialists and conservatives, Lutherans and Catholics, Prussians and Bavarians fought side by side, with Catholics and socialists striving to show that they were just as German and patriotic as the others. So, too, did the Jews. But in their case, prewar animosity, as expressed, for instance, in the historian Heinrich Treitschke's infamous 1880 "the Jews are our misfortune" article, culminated in the "Jew count" of 1916, which strove to measure whether German Jews were doing their part in defense of the Reich, and, after the war, in the stab-in-the-back legend that created the raison d'être for the radical right and the rise of the Nazis in the 1920s. The German nation was forged again by blood and iron, and the vaunted *Frontgemeinschaft* (community of the front) gave birth to the *Volksgemeinschaft* (the community of the nation, or the race); but the Jews, emancipated, given equal rights, and deeply integrated into German society, were excluded from the vision of a racially united Germany, and were associated with defeat in the war and misery and degeneration in its aftermath.[14] For the Nazis, there was no clear definition of an Aryan but that he or she contained no Jewish blood. The true German held a plow in one hand and a gun in the other; the Jew was innately unable to either fight or work. If Germany had to liberate itself from the Jews by way of extermination through labor, Zionists came to believe that Jews could be liberated from their essence as *Luftmenschen*—rootless "air people" associated with wheeling and dealing and impractical contemplation—only by learning to work the land with a plow in one hand and a gun in the other.[15]

In Galicia, especially in its eastern part, which contained the largest concentration of Ukrainians (known then as Ruthenians) and of Jews in the Austrian Empire, emancipation created two nations, the Ukrainians and the Jews. Neither one nor the other awoke from their slumber instantaneously. It took, indeed, Sisyphean labor by nationalizers, who were just as busy also among Polish villagers, to persuade peasants and town dwellers that they were, indeed, part of some larger whole, that recognizing this would give greater meaning to their existence and improve their material conditions, and that the others, those who did not belong to their nation, were hostile to them and threatened their material existence and their newly found identity.

The nationalizers worked hard disseminating their message, through literacy campaigns, schooling and education, pamphlets and newspapers, lectures and clubs and societies, employing students and priests, writers and poets, songs and music. At times they despaired, traveling from one wretched village to another, seeing the peasants mired in poverty and illiteracy, in drink and violence. Why had the peasants not seized their newly found freedom after emancipation and built for themselves successful, prosperous farms? The plots were too small, they had no access to better knowledge of farming or better tools to husband the land. But they were also exploited, as the nationalizers saw it, more than ever before by the newly emancipated Jews, who could now also live in the villages, own taverns where they sucked the last coin from the peasants for cheap alcohol and thus drove the new nation into alcoholism, poverty, and disease. As the popular Ukrainian author Ivan Franko wrote in his many novels and stories, the Jews were the misfortune of the emerging Ukrainian nation; one emancipated group was debilitating and sucking the blood of another.[16]

How many peasants bought into this rhetoric and if so, when did they? In this case too, the First World War and its aftermath were pivotal, in Galicia as in many other parts of Europe, East and West. The war militarized and divided the groups residing in this province; the Poles joined the Polish legions and fought not for the emperor but for the resurrection of Poland. Poland, they sang, is not yet lost. The Ukrainians joined Ukrainian legions, and then formed the Ukrainian Galician Army, hoping to create an independent western Ukrainian republic, which they eventually established just as the empire collapsed, only to see it snatched from their hands and incorporated into the Second Polish Republic following a bitter war with the Poles, replete with massacres of civilian populations and pogroms against Jewish communities accused by each side of supporting the other.[17] Indeed, during the war, it was mostly the Jews who fought for the emperor, fearing the outcome of imperial collapse and the establishment of nation-states led by ethno-nationalists.[18] In Galicia, by the end of this cycle of violence from 1914 to 1921, nationalism had come to play a much more prominent role in people's lives and experiences than in the prewar era. Over the next two decades it only spread and deepened, as the Polish state's attempts to suppress Ukrainian nationalism by brutal police actions and prohibitions on nationalist organizations, as well as colonization of these lands by Poles brought in from the west and given preferential support by the government, led to the creation of underground Ukrainian nationalist organizations dedicated to terrorism and the establishment of a Pole-free and Jew-free Ukraine. By the 1930s the evidence indicates that large numbers of Ukrainian peasants supported nationalist organizations and parties.[19] As mentioned by Dalle Mulle, Rodogno, and Bieling in the introduction to this volume, and shown by several other contributions, the space for national indifference shrank considerably during the interwar period.

As for the Jews, Jewish nationalism and eventually Zionism developed belatedly. The Jewish writer and Nobel Prize laureate Shmuel Yosef Agnon recalled the arrival of socialism and Zionism among the Jewish population of his hometown Buczacz at the dawn of the twentieth century as a major upheaval.[20] Both threatened the traditional Jewish way of life and were carried mostly by the young. The Jews, of course, had a sense of their separate identity long before nationalism came on the scene, and their insistence on keeping themselves apart from non-Jews, along with restrictions by Christian regimes on Jewish occupations and sites of residence, meant that they lived both together with and apart from their Gentile neighbors. But emancipation brought great promise to the Jews, just as it did to the serfs. Now they could leave their sites of residence, enter educational institutions, take up occupations previously barred to them, and generally "come out of the ghetto," as the saying went, and become part of mainstream society.[21] But that also meant abandoning, or at least attenuating, reforming, or changing their traditional Jewish identity, their membership in a community, long-held customs and habits, and stepping out into a world that was hardly always welcoming and often suspicious and resentful of their success. There were those who left their Galician towns between the mid-nineteenth century and the First World War and found alternative ways of life, some at the great capitals of Vienna and Berlin as writers, actors, scholars, scientists, and so forth; others heading to Palestine, and many, many more crossing the continent and the ocean to North America and other parts of the world, fleeing poverty and prejudice, and hoping for a better life.[22]

But how many Jews were swayed by nationalism and Zionism, the notion that the Jews are not just a people united by religion, birth, and fate, but also a nation that must modernize itself, adapt to the brave new world of the twentieth century, and seek its own autonomy or independence, if not, indeed, its own land? In Galicia, where the *Bund*, the Jewish workers' movement, was weak, Jewish nationalism became the alternative even before the First World War.[23] But it was only in the wake of the war, which saw the destruction of countless Jewish communities by the Russian army, massive displacement of populations, and the emptying of many towns, that Zionism began to play an important role, not least in response to the ever more active nationalist policies of the new Polish government and the growing militancy and antisemitism of Ukrainian nationalism. By the 1930s the Zionists were a potent, if not the strongest, single political movement in Galicia, even if for many Jews this did not imply actually wanting to set off to Palestine but rather a political and national identity.[24]

What appears by all accounts more than likely is that on the eve of the Second World War, which in Galicia meant the takeover of the province by the Soviet Union for the next two years, a combination of violent events and nationalizing efforts had ensured that large parts of the population identified themselves as members of one of the three main groups in the region. However, as many other contributions to this volume have shown for different European countries, both in the East and the West of the continent, this does not mean that there were no overlaps, ambiguities, or attempts to defy national divisions by way of other allegiances and ideologies. In Galicia, significant numbers of Poles and Ukrainians had intermarried for generations, although traditionally the sons of such unions took up their father's religion and the daughters took up their mother's faith, thus perpetuating the ethno religious divide between Polish Roman Catholics and Ukrainian Greek Catholics (the main religion of Ukrainians in Galicia). Local socialists had tried since the beginning of the century to create a non-ethnic sense of identity and solidarity between mostly Jewish working-class town dwellers and mostly Ukrainian peasants. But by the 1930s peasants identified socialists and communists with Jews and preferred joining nationalist organizations. Some Jews abandoned their Jewish origins and identity and became active socialists, anarchists, and communists; but they were a small minority. Relations between the groups persisted, and by all accounts there were still friendships, at least among the young. But the ethno-national divide was growing and deepening. When the war broke out, violence also erupted. As the German consul in Lwów (Lviv), Dr. Gerhard Seelos, wrote in August 1939, "in case of an armed conflict … the Ukrainians" would "rise up as one man" and "drive out or slaughter the Poles." But like many others, even this official of the Nazi government could not anticipate the scale of the horror that was about to envelop Galicia.[25] The various invaders and occupiers did their worst. But much of the violence also came from within these communities, exercised against friends and neighbors, schoolmates and acquaintances, colleagues and even at time spouses and children. Nationalism had learned not only to hate but also to murder.[26]

Aftermath and beyond

The ethno-nationalists' quest for homogeneity since the latter third of the nineteenth century was accomplished in Galicia by their enemies: Nazi genocidal policies against the Jews; ethnic cleansing of the Poles by Ukrainian nationalist under the cover of German occupation; Soviet decapitation of elites in 1939–41; and then Polish-Ukrainian population exchange after reoccupying the area in 1944. By the late 1940s what had been eastern Galicia, now West Ukraine, was primarily inhabited by Ukrainians, some of them deported from Polish territories.[27]

Poland, too, accomplished ethno-national homogeneity. Moved to the west, into lands that were emptied of their German inhabitants, its large Jewish population had almost entirely been murdered, and its Ukrainian inhabitants largely deported. From an interwar count of only 60 percent ethnic Poles it became, and until the present war in Ukraine remained, almost purely Polish and Roman Catholic.[28] Things in Germany and France looked different. While Germany had become almost entirely *judenfrei* once the postwar DP camps were emptied, it soon took in large numbers of mostly Turkish guest workers, albeit remaining highly reluctant to absorb them as citizens for decades thereafter. Since the fall of communism, Germany has also taken in large numbers of Jews from Russia, although the Jewish community in Germany today is still a far smaller than its very modest prewar predecessor.[29] In France, on the other hand, the number of Jews doubled after the war, many of them coming from North Africa. France's colonial legacy also meant that it has taken in large numbers of North and sub-Saharan Africans and Southeast Asians. Yet since the Algerian War, and under the pressure of anti-immigrant sentiments, France has again begun defining its citizenship more along ethnic lines and has made naturalization increasingly difficult.[30]

Developments in recent years, such as the rise of the Law and Justice party in Poland since 2005, the election of Viktor Orbán as prime minister of Hungary in 2010, the Brexit referendum in the United Kingdom and the election of Donald Trump as president of the United States in 2016, and the success of Marine Le Pen to garner over 40 percent of the vote in the French presidential elections of 2022, indicate that radical ethno-nationalism, accompanied or encouraged by a growing socioeconomic gap, anti-immigration sentiments, distrust of democratic institutions, endemic corruption, and conspiracy theories spreading like wildfires on social media, is on the rise in all parts of Europe. Just as inevitably, it also includes a perceptible rise in antisemitism. Popular sentiments toward homogeneity, as expressed by English supporters of Brexit, are probably both pre-national and given a certain ideological panache by nationalist rhetoric. Critics have rightly noted that countries like Poland, which resisted taking in any Syrian refugees, is accommodating vast numbers of Ukrainians. Yet in fact, this is not at all "natural," considering that Poland's nationalist government passed memory laws against Ukraine for what it depicts as the Ukrainian nationalists' genocide of Poles in Eastern Poland in 1943–4, and fiercely protected its border with Ukraine as the perceived eastern boundary of Europe.[31] It is nonetheless encouraging to see European countries mobilizing to help Ukraine, even if this is clearly meant to deter an expansionist Russia feared by its smaller and most vulnerable neighbors. Whether the Russian invasion of Ukraine in February 2022, which is likely to change European politics in profound ways we can still not clearly anticipate, will lead to growing nationalism, including calls for greater ethnic homogeneity, is hard to say. But, as I have argued here, nationalism thrives on war and conflict. While I believe that Europe has no choice at the moment but to face up to a clear Russian threat, I fear that the trend toward greater nationalism, exclusion, and intolerance that was already on the rise before the Russian aggression will continue and even accelerate. If we should celebrate a lack of indifference to the fate of Ukraine, four years of Donald Trump's presidency in the United States, the widespread support for Marine Le Pen in France, the creation of new-fangled authoritarianisms, often kleptocratic and bound up with religion, as in Russia and Turkey, the Han-national-communist violent suppressions of minorities in China, and the fear, rage, and militancy that the war in Ukraine may spread around the continent, do not bode well for the future of national indifference.

Notes

1. See references to the relevant literature in Emmanuel Dalle Mulle, Davide Rodogno and Mona Bieling's introduction to this volume.
2. Tony Judt, "Israel: The Alternative," *New York Review of Books*, October 23, 2003, https://www.nybooks.com/articles/2003/10/23/israel-the-alternative/ (accessed June 28, 2022).
3. For a particularly frightening statement on Russian goals in Ukraine, literally calling for genocide in the sense of eradicating Ukraine and wiping it off the map, see Timofey Sergeytsev, "What Should Russia Do with Ukraine?" published in the Russian state-owned news agency *RIA Novosti* on April 3, 2022, https://ria.ru/20220403/ukraina-1781469605.html (accessed June 28, 2022).
4. On these competing narratives see, e.g., NPR interview with Timothy Snyder, "How Ukraine's History Differs from Putin's Version," February 26, 2022, https://www.npr.org/2022/02/26/1083332620/how-ukraines-history-differs-from-putins-version (accessed June 28, 2022).
5. I was a soldier in that war and vividly recall the troops' sentiments. But this incident was related to me by my late father, a journalist and an author, who was serving at the time as one of those morale-boosters. On the "primary group" thesis and my critique of it, see Omer Bartov, *Hitler's Army: Soldiers, Nazis, and War in the Third Reich* (New York: Oxford University Press, 1991), 29–58.
6. See, e.g., Shoshana Felman and Dori Laub, *Testimony: Crises of Witnessing in Literature, Psychoanalysis, and History* (New York: Routledge, 1992), 86–92.
7. See, e.g., Joshua Shanes, *Diaspora Nationalism and Jewish Identity in Habsburg Galicia* (New York: Cambridge University Press, 2012); Kai Struve, *Bauern und Nation in Galizien: Über Zugehörigkeit und soziale Emanzipation im* 19. Jahrhundert (Göttingen: Vandenhoeck & Ruprecht, 2005); Keely Stauter-Halsted, *The Nation in the Village: The Genesis of Peasant National Identity in Austrian Poland, 1848–1914* (Ithaca: Cornell University Press, 2001); Omer Bartov, "The Return of the Displaced: Ironies of the Jewish-Palestinian Nexus, 1939–1949," *Jewish Social Studies* 24, no. 3 (2019): 26–50.
8. Omer Bartov, *Anatomy of a Genocide: The Life and Death of a Town Called Buczacz* (New York: Simon and Schuster, 2018), 15–29, 33–6.
9. Eugen Weber, *Peasants into Frenchmen: The Modernization of Rural France, 1870–1914* (Stanford: Stanford University Press, 1976).
10. Hagen Schulze, *The Course of German Nationalism: From Frederick the Great to Bismarck, 1763–1867* (New York: Cambridge University Press, 1991); Jonathan Sperber, *The European Revolutions, 1848–1851*, 2nd ed. (New York: Cambridge University Press, 2005).
11. David Sorkin, *Jewish Emancipation: A History across Five Centuries* (Princeton: Princeton University Press, 2019); Arthur Hertzberg, *The French Enlightenment and the Jews* (New York: Columbia University Press, 1968); Uriel Tal, *Christians and Jews in Germany: Religion, Politics, and Ideology in the Second Reich, 1870–1914* (Ithaca: Cornell University Press, 1975).
12. Zeev Sternhell, *Maurice Barrès et le nationalisme français* (Brussels: Éditions Complexe, 1985); Eugen Weber, *Action Française: Royalism and Reaction in Twentieth Century France* (Stanford: Stanford University Press, 1962); Ernst Nolte, *Three Faces of Fascism: Action Française, Italian Fascism, National Socialism*, trans.

Leila Vennewitz (London: Weidenfeld and Nicolson, 1965); Herman Lebovics, *True France: The Wars over Cultural Identity, 1900–1945* (Ithaca: Cornell University Press, 1992).

13   Alon Confino, *The Nation as a Local Metaphor: Württemberg, Imperial Germany, and National Memory, 1871–1918* (Chapel Hill: University of North Carolina Press, 1997); Celia Applegate, *A Nation of Provincials: The German Idea of Heimat* (Berkeley: University of California Press, 1990).

14   Heinrich von Treitschke, "A Word about Our Jewry (1880)," in *The Jew in the Modern World: A Documentary History*, ed. Paul Mendes-Flohr and Yehuda Reinharz, 2nd ed. (New York: Oxford University Press, 1995), 343–6; Werner T. Angress, "The German army's 'Judenzählung' of 1916: Genesis—Consequences—Significance," *Leo Baeck Institute Yearbook* 23 (1978): 117–37; George L. Mosse, *Fallen Soldiers: Reshaping the Memory of the World Wars* (New York: Oxford University Press, 1990).

15   Nazi posters are replete with this image, as are Zionist ones. This is also an image used by Israeli Defense Minister Moshe Dayan in a famous speech he made in 1956: "We are a generation of settlers, and without a steel helmet and the muzzle of a canon we will not be able to plant a tree and build a home." See https://www.makorrishon.co.il/nrg/online/1/ART2/239/021.html (accessed June 28, 2022).

16   Omer Bartov, *Tales from the Borderlands: Making and Unmaking the Galician Past* (New Haven: Yale University Press, 2022), 159–74; John-Paul Himka, *Galician Villagers and the Ukrainian National Movement in the Nineteenth Century* (New York: St. Martin's Press, 1988); John-Paul Himka, *Religion and Nationality in Western Ukraine: The Greek Catholic Church and the Ruthenian National Movement in Galicia, 1867–1900* (Montreal: McGill-Queen's University Press, 1999).

17   Bartov, *Anatomy of a Genocide*, 37–81; Omer Bartov, ed., *Voices on War and Genocide: Three Accounts of the World Wars in a Galician Town* (New York: Berghahn Books, 2020), 21–137.

18   Marsha L. Rozenblit, *Reconstructing a National Identity: The Jews of Habsburg Austria during World War I* (New York: Oxford University Press, 2001). Pieter M. Judson and Marsha L. Rozenblit, eds., *Constructing Nationalities in East Central Europe* (New York: Berghahn Books, 2005).

19   Bartov, *Anatomy of a Genocide*, 82–128.

20   Bartov, *Tales from the Borderlands*, 191; Bartov, *Anatomy of a Genocide*, 30–1.

21   Jacob Katz, *Out of the Ghetto: The Social Background of Jewish Emancipation, 1770–1870* (Cambridge: Harvard University Press, 1973).

22   Bartov, *Tales from the Borderlands*, 174–228; Bartov, *Anatomy of a Genocide*, 29–36.

23   Shanes, *Diaspora Nationalism*.

24   S. An-Ski, *The Enemy at His Pleasure: A Journey through the Jewish Pale of Settlement during World War I*, ed. and trans. Joachim & Neugroschel (New York: Metropolitan Books/H. Holt, 2003); Brian Porter, *When Nationalism Began to Hate: Imagining Modern Politics in Nineteenth-century Poland* (New York: Oxford University Press, 2000); Joanna B. Michlic, *Poland's Threatening Other: The Image of the Jew from 1880 to the Present* (Lincoln: University of Nebraska Press, 2006); Grzegorz Rossoliński-Liebe, *Stepan Bandera: The Life and Afterlife of a Ukrainian Nationalist: Fascism, Genocide, and Cult* (Stuttgart: Ibidem Verlag, 2014); John-Paul Himka, *Ukrainian Nationalists and the Holocaust: OUN and UPA's Participation in the Destruction of Ukrainian Jewry, 1941–1944* (Stuttgart: Ibidem Verlag, 2021); Bartov, *Anatomy of a Genocide*, 37–128; Yisrael Gutman et al., eds., *The Jews of Poland between the World Wars* (Hanover: University Press of New England, 1989).

25 Bartov, *Anatomy of a Genocide*, 127–8.
26 Bartov, *Tales from the Borderlands*, 189–215, 220–3; Bartov, *Anatomy of a Genocide*, 101–23; 158–69, 179–82, 234–64.
27 Ibid., 271–4, 284–8.
28 See, e.g., Gregor Thum, *Uprooted: How Breslau Became Wrocław during the Century of Expulsions*, trans. Tom Lampert and Allison Brown (Princeton: Princeton University Press, 2011).
29 See, e.g., Rita Chin, *The Guest Worker Question in Postwar Germany* (New York: Cambridge University Press, 2007); Olaf Glöckner and Haim Fireberg, *Being Jewish in 21st-Century Germany* (Berlin: De Gruyter Oldenbourg, 2015).
30 See, e.g., Mary Dewhurst Lewis, *In the Boundaries of the Republic: Migrant Rights and the Limits of Universalism in France, 1918–1940* (Stanford: Stanford University Press, 2007); Todd Shepard, *The Invention of Decolonization: The Algerian War and the Remaking of France* (Ithaca: Cornell University Press, 2008).
31 Omer Bartov, "Criminalizing Denial as a Form of Erasure: The Polish-Ukrainian-Israeli Triangle," in *Memory Laws and Historical Justice: The Politics of Criminalizing the Past*, ed. Elazar Barkan (London: Palgrave, 2022), 195–221.

Index

Abdülhamid II 62, 63
activism 51, 201, 249, 250, 274
　activists 6, 8, 10–12, 24, 25, 27, 51, 96, 107, 140, 161, 176, 177, 179, 180, 185, 233–240, 242, 246–248, 250, 257–260, 262, 264, 274, 275
Aegean Sea 66, 88, 90
Agudah Israel 131, 137
Albania (Albanian) 64, 68, 72–74, 260
Alliance Israélite Universelle 126, 134
Allies, Allied powers 2, 30, 67–69, 86–88, 93, 96, 135, 155, 214
Alsace 11, 92, 94, 153, 154, 211–224
Alsace–Lorraine 4, 5, 7, 9, 85–87, 91–97, 172, 211–216
Ammende, Ewald 242, 245, 248
Anatolia 61, 62, 64, 66, 67, 69, 74, 75, 85
Anderson, Mosa 267, 269–271
Ankara 61, 67, 69, 70, 73
antisemitism 75, 113, 128, 131, 132, 135, 156, 186, 237, 243, 248, 286, 288 290, 292
Armenia (Armenian) 64, 66, 68, 69, 73, 74, 89, 90, 150, 152, 153, 236, 242, 265, 284
　Armenian genocide 62, 89
armistice 61, 62, 66, 67, 85, 91, 200, 211, 215
Asia Minor 5, 9, 61, 66, 69–71, 85–91, 93, 95–97, 262
assimilation 5, 6, 10, 11, 39, 40, 45, 54, 63–66, 73–75, 93, 94, 105, 108–110, 112, 113, 115–117, 119, 128, 173, 181, 191, 198, 204, 235, 244, 245, 248, 262
Athens 262, 263
Ausgleich 41, 43, 45
Auslandsdeutsche 241, 247
Austria (Austrian) 3, 9, 21, 22, 25–29, 31, 33, 34, 41, 44, 45, 47, 52, 53, 68, 127, 129, 238, 244

Austrian Empire 25, 288, 289
Austria-Hungary (Austro-Hungarian) 8, 21–23, 28–33, 41, 43, 45, 49, 50, 64, 66, 108, 127, 133, 148, 155, 236, 287
Austro-Hungarian Empire 66, 133
autonomy 28, 32, 37, 47, 54, 68, 108–111, 113–119, 121, 133, 134, 137, 138, 149, 150, 154, 182, 218, 221, 222, 241, 246, 249, 260, 261, 290
　non-territorial/cultural autonomy 10, 38, 117, 126, 127, 130, 133, 136–139, 141, 151, 241, 243, 244, 247
　territorial autonomy 117, 118, 128
Azerbaijan 150, 153

Balfour, Lord Arthur 214, 215
Balkans 2, 66, 75, 153, 258, 259, 263, 264, 266, 269–273
　Balkan Wars (see war)
Baltia, Herman 115
Baltic 4, 6, 128, 137, 138, 161, 163, 236, 241, 243, 244, 247, 258
Barcelona 110, 111
Basque Country 1, 108, 110–115, 117, 118, 234, 238, 239, 242
Belarus (Belarusian) 127–129, 131, 137, 149–160, 162, 164, 173, 174, 181, 285
Belgium (Belgian) 7, 10, 106–109, 114–119, 238 (4, 115–117, 260)
Belgrade 262, 263, 272
Benes, Edvard 237
Berlin 115, 129, 137, 155, 164, 233, 237, 241, 290
Bessarabia 132, 149, 153, 156, 157, 162
bilingualism 6, 116, 117, 179, 201, 216
Biscay 114, 111
Bloc of National Minorities (*Bloc Mniejczości Narodowych*) 129, 131, 137
Bohemia 26, 30, 32, 47, 162, 201

Bolshevism (Bolshevik/s) 10, 127, 128, 135, 136, 147–150, 152, 153, 155–158, 162, 182, 234
  Bolshevik revolution (see revolution)
Bolzano/Bozen 109, 112
borderlands 10, 63, 129, 149, 171–173, 180–186
Bosnia Herzegovina (Bosnian) 33, 72
Brandsch, Rudolph 134, 135, 139, 140
Brătianu, Ion 125, 157
Britishness 42–46, 50, 199
Brussels 115, 116
Bucharest 154, 156, 260, 263, 272, 284
Bund 130, 132, 137, 138, 290
Bukovina 132–134, 162, 164
Bulgaria (Bulgarian) 3, 12, 64–66, 68, 70, 71, 105, 132, 152, 154, 156, 191, 235, 237, 257–275

Calvinism 46, 47
Catalonia 2, 4, 108, 110–115, 117, 118, 234, 236–240, 242, 250
Catholicism (Catholic) 11, 39, 45–49, 53, 56, 116, 171, 175–180, 183, 184, 186, 191–193, 196, 198–204, 215, 220, 288, 291
  Catholic Church (see Church)
Caucasus 66, 75, 164, 236
Cauwelaert, Frans van 116, 117
China (Chinese) 159, 161, 163, 292
Church 46–48, 171, 221
  Anglican Church 39, 45–47, 54, 55
  Catholic Church 25, 47, 199, 219
  Church of England 46, 47, 49
  Church of Ireland 39, 46, 55, 195, 198, 199, 201
  Church of Scotland 45–47
  Free Church 46, 47
  Greek Catholic Church 186
  Roman Catholic Church 47, 186
  United Church of England and Ireland 46, 47
civil war (see war)
civilization 3, 8, 12, 28, 29, 88, 105, 118, 161, 172, 173, 180, 182–185, 261, 288
Clark, Hilda 269–273, 275
Clemenceau, Georges 88, 94, 215
collectivization 10, 149, 158, 159
colonialism 160
  anti-colonialism 233, 234, 239, 241, 270

Committee of Union and Progress (CUP) 62–64, 66–68, 74
Communism 1, 132, 140, 148, 150–154, 156, 158–164, 184, 234, 240, 242, 291, 292
  Communist International 148, 153, 155–157, 160, 163, 240
Congress of European Nationalities (CEN) 11, 233–235, 240, 242–250
Constantinople 88, 90
Cork 194, 195, 197, 202
cosmology, vernacular 11, 172, 173, 180, 184, 185
coup 64, 109, 112, 117, 131, 138, 158, 174
Crimea 152, 153, 158, 238
Croatia (Croatian) 42, 53, 108, 109, 112, 236
crownlands 27, 30, 31, 34
Curzon, Lord George 88, 155
Czechoslovakia (Czechoslovak) 4, 21, 23, 27, 32, 68, 111, 119, 127, 128, 151, 155, 160, 162, 175, 247, 260
Czech (Czechs) 28, 45, 47, 111, 201, 237, 260, 284

deportation 61, 66, 73–75, 85–91, 97, 161, 261
Deutscher Verband (DV) 110
diaspora 152, 153, 160, 233, 242
Dickinson, Lord Willoughby 239, 246
dictatorship 30–32, 107–113, 119, 238
discrimination 2, 62, 95, 96, 113, 125, 131, 134, 150, 153, 198, 199, 284
dissimilation 65, 66, 74, 248
Distanzliebe 126
Dmowski, Roman 125
Dniester 153, 156, 167, 162
Dragnewa, Dr. Z. 264, 265, 272
Dual Monarchy 9, 22, 33, 41, 43, 44, 47, 48, 51, 53, 55, 56
Dublin 51, 192–194, 199–201

Eastern cantons 115, 117, 119
Easter Rising 48, 192, 200
education 2, 10, 22, 25–27, 44, 45, 53, 70, 107, 110–112, 114–117, 125–127, 132–134, 136–138, 150, 151, 155, 174–176, 178, 180, 181, 183, 185, 189, 199, 201, 215–217, 220, 257, 260, 262–264, 286, 288–290

emancipation 12, 46, 287–290
Enlightenment 126, 288
Entente 67, 88, 236, 237
Estonia (Estonian) 7, 68, 107, 117–119, 130, 136, 139, 191, 242–244, 246, 247
Eupen 108, 115
Eupen-Malmedy 87

fascism 118, 160, 234, 238
   anti-fascism 234, 238, 240, 242, 243, 248
Fianna Fáil 199, 201
Finland (Finnish) 153, 161–163, 191
Fiume 33, 219
Flanders 108, 115–117, 119, 241
France (French) 4, 6, 11, 12, 32, 42, 45, 50, 65, 85, 86, 88, 89, 91–96, 105, 108, 115–117, 119, 126, 151, 155, 156, 160, 203, 211–24, 234, 236, 238–240, 242, 263, 270, 274, 285, 287, 288, 291, 292
Franco, Franciso 108, 114, 115, 160
francophone 108, 116, 117

Gaelic 11, 48, 198, 200, 201
Galicia (Austria-Hungary, Poland) 26, 128, 130, 131, 148, 149, 151, 153–155, 162, 163, 171, 176–178, 180–184, 287, 289–291
Galicia (Spain) 235, 238, 239
Gegenwartsarbeit 130, 133
Generalitat 114, 115
Geneva 2, 8, 139, 163, 233, 234, 237, 239, 240, 242, 258, 261, 264–266, 269, 270, 274
genocide 62, 66, 89, 159, 163, 284, 287, 292
Georgia (Georgian) 149–151
Germany (German) 4, 10–12, 22, 25, 26, 28, 29, 32, 34, 44, 45, 64, 65, 85, 86, 92–96, 108, 109, 111–113, 115–119, 126–140, 152–154, 156–158, 160–163, 175, 181, 195, 196, 201, 203, 204, 211, 213–219, 222–224, 233–235, 237–243, 245, 247–249, 260, 270, 287–289, 291, 292
   Germanization 65, 95, 128, 132, 137
   Nazi Germany (see Nazism)
Gladstone, William 41, 55
Gökalp, Ziya 64–66

Gourd, Emilie 265, 266
Grabski, Stanislaw 174, 175, 176
Great Britain (British) 3, 4, 9, 39–48, 52–56, 88–92, 95, 126, 127, 153, 191–201, 203, 214, 234, 235–237, 239, 240, 263, 267, 269, 270, 273, 284, 285
   British Empire 9, 153
Great Depression 132, 135
Great Famine 52, 53
Greece (Greek) 3, 12, 61, 62, 64–66, 68–74, 88–91, 93–95, 105, 152, 191, 237, 258, 260–265, 267–269, 271–274
   Greek Catholic 171, 175–180, 183, 186, 291
   Greek Catholic Church (see Church)
   Greek Orthodox 61, 66, 69, 71–73, 88, 90
Gruenbaum, Yitzhak 129–132, 139, 140

Habsburg Empire 5, 6, 9, 23, 25, 50, 51, 110, 129, 155
Habsburgtreue 43, 50
Hamidian Period 61–63, 74
Hasbach, Erwin 129–132, 139, 140
Hasselblatt, Werner 243, 248
Helsinki 130, 154, 163
Hitler, Adolf 113, 140, 163, 248
Hohenzollern 22, 258
Holodomor 159, 184
Holy Roman Empire 25, 28
homogeneity (homogenization) 1–6, 8–10, 12, 40, 61, 65, 66, 74, 88, 93, 96, 97, 105, 106, 109, 110, 114, 115, 117, 127, 164, 192, 275, 287, 291, 292
human rights 235, 239, 248
Human Rights League 146, 236, 239
Hungary (Hungarian) 8, 22, 25–31, 41, 42, 45, 47, 52, 53, 68, 12, 132–134, 155, 157, 162, 219, 233, 240–242, 245, 247, 249, 260, 265, 285, 292
Hutsul 32, 172, 182–184

immigrants 64, 66, 72–75, 238
imperialism 44, 148, 162, 200
independence 2, 3, 44, 55, 62, 64, 68, 108, 116, 127, 131, 135, 138, 155, 162, 184, 191, 193, 194, 198, 202, 235, 286, 290

internationalism 86, 150, 151, 153, 233, 234, 240, 242, 250, 257, 259, 260, 264, 265, 274
Inter-Parliamentary Union (IPU) 250
Ireland (Irish) 7, 9, 11, 12, 31, 32, 39–43, 45–56, 154, 171, 191–204, 203, 204, 234–237, 239, 241, 270
    Irish Free State 51, 191, 193, 195–204
    Irish Republican Army (IRA) 51, 191, 234
    Irish Revolution (see revolution)
irredentism 133, 134, 148, 149, 151, 153, 157, 158, 160–163, 233, 235, 249, 250, 267
Islam (Muslim) 9, 33, 61–63, 67, 68, 260, 262, 271
Israel (Israeli) 12, 131, 137, 284–287
Istanbul 69, 70, 75, 238, 242
Italy (Italian) 6, 10, 12, 23, 28, 29, 32, 45, 88, 91, 106–115, 118, 119, 147, 160, 219, 234, 235, 238, 242

Jabotinsky, Zeʼev (Vladimir) 130, 132
Jászi, Oszkár 41, 44, 45, 48, 49, 53
Japan (Japanese) 159, 160, 162
Jews (Jewish) 10, 63, 65, 70, 74, 75, 118, 125–140, 152–154, 156, 163, 172, 173, 181, 184–186, 234, 236, 237, 239–243, 247, 278, 260, 283, 284, 286–292

Karavéloff, Catherine 267–269, 271–273, 279
Karelia 153, 154, 163, 166
Kazakhstan (Kazakh) 151, 153, 159, 161
Kemal, Mustafa (Atatürk) 73, 88, 89, 100
Kharkiv 148, 152, 158
kin-state 108, 126, 233, 241, 246
korenizatsiya 150–152
Krabbe, Ludvig de 246, 247, 249
Kremlin 148, 163
Kurchinskii, Mikhail 246, 255
Kurdistan (Kurdish) 62, 66, 68, 75, 81
Kyiv 148, 153, 166

Laserson, Max 137–140,
Latvia (Latvian) 10, 14, 68, 120, 125–127, 135–138, 140, 191, 243, 244
League of Nations 2–4, 6–8, 11, 12, 33, 68, 70, 71, 73, 75, 78, 79, 107, 111, 118, 125, 126, 128, 131, 134, 136, 139, 148, 154, 157, 160, 163, 165, 166, 174, 175, 213, 214, 233, 234, 237–243, 245–250, 252, 254, 256, 257, 264, 266–268
    International Federation of League of Nations Societies 239, 245, 246
    League of Nations' Assembly 107, 118
    League of Nations' Council 2, 68, 70, 245, 271
    League of Nations' Mandates 3, 16, 279
    League of Nations' Minorities Section 2, 8, 12, 105, 246, 259, 260, 263, 265–269, 274, 277, 278
    League of Nations' minority system/regime 9, 61, 67–69, 105–107, 154, 213, 235, 237, 239, 249
    League of Nations' minority treaties (see minority)
Lenin 147–151, 153
liberalism 46, 56, 94, 106, 109, 110, 112, 114, 132, 134, 139, 236, 249, 250, 259
    liberals 26, 41, 44, 54, 117, 137, 202, 234, 235, 238–240, 242, 247
    liberal–democracy 7, 28, 88, 94, 96, 97,
    liberal Italy 108–111, 118, 119
    liberal minority policy 8, 26, 109, 110, 118, 136
Lithuania (Lithuanian) 4, 14, 68, 120, 127, 174, 236
Ljubljana 34, 263
Lloyd George, David 54, 88, 214
Locarno Agreements 94, 96
London 40, 197, 198, 200, 233, 234–237, 242
loyalism 11, 38, 49–51, 60, 191–205, 225
Lutherans 47, 288
Luxembourg, Rosa 164
Lviv (Lwów) 148, 155, 177, 291

Macedonia (Macedonian) 12, 64, 236, 242, 250, 257–262, 264–277
    Macedonian Revolutionary Organization 259, 260, 262, 266
    Macedonian Women's Union (MWU) 259, 266–268, 272
Madrid 115, 160
Magyar 45, 47, 58, 242, 249
    Magyarization 27, 34, 132

majority 2, 13, 21–23, 39, 46, 51, 56, 67, 90–92, 100, 108, 110–113, 116–118, 126, 128, 129, 131, 132, 134, 136–139, 150, 152, 155, 171, 178, 179, 192, 193, 195, 198–200, 203, 205, 214, 215, 238, 260, 261, 284, 287
  majority–minority relations 4–7, 9, 10, 105–108, 118, 120, 136, 137, 199, 245

Malinoff, Julia 264–266, 278

Mancomunitat 111, 121

Manchuria 160, 161

Marchlewski, Julian 148, 164

Marxism 150, 162, 234

Masaryk, Tomáš Garrigue 21–24, 28, 32, 34, 237

millet 63, 76

minority 2–7, 9, 10, 11, 13, 16, 19, 21–24, 26, 27, 33, 34, 36, 39–46, 48, 51, 53, 55, 56, 61, 66–72, 74, 75, 78, 79, 85, 88, 90–95, 97, 100, 105–119, 125–139, 143, 147, 148, 152, 154–157, 159, 160–162, 164, 212, 213, 224, 231, 233–235, 237–250, 255–263, 268, 269, 271–275, 277, 284, 291, 292
  majority-minority relations (see majority)
  minority nationalism (see nationalism)
  minority organizations/representatives 2, 5, 7, 8, 10, 11, 107–112, 114, 118, 119, 126, 128, 139, 154, 155, 175, 217, 223, 233, 234, 236–245, 247–250, 252, 254, 256, 258–266, 268, 269, 272–275, 286, 290
  minority petitions (see petitions)
  minority protection 3, 7, 10, 61, 67–69, 79, 105–107, 118, 125, 130, 132, 136, 139, 149, 154, 157, 235, 237, 239, 243, 245–247, 249, 250, 257
  minority question/problem/issue 1, 3–5, 9, 11, 12, 62, 67, 69, 79, 83, 105–107, 115, 116, 120, 121, 123, 164, 165, 169, 174, 175, 235, 245, 246, 250, 254, 258, 260, 263, 264, 274
  minority rights 2, 7, 8, 11, 13, 14, 27, 66–68, 70, 78, 79, 85, 86, 110, 117, 119, 125–127, 129–131, 134, 136, 139, 154, 175, 213, 235, 239, 240, 243–246, 248, 250, 258

Minorities Section (see League of Nations)

minority system/regime (see League of Nations)

minority treaties 2–4, 8, 111, 118, 241, 14, 68, 86, 107, 111, 118, 125, 128, 130, 132, 136, 139, 154, 157, 176, 237, 238, 240–242, 258, 264, 265, 268, 270, 274, 275

mobilization 1, 10, 11, 12, 29, 51, 54, 55, 62, 69, 85, 89, 91, 106, 108, 147, 171, 177, 180, 231, 247, 250, 258, 264, 265, 272, 283, 284, 286, 292

Moldavia (Moldavian) 152, 153, 156, 157, 162, 163

monarchy 9, 11, 22, 24, 26, 28, 29, 31, 33, 34, 41–44, 47–53, 55–58

Moravia 25, 32, 37, 38, 111

Moscow 148, 149, 151, 154–160, 163, 234, 238

Motzkin, Leo 241

Mulhouse 218, 224

multiethnicity 63, 105, 163, 164, 174, 237, 286

multinationalism 1, 21, 22, 24, 40–45, 47, 49, 51, 52, 60, 63, 127, 147–149, 151, 164, 236, 249

Muslim (see Islam)

Mussolini, Benito 108, 109, 112, 113, 116, 118, 119, 123, 242

Napoleon, Bonaparte 219, 287

national indifference 6, 7, 9–12, 21, 22, 24, 29, 31, 35, 51, 56, 101, 120, 171–173, 180, 182, 185, 186, 192, 193, 199, 201, 203, 261, 271, 283, 284, 286, 290, 292

nationalism 1, 4–7, 9, 12, 13, 22, 35, 44, 47, 51, 58, 61–64, 74, 76, 81, 86, 116, 120, 125, 126, 151, 152, 159, 162, 171–173, 180, 182, 184, 185, 187, 192, 235, 249, 250, 260, 264, 283–285, 287–292
  civic nationalism 113, 214, 288
  ethnic nationalism 185, 233, 234, 236, 237, 250, 285, 287, 288, 291, 292
  homeland nationalism 258, 265, 268, 273, 274
  minority/sub-state nationalism 113, 235

nationalism and religion 61, 62, 74, 76, 198
nationality 6, 11, 13, 22, 23, 26, 35, 37, 39–41, 43, 45, 47, 55, 56, 61, 63, 64, 65, 70, 72–74, 80, 96, 147, 149–153, 157, 161–163, 175–177, 181, 189, 201, 221, 235–237, 240, 241, 243, 244, 246, 249, 250, 258, 259–262, 271, 274
   minority nationality 39–45, 48, 55, 108
   nationality policy 10, 62–64, 66, 74, 148, 234
   principle of nationality 21, 235, 239–241, 249
nationalizing state 5, 8, 10, 16, 249, 257, 260, 274, 275
nation-building 4, 11, 16, 61–63, 70, 73–75, 78, 81, 89, 109, 181, 213, 249
nationhood 5, 6, 8, 12, 43, 22–26, 29–31, 33, 35, 36, 65, 151, 164, 214, 269
Nazism (Nazi) 113, 115, 139, 140, 223, 234, 245, 248, 255, 286, 288, 289, 291, 294
Netherlands (Dutch) 43, 57, 116, 234, 239, 276
neutrality 136, 192, 215, 226, 265, 266
non-conformism 45, 46, 54, 240
non-territorial autonomy (NTA) (see autonomy)
Northern Ireland (Northern Irish) 40, 41, 195, 196, 201
Norway (Norwegian) 43, 49
numerus clausus 131, 133, 143

OGPU (Joint State Political Directorate) 152, 153, 158, 160
Option Agreement 113, 124
Ottoman Empire (Ottoman) 3, 8, 9, 21, 22, 61–64, 66–72, 74, 76, 78, 87, 88, 91, 157, 236, 258, 260, 261
   ottomanism 62–64, 66

pacifism 269, 271, 273
Paderewski, Ignacy 125
Palestine 126, 140, 152, 284, 290
Paris 3, 156, 162, 212, 213, 216, 217, 221, 233–239, 241, 242
   Paris Peace Conference 1–3, 6, 7, 67, 85–87, 90–92, 94, 95, 97, 105, 125, 135, 172, 174, 175, 211, 214, 233, 237, 249, 258
   Paris system 6, 9–11, 85–87, 90, 91, 93, 96, 98
Permanent Court of International Justice (The Hague) 70, 154
petitions 32, 156, 176–178, 257, 264
   petitions to the League of Nations' Minorities Section 2, 11, 107, 154, 241, 242, 245, 258, 266, 268, 269, 275, 279
Piedmont policy 147, 148, 151–153, 158, 159, 162, 164
Piłsudski, Józef 113, 131, 148, 155, 159, 162
plebiscite 11, 92, 102, 119, 124, 171, 187, 201, 214, 215
   Grasbki's Plebiscite 171–180, 182, 184
pogrom 31, 75, 113, 128, 203, 237, 289
Poincaré, Raymond 92, 211, 214, 217
Poland (Polish) 2, 7, 10–12, 14, 23, 28, 32, 35, 65, 68, 107, 113, 119, 120, 123, 125, 127–133, 135–137, 143, 148, 149, 151–162, 164–166, 171–188, 191, 195, 196, 201, 203, 204, 235, 237, 238–241, 247, 249, 265, 284–287, 289–292
Polesia 173, 181, 187, 189
Polish–Lithuanian Commonwealth 186, 287
Popular Front 115, 160
population exchange/transfer 1, 4, 13, 62, 70–73, 78, 80, 88, 94, 262, 291
Prague 126, 272
Presbyterianism 45, 46, 49, 201, 205
Protestantism 11, 44–47, 53, 56, 65, 134, 193–203, 205, 209, 214, 220, 239
Prussia (Prussian) 43, 92, 128, 129, 134, 157, 211, 287, 288

Quakers 269–271
Queen Victoria 48, 49, 200

racism (race) 4, 8, 12, 67, 70, 72–74, 105, 156, 161, 234, 236, 237, 246, 261, 268, 284, 285, 288
Red Army 148, 149, 153, 160–163,
refugees 33, 66, 69, 71, 160, 162, 191, 195–197, 207, 221, 259, 261, 262, 264–266, 271–272, 274, 292

Renan, Ernest 92, 214
resistance 9, 11, 26, 42, 76, 89, 109, 110, 116, 131, 139, 162, 192, 200, 217, 222, 270, 288
revolution 24, 31, 32, 42, 148, 150, 153, 162, 164
    Bolshevik revolution 23, 135, 147–149, 214
    French Revolution 12, 42, 48, 92, 217, 219, 287
    Irish Revolution 11, 42, 51, 191, 192, 196, 197, 199, 202–204
    Young Turks Revolution 9, 63, 74,
Riga (see Treaty)
Romania (Romanian) 3, 10, 12, 14, 23, 31, 35, 68, 105, 120, 125, 127, 132–137, 140, 144, 153, 154, 156, 157, 165, 235, 237, 240, 242, 253, 272, 273, 284
Romanov Empire (see Russian Empire)
Royal Irish Constabulary (RIC) 48, 56, 193, 196, 197, 202
Russia (Russian) 3, 12, 30, 32, 44, 63, 64, 127, 129, 132, 136, 149, 150, 153–155, 157, 158, 265, 285, 286, 292, 293
    Russian Civil War (see war)
    Russian Empire 21, 125, 127, 130, 133, 147–149, 159, 186, 258, 284, 285
    Russian Revolution (see revolution)
    Russification 132, 137
    Russian Soviet Federative Socialist Republic (RSFSR) 149–152, 154, 214
Russki 178, 179, 181–183, 188
Rusyn 176–179, 183
Ruthenia 151, 155, 157, 162, 163, 167, 181, 289

Sardinian nationalists 234, 238
Schickele, René 92, 102
Schiemann, Paul 137–140, 235, 243–250, 255
Schleswig 87, 99, 247
Schuman, Robert 220, 221
Scotland 2, 39–50, 52–56, 192
Sejm 129–131, 175, 177
self-determination 1, 2, 9, 13, 21, 23, 32, 33, 67, 85, 86, 88, 90–93, 97, 105, 109, 126, 147, 154, 156, 172, 174–176, 187, 211, 215, 219, 234, 235–237, 241, 249
separatism 50, 51, 112, 113, 158, 191, 203, 239, 249, 285
Serbia (Serb) 12, 25, 30, 35, 258, 260–262 265, 267–272, 274, 284
Seton-Watson, Robert W. 53, 237
Sheepshanks, Mary 263, 268–273
Sinn Féin 41, 234
Slav (Slavic) 24, 47, 53, 65, 128, 134, 161, 174, 175, 178, 242, 260–262, 270, 271, 274, 276, 277
Slovakia (Slovak) 25, 35, 47, 111, 162, 236
Slovenia (Slovene) 25, 30, 34–36, 108, 109, 112, 234, 238, 258, 260–262, 267, 268, 270, 274
Smuts, Jan 3, 35
Smyrna 68, 69, 85, 88–91, 93–95, 101
Sofia 262, 263, 266, 272, 273
South Africa (South African) 3, 35
South Tyrol 87, 99, 108–111, 113, 116, 124, 234, 238
sovereignty 1–3, 5, 9, 10, 31, 32, 85, 86, 96, 97, 105, 125, 135, 136, 156, 157, 174, 212–214, 217, 219, 224, 235, 245, 246, 258, 265, 268
Soviet Union 1, 2, 10, 147–165, 182, 214, 234, 238, 285, 291
    Sovietization 147, 148, 153
    Soviet nationality policy (see *korenizatsiya*)
Spain (Spanish) 2, 4, 10, 106–115, 117–119, 121, 160, 234, 238, 242
Stalin, Iósif 148–151, 158–164
Strasbourg 85, 92, 211, 217–220, 222, 227
St. Vith 108, 115
Sweden (Swedish) 43, 49, 276
Switzerland (Swiss) 235, 237, 239, 241, 263, 265, 276

Tajikistan (Tajik) 151, 153
Tanzimat 62–64
Tatarbunary uprising 156, 157
Tatars 64, 152, 158
Third Reich 223, 250
Thrace 64, 67, 69, 71, 81, 262
Thugutt, Stanisław 175, 177, 181, 187

Toynbee, Arnold 3, 89
Transcaucasia 150, 151
Transylvania 31, 132, 134, 242
Treaty 134, 154, 260, 264
    Anglo–Irish Treaty 194, 198, 208
    minority treaties (see minority)
    Treaty of Lausanne 9, 61, 66, 69, 70, 72, 79, 87
    Treaty of Riga 140, 148, 149, 153, 155, 162
    Treaty of Sèvres 67–70, 87, 90, 91, 97
    Treaty of Versailles 93, 94, 96, 97, 115, 130, 132, 154, 215
Turkey (Turkish) 3, 4, 9, 14, 35, 61–81, 87–90, 93, 95, 97, 100, 106, 120, 157, 191, 226, 260, 262, 271, 284, 292
    Turkification 62, 64–66, 74, 75, 77
tutejsi 173, 180–182, 189

Ukraine (Ukrainian) 12, 148, 156, 157–159, 162, 167, 171, 285, 286, 290–293
    Russian invasion of Ukraine 12, 285, 292
    Soviet Socialist Republic of Ukraine 148–153, 155–159, 162–164
    Ukrainianization 154, 158, 159
Ulster 4, 5, 52, 191, 193, 196, 203, 205
unionism 41, 45, 52, 56, 62, 64, 67, 193, 194, 196, 198–202, 204, 205
United Kingdom 8, 9, 38–57, 76, 205, 235, 292
United States (American) 23, 88–91, 95, 102, 125, 140, 215, 235, 237, 263, 276, 285, 286, 292
Upper Silesia 4, 5, 14, 87, 107, 120, 175, 187, 203
USSR (see Soviet Union)
Uzbekistan 151, 161

Venezia Giulia 108–111
Venizelos, Eleftherios 88
Verband der Deutschen Minderheiten in Europa (VDM) 242–243, 248, 255, 256

Vienna 26, 155, 156, 162, 166, 233, 234, 237, 238, 241, 242, 290
Vilfan, Josip 238, 243–245, 248
violence 4, 5, 9, 10, 31, 85–93, 95–97, 100, 105, 109, 110, 112, 113, 162, 167, 191, 192, 194, 195, 198, 203, 223, 260–264, 266, 267, 270, 271, 283, 284, 289, 291
Volhynia 142, 162, 171, 172, 176, 187

Wales (Welsh) 4, 39, 40, 45–50, 52–56, 197, 249
Wallonia 4, 116, 117, 124
war 10, 41, 42, 44, 45, 50, 63, 64, 69, 71, 85, 87, 94, 97, 125, 153, 156–161, 163, 164, 191, 192, 203, 211, 216, 257, 259, 261, 263, 264, 272, 280, 283, 285, 291, 292
    Balkan Wars 62, 64, 70, 71, 88, 99, 260, 262, 264
    Cold War 149, 246
    First World War 1–3, 5, 8, 9, 12, 13, 15, 23, 24, 28, 30, 31, 45, 48, 54, 56, 62, 64–66, 68, 70, 71, 74, 77, 78, 80, 85, 86, 88, 89, 91–95, 97, 100, 102, 106, 108–111, 115–118, 128, 129, 135, 162, 192, 195, 200, 211–215, 220, 221, 224, 233, 235–237, 249, 250, 258, 264, 283, 284, 288–290
    Greco–Turkish War 61, 62, 67, 88–91, 95, 100
    Irish Civil War 191, 194, 195, 200
    Irish War of Independence 191, 194, 202
    Russian Civil War 147, 149, 153, 161–163, 233
    Russo–Polish War 148, 155, 195
    Second World War 1, 2, 4, 5, 12, 13, 95, 106, 118, 140, 164, 217, 223, 224, 286, 291, 292
    Spanish Civil War 108, 114, 115, 119, 121, 160, 163, 238
    Yom Kippur War 286, 287, 293
Warsaw 129, 131, 148, 154, 158, 164, 181, 238, 284
Weill, Georges 217, 219, 220, 222

Women's International League for Peace and Freedom (WILPF) 8, 11, 12, 257–275, 279, 280
Wilson, Woodrow 35, 67, 86, 88, 125, 241
  Fourteen Points 92, 102, 127, 215, 237
women's suffrage 257, 264, 265

Yiddish 131, 137, 138, 152
Young Turks 9, 61–64, 66, 70, 74, 88
Yugoslavia 1, 23, 32, 33, 68, 154, 164, 261, 270, 272, 274, 285

Zionism 126, 128–133, 137, 138, 236, 241, 284, 287–290

www.ingramcontent.com/pod-product-compliance
Lightning Source LLC
Chambersburg PA
CBHW071803300426
44116CB00009B/1182